Platform-Mediated Tourism

This book presents theoretical and empirical perspectives on platform-mediated tourism, with a special focus on Airbnb. The case studies included in this volume show that the impacts of short-term renting on neighbourhoods, residents, and tourism operators are uneven, but increasingly significant.

During the past decade, digital platforms for short-term rental, transport, social dining etc., have enabled the development of a new generation of entrepreneurs in tourism and mobility. The mediation of services through digital platforms was initially presented as a form of a sharing economy led by non-professional providers, but it has grown into a new form of capitalist speculation. The inadequacy of existing legal frameworks in regulating platform-mediated activities has generated reactions by social movements, especially for the protection of housing rights. With the outbreak of Covid-19, the downfall in the mobility and tourism economy has revealed the acuteness of the structural crisis of cities and of labour based on platform-mediated activities. In Europe, networks of cities are taking action against platforms to regain their control over data that is needed to regulate platform-mediated tourism services, and the rights of residents in tourism cities.

The authors in this edited volume explore issues of social justice in terms of residents' quality of life, working conditions, the housing market, urban structure, the morality of operators who navigate through normative loopholes, and the responsibility issues of platform companies holding data on short-term rentals.

The chapters in this book were originally published in the *Journal of Sustainable Tourism*.

Paola Minoia is Associate Professor in Geography, University of Turin, Italy, and Senior Lecturer in Global Development Studies, University of Helsinki, Finland. Her interests intersect the fields of geography, political ecology, and development studies with a focus on territoriality, state and community relations, socio-environmental justice, eco-cultural knowledges, tourism, and sustainability.

Salla Jokela is University Lecturer at the Faculty of Social Sciences, Tampere University, Finland. She teaches in the Bachelor's degree programme in Sustainable Urban Development. Her research has focused on urban tourism, visual culture, identity politics, city branding, and urban discourses.

Platform-Mediated Tourism

Social Justice and Urban Governance before and during Covid-19

Edited by
Paola Minoia and Salla Jokela

Routledge
Taylor & Francis Group

LONDON AND NEW YORK

First published 2023
by Routledge
4 Park Square, Milton Park, Abingdon, Oxon OX14 4RN

and by Routledge
605 Third Avenue, New York, NY 10158

Routledge is an imprint of the Taylor & Francis Group, an informa business

British Library Cataloguing in Publication Data
A catalogue record for this book is available from the British Library

ISBN13: 978-1-032-13730-8 (hbk)
ISBN13: 978-1-032-13733-9 (pbk)
ISBN13: 978-1-003-23061-8 (ebk)

DOI: 10.4324/9781003230618

Typeset in Myriad Pro
by Newgen Publishing UK

Publisher's Note
The publisher accepts responsibility for any inconsistencies that may have arisen during the conversion of this book from journal articles to book chapters, namely the inclusion of journal terminology.

Disclaimer
Every effort has been made to contact copyright holders for their permission to reprint material in this book. The publishers would be grateful to hear from any copyright holder who is not here acknowledged and will undertake to rectify any errors or omissions in future editions of this book.

Contents

Citation Information

The chapters in this book, except chapter 10, were originally published in the *Journal of Sustainable Tourism,* volume 30, issue 5 (2022). Chapter 10 was originally published in volume 29, issue 10 (2021) of the same journal. When citing this material, please use the original page numbering for each article, as follows:

For any permission-related enquiries please visit:
www.tandfonline.com/page/help/permissions

Notes on Contributors

Rodney W. Caldicott is an adjunct fellow within the School of Business and Tourism at Southern Cross University, Australia, though currently an international scholar in residence at the Faculty of Interdisciplinary Studies at Khon Kaen University (Nong Khai Campus), Thailand. His political geography and policy studies background focuses his research on consumer-driven "alternative" tourism, leisure and lifestyle pursuits, and their associated contributions and impacts on local communities.

Filippo Celata is Professor in Economic and Political Geography at the University of Rome La Sapienza, Italy. His main research interest has recently been the impact of digital platforms on socio-spatial relations, tourism practices, and cities. He coordinates the Research Project of National Relevance "The short-term city: digital platforms and spatial (in)justice".

Deborah Che is a lecturer in the School of Business and Tourism at Southern Cross University, Australia. Her research interests include sustainable economic development, natural resource-based tourism development and marketing, cultural/heritage tourism, and arts-based economic diversification strategies. A common theme in Dr. Che's research involves the interconnection between economic restructuring and shifting land uses.

Guangwu Chen is an assistant professor at the School of Environment, Beijing Normal University, China. His research interest centres around sustainable consumption and digital economy. Guangwu is also a visiting research fellow at the UNSW Sydney, Australia.

Mingming Cheng is a senior lecturer in digital marketing in the School of Marketing, Curtin University, Australia. His research interests include the sharing economy, data science, digital marketing, and Chinese tourists.

Mathilde Dissing Christensen is a lecturer at the School of Geography and Planning at Cardiff University, Wales, UK. Her research interest lies in the areas of mobilities, technologies, and everyday practices.

Agnese Cretella is a social scientist whose research examines the intersection between food and urban studies. Her academic focus revolves around urban food governance and new urban developments in cities. She was a postdoctoral research with SHARECITY.

Anna Davies is Chair of Geography, Environment and Society at Trinity College Dublin, Ireland, where she directs the Environmental Governance Research Group. She is Principal Investigator of the ERC-funded project SHARECITY: examining the practice and potential of ICT-mediated urban food sharing.

Gebeyaw Ambelu Degarege is currently a lecturer in the Department of Tourism, Sport, and Society, Lincoln University, New Zealand. Gebeyaw's current research interests lie in the wider field of tourism and sustainable development

Deborah Edwards is Associate Professor at the UTS Business School at University of Technology Sydney, Australia. Deborah's research interests are in business event impacts and expenditure studies, tourist spatial behaviour, sustainable tourism management, urban precincts, tourism planning, tourism sustainability, and crowd control.

Ferne Edwards was awarded a PhD in cultural anthropology from the Australian National University. She has more than 16 years international research and university teaching experience on sustainable cities, urban food systems, and social movements. She was a postdoctoral research with SHARECITY.

Anna Farmaki is Assistant Professor at the School of Management and Economics at the Cyprus University of Technology, Republic of Cyprus. Her research interests lie in the areas of tourism planning and development and tourist behaviour.

Lluís Garay-Tamajon is Associate Professor at Universitat Oberta de Catalunya (UOC), Barcelona, Spain. His main areas of research interest concern diverse forces transforming the tourism activity, particularly the collaborative, co-creative, sustainable, and responsible processes causing disruptive impacts on urban and rural socio-economic environments and organizations. Lluís is the coordinator of the NOUTUR research group (UOC) which aims to analyse the impacts that tourism and leisure activities are causing within the contexts of destinations (territories), organisations (both business and non-business), and consumption patterns (both tourists and residents).

Salla Jokela is University Lecturer at the Faculty of Social Sciences, Tampere University, Finland. She teaches in the Bachelor's degree programme in Sustainable Urban Development. Her research has focused on urban tourism, visual culture, identity politics, city branding, and urban discourses.

Antonios Kaniadakis is Lecturer in Information Technology Management at Queen Mary University of London, UK. His primary research interest is socio-technical analyses of ICT although more recently he started to investigate the role of social media as marketing platforms.

Linglong Ma completed his master's degree in Management Studies with a major in tourism at the University of Waikato, and worked as a research assistant with the China-New Zealand Tourism Research Unit at the Waikato Management School. His research interests relate to the impacts of tourism and how communities adapt to tourism-induced change. He currently works in Xi'an where he has an interest in the issues of heritage and tourism in that city.

Susan Houge Mackenzie is an associate professor in the University of Otago Department of Tourism in Dunedin, New Zealand. She investigates links between adventure and psychological well-being across tourism, recreation, and education contexts using psychological frameworks (e.g., self-determination theory, flow theory).

Brigida Marovelli has a PhD in Social Anthropology from Brunel University, West London, UK, with a thesis exploring the dynamic relationship between place, history, and landscape in an urban food market, Catania, Sicily. She was a postdoctoral researcher with SHARECITY.

Paola Minoia is Associate Professor in Geography, University of Turin, Italy, and Senior Lecturer in Global Development Studies, University of Helsinki, Finland. Her interests intersect the fields of geography, political ecology, and development studies with a focus on territoriality, state and community relations, socio-environmental justice, eco-cultural knowledges, tourism, and sustainability.

Sabine Muschter holds a PhD from the School of Business and Tourism at Southern Cross University (SCU), Lismore, Australia where she maintains her academic interests as a research assistant. Her doctoral research focused on the decision-making process of European international students to study abroad and their ensuing travel behaviour during their stay in Australia.

Soledad Morales-Perez is Associate Professor of Economics and Business Studies at the Universitat Oberta de Catalunya (UOC), Barcelona, Spain, and member of the UOC tourism research group, NOUTUR. At present, her research interests include the analysis of collaborative economies in socio-spatial transformations of tourism spaces, new narratives and measurement of tourist sustainability, and event tourism impacts in public space.

Filipa Perdigão Ribeiro is Professora Adjunta at the University of the Algarve, School of Management, Tourism and Hospitality, Portugal. Her current research interests focus on links between language(s), discourse, and tourism in their multiple facets. She regularly reviews language and tourism papers for journals and scientific meetings and is a researcher at CiTUR – Centre for Tourism Research, Development, and Innovation (Portugal).

Antonello Romano is PhD candidate in Economic Geography at Dep.MEMOTEF, La Sapienza University Rome, Italy, and Geographic Data Scientist at Ladest Lab., DISPOC, University of Siena, Italy.

Antonio Paolo Russo is an associate tenured professor at Department of Geography, University Rovira i Virgili, Tarragona, Spain. His research interests include tourism mobilities and the transformations they produce in the physical, social, and cultural environments of cities as well as rural environments; digital technologies as catalysts of urban change; social exclusion and citizen empowerment at tourist places; local identities and their negotiation and hybridization under the forcefield of tourism; planning solutions for resilient cities; and cultural affirmation of marginalised groups in world tourism cities.

Chris Ryan is Professor of Tourism Management at The University of Waikato Management School, Hamilton, New Zealand; Chris is interested in tourist behaviours, motivations, and the social, environmental, and economic consequences of those behaviours with a specific interest in China and cultural differences. He utilises both quantitative and qualitative techniques including discriminate analysis, SEM, regressions etc., and textual analysis software.

Giacomo-Maria Salerno is Postdoctoral Research Fellow at DICEA – Department of Civil, Building and Environmental Engineering, Sapienza – University of Rome, Italy. The title of his research project is "The territorial effects of the tourist industry. Spectacularization, museification and commodification of urban contexts". His research has a strong focus on the strategies elaborated by social movements in contrast to touristification processes.

Dimitrios Stergiou is Assistant Professor at the School of Social Sciences at the Hellenic Open University, Greece. His research interests are concerned with tourism management and tourism education.

Kate Torkington is Professora Adjunta at the School of Management, Hospitality and Tourism, University of the Algarve, Portugal. Her current research interests include discourses of and about tourism; language practices in tourism and migration contexts; place-identities; sustainability practices in tourism; slow tourism and responsibility in tourism.

Tania von der Heidt is Senior Lecturer in the School of Business and Tourism at Southern Cross University, Australia. She currently teaches in Marketing Principles, Competitive Strategy, and Sustainable Business Management for the undergraduate business degree domestically and off-shore (Tianjin). Dr von der Heidt's primary research area is creative problem solving and collaboration in product innovation for sustainability marketing and business.

Julie Wilson is Associate Dean for Research of the Faculty of Economics and Business and member of the NOUTUR Research Group at the Universitat Oberta de Catalunya (UOC), Barcelona, Spain. She is currently Chair of the International Geographical Union (IGU) Commission on Tourism, Leisure and Global Change. Her research interests include the role of tourism in the transformation and socio-spatial evolution of place (urban and rural), the role of culture and creativity in sustainable tourism, and evolutionary economic geography approaches to urban and regional development.

Lixiao Xu is an assistant professor at the School of Environment, Beijing Normal University, China. Her expertise is in the big data analysis and visualization. She conducts interdisciplinary studies by developing quantitative models.

Platform-mediated tourism: social justice and urban governance before and during Covid-19

Paola Minoia (iD) and Salla Jokela (iD)

ABSTRACT

During the past decade, digital platforms like Airbnb and Uber have enabled the development of a new generation of entrepreneurs in tourism and mobility. The mediation of services through digital platforms was initially presented as a form of a sharing economy led by non-professional providers, but it has grown into a new form of capitalist speculation. This special issue presents theoretical and empirical perspectives on platform-mediated tourism by focusing on Airbnb, which is the most notable digital platform specialising in short-term property rental. The case studies included in this issue show that the impacts of short-term renting on neighbourhoods, residents, and tourism operators are uneven, but increasingly significant. The authors explore issues of social justice in terms of residents' quality of life, working conditions, the housing market, urban structure, and the morality of operators who navigate through normative loopholes. They also examine the governance challenges caused by the inadequacy of existing legal frameworks to better regulate platform-mediated activities, and the reactions generated by social movements and city governments. With the outbreak of Covid-19, networks of cities are taking action against platforms to regain their control over data that is needed to regulate platform-mediated tourism services.

Introduction

During the past decade, Internet-based peer-to-peer service platforms have enabled the development of a new generation of entrepreneurs in tourism and mobility. Services that were traditionally in the hands of specialised and certified companies like hotels, restaurants, and taxis, have been integrated with non-professional services, and partly substituted by (in theory) non-professional services. Along with this development, Airbnb, Uber, and many more have become an integral part of smart city imaginaries and platform ecosystems, driven by the development of digital technologies and the emergence of "app economy" (Barns, 2020, p. 81; Söderström & Mermet, 2020). The diffused supply of services enabled by these platforms was initially considered to be one form of the "sharing economy," but a remarkable part of it is growing into a new form of capitalist speculation. Sometimes seen as a driver of revitalising neighbourhoods, sometimes as a gentrifier or a disruptive business model, it has rapidly become a driving force of change in tourist cities, with a processual formation of meanings, cultures, services, and infra-structures involving a multitude of actors and serving different purposes and users (Köhler et al. 2019). Not only are digital platforms enabling new types of economic activity such as short-term letting of apartments and flexible provision of taxi services, but they are also shaping the ways in which places are made, perceived, and used.

Some of the more drastic impacts of digital platforms in cities are caused by the short-term rental of properties through digital platforms like Airbnb. These include the generation of new forms of inequality through processes like the financialisation of housing, gentrification, touristifi-cation, and deterioration of working conditions. In situations of stress, when residential functions are shrinking due to over-touristification of urban areas, these processes may involve contest-ation and lead to residents attempting to reclaim their rights to the city. Especially in major tour-ist cities like Barcelona and Venice, processes of eviction of residents have changed the popular urban character. For displaced residents, gentrified neighbourhoods are turning into memorial sites of lost identity practices (Navaro-Yashin, 2009). These processes are evidenced by a growing body of literature on critical urban and tourism studies to which this special issue contributes.

By collating explorations of hosts' behaviours and urban changes associated with platform tourism, this special issue continues the discussion on one of the major paradigmatic phenom-ena of our time: the neoliberal globalisation of cities and its consequences in terms of social just-ice and urban governance. Neo-liberalisation has unfolded from the 1970s onwards as a reaction to the crisis of profitability in the global economy (Brenner & Theodore, 2002; Harvey, 1989; Pinson & Journel, 2016). This process has involved a shift from the Fordist-Keynesian system to a Post-Fordist regime of flexible accumulation, underpinned by intellectual currents that have focused on promoting market-orientation as the basis of urban life and new regulatory arrange-ments (Rossi & Vanolo, 2015). As part of this process, cities have turned into "entrepreneurial" actors, which compete against each other to secure a central position in global flows of capital, skilled labour and tourists (Harvey, 1989; Rossi, 2017). Strategies to increase the attractiveness and competitiveness of cities have included investment in cultural infrastructure and innovation, urban regeneration projects, and – increasingly after the financial crisis of 2008 – the promotion of self-responsibilised citizenship and self-entrepreneurialism as a way of fostering vibrant urban life and "authentic" experiences (Rossi, 2017).

We have drawn on critical urban scholars' notion of cities as socially constituted entities (e.g., Fainstein, 2014; Lefebvre, 1968, Harvey, 1973; Zukin, 1980). This means that our focus is on the interactions between urban residents, economic ownership, and government that underlie tour-ism and hospitality, as well as the outcomes that these social relations produce in terms of social justice and urban governance (Fainstein, 2014; Fainstein et al., 2003). Digitally-enabled platforms in tourism, hospitality and leisure are the "next step" in the social constitution of cities under the neoliberal ideals of market-oriented urbanism. Previously, cities responded to changes in their competitive environments through a range of strategies, such as the regeneration of urban cores and waterfronts, and the attraction of mega-events and brands (Rossi, 2017). These develop-ments have directed attention to questions of social sustainability, such as the rights of the mid-dle class in relation to those of the poor (Fainstein et al., 2003; Jamal & Higham, 2020). While these questions are still relevant, the more recent developments driven by digital platforms are raising new questions as to how neoliberal globalisation escapes from global regulations and dir-ectly produces impacts locally, creating new pressures on local communities and their represen-tatives, and calls for responses from them.

The aim is for these contributions to bridge academic and policy-relevant discussions within tourism and urban studies. The case studies from Europe, Australia, New Zealand and the United States have a particular focus on the short-term rental (STR) Airbnb platform. In addition, one paper examines the peer-to-peer social dining platforms VizEat and EatWith. Each study draws on explicit theories and conceptualisations: the performance approach (Christensen, 2020); moral identity theory (Farmaki et al., 2019); the social practice theoretical framework (Davies et al.,

2020); GIS-based morphology of the tourist city (Celata & Romano, 2020); the short-term city (Salerno & Russo, 2020); rights to the city (Torkington & Ribeiro, 2020); social movements as transnational assemblages and politicisation through digital protests (Wilson et al., 2020); externalities, community perceptions and regulatory responses (Muschter et al., 2020); evolutionary economics and gentrification (Ryan & Ma, 2020); social representation theory (Cheng et al., 2020); and workforce income accounting (Chen et al., 2021). Through the case studies, the authors address various sustainability issues caused by the diffusion of platform capitalism in urban tourism, illustrating a crisis that the outbreak of Covid-19 has made even more evident. Before presenting the themes and articles included in this special issue, we delve into the background of platform-mediated tourism services as performing agents in urban restructuring, as well as their consequences for social justice.

The emergence of digital platforms as drivers of tourism development

While the impacts of internet-based tourism platforms on cities have become evident only relatively recently, the existence of a peer-to-peer market of tourism services is nothing new. Even before the creation of Airbnb in 2008, scattered offers of private lodging, as well as home cooking, tourist guiding and transportation, food delivery etc., existed worldwide, especially informally. What is different is that now an increasing proportion of the offers is managed by private entrepreneurs and mediated through platforms, positioning STRs and other so-called shared services as structural components of the tourism services offer. This change is based on other large-scale social transformations, including a shift from mass to 'post-Fordist', individualised or "collaborative" (tourism) consumption (Nilsson, 2020); the introduction of an entirely new business model and economic infrastructure around digital platforms (Barns, 2020; Srnicek, 2017; Zuboff, 2019); and the emergence of self-entrepreneurship and post-work ethos as the basis of urban citizenship (Farmaki et al., 2019 in this issue; Hua & Ray, 2018; Stabrowski, 2017).

The origins of peer-to-peer platforms in tourism can be traced to new business models and technological innovations that started to transform tourism from the 1990s onwards. These included the emergence of low-cost airlines with dense networks, the development of computer technology, the availability of the commercial Internet and, finally, in the 2010s, the growing popularity of smartphones offering fast access to social media and expanding repositories of user-generated content. Social media and peer-to-peer marketplaces created new preconditions for tourism production and consumption, breaking tourists' dependence on large tour operators and enabling increasingly flexible, specialised and individualised travel (Nilsson, 2020). The integration of social networking in global consumerism and increased mobility brought changes in the hospitality sector, starting with home swapping webpages, where suppliers and demanders are part of a peer community without any third-party mediation (Russo & Quaglieri Domínguez, 2016). These webpages paved the way for a new business model invented by a new generation of entrepreneurs who harnessed the opportunities offered by the increasingly social Internet for profit making (Srnicek, 2017; Zuboff, 2019). These entrepreneurs developed digital platforms that specialised in the mediation of accommodation and other tourism services, tapping successfully into what was known as the "sharing economy" - a form of economy that is based on consumers giving each other temporary access to underutilised physical assets and driven by values such as "transparency, humanness, and authenticity" (Botsman, 2015; Frenken et al., 2015).

It followed that digital platforms were discursively aligned with progressive urban politics associated with the peer-to-peer collaborative model, technological advances, and open, ubiquitous and mobile internet (Barns, 2020; Oskam, 2019). They have also been referred to as "liberation technology," allegedly able to "expand political, social, and economic freedom" (Diamond, 2010, p. 70). Because Airbnb and its many counterparts were repeatedly discussed in this framework, many policymakers, tourists, and residents initially praised them for introducing a "green" and inclusive transition to tourism and hospitality. New digital peer-to-peer platforms were associated with enabling more efficient use of resources, creating employment, and empowering residents through the decentralisation of the economy (Botsman & Rogers, 2010; Fang et al., 2016). Since then, the marketing of Airbnb has relied heavily on promoting an idealistic view of the authenticity of the Airbnb community as well as the neighbourhoods in which its listings are located, giving tourists the impression that by choosing Airbnb they can "live like a local" (Oskam & Boswijk, 2016, Paulauskaite et al., 2017). Accordingly, the activities enabled by Airbnb have been associated with the generation of social capital in alignment with a quest for just, inclusive societies (Jung et al., 2016).

However, in recent years, increasingly critical concerns have been voiced with regard to the impacts of the business model of Airbnb and other peer-to-peer service platforms in tourism. Several researchers have shown that digital platforms are based on accumulation of capital through extraction, management and analysis of data enabled by the facilitation of transactions and exploitation of people searching for self-actualisation and efficient, meaningful ways of life (Boswijk, 2013; Brand & Rocchi, 2010; Oskam & Boswijk, 2016; Srnicek, 2017; Zuboff, 2019). The emergence of this new business model has been documented in detail by Nick Srnicek (2017) and Shoshana Zuboff (2019). While their approaches differ in some respects, they share the view that we have recently witnessed the emergence of an entirely new form of capitalism, which they termed "platform capitalism" or "surveillance capitalism," respectively. This form of capitalism is based on a business model that utilises companies' ability to derive data and turn it into products and predictions that can be further sold to advertisers and other external parties, while outsourcing everything else, including workers, maintenance and training (Srnicek, 2017, pp. 33–35; Zuboff, 2019).

Policymakers have embraced this new form of capitalism for at least two reasons. First, it has enabled the capitalist system to respond to the declining profits from manufacturing industries and renew itself in the aftermath of the crisis of the "dot-com" sector that was related to the early phase of commercialisation of the internet in the 1990s (Srnicek, 2017). Secondly, this form of capitalism has seemed largely unavoidable because it has been in the interests of the digital platforms to portray the technology behind their operations as an autonomous force with inevitable implications for our economic system, consumption patterns and ways of life (Zuboff, 2019). As a consequence, the data-driven business model has been flexibly adapted to the most recent manifestations of "urban entrepreneurialism" (Harvey, 1989; Rossi, 2017) - an urban condition that emphasises the market principle as the basis of the operation of the city and directs attention from the channelling of capital from innovation centres, technology parks and cultural building projects towards more spontaneously produced and ephemeral spaces that foster value production through urban culture and digitally enabled "sharing economy" (Moisio, 2018; Rossi, 2017). Furthermore, in many cities, businesses based on digital platforms have been reconciled with "smart city" imaginaries, which, according to Vanolo (2014), are seemingly neutral but powerful devices in attracting investments and creating "smart citizens." Through this development, cities themselves have become increasingly conceptualised as platforms that encourage entrepreneurial activity and produce new urban subjects who use the urban space in creative ways, participate in value creation, and take responsibility for their own wellbeing and livelihoods (Barns, 2020; Jokela, 2020; Rossi, 2017).

As part of this self-responsibilised and self-governed urban citizenship, the urban middle class has used digital platforms to facilitate self-entrepreneurship as a way of coping with the economic insecurity associated with the financial crisis of 2008. In Southern Europe, the recession followed a decade of urban regeneration interventions, also involving EU funding, that improved the attractiveness of city centres as spaces for leisure and consumption, paving the way for private entrepreneurial investments and processes of gentrification (Semi & Tonetta, 2019). The entanglement of urban entrepreneurialism and digital platforms has manifested itself in what Filip Stabrowski (2017) calls "spaces of domestic entrepreneurialism" - that is, homes and neighbourhoods where people have adopted an entrepreneurial attitude. As Torkington and Ribeiro (2020) show in this issue, this is especially evident among young people who are renting apartments to tourists or temporary residents as part of their flexible lifestyles, which involve the accumulation of economic and social capital for the purpose of maintaining cosmopolitan cultural identities and making individualist decisions. This view of individualism and cosmopolitanism is aligned with an imaginary of a post-work and post-capitalist society, in which automation and robotics are freeing people from the oppressiveness of capitalist working conditions to enjoy leisure activities and self-actualisation (Snape et al., 2017). The platforms promote this view by portraying their users as "peers": white and empowered to earn "what they need" flexibly, to maintain their personal lifestyles.

While this image is powerful, it is largely at odds with reality. As Cheng et al. (2020) show in this issue, Airbnb has contributed to an alteration of labour force structures, leading to an increase in jobs that are low-paid, seasonal, and outsourced through external companies. Several other studies have shown that a large proportion of workers in the platform mediated industry (Airbnb apartment cleaners, Uber drivers, Wolt or Foodora bike deliverers) are working class women and immigrants, who are non-unionised and missing income stability or social protection, which are integral to decent work as defined by the International Labour Organization (Acevedo, 2016; De Stefano, 2016; Hua & Ray, 2018; Sundararajan, 2016; Williams & Horodnic, 2017). With the professionalisation of the STR market, the services offered by this precarious and mostly informal workforce cover all the tasks that customers would expect from the official hosts, from the management of reservations, to reception, cleaning, laundry, and on-site availability.

In addition to labour casualisation, there are also other mechanisms through which peer-to-peer platforms in tourism reduce the quality of life of residents and especially that of vulnerable groups. The wide use of residences in the tourism industry has serious impacts on the real estate market and thus on housing affordability, and is a cause of population change and social exclusion. These are other critical dimensions of the sustainability of the Airbnb model.

Sustainability and social justice

Short-term rentals (STRs) and other tourism services mediated by digital platforms interact with policies on sustainability globally expressed through the Sustainable Development Goals (SDG) introduced by the United Nations in 2015. In particular, they relate with: SDG11 "Sustainable cities and communities", especially for target 11.1 "By 2030, ensure access for all to adequate, safe and affordable housing and basic services"; SDG12 "Responsible consumption and production", target 12.B "Develop and implement tools to monitor sustainable development impacts for sustainable tourism that creates jobs and promotes local culture and products"; and SDG8 "Decent work and economic growth", target 8.8 "Protect labour rights and promote safe and secure working environments for all workers". Therefore, in this section we will discuss how these platforms affect the local dynamics on housing, culture and production, and labour in tourist cities, all relevant components of social justice.

The fact that digital peer-to-peer service platforms in tourism position themselves primarily as intermediaries or enablers of "sharing" has an impact beyond those who depend economically on the platforms. Research has shown that the high profitability of short-term renting compared to long-term renting creates a gap between actual and potential rental income, encouraging homeowners, companies, and real estate investors to convert apartments from residential use into tourist accommodation (Wachsmuth & Weisler, 2018; Yrigoy, 2019).

This business of networked hospitality thus encourages multiple listings that have little to do with the original idea of home sharing, but rather use apartments as a commodity for financial investment (Gil & Sequera, 2020; Jokela & Minoia, 2020; Rolnik, 2013, Oskam, 2019). Many studies have shown that these forms of transnational gentrification cause disruptive social, spatial and economic transformations of urban and rural landscapes (Hayes & Zaban, 2020a). The globalisation of rent gaps has caused severe problems of housing affordability, social polarisation and displacement of residents in the affected areas (Cocola-Gant, 2016; Cocola-Gant & Gago, 2019; Yrigoy, 2019). While gentrification and depopulation of city centres are not new phenomena, the platformisation of tourism has accelerated these processes, transforming residential homes into tourist accommodation and causing a loss of neighbourhood businesses and social services that were devoted to residents (Lees, 2012; Sequera & Nofre, 2020). Professionalisation and densification of STRs thus constitute a threat to residents' right to affordable housing, paving the way towards built spaces without residents, or "short-term cities" (Salerno & Russo, 2020, in this issue). Empirical studies show the global dimension of these effects, e.g., in New York City (Wachsmuth & Weisler, 2018), Barcelona (Garcia-López et al., 2020), Raglan in New Zealand (as illustrated by Ryan & Ma, 2020 in this issue) Cuenca in Ecuador, (Hayes & Zaban, 2020b), Jerusalem (Zaban, 2020), and San Miguel de Allende in Mexico (Navarrete Escobedo, 2020).

Traditional businesses are replaced by new ones designed to match global tastes, especially in situations of "overtourism" - the overcrowding of popular tourist areas – where the lack of everyday life-services decrease residents' quality of life (Dodds & Butler, 2019). In popular touristic cities, an alliance between platforms such as Google Maps, Airbnb and Uber, creates "superserved" areas and directs people to areas and routes that are already crowded. This further jeopardises the principles of the sharing economy, such as authentic encounters between hosts and guests. Studies have also shown that the use of authenticity as a competitive edge for tourism business may lead to a situation in which the local setting becomes commodified through "staged authenticity" that is adapted to tourists' desires and expectations at the expense of locals' needs (Chhabra et al., 2003; MacCannell, 1973; Minoia, 2017; Ye et al., 2018). Interactions between hosts and guests are limited and depersonalised, more focused on the service uses than on the human relationship (Ert & Fleischer, 2019; Jung et al., 2016).

Also, work is challenged by the logic of profit making on tourism, especially in neoliberal markets that overlook issues of economic distribution and workers' rights. Bianchi and de Man (2021, p. 358) recognise a "hidden dimension of sustainability" in the systemic presence of exploitation and informality that are overshadowed by orthodox managerial studies on tourism economy. Outsourcing, sub-contracting and occasional calls make the traceability of work arduous. The "demand-economy" of platforms has further exacerbated the already precarious conditions of workers in low-income service sectors, whose conditions depend on race, gender and class (van Doorn, 2017). As explained in the previous section, platforms are active infrastructural agents in the fragmentation of the workforce, hired in the form of independent contractors rather than employees. These service-agreements are beneficial to entrepreneurs who avoid the costs of employment, but erode employee protection with respect to accidents, unemployment, and their unity in collective bargaining.

Cause-and-effect relationships involved in these interconnected processes - the emergence of professional hosts, overtourism, increasing rent prices, the flight of residents from popular tourist areas and work insecurity - are complex and context-specific. Policy-makers have only recently started to address the real impacts of peer-to-peer platforms in tourism. In many cities, fines and lawsuits have been advanced against Airbnb and there have been attempts to impose the cancellation of unlicensed listings. For example, Barcelona, Paris and Amsterdam have imposed rental caps (maximum number of days per year) as to limit the STRs of apartments, but the enforcement of the regulations is difficult because of the lack of access to data on rentals. In the EU, the activities of digital intermediation services like Airbnb are regulated under the directive on electronic commerce in compliance with a ruling of the European Court of Justice. According to this ruling, Airbnb is a provider of an information society service rather than a real estate agent that would be subject to more stringent regulation (Curia, 2019; Feuer, 2019). As a result, Airbnb has been able to avoid cooperating with the cities by giving them access to its data (van Sparrentak, 2020). Nevertheless, these trials show that a stronger political awareness has been formed, especially in large cities. Debates on the future of tourism within a remaking of the city as a complex functioning ecosystem continue, as the following section based on the case studies presented in the articles in the special issue shows.

Themes addressed in this special issue

The articles in this special issue articulate the critical aspects of peer-to-peer platforms and tourist cities, through the following themes: socio-legal loopholes and morality in hosting performativity; STRs as drivers of gentrification, financialisation of housing, impacts on neighbourhoods; diverse stakeholder positions, and government responses.

a. Socio-legal loopholes and performative morality

Authors have observed a fundamental problem of framing the platform-mediated services. Julie Wilson et al. (2020) define platforms as socio-technical assemblages for trading, although they are promoted as enablers of non-professional sharing practices. This confusion in their very definition creates socio-legal uncertainties and loopholes that are used instrumentally by entrepreneurs, as argued by Mathilde Dissing Christensen (2020). The absence of official regulatory frameworks has directed attention to the diffused responsibilities of "communities of practice" formed around the platforms. The study by Farmaki et al. (2019) shows that the perceptions of moral responsibilities of Airbnb hosts and their subsequent efforts to self-regulate their behaviour vary depending on the degree of the hosts' professionalism. The lack of official regulatory frameworks may reduce the hosts' willingness to adhere to law, because hosts can justify irresponsible behaviour by claiming that other hosts are behaving in the same way. The stabilisation and wide diffusion of these practices produce forms of illegality that have impacts on taxation and on the public control over the use of residential apartments for tourist accommodation, this being what concerns STR. A range of unethical acts against guests (e.g., cheating on service quality) and society (e.g., causing disturbance to neighbours, or hiding the business to avoid paying tax) become consolidated in the absence of specific regulations and due to low risk of being detected and sanctioned. Muschter et al. (2020) have shown that hosts are in favour of unrestricted STR letting, whereas non-hosts would prefer a stricter code. In the case of social dining, Davies et al. (2020) note that while platforms claim that they have insurance for hosts and guests, the parameters of that insurance are poorly known by those involved in social dining. In alignment with previous studies (Edelman & Luca, 2014, Kakar et al., 2018, Piracha et al., 2019), Christensen (2020) claims that whiteness, high education levels, good socio-economic status and pleasant physical appearance pave the ground for stronger positions, while different conditions may cause marginalisation and exclusion from either sides of the transaction.

b. Gentrification, financialisation of housing, and impacts on neighbourhoods

Contrary to a popularised narrative of Airbnb as a facilitator of sharing of underutilised rooms in hosts' homes, the databases of *insideairbnb*.com and *AirDNA* reveal that a large proportion of listings are of entire apartments, and that professional enterprises handle multiple listings. Tourism platforms are therefore discussed as drivers of commodification, consumption, and financial speculation over social goods that feed the industry: private homes, public spaces and neighbourhoods. Multiple acquisitions in the same buildings that lead to hotelisation of buildings show the speculative nature of these hosting activities, extracting value from social goods (Salerno & Russo, 2020). STRs channelled through platforms, increase the rent gap in tourist areas, and accelerate financialisation of housing, i.e., investments ensuring capital gains that outstrip interest rates on bank deposit accounts (Ryan & Ma, 2020; Wilson et al., 2020). In Italian tourist cities, the acceleration of speculation in STRs is particularly concentrated in areas that are crucial for the residents' sense of belonging (Celata & Romano, 2020). Housing stress especially hits the lower and middle classes even when their jobs remain in the tourist city, as illustrated by Cheng et al. (2020) in the case of Queensland, Australia.

Tourism-driven speculation on properties is also studied in relation to its effects on resident communities. Ryan and Ma (2020) contribution presents the example of Raglan in New Zealand, a small coastal town, in which STRs have affected several dimensions of place attachment and identity. Torkington and Ribeiro (2020) on Lisbon and Porto, as well as Muschter et al. (2020) on Byron Shire in New South Wales, Australia, expand the discussion on the transformation of public spaces as centres of leisure and entertainment. Many of the authors in this collection (Cheng et al., 2020; Muschter et al., 2020; Ryan & Ma, 2020; Salerno & Russo, 2020; Torkington & Ribeiro, 2020; Wilson et al., 2020) have observed an increased perception of risk, noise and discomfort from living in places where residents can no longer recognise their neighbours. At the same time, increasing cost of urban services such as waste, parking lots, traffic, public toilets, street cleaning and maintenance have to be borne by local taxpayers. These higher costs, together with increases in prices of food and other everyday supplies, make residents' lives harder especially in over-touristed cities where residents are forced to use services designed for tourists (Salerno & Russo, 2020).

c. Diverse positions and government responses

Different groupings and positionalities can be recognised in relation to platform-mediated services: a) hosts, who can have different interests depending on their status as resident or non-resident hosts, non-commercial or entrepreneurs, responsible or opportunistic, non-professional or holding multiple listings with high financial returns; b) workers, on flexible work conditions based on-demand and without social insurance; c) guests of STRs or customers of social dining platforms; d) residents, individually impacted, or members of housing companies, residents' associations or wider social movements; e) the hotel industry, mostly positioned against the rise of STRs; f) *sharing*-advocates and other tourism-related businesses; g) platforms; and h) local authorities, reacting in different ways, from laissez-faire, to semi-interventionist or strongly regulating policies.

Within all groups, different sensitivities, political orientations, agency and organising settings exist, as the Byron Shire community survey presented by Muschter et al. (2020) shows. Effects of platform-mediated services are not uniform and different social groups are affected in different ways depending on their positions in relation to the platforms, as well as the economic interests and social rights that the parties involved seek to protect. An interesting case is the impact felt by the traditional hotels of Queenstown, New Zealand, suffering from a loss of personnel attracted by the new flexible work offered by STRs (Ryan & Ma, 2020). The case of Sydney presented by Chen et al. (2021) shows the extreme vulnerability of the hyper-exploited workforce, that has been the most severely hit by the Covid-19 pandemic. The atomisation of workers, and the invisibility of professional hosts, keep problems submerged and unaddressed. Residents have been reacting in different ways. In the case of Copenhagen illustrated by Christensen (2020), shareholder assemblies are entitled to control apartments' uses and oppose their conversion into tourist accommodation. However, the most common visible reaction is through protests.

Social media provide spaces of protests. The digital amplification of activism transcends local spaces of communities by permitting remote participation of ex-residents of tourism cities and supportive outsiders (Torkington & Ribeiro, 2020; Wilson et al., 2020). An example of international movement is the Southern Europe against Touristification (SET) described by Salerno and Russo (2020), which involves local movements and researchers, claiming housing rights and preservation of local commerce, public services, jobs, and urban environments in tourist cities.

Muschter et al. (2020) indicate three main regulative options taken by local governments: laissez-faire, co-regulative, and interventionist including prohibitions and penalties. The Italian case studies show a laissez-faire attitude caused by the fear of losing tourist market quota (Celata & Romano, 2020; Salerno & Russo, 2020). In those cases, reactions by local authorities are limited to the production of decalogues for "educating" tourists to behaviours of "public decency", or to the proposal of entry tickets, gates or other mechanisms to limit the number of tourists entering in peak periods. With regard to platform-mediated STRs, the purpose of a recently introduced obligation for hosts to register is to increase taxation entries instead of restricting hosting in apartments or regulating work service.

Some other cities have used stronger initiatives to limit the expansion of STRs. As we have discussed before, many cities have requested Airbnb to collaborate with them with the aim of regulating STR and collect taxation to forward directly to the fiscal authorities. Most of these trials failed in the pre-Covid era, apart from the city of Philadelphia, which signed an agreement with Airbnb in 2016 (Christensen, 2020).

Covid-19 pandemic: reclaiming the city

When this special issue was conceived, travel and mobility were still growing at a fast pace, as Covid-19 had not yet manifested itself. However, with the pandemic, the consequences of Airbnb and other digital peer-to-peer service platforms in cities have become especially evident, as the most touristified areas have been emptied of people, shops have closed, and an economic crisis has affected workers in this volatile market (Chen et al., 2021 in this issue; Cherici, 2020). This situation calls for a rethink of the relationship between the platforms and urban development, searching for more effective ways to govern with progressive visions of sustainable cities and communities. While some commentators have predicted that the pandemic will take STR platforms back towards the original idea of sharing idle spaces, others find this unlikely. For instance, Dolnicar and Zare (2020) point out that increasingly many professional hosts may return to the long-term rental market to avoid the consequences of future shocks, whereas Agustín Cocola-Gant (2020) maintains that these hosts are likely to continue to extract value from the short-term rental market. This is because the flexibility of the short-term rental market matches professional hosts' view of properties as financial assets, enabling them to use and sell their properties as they wish without entering into stable contracts with long-term tenants, or being constrained by them (Cocola-Gant, 2020).

Thus, while the pandemic has affected the demand for short-term holiday rentals, there is no justification for assuming that this will automatically lead to a significant increase in the supply of apartments in the long-term rental market, let alone a return to the situation that preceded the platformisation of tourism. For instance, Salerno and Russo (2020), and Celata and Romano (2020), both in this issue, have noticed a small increase in the number of apartments being offered on the medium and longer-term rental market, but with some caution, expecting that tourists will soon fill in the emptiness again. Furthermore, as Cocola-Gant (2020) writes, there is evidence that many professional hosts are increasingly using the services of short-term rental management agencies to move properties flexibly between platforms and adjust the prices and lengths of rental contracts to favour mid-term stays until the short-term holiday rental market has recovered. By giving impetus to this kind of flexibility, the ongoing pandemic may foster the incorporation of mid-term renting of apartments into the exploitative logic of digital platforms. For example, if student apartments start to be viewed as financial assets that can be promoted through platforms and managed by agencies, conditions of rental contracts are likely to change accordingly. Increasingly, many tenants may have to enter contracts without being able to view their future homes first.

Furthermore, as discussed by Christensen (2020) in this issue, the halt to tourism is paid by hosts operating through STR platforms and especially their laid-off workforce. For instance, Chen et al. (2021, this issue) point out that according to AppJobs - a digital gig economy platform - half of the workers employed in App-based jobs have lost their jobs since the beginning of the Covid-19 pandemic. In the Greater Sydney area in Australia, Airbnb hosts have suffered 6.5 times more than the platform itself. As a result, hosts' associations have claimed from national governments the right to subsidies, as given to private companies as compensation. However, in most cases, they have not been eligible for any employment-based social insurance because of the

informal nature of their business. Airbnb established a $250 million fund to compensate the eco-
nomic losses of Airbnb hosts around the world during the first months of 2020 by covering 25%
of the host's cancellation fees, but this support has been limited (Airbnb, 2020; Chen et al., 2021
in this issue; Fishman, 2020).

Workers on other platforms have been affected by the Covid-19 pandemic in different ways.
Informal workers in Airbnb, like cleaners or maintenance workers, are the most vulnerable
groups, as they lack employment-based social security (Sundararajan, 2016). The majority of Uber
drivers have lost their jobs, although some have been involved in delivery of food and drugs or
providing transport to hospitals (Hua & Ray, 2020, Spurk & Straub, 2020). .

The current pandemic has both revealed and exacerbated the negative effects of tourism platforms. The situation calls for new regulations to support cities' efforts to mitigate the harmful
impacts. A few local governments have started new actions, especially for the re-urbanisation of
city centres. Amsterdam has required every host to request a permit and to register all visitors
and has banned STRs in three districts of the old town (De Jong, 2020; Ivens, 2020). In France, a
new law has disposed specific regulations for Airbnb locations (Heikkilä, 2020). Barcelona has
activated stronger control over STRs and has limited their activity (Sequera & Nofre, 2018; Wilson
et al., 2020 in his issue). However, national legislation has found it to be difficult to address the
loopholes of the business logic of the platforms (Christensen, 2020 in this issue; Guttentag,
2017). Dorrit De Jong (2020) points out that as long as the platforms do not make registration
mandatory, it is practically impossible for cities to enforce the new regulations to control rentals
and fiscal compliances.

New promising initiatives have also been introduced at the European level. A new alliance of
European cities (involving Amsterdam, Athens, Barcelona, Berlin, Bologna, Bordeaux, Brussels,
Cologne, Florence, Frankfurt, Helsinki, Krakow, London, Milan, Munich, Paris, Porto, Prague,
Utrecht, Valencia, Vienna and Warsaw) has published a "Position Paper on better EU-legislation
of Platforms offering Short-Term Holiday Rentals". The aim is to regain control over data on tourist apartments and limit STRs in residential buildings. Moreover, the European Commission
(2020) has prepared a Digital Services Act package that contains interesting rules for the e-com-
merce, including Airbnb. According to Cox (2020), the Act should enable the access to neigh-
bourhood-level data with addresses and intervene in the regulation of registrations and permit
systems. Moreover, it should introduce the principle of platform accountability, i.e., storing only
listings that have permit ID numbers.

Conclusions

In this paper, we proposed a discussion on global platforms mediating tourism services, the
manifestations of which are contingent on the local cultural, societal and regulatory contexts.
Through case studies of tourism cities in Europe, Australia, New Zealand and the USA, we could
observe the platform mediated peer-to-peer services in tourism as performative agents in cities.
The literature emphasises the various forms of urban disruption caused by platforms, especially
Airbnb, and the range of interests at stake, the forms of contestation and political reactions.
Lines of argumentation have moved across tourism studies and urban studies and have touched
on a complex arena of intertwined phenomena: entrepreneurial performances in tourism; neo-
liberal political and legal systems protective of the platforms' ownership of data; poor governance mechanisms of control of the gentrification of neighbourhoods and financialisation of
housing, considered to be investment assets with high rentability.

The performativity of operators through platforms has produced a direct impact on the principles according to which the economy operates. Zuboff (2019) claims that one of the main challenges in addressing the ethical issues related to what she has termed "surveillance capitalism" is
that we rely on outdated terminology that is based on old regulatory frameworks. For example,

talk about "monopolistic tendencies" of big tech companies is based on a twentieth-century imagination, which may keep us from seeing some of the new threats posed by digital tracking done by these companies. Similarly, the discursive alignment of digital peer-to-peer platforms with sharing economy, collaborative economy or other alternative modes of economy veils the capitalist logic that explains the success of these platforms, as well as some of the drastic impacts it is having on our cities – and now, with the pandemic, on the middle-classes affected by the crisis. An intersectional approach is needed "to explore the multifaceted relationships between social groups and structures" (Mooney, 2018, p. 175). It is important to look beyond simple indicators of economic growth and income, and to try to comprehend the positions of the disadvantaged actors.

At the European level, some initiatives have seen stronger agency of city administrators and the Commission, to regain control over the data possessed by platforms. Data will help local governments to enforce their decisions on maximum rental day limits, tax collection and safety-regulations, and to revive residence rights in tourist areas. Moreover, data can also reveal the concentration of apartments in the hands of large corporations. This is proving to be a growing public awareness of the fallacy of STR platforms as *sharing* models and of hosts as local casual residents. It will be important to address other related social problems politically, such as the reality of an industry that uses low-paid labour that find it difficult to find a place to live in those unaffordable city areas. The importance of sharing analyses and successful practices to govern tourist cities, and of data sovereignty reclaimed by networks of cities, aligned with a long-expressed call by social movements, can support new commonly enforced practices on a large scale, leading to a sustainable turn that will finally prioritise cities as equitable living places.

Acknowledgements

We are grateful for the University of Helsinki and Academy of Finland (RELATE Centre of Excellence 2017–2019, grant number 307348) for supporting this research. We also thank the anonymous reviewers for their helpful comments on earlier drafts of the manuscript, and Xavier Font for the great support he has given throughout the editorial process of this special issue.

Disclosure statement

No potential conflict of interest was reported by the authors.

ORCID

Paola Minoia iD http://orcid.org/0000-0003-0760-5785
Salla Jokela iD http://orcid.org/0000-0002-9020-2049

References

Acevedo, D. D. (2016). Regulating employment relationships in the sharing economy. *Employee Rights and Employment Policy Journal, 20*, 1–35.

Airbnb. (2020). *$250M to support hosts impacted by cancellations.* https://www.airbnb.com.au/resources/hosting-homes/a/250m-to-support-hosts-impacted-by-cancellations-165

Barns, S. (2020). *Platform urbanism: Negotiating platform ecosystems in connected cities.* Palgrave Macmillan.

Bianchi, R. V., & de Man, F. (2021). Tourism, inclusive growth and decent work: A political economy critique. *Journal of Sustainable Tourism, 29*(2–3), 3, 353–371. https://doi.org/10.1080/09669582.2020.1730862

Boswijk, A. (2013). The power of the economy of experiences: New ways of value creation. In J. Sundbo & F. Sørensen (Eds.), *Handbook on the experience economy* (pp. 171–176). Edward Elgar.

Botsman, R. (2015, May 27). Defining the sharing economy: What is collaborative consumption and what isn't? *FastCompany.* https://www.fastcompany.com/3046119/defining-the-sharing-economy-what-is-collaborative-consumption-and-what-isnt

Botsman, R., & Rogers, R. (2010). *What's mine is yours: The rise of collaborative consumption.* Harper Collins Publishers.

Brand, R., Rocchi, S. (2010). Rethinking value in a changing landscape. A model for strategic reflection and business transformation. *A Philips design paper.* http://www.rickdevisser.com/assets/economic-paradigms-paper.pdf

Brenner, N., & Theodore, N. (2002). Cities and the geographies of "actually existing neoliberalism. *Antipode, 34*(3), 349–379. https://doi.org/10.1111/1467-8330.00246

Celata, F., & Romano, A. (2020). Overtourism and online short-term rental platforms in Italian cities. *Journal of Sustainable Tourism*, 1–20. https://doi.org/10.1080/09669582.2020.1788568

Chen, G., Cheng, M., Edwards, D., & Xu, L. (2021). COVID-19 pandemic exposes the vulnerability of the sharing economy: A novel accounting framework. *Journal of Sustainable Tourism*, 1–18. https://doi.org/10.1080/09669582.2020.1868484

Cheng, M., Houge Mackenzie, S., & Degarege, G. A. (2020). Airbnb impacts on host communities in a tourism destination: An exploratory study of stakeholder perspectives in Queenstown, New Zealand. *Journal of Sustainable Tourism*, 1–19. https://doi.org/10.1080/09669582.2020.1802469

Cherici, S. (2020). Cities as empty shells: Urban tourism in a post-pandemic world. *Green European Journal, 20*, 80–87.

Chhabra, D., Healy, R. G., & Sills, E. (2003). Staged authenticity and heritage tourism. *Annals of Tourism Research, 30*(3), 702–719. https://doi.org/10.1016/S0160-7383(03)00044-6

Christensen, M. D. (2020). Performing a peer-to-peer economy: How Airbnb hosts navigate socio-institutional frameworks. *Journal of Sustainable Tourism*, 1–17. https://doi.org/10.1080/09669582.2020.1849231

Cocola-Gant, A. (2016). Holiday rentals: The new gentrification battlefront. *Sociological Research Online, 21*(3), 112–120. https://doi.org/10.5153/sro.4071

Cocola-Gant, A. (2020, May 25). Short-term rentals, Covid-19 and platform capitalism. *Blog post.* http://www.albasud.org/blog/en/1220/short-term-rentals-covid-19-and-platform-capitalism

Cocola-Gant, A., & Gago, A. (2019). Airbnb, buy-to-let investment and tourism-driven displacement: A case study in Lisbon. *Environment and Planning A: Economy and Space,* https://doi.org/10.1177/0308518X19869012

Cox, M. (2020, November 18). Founder of Inside AirBnB. Talk in the event *"Affordable Housing - Airbnb and the digital services act"* organized by Greens/EFA in the European Parliament.

CURIA Court of Justice of the European Union (2019). Judgement in case C-390/18 Airbnb Ireland. Press release No 162/19.

Davies, A., Cretella, A., Edwards, F., & Marovelli, B. (2020). The social practices of hosting P2P social dining events: Insights for sustainable tourism. *Journal of Sustainable Tourism*, 1–16. https://doi.org/10.1080/09669582.2020.1838526

De Jong, D. (2020, November 18). Dutch Greens/City Council of Amsterdam. Introduction to the event *"Affordable Housing - Airbnb and the digital services act"* organized by Greens/EFA in the European Parliament.

De Stefano, V. (2016). The rise of the" just-in time workforce": On demand work, crowdwork, and labor protection in the" gig economy. *Comparative Labor Law and Policy Journal, 37*(3), 461–471.

Diamond, L. (2010). Liberation technology. *Journal of Democracy, 3*, 69–83.

Dodds, R., & Butler, R. W. (Eds.). (2019). *Overtourism: Issues, realities and solutions.* De Gruyter.

Dolnicar, S., & Zare, S. (2020). COVID19 and Airbnb – Disrupting the disruptor. *Annals of Tourism Research, 83*, 102961. https://doi.org/10.1016/j.annals.2020.102961

Edelman, B. G., Luca, M. (2014). Digital discrimination: The case of Airbnb.com. *Harvard Business School NOM Unit Working Paper* No. 14–054. https://doi.org/10.2139/ssrn.2377353

Ert, E., & Fleischer, A. (2019). The evolution of trust in Airbnb: A case of home rental. *Annals of Tourism Research, 75*(3), 279–287. https://doi.org/10.1016/j.annals.2019.01.004

European Commission (2020). The Digital Services Act package. In: Shaping Europe's digital future (website) https://digital-strategy.ec.europa.eu/en/policies/digital-services-act-package

Fainstein, S. S. (2014). The just city. *International Journal of Urban Sciences*, *18*(1), 1–18. https://doi.org/10.1080/12265934.2013.834643

Fainstein, S. S., Hoffman, L. M., & Judd, D. R. (2003). Introduction. In L. M. Hoffman, S. S. Fainstein, & D. R. Judd (Eds.), *Cities and visitors: Regulating people, markets, and city space*. Blackwell Publishing, 1-19.

Fang, B., Ye, Q., & Law, R. (2016). Effect of sharing economy on tourism industry employment. *Annals of Tourism Research*, *57*, 264–267. https://doi.org/10.1016/j.annals.2015.11.018

Farmaki, A., Stergiou, D., & Kaniadakis, A. (2019). Self-perceptions of Airbnb hosts' responsibility: A moral identity perspective. *Journal of Sustainable Tourism*, 1–21. https://doi.org/10.1080/09669582.2019.1707216

Feuer, W. (2019). Europe's top court just delivered Airbnb a major victory as the company prepares to go public. *CNBC*. https://www.cnbc.com/2019/12/19/airbnb-wins-legal-victory-from-europes-top-court-as-it-looks-to-ipo.html

Fishman, S. (2020). Help for AirBNB hosts affected by the coronavirus outbreak. *Nolo* https://www.nolo.com/legal-encyclopedia/help-for-airbnb-hosts-affected-by-the-coronavirus-outbreak.html

Frenken, K., Meelen, T., Arets, M., & Van de Glind, P. (2015, May 20). Smarter regulation for the sharing economy. *The Guardian*. https://www.theguardian.com/science/political-science/2015/may/20/smarter-regulation-for-the-sharing-economy

Garcia-López, M. A., Jofre-Monseny, J., Martínez-Mazza, R., & Segú, M. (2020). Do short-term rental platforms affect housing markets? Evidence from Airbnb in Barcelona. *Journal of Urban Economics*, *119*, 103278. https://doi.org/10.1016/j.jue.2020.103278

Gil, X., & Sequera, J. (2020). The professionalization of Airbnb in Madrid: far from a collaborative economy. *Current Issues in Tourism*, 1–20. https://doi.org/10.1080/13683500.2020.1757628

Guttentag, D. (2017). Regulating innovation in the collaborative economy: An examination of Airbnb's early legal issues. In D. Dredge & S. Gyimóthy (Eds.), *Collaborative economy and tourism: Perspectives, politics, policies and prospects* (pp. 97–128). Springer.

Harvey, D. (1973). *Social justice and the city*. Johns Hopkins University Press.

Harvey, D. (1989). From managerialism to entrepreneurialism: The transformation in urban governance in late capitalism. *Geografiska Annaler: Series B, Human Geography*, *71*(1), 3–17. https://doi.org/10.1080/04353684.1989.11879583

Hayes, M., & Zaban, H. (2020a). The coloniality of UNESCO's heritage urban 3060 landscapes: Heritage process and transnational gentrification in Cuenca. *Urban Studies*, *57*(15), 3009–3024. https://doi.org/10.1177/0042098019888441

Hayes, M., & Zaban, H. (2020b). Transnational gentrification: The crossroads of transnational mobility and urban research. *Urban Studies*, *57*(15), 3009–3024. https://doi.org/10.1177/0042098020945247

Heikkilä, M. (2020). In blow to Airbnb, EU court rules cities can restrict short-term rentals. *Politico*. https://www.politico.eu/article/eu-court-rules-cities-can-restrict-short-term-rentals-in-blow-to-airbnb/

Hua, J., & Ray, K. (2018). Beyond the precariat: Race, gender, and labor in the taxi and Uber economy. *Social Identities*, *24*(2), 271–289. https://doi.org/10.1080/13504630.2017.1321721

Hua, J., & Ray, K. (2020, August 20). *Spent lives: Taxi driving and the uber economy*. Webinar organized by the University of Edinburgh Business School with Julietta Hua and Kasturi Ray in discussion with Rashné Limki.

Ivens, L. (2020). Verbodsgebieden vakantieverhuur van kracht. *Gemeente Amsterdam*. https://www.amsterdam.nl/bestuur-organisatie/college/wethouder/laurens-ivens/persberichten/verbodsgebieden-vakantieverhuur-kracht/

Jamal, T., & Higham, J. (2020). Justice and ethics: Towards a new platform for tourism and sustainability. *Journal of Sustainable Tourism*, *29*(2), 3, 143–157. https://doi.org/10.1080/09669582.2020.1835933

Jokela, S. (2020). Transformative city branding and the evolution of the entrepreneurial city: The case of 'Brand New Helsinki. *Urban Studies*, *57*(10), 2031–2046. https://doi.org/10.1177/0042098019867073

Jokela, S., & Minoia, P. (2020). Nordic home-sharing utopia: A critical analysis of Airbnb in Helsinki. *Scandinavian Journal of Hospitality and Tourism*, *20*(3), 227–245. https://doi.org/10.1080/15022250.2020.1774412

Jung, J., Yoon, S., Kim, S., Park, S., Lee, K. P., & Lee, U. (2016). *Social or financial goals?* [Paper presentation]. Comparative analysis of user behaviors in Couchsurfing and Airbnb. Proceedings of the 2016 CHI conference extended abstracts on human factors in computing systems, 2857–2863. https://doi.org/10.1145/2851581.2892328

Kakar, V., Voelz, J., Wu, J., & Franco, J. (2018). The visible host: Does race guide Airbnb rental rates in San Francisco? *Journal of Housing Economics*, *40*, 25–40. https://doi.org/10.1016/j.jhe.2017.08.001

Köhler, J., Geels, F. W., Kern, F., Markard, J., Onsongo, E., Wieczorek, A., Alkemade, F., Avelino, F., Bergek, A., Boons, F., Fünfschilling, L., Hess, D., Holtz, G., Hyysalo, S., Jenkins, K., Kivimaa, P., Martiskainen, M., McMeekin, A., Mühlemeier, M. S., ... Wells, P. (2019). An agenda for sustainability transitions research: State of the art and future directions. *Environmental Innovation and Societal Transitions*, *31*, 1–32. https://doi.org/10.1016/j.eist.2019.01.004

Lees, L. (2012). The geography of gentrification: Thinking through comparative urbanism. *Progress in Human Geography*, *36*(2), 155–171. https://doi.org/10.1177/0309132511412998

Lefebvre, H. (1968). *La droit à la ville*. Éditions Anthropos.

MacCannell, D. (1973). Staged authenticity: Arrangement of social space in tourist settings. *American Journal of Sociology, 79*(3), 589–603. https://doi.org/10.1086/225585

Minoia, P. (2017). Venice reshaped? Tourism gentrification and sense of place. In N. Bellini & C. Pasquinelli (Eds.), *Tourism in the City-Towards an integrative agenda on urban tourism* (pp. 261–274). Springer.

Moisio, S. (2018). *Geopolitics of the knowledge-based economy*. Routledge.

Mooney, S. (2018). Illuminating intersectionality for tourism researchers. *Annals of Tourism Research, 72*, 175–176. https://doi.org/10.1016/j.annals.2018.03.003

Muschter, S., Caldicott, R. W., von der Heidt, T., & Che, D. (2020). Third-party impacts of short-term rental accommodation: A community survey to inform government responses. *Journal of Sustainable Tourism*, 1–20. https://doi.org/10.1080/09669582.2020.1860067

Navaro-Yashin, Y. (2009). Affective spaces, melancholic objects: Ruination and the production of anthropological knowledge. *Journal of the Royal Anthropological Institute, 15*(1), 1–18. https://doi.org/10.1111/j.1467-9655.2008.01527.x

Navarrete Escobedo, D. (2020). Foreigners as gentrifiers and tourists in a Mexican historic district. *Urban Studies, 57*(15), 3151–3168. https://doi.org/10.1177/0042098019896532

Nilsson, J. H. (2020). Conceptualizing and contextualizing overtourism: The dynamics of accelerating urban tourism. *International Journal of Tourism Cities, 6*(4), 657–667. https://doi.org/10.1108/IJTC-08-2019-0117

Oskam, J. A. (2019). *The future of Airbnb and the "sharing economy": The collaborative consumption of our cities*. Channel View Publications.

Oskam, J. A., & Boswijk, A. (2016). Airbnb: The future of networked hospitality businesses. *Journal of Tourism Futures, 2*(1), 22–42. https://doi.org/10.1108/JTF-11-2015-0048

Paulauskaite, D., Powell, R., Coca, -Stefaniak, J. A., & Morrison, A. M. (2017). Living like a local: Authentic tourism experiences and the sharing economy. *International Journal of Tourism Research, 19*(6), 619–628. https://doi.org/10.1002/jtr.2134

Pinson, G., & Journel, M. C. (2016). The neoliberal city: Theory, evidence, debates. *Territory, Politics, Governance, 4*(2), 137–153. https://doi.org/10.1080/21622671.2016.1166982

Piracha, A., Sharples, R., Forrest, J., & Dunn, K. (2019). Racism in the sharing economy: Regulatory challenges in a neo-liberal cyber world. *Geoforum, 98*, 144–152. https://doi.org/10.1016/j.geoforum.2018.11.007

Rolnik, R. (2013). Late neoliberalism: The financialization of homeownership and housing rights. *International Journal of Urban and Regional Research, 37*(3), 1058–1066. [Database] https://doi.org/10.1111/1468-2427.12062

Rossi, U. (2017). *Cities in Global Capitalism*. Polity Press.

Rossi, U., & Vanolo, A. (2015). Urban neoliberalism. In J. D. Wright (Ed.), *International encyclopedia of the social and behavioral sciences* (pp. 846–853). Elsevier.

Russo, A. P., & Quaglieri Domínguez, A. (2016). Home exchanging: A shift in the tourism marketplace. In J. Rickly Boyd, K. Hannam, & M. Mostafanezhad (Eds.), *Tourism and leisure mobilities: Politics, work and play* (pp. 147–160). Routledge.

Ryan, C., & Ma, L. (2020). Social consequences of airbnb–a New Zealand case study of cause and effect. *Journal of Sustainable Tourism*, 1–21. https://doi.org/10.1080/09669582.2020.1860073

Salerno, G. M., & Russo, A. P. (2020). Venice as a short-term city. Between global trends and local lock-ins. *Journal of Sustainable Tourism*, 1–20. https://doi.org/10.1080/09669582.2020.1860068

Semi, G., & Tonetta, M. (2019). Plateformes locatives en ligne et rente urbaine à Turin: Les classes moyennes face à l'austérité. *Annales de Géographie, N° 727*(3), 40–61. https://doi.org/10.3917/ag.727.0040

Sequera, J., & Nofre, J. (2018). Shaken, not stirred: New debates on touristification and the limits of gentrification. *City, 22*(5–6), 843–855. https://doi.org/10.1080/13604813.2018.1548819

Sequera, J., & Nofre, J. (2020). Touristification, transnational gentrification and urban change in Lisbon: The neighbourhood of Alfama. *Urban Studies, 57*(15), 3169–3189. https://doi.org/10.1177/0042098019883734

Snape, R., Haworth, J., McHugh, S., & Carson, J. (2017). Leisure in a post-work society. *World Leisure Journal, 59*(3), 184–194. https://doi.org/10.1080/16078055.2017.1345483

Söderström, O., & Mermet, A.-C. (2020, May). When Airbnb sits in the control room: platform urbanism as actually existing smart urbanism in Reykjavík. *Frontiers in Sustainable Cities, 2*, 1–7. https://doi.org/10.3389/frsc.2020.00015

Spurk, D., & Straub, C. (2020). Flexible employment relationships and careers in times of the COVID-19 pandemic. *Journal of Vocational Behavior, 119*, 103435. https://doi.org/10.1016/j.jvb.2020.103435

Srnicek, N. (2017). *Platform capitalism*. Polity Press.

Stabrowski, F. (2017). People as businesses': Airbnb and urban micro-entrepreneurialism in New York City. *Cambridge Journal of Regions, Economy and Society, 10*(2), 327–347. https://doi.org/10.1093/cjres/rsx004

Sundararajan, A. (2016). *The sharing economy: The end of employment and the rise of crowd-based capitalism*. MIT Press.

Torkington, K., & Ribeiro, F. P. (2020). Whose right to the city? An analysis of the mediatized politics of place surrounding alojamento local issues in Lisbon and Porto. *Journal of Sustainable Tourism*, 1–20. https://doi.org/10.1080/09669582.2020.1849230

United Nations. (2015). *Sustainable development goals*. http://www.un.org/sustainabledevelopment/sustainable-development-goalsvan

van Doorn, N. (2017). Platform labor: On the gendered and racialized exploitation of low-income service work in the 'on-demand' economy. *Information, Communication & Society, 20*(6), 898–914. https://doi.org/10.1080/1369118X.2017.1294194

Vanolo, A. (2014). Smartmentality: The smart city as disciplinary strategy. *Urban Studies, 51*(5), 883–898. https://doi.org/10.1177/0042098013494427

van Sparrentak, K. (2020). Introductory note. Airbnb and the digital service act. Possibilities for regulating online short-term rental to ensure affordable housing (webinar).

Wachsmuth, D., & Weisler, A. (2018). Airbnb and the rent gap: Gentrification through the sharing economy. *Environment and Planning A: Economy and Space, 50*(6), 1147–1170. https://doi.org/10.1177/0308518X18778038

Williams, C. C., & Horodnic, I. A. (2017). Regulating the sharing economy to prevent the growth of the informal sector in the hospitality industry. *International Journal of Contemporary Hospitality Management, 29*(9), 2261–2278. https://doi.org/10.1108/IJCHM-08-2016-0431

Wilson, J., Garay-Tamajon, L., & Morales-Perez, S. (2020). Politicising platform-mediated tourism rentals in the digital sphere: Airbnb in Madrid and Barcelona. *Journal of Sustainable Tourism*, 1–22. https://doi.org/10.1080/09669582.2020.1866585

Ye, S., Xiao, H., & Zhou, L. (2018). Commodification and perceived authenticity in commercial homes. *Annals of Tourism Research, 71*, 39–53. https://doi.org/10.1016/j.annals.2018.05.003

Yrigoy, I. (2019). Rent gap reloaded: Airbnb and the shift from residential to touristic rental housing in the Palma Old Quarter in Mallorca. *Urban Studies, 56*(13), 2709–2726. https://doi.org/10.1177/0042098018803261

Zaban, H. (2020). The real estate foothold in the Holy Land: Transnational gentrification in Jerusalem. *Urban Studies, 57*(15), 3116–3134. https://doi.org/10.1177/0042098019845614

Zuboff, S. (2019). *The age of surveillance capitalism: The fight for a human future at the new frontier of power*. Public Affairs.

Zukin, S. (1980). A decade of the new urban sociology. *Theory and Society, 9*(4), 575–601. https://doi.org/10.1007/BF00148354

Performing a peer-to-peer economy: how Airbnb hosts navigate socio-institutional frameworks

Mathilde Dissing Christensen (iD)

ABSTRACT

Airbnb is commonly seen as emblematic of the disruptive forces of peer-to-peer platforms, and often attracts attention due to its relationship to existing socio-institutional frameworks. This article investigates how existing societal structures are navigated, remade or challenged through Airbnb hosting. In taking a performative approach to the economic forms found in collaborative economies, this article introduces a novel way of thinking about such changes. In examining performances of Airbnb hosts performances this article endeavours to move beyond distinctions of commercial, cultural and private, but rather perceives such categories as performatively constructed through ongoing framings. Through 33 qualitative interviews with hosts in Copenhagen, Denmark and Philadelphia, United States, this article explores how hosting becomes entangled with social and institutional frameworks through host performances. First, the article explores host strategies for navigating and making sense of local legislation. Second, the article moves to the theme of taxation and discusses how hosts balance public obligations with personal profit. Finally, the article addresses how hosting is negotiated in relation to neighbour relations and implications for local communities. The article contributes with insights into how Airbnb hosting is transforming urban landscapes, as well as discussions on the heterogeneity of economies.

Introduction

Airbnb has been the subject of worldwide press attention in attempts to understand its impact on urban dwellers, local neighbourhoods and legislative landscapes. Public discourse often emphasizes negative impacts, as Airbnb is criticized for feeding the urban housing crises and eroding local communities. This is perhaps most clearly illustrated by a strongly worded opinion piece claiming that "Airbnb is a parasitic monster that squats over cities and hoovers up vast sums of money in its slimy proboscis" (Poole, 2018). Airbnb is widely accused of disrupting established socio-institutional frameworks (see Guttentag, 2015) impacting a variety of heterogenous stakeholders (Cheng et al., 2020). Multiple papers link Airbnb to gentrification (see for instance Cocola-Gant & Gago, 2019; Mermet, 2017; Wachsmuth & Weisler, 2018), local tenants being evicted in favour of more profitable short-term rentals and perceived negative socio-economic and environmental impacts (Stergiou & Farmaki, 2020). Other research documents the economic effect on budget hotels (Zervas et al., 2017), potentially based on the ability to open Airbnbs outside hotel districts (Gutiérrez et al., 2017), expanding touristic "bubbles" (Ioannides et al., 2019) and feeding overtourism (Celata & Romano, 2020).

Such discussions clearly illustrate that economic activities do not occur in a vacuum. Rather, economic performances are always intimately entangled with socio-institutional contexts and unfold in interaction with existing legislative and social structures. Rules and legislation can (at least momentarily) serve to stabilize certain moral aspects of markets, or conversely become destabilized if not adhered to as new market configurations challenge existing frameworks. Guttentag (2017) reports that short-term rental regulations make a large proportion of listings illegal. van Doorn recently argued that Airbnb is a "regulatory entrepreneur" for whom changing existing laws are an integral part of its business plan (2019). Researchers additionally argue that platforms like Airbnb have significant control over materiality, governance and everyday lives in contemporary cities through control over code and data (Söderström & Mermet, 2020). In fact, Airbnb has been criticized for producing "information asymmetries" (Dredge, 2017), as its control over data is incremental to the governmentality of the platform (Minca & Roelofsen, 2019).

Whereas van Doorn explores Airbnb as a new institutional form which strategically utilizes hosts as part of the "toolbox" of platform urbanism, this article takes host performances as the starting point. Rather than attending to deliberate attempts to affect legislative processes, the objective of this article is to explore how existing societal structures are navigated, remade or challenged through hosting performances. Although digital platforms are constantly remaking those structures, limited qualitative attention has been devoted to exploring the experiences of this new category of workers (for exceptions see Farmaki et al., 2019; Knaus, 2020; Meged & Christensen, 2017; Ravenelle, 2017; Roelofsen, 2018). Airbnb does not fit neatly into existing legislative frameworks, but rather criss-crosses existing legislative structures. Consequently, strategies of navigating the socio-institutional embeddedness of Airbnb hosting become an integral part of host performances. I perceive the socio-institutional context not solely as constituting a frame within which certain types of host performances are made possible, but rather as an active performance in its own right, informing, as well as being remade through everyday performances. As hosts navigate social structures, develop creative interpretations, comply with some rules whilst ignoring others, socio-institutional frameworks develop along such performances, sometimes through legislative adaptions, sometimes gradually as the performative forces of certain rules are diminished.

The article focuses analytically on three different themes. First, it explores host strategies for navigating local legislation. Second, the theme of taxation is discussed in relation to how hosts negotiate public obligations with personal profit. Finally, the article addresses how hosting is negotiated in relation to neighbour relations and implications for local communities.

Doing a peer-to-peer economy

In this section, I explore how distinctions between economic and cultural categories have been theorised in relation to peer-to-peer economies and discuss how a performative approach can help aid this discussion.

Airbnb is often argued to represent a new mode of economic organization, intersecting previous distinctions and understandings of the economic. Much critique is based on the presumption that peer-to-peer platforms are utilizing legislative loopholes by rearranging established relationships and transgressing existing boundaries between public and private categories. Consequently, peer-to-peer platforms offer complex entanglements of what is considered commercial and non-commercial. Peer-to-peer platforms are often based on opening up resources previously considered private for public audiences, and negotiation of these categories can be an essential normative underlining for users (Koch, 2020). Additionally, Ravenelle (2017) argues that sharing is often seen as a misleading descriptor for users of peer-to-peer economies, which often reject both notions of sharing, as well as entrepreneurial descriptors, in favour of terminologies of work.

This points towards the embedded paradox emphasised by Richardson (2015) that peer-to-peer economies are framed simultaneously as part of a capitalist economy and as an alternative. This tension is mirrored in various terminologies, which often imply that the cultural is being performed in a new way, albeit within an economic context (Dredge & Gyimóthy, 2015). Such observations highlight the relevance of research exploring the heterogeneity of economic activity through entanglements of culture and economy. Scholars have long argued that economies take diverse forms and are informed by various rationalities reaching beyond profit-maximizing behaviours (see e.g. Amin & Thrift, 2007; Gibson-Graham, 2008; Polanyi, 1957; Zelizer, 1994). A common aim of such research is the endeavour to avoid presuppositions of what the economy is, but rather to engage with "ontological reframing" by exploring performances as constructive or deconstructive social components (Gibson-Graham, 2008). Such theoretical endeavours challenge positivistic understandings of the market as an autonomous reality, and argue that such processes are not "pre-given entities, already bounded, identifiable and knowable" (Butler, 2010, p. 147). The core argument is that economic theories not only describe economic phenomena, but are in fact simultaneously shaping them (see e.g. Butler, 2010; Callon, 1998; Gibson-Graham, 2008). Although often debated though the discipline of economics, performative agency extends outside academic institutions and is also installed in the mindsets of citizens, reproduced through their values and agency.

A main dividing line in theories of performativity is between those who construe performativity as a formal quality of language and those who understand it as an embodied practice. Butler represents a linguistic definition, emphasizing the repetitive power of discourse which produces that which it simultaneously regulates (Butler, 1990). Rather than giving priority to linguistic performances, Gregson and Rose (2000), argue that performative effects are present in all social practice. Thus, all performances are seen as interrelational and saturated with power, not only linking subjects together but also bridging the divide to performativity, as they express already established forms of knowledge.

Callon (2010) argues that the performative nature of the economic implies demarcation between that which is economic and that which is not. He, thus, abandons the concept of "the economy" in order to focus on processes of "economization" and "marketization" to comprehend the processes through which part of the world is perceived or qualified as economic. Consequently, continuous definition or framing is integral to any process of marketization, as markets are perceived predominantly as a construction of boundaries "where certain entities and behaviours become disentangled from other systems and temporarily stabilized as appropriate, rational, or even necessary" (Callon, 1998 in Muellerleile, 2013, p. 1630).

The performative framework conceptualizes how a multitude of performances are co-constitutive of what is perceived as being economic. As such, technologies, which support the development of peer-to-peer platforms, are organizing new networks around short-term hospitality rentals, by introducing new types of actors previously engaged in commercial hospitality. This in turn results in changes of the mundane and repeated acts of delimitation that seek to maintain a separation among economic, social and political spheres. Hosting performances can serve to reinforce or challenge existing formal and informal understandings of which aspects of hospitality are perceived as private matters and which are not, and such performances have performative effects. Consequently, framing of economies does not solely occur in legislative documents, but also in public discourse and everyday performances.

The processual focus of Callon's framework proves especially useful when analysing economic instability and change. The disruption caused by the emergence of peer-to-peer platforms is clearly challenging existing framing(s) of the economic. Thus, agents (and activities) that have previously largely been considered outside of the economic sphere are subjected to a process of "economization." As the scale of such performances increases, they are considered to be "economic activities" that change the balance between economic, social and political spheres. As private homes become occasional hotels, relationships between neighbours are challenged and legislative assemblies struggle to keep up with the economic reframing. This performative perspective demands sensitivity in analysing networks that are in the process of reframing or reconfiguration, with attention to everyday performances.

By reassembling networks of touristic accommodation, new technologies alter perceptions about which performances are "economized" and since the network is unstable, the "economization" of such behaviours is debatable, subject to political discussion and (re)definition. Therefore, discursive battles to define the "collaborative economy," either through utopian imagery as "the sharing economy" (Botsman & Rogers, 2010) or the more dystopian "Platform Capitalism" (Srnicek, 2017), can be seen as an expression of a framing or economization, with performative effects on how to re/disentangle certain performances, economize some behaviours and stabilize the network. As a result, there are multiple crosscurrents; the different implications of this stabilization process remain unsettled. In attending to the immediate level by studying this reconfiguration from the point of production, the performances of Airbnb hosts, this article offers both insights into the performances of a specific touristic phenomenon, but also adds to wider theoretical discussions of the entanglements of economic, cultural and digital performances.

Method

In order to develop insights into the performances of hosts, in-depth qualitative interviews were employed. The narrative work done in an interview does not offer a direct reflection of an objective reality but can be seen as part of a cognitive process of establishing perceptions and attitudes. As such, the construction of narratives occurring during the interview situation can be understood as an integral element of the performance, as meanings are articulated and legitimized in this process (Haldrup, 2004).

Thirty-three Airbnb hosts based in Copenhagen (CPH), Denmark and Philadelphia (PHL), United States were interviewed. Interviewing hosts in two destinations was in part a matter of convenience, as well as an attempt to collect accounts from two different socio-institutional contexts: a social democratic welfare state, and a more free-market capitalist society. The two cities are not only embedded in different national contexts but have their own distinct characteristics (see Table 1). Copenhagen has 720,000 inhabitants (Copenhagen Municipality, 2018; Frederiksberg Municipality, 2018), compared to Philadelphia, which has 1,580,000 inhabitants (United States Census Bureau, 2018). The touristic profiles of the two cities vary, as Copenhagen has higher levels of tourist activity with more than 8 million booked hotel room nights in 2017 (Visit Copenhagen, 2017) compared with 1.1 million room nights in Philadelphia (Visit Philadelphia, 2018).

Copenhagen has five times as many active Airbnb hosts as Philadelphia, not accounting for differences in population size. However, Philadelphia has a higher percentage of multi-listing hosts, running 64% of listings compared to 22% in Copenhagen. This number parallels the percentage of hosts who administer solely one listing, which is 94% in Copenhagen compared to 73% in Philadelphia. A total of 81% of all Copenhagen listings are for an entire home, compared to 56% in Philadelphia.

Such patterns indicate high variability in the ways hosting is performed, both within and across different destinations. Hosts were recruited by snowballing extended networks, in Facebook groups for Airbnb hosts, and through contacting hosts from previous visits. In an effort to collect a large variety of accounts, a sample with maximum variation was constructed in relation to demographic features such as age, gender, race and class, but also for the types of listings, accounting for hosts with both single and multiple listings, offering private rooms, shared rooms, as well as full homes. The sample of interviewees included hosts who drew on multiple discourses when describing their role; hosts managing multiple listings describing themselves as entrepreneurs; hosts in precarious conditions relying on Airbnb as a source of income and hosts utilizing the discourses of the "sharing economy" and community.

I interviewed only a few hosts with a minority background. This is likely to be an extension of the skewedness towards whiteness amongst Airbnb hosts shown by Cansoy and Schor (2016) or Edelman et al. (2017). Education has also been seen as key to understanding Airbnb participation, as highly educated populations participate at higher rates (Andreotti et al., 2017; Cansoy & Schor, 2016). This resonates with the interviewees of this study, who had significantly higher educational levels compared to the general population.[1]

Interviews were carried out in 2017 and 2018 at a place of the interviewees choosing, most frequently within the Airbnb listing, lasting between 40 min to 2 hours. The conversations were structured through a series of open-ended questions exploring various aspects of hosting. All interviews were audio recorded, transcribed verbatim, whilst giving pseudonyms and deleting identifying features, and finally coded into broad thematic categories. The coding was conducted by the researcher by manually reading through the transcriptions numerous times, interpretating and developing themes.

Navigating legislation

When hosting on Airbnb, hosts often have to navigate confusing legislative landscapes. I will explore host strategies for navigating and argue that whilst confusion can provide openings for opportune interpretations it simultaneously creates uncertainties. Strategies range across a spectrum between evasion and engagement. A commonly used strategy was one of direct evasion, which Julie describes as a reaction to being overwhelmed:

> I have to honestly admit, that when they change something or write that something new has happened, I simply don't read it. I close my eyes and say that I read it. But that isn't too smart, because it is your own home and responsibility. [...] But you also wouldn't read it when Apple sends out something new on iTunes. You just click accept (Julie, CPH).

This provides insights into digital cultures, where the sheer amount of terms and conditions often lead users to disengage, and simply "click accept." Such digital performances become entangled with Airbnb hosting in spite of ambivalent feelings. As an integral part of evading strategies few hosts looked extensively into rules and legislation before engaging with hosting. Rather, interviewees describe an approach of "jumping right in":

> I made a lot of assumptions, and I assumed like, if there are dozens of people doing this, it might be illegal, but there isn't an impending danger. Otherwise they would have shut the site down ... People wouldn't be booked solid for months in advance. So, I just kind of jumped right in (Logan, PHL).

Logan's assumptions about the legality of hosting were based on the popularity and consequent normalization of Airbnb. "It might be illegal, but there isn't an impending danger," denotes that the sheer volume of users is perceived as a counterweight to existing rules and regulations. Thus, popularity becomes a stabilizing force of the Airbnb market, indicating legitimacy whilst complicating legislative reactions. Paradoxically, the widespread scale afforded by Airbnb is pushing hosting into the public eye and raises questions about the legality of peer-to-peer hosting. The substantial economic flow through the platform is increasingly pressuring legislators into reacting to performances previously considered private, as increasing numbers are affected by the undesirable impacts of Airbnb, as with regard to housing prices (see Horn & Merante, 2017; Wachsmuth & Weisler, 2018), eroding local communities (see Harris, 2018; Poole, 2018) or effects on local hotels (see Zervas et al., 2017).

Countering strategies of evasion, other hosts engage more directly with legislative structures. Helen demonstrates an alternate experience and proclaims that she found requirements fairly easy to navigate:

> It was pretty straightforward to me. But I also owned a business beforehand. [...] You have to have occupancy stuff and rental licences, and vacant property licences if it's vacant for a period of time. You know stuff like that. But I knew, because I'd already been in that system to some degree (Helen, PHL).

Helen rationalizes that the "straightforwardness" of the system might be rooted in her previous business experience. This indicates that legislative frameworks are designed in a manner that resonates with a professional approach, and that professional skills significantly eases navigating the system. This brings up considerations about the diversity of users. Airbnb offers low entry requirements to participate in commercial hospitality. Many users will be new to running a business and potentially challenged in navigating existing legislation, especially as rules crisscross multiple legislative frameworks. As such, patterns connected to strategies of navigating legislation, evasion or engagement, were more related to business experience than local contexts. Steve found rules and regulations more difficult to navigate:

> On their [Airbnb's] website it just says, just go to Philadelphia's website to understand your rules and regulations. So basically, they are leaving it up to us to understand everything and it is really confusing as to how it all works. It is really convoluted. So, we are kind of just playing dumb a little bit and just waiting for them to see what they are going to do (Steve, PHL).

Although hosting via Airbnb on a large scale, Steve did not share Helen's business experience and feels compelled to learn from "convoluted" public webpages. Additionally, Steve utilizes an evading strategy of "playing dumb," awaiting reactions from the official side. This strategy carries a striking resemblance with the forgiveness over permission strategy often associated with Airbnb (Varma et al., 2016). Steve's strategy, moreover, relies on Airbnb hosting remaining within an understanding of being "private" rather than "commercial." Strategies of positioning peer-to-peer interactions within the private domain rely on staying nonvisible in the public eye and consistently remaining within a private framing. Thus, Steve explains being paid a visit from the local council, presumably after having noticed the word "hostel" in a listing[2]:

> We actually got a rude awakening when somebody from the city knocked on our door one day and asking us. Thinking that we were an actual hostel. Because one of our listings at one point mentioned hostel and I think they have some kind of city council that goes through all of these listings, that like screens them to see if they were being used for the wrong reasons or they needed some kind of permit that they didn't already have [...] He said that since the whole unit itself is shared between everyone it is ok, and it is essentially just an owner-occupied rental. Then you can rent it out up to 180 days, which they don't enforce. So, after 180 days you are kind of changing the nature of what it was intended for, as residential, and it is becoming more commercial (Steve, PHL).

Beyond the council not recognizing hosting as a fully private affair screening listings that might fit a more commercial framework, this indicates that there is a divergence in perception about what ought to be categorized as private versus commercial. Additionally, Steve addresses a hierarchy of rules and questions the nature of such rules, which are not enforced and thus lose their performative function, "after 180 days you are kind of changing the nature of what it was intended for, as residential, and it is becoming more commercial" – indicates a formalized process of framing. Here, formal boundaries are constructed in what Callon conceptualizes as a process of marketization, where certain performances become disentangled from the private sphere and reframed as part of the economic and commercial sphere. As a result, agents and behaviours previously considered separate from the commercial are repositioned, as hosts are considered as performing economic activities and transgressing boundaries between economic, social and political realms. This in turn affects the performances of the individual Airbnb hosts trying to predict, affect and navigate the changing circumstances in a process of reconfiguration and reframing.

This reconfiguration creates unpredictable legislative circumstances. Economies are never quite stable, but continuously reshaped through performance. This is especially true in this case, since Airbnb is producing instability in existing markets which have not quite stabilized yet, especially not in relation to socio-institutional contexts. Although continuous change is a condition in all markets, the dramatic reconfiguration caused by the disruption strategy of Airbnb brings this instability front and centre. Thus, legislative frameworks and workers struggle to define what should be perceived as economic, and which rules should apply. All of this indicates that Airbnb is in the process of "economization" and being framed within an economic context.

Legitimizing Airbnb

Airbnb represents contested performances and a process of framing and stabilizing is currently being debated in multiple localities. In this section I will investigate hosts' positions on future legislation. I argue that although hosts welcome the legitimacy offered by formal legislation, opinions on the content of such legislation are directly informed by the hosts' own approach to hosting.

Hosts' reflections on regulatory initiatives reveal complex entanglements of their individual hosting, as well as their distinctions between harmless private behaviour and corporate businesses which have emerged between considerations of common good and self-interest. Hosts were very much aware that Airbnb hosting carried undesired consequences. This is addressed by Jacob who speaks of the challenges of creating distinctions between corporate performances and small scale "harmless" hosting:

> Not because there is a problem with renting out a lot. But then it starts to resemble a hotel. And then it is unequal competition, because hotels have a lot of safety requirements, just like the taxis do. There needs to be a balance. And I don't think we compete with the hotels in the area. It is just a single apartment. But if you start to have twelve beds in a two-bedroom apartment, then it is looking a lot like a hotel (Jacob, CPH).

Jacob addresses a "need for balance," as he understands Airbnb hosting through a spectrum related to the level of competition towards existing businesses and presents a moral imperative based on unfair competitive advantages. His perceptions are focused on the individual hosts and not on the cumulative consequences of multiple hosts. Julie adds an additional angle to the moral imperatives, articulating a desire for clearing up legislative circumstances. She considers the current situation as unfair, since other businesses are subjected more directly to rules and regulations which Airbnb hosts seem to circumvent:

> All other businesses that start up, large or small, are subjected to laws and regulations. So, I think it would be fair in this case as well. But I am also a stickler for the rules. It makes things more credible and I feel like everything is under control. It might be a false sense of security that everything is right (Julie, CPH).

Simultaneously, Julie argues that regulations designed to apply more directly to Airbnb would help legitimize peer-to-peer hosting through direct embeddedness in social rules. In addition to achieving legitimacy, the vague framing of Airbnb hosting leaves hosts in positions of uncertainty, manifested, for instance, through attempts to ensure sufficient insurance.

Questions about forthcoming legislation occupied the minds of Copenhagen hosts more than their Philadelphian counterparts, as future legislation was widely discussed, and Danish papers frequently published stories about the issue, whereas the topic was less contested in Philadelphia. In Philadelphia a key reference point occurred in July 2015, as the city council passed an ordinance permitting short-term rentals, only a few months before the city welcomed the Pope, along with thousands of pilgrims (Winberg, 2018).

> Philadelphia did pass a thing where they intentionally said that they would support Airbnb, so I mean there was a big hush, in Philadelphia around the time of the Pope's arrival, where they changed a lot of that legislation, to really encourage Airbnbs (Helen, PHL).

In the aftermath of this ordinance, Airbnb hosting underwent massive growth. This is illustrative of the embedded nature of economic performances, as hospitality markets are shaped through social relationships, and mega-events can create pressure and serve to open up certain performances. Here, the papal visit served not only to ease the legislative landscape, but also to normalize hosting as the massive influx of guests created a demand for accommodation and tempted many to initiate hosting.

Consequently, Philadelphian hosts expressed little concern about the future legislative landscape:

> Philadelphia feels pretty comfortable. But just hearing about the horror stories in New York and how they are like fining everyone. It is kind of scary to see in five to ten years – what can happen! The hotels didn't really expect it to be such a big player until recently (Steve, PHL).

Steve reveals growing uncertainty, acknowledging that the scope of Airbnb might pressure the city to react and look to other major American cities, enforcing restrictive regulations. This speaks to the larger embeddedness of economies and the performative effects of media, as agents consider how issues are managed elsewhere and anticipate similar local solutions. Anticipation in this context involves deciphering different rationalities behind legislation; in Steve's example, the hotel industry is lobbying for restrictions, or in Matt's case, trying to rationalize which hospitality performances are likely to be affected:

> The legislation seems to be more targeted towards the other situation, where neighbours are complaining because people are renting out their apartment or entire house. They are setting up apartment buildings with units for Airbnb. I feel like legislation and people focus on that aspect of it as opposed to someone like me, who is renting out my own space, a room, not making a whole bunch of money (Matt, PHL).

Matt addresses multiple conditions driving the debate about further legislation – complaining neighbours, modes of hospitality that involve listing entire dwellings on Airbnb – and notes that legislation seems to be focused on those aspects. However, he rationalizes that these concerns do not reflect his hosting, as he is cohabitating and "not making a whole lot of money," thereby actively creating distinction between commercial and less commercial businesses.

In Copenhagen the growth of Airbnb has been steadier. However, for a city roughly half the size of Philadelphia, there is significantly more Airbnb activity. This potentially makes Airbnb more contested (as seen in public debate see Hansen & Fabian, 2017; Leth et al., 2017) and a pressing theme on the minds of hosts:

> I would probably prefer that there were some restrictions. As long as it is restrictions where you have to live there, it wouldn't matter [to her] (Birgitte, CPH).

Birgitte echoes a large proportion of Copenhagen hosts who welcome legislation and favour regulations which impose restrictions, where "you have to live there." This indicates partly a moral imperative favourable towards cohabitating modes of hospitality, and partly a tendency to favour only legislation that does not collide with one's own manner of hosting. This moral imperative towards cohabitation or host-occupied listings is additionally expressed in local regulations. The majority of Copenhagen dwellings are covered by a residence requirement specifying that the dwelling must not be vacated for more than six consecutive weeks, thus, attempting to limit the scope of real estate speculation. However, dwellings which have never had a registered address (as is the case for new developments) are not covered, leaving 2700 dwellings[3] exempt from this requirement (Lund, 2017). Encompassing all dwellings in this requirement, and actively enforcing it, would eliminate the range of opportunities for legally running Airbnb listings in non-occupied dwellings.

In 2018, as an international first, Airbnb reached an agreement with the Danish government agreeing to report the full rental income of individual hosts (Regeringen, 2018). The agreement allow non-cohabitating hosts to rent out for a maximum of 70 days a year, fixing an annual tax-exempt amount at 28,000 DKK (equivalent of 4340 USD) provided that hosting is offered through a third-party company which reports all rental income of hosts.[4] Through this agreement Airbnb hosting is gradually stabilized and embedded into socio-institutional frameworks. Getting an agreement that ensured automatic reporting of full host income was essential in addressing concerns that connect Airbnb hosting with tax avoidance. This raises questions as to how hosts negotiate redistributional requirements, and their diverse strategies for navigating tax obligations.

Taxation

Airbnb has been considered controversial in relation to taxation, as the company has long avoided reporting earnings of individual hosts to tax authorities, leaving hosts to report income without providing tax authorities with the opportunity to control their self-reporting. In this section, I explore how hosts navigate the tension between optimising profits and societal obligations related to taxation.

In Philadelphia, the 2015 ordinance ensured that Airbnb would collect and remit occupancy or hotel taxes, consisting of 8.5% of the total amount received by hosts. Additionally, hosts have responsibility for reporting income at city, state and federal levels. At the time of the interviews, Copenhagen hosts were not subjected to direct reporting between Airbnb and tax authorities. Consequently, hosts in both destinations had considerable agency in navigating public obligations towards economic redistribution.

The theme of tax emerged stronger amongst Copenhagen hosts compared to Philadelphia. This is likely because taxation was debated more in Danish media, and perhaps because the tax percentage is relatively high in Copenhagen, making it a frequent topic of conversation. Additionally, in a country with a high level of digital integration, reporting income manually was unusual, and often perceived as troublesome.

Copenhagen hosts had different experiences with the transparency of the tax system. Unlike many hosts, Jane states that tax authorities were useful in explaining guidelines. Such guidelines vary depending on whether the host owns, rents or is part of a co-op housing association, as there were different guidelines for calculating tax-exempt amounts[5] (Skat.dk, 2017):

> You can just access the tax webpage. There are some very clear rules and they are written in a straightforward language. Someone born and raised in Denmark would easily understand those rules. If they claim otherwise, they are just trying to be oppositional. And we pay our taxes, we report it. But we would very much like it to be reported automatically, so we didn't have to [report it manually[6]]. Also, because we don't want it to be an argument that people are not paying their taxes [from Airbnb income] (Jane, CPH).

Jane perceives narratives about confusing tax guidelines as unreliable and welcomes a digital reporting system, partly out of convenience, but more so to eliminate suspicions about tax evasion and legitimize Airbnb hosting. This notion was echoed by multiple Copenhagen hosts, who often found manually reporting inconvenient and berated Airbnb for not reporting automatically. However, not all hosts welcomed automated digital reporting, as several acknowledged deliberately avoiding paying taxes. Christine explains that she abandoned researching tax regulation after she learned of the lack of digital enforcing:

> It was a little confusing and then there is the whole thing with Airbnb not reporting it to the tax authorities. Then I thought I wouldn't have to worry about it (Christine, CPH).

Christine concluded that without repercussions, there was no cause to pay taxes, and prioritized private profit over collective obligations. Others expressed more hesitant negotiations leading to the same result. Thomas explains that Airbnb income remains more or less untouched in a separate account:

I am keeping an eye open, maybe they will say that you need to pay this or that. But I do know that you have to report it yourself. And I could just do that, but I haven't taken that decision yet (Thomas, CPH).

Beyond pointing towards tax evasion, this is illustrative of his relationship to the Airbnb income, as something not quite an actual income, but just "something extra." Thomas describes a moral limbo, knowing that whilst he ought to report his income, he nevertheless has not done it yet (in spite of the interview being conducted a month after the reporting deadline). Simultaneously, he express doubt about the stability of the tax loophole, as he dares not touch his Airbnb income in case of retroactive tax claims. The instability of Airbnb's economic system is thus leading some hosts into calculative performances, managing risks and preparing caution-ary measures.

Anna, who negotiates tax avoidance through the moral pressures of family and kin, also expresses management of risk. Her experience is illustrative of the multiple ways social relation-ships are entangled with hosting, creating moral pressure and concern for financial stability:

I haven't been paying taxes from my Airbnb income... And it worries my daughter and son-in-law. He keeps saying that we should sit down and set up a corporate structure, so I can make the most of my Airbnb, but still do it legally. [...] The tax authorities can go back up to five years on your tax returns. The question is if they would actually do it. One of the things I have been thinking is that if they do that someday I will close my Airbnb profile. Then it is gone! [...] And then I will make a new one and be completely legitimate (Anna, CPH).

Anna is presupposing that tax authorities will not retroactively check her Airbnb income. Thus, an assumption of non-cooperating systems is integral to her rationality. Simultaneously, her plans for navigating implementation of automatic reporting relies on an expectation of low digital memory, as she assumes her data to be untraceable upon deleting her listing. This approach contains several potential pitfalls and indicates the uncertainty hosts can experience navigating novel and uncertain economic and socio-institutional configurations.

A final group of hosts navigated tax guidelines by staying within their tax-exempt amount,[7] thus, legally not paying tax, and equally importantly, not having to deal with manually reporting:

I am determined to not have to pay anything. Because if that was the case I simply wouldn't make enough to make it worthwhile (Ingrid, CPH).

Last year I was nearly there, and I then stopped accepting requests. The app shows how much you have made this year and when I was close to the amount, I questioned whether it made sense when you had to pay 60% in taxes. [...]. Because I don't want to bother with it on my tax return and I don't want to cause any trouble (Caroline, CPH).

Consequently, these hosts avoid earning more than the tax-exempt amount. This strategy was most commonly found amongst non-cohabitating hosts who often found that the tax-exempt amount aligns with their needs. They noted that the inconvenience of hosting is not sufficiently rewarded when paying tax, or if they "have to bother with it on their tax return." Simultaneously, they distance themselves from tax evasion and simply choose to stop for the year before being required to report the income. This sort of economic performance is emblem-atic of the socio-institutional embedding of economies, and how social regulatory frameworks shape economic performances, sometimes in unforeseen ways. As such, the tax-exempt amount effectively regulates rental activity for some hosts.

Philadelphian hosts expressed general relief that occupancy taxes were being handled dir-ectly, signalling a welcoming attitude towards simplifying the reporting configurations and an authorized way of handling this public obligation:

I think that Airbnb worked out a deal with both the state and the city that now guests pay the taxes directly through Airbnb. So, I still pay all income taxes, city, state and federal on the income (Carol, PHL).

As Carol points out, Philadelphian hosts are, in addition to the occupancy taxes, responsible for reporting their income. No hosts admitted to not fulfilling this requirement, but often talked about their strategies for deducting expenses connected to the dwelling in a manner that minimized tax significantly:

> Airbnb sends a form of how much money I made, and then I write off. It is great because I can write off 75% of my insurance, my utilities, if I buy something for the rooms specifically. That is all a write off. My cell phone, because I want to be able to respond at any time because of Airbnb. Writing that off (Anna, PHL).

Thus, navigating and minimizing tax obligations requires skills and knowledge about which expenses qualify for deduction. This speaks to the previous point about prior business experience easing some aspects of hosting performances and indicates that Airbnb hosting can support the development of such skills. The multiple ways of negotiating tax evasion illustrate the complex ways in which hosting is entangled with socio-institutional contexts, where self-interest is weighed against collective obligations, and risks are weighed against both moral pressures and strategies for managing consequences.

Beyond questions of taxation, the tensions between individual liberties and collective responsibilities have been a focal point in other controversies surrounding Airbnb. A frequently emerging theme is the way in which Airbnb hosting can have negative effects on local communities and neighbour relations.

Community and neighbour relationships

In addition to navigating official rules and taxation, hosting is entangled with situated relationships. Airbnb is often contested within local communities and critiqued in the media for contributing to rising housing costs (Lee, 2016), adding to the experience of overtourism, where the amount of visitors results in negative perceptions (Manjoo, 2018), or bringing unsafe strangers into buildings (Francis, 2014). Such tensions illuminate how Airbnb affects multiple individuals beyond users and is indicative of how the current reconfiguration of hospitality is opening up new touristic territories. Through this section, I will explore how hosts manoeuvre and navigate their relationship with local communities in the light of such controversy. Many hosts had experiences with discontented neighbours:

> You are probably going to ask me if there have been complaints in the building and of course there have (Karen, CPH).

Karen situates complaints as almost a certainty, expressing awareness of the often-negative attitudes of neighbours. Interviewees employ various strategies for navigating discontent. For instance, Anna perceives the causes for neighbourly complaints as absurd and contradictory:

> Some of the neighbours have become provoked that we are renting out through Airbnb. They feel like it is bothering them. They say that they never see me around[8] anymore. But I just moved 50 metres, so they can see me as much as ever. The next thing is that there are so many tourists around, we dont know them! And then the windows are always dark! But how can there be 'so many tourists' and also dark windows? I told them that tourists also turn on the light. [...] There is no doubt that some are really pissed. Some of us understand it as envy though (Anna, CPH).

Anna addresses practical concerns from her neighbours and highlights how Airbnb hosting contributes to tensions in local communities, as undesirable consequences are not necessarily distributed to those who reap the rewards. However, she discards these concerns as irrational and legitimizes her activities through the perceived irrationality of her neighbours.

Neighbourly concerns can also be focused on notions of safety. Such concerns were solely activated by Philadelphian hosts, indicating that safety apprehensions are more predominant in their minds compared to Copenhagen hosts. Logan explains:

> I feel like a lot of my neighbours kind of didn't understand that. Like there are a lot of people who grow up in Philadelphia and they never leave Philadelphia, or they never leave Pennsylvania, they never leave

America. Like, their mentality is like other Americans, other Philadelphians and sort of like always assume the worst. (Logan, PHL).

This implies that negotiation of safety is navigated in community relations, where discourses about dangerous strangers are activated in the mindsets of people who experience having new neighbours on a weekly basis. As such, the perception of the urban as "a world of strangers" often found in urban theory is challenged (Lofland, 1973; Simmel, [1903] 1950; Tonkiss, 2003). The urban dweller might treat strangers with indifference in public spaces, but on the spatial scale of the home street, or the building, strangers are recognized and not necessarily welcomed. This contrasts with the experiences of hosts, who have chosen to engage with hosting and perceive their guests as known, others, having become familiarized online. Additionally, Logan distinguishes between himself as cosmopolitan and open-minded and his neighbours whom he perceives to be provincial and not equipped to comprehend his international travellers. Although negative impacts of tourism are highly debated in many cities, hosts did not connect to such narratives. Rather, they argue that tourists attracted to their listing, and Airbnb in general, are easily absorbed into the complex fabric of the city. Thus, their guests are, in their opinion, hard to differentiate and blend in with city dwellers. This echoes well with the work of Colomb and Novy (2016) and Larsen (2019), which explores multiple types of tourists, many of whom can be difficult to distinguish from local populations. This is especially true in urban settings characterized by certain anonymity, where guests are not easily distinguished from locals. Although Logan indicated that his neighbours would not approve, he nevertheless ran his listing successfully, and his neighbours were rarely able to identify the tourists visiting.

The Copenhagen Co-op association[9] provides an interesting case for the negotiation of collective and private interest. Residents co-own their building(s), and the housing association puts neighbourly negotiation under pressure by developing guidelines for members to comply with and balance everyone's concerns. Some associations had existing regulations about short-term rentals, others have no guidelines and some have been developing guidelines in the wake of Airbnb. Therefore, Airbnb hosting becomes embedded differently across various housing associations, and hosts navigate and manoeuvre such guidelines differently. One strategy involves skirting the edges of the guidelines of the housing association, by utilizing that frameworks do not explicitly specify rules:

Our statutes do not specify anything. So, I allowed myself. I didn't ask beforehand, but I allowed myself (Thomas, CPH).

Thomas demonstrates awareness that his hosting might not be positively received, by trying to minimize encounters between neighbours and guests; his guests are only allowed to use the front door and not the shared communal backyard. Several other hosts explained that their co-op associations have guidelines in place limiting, but not forbidding, Airbnb hosting:

In our housing association you are only allowed to rent out from May to October. There are many who do it when the association doesn't want them to. They are really taking chances (Peter, CPH).

We have the rule within our housing association that you are allowed to rent out for the equivalent of seven weeks (Julie, CPH).

Peter explains how his association allows Airbnb during the most popular tourist season, coinciding with the timeframe where most locals spend the majority of their holiday. Julie explains the same pattern of considering established holiday rhythms through a time limit of seven weeks. This seems in line with the "traditional" Danish pattern of six weeks of annual holiday. Both of these guidelines support Airbnb hosting, where the home is utilized as a resource during timeframes where the hosts would leave the home vacant. Peter additionally addresses that not everyone seems to abide by their rules, and later confesses to having breached this rule himself. This addresses performances of creating flexibility within existing timeframes, as well as uncertainty; Peter points out "they are really taking chances," since housing associations have the authority to evict shareholders. Christine elaborates on this experience, as she was using Airbnb without the consent of her housing association:

> It wasn't really legit. Because my co-op association discovered it and wrote to me that they had learned that I was renting out through Airbnb and that I had to stop immediately (Christine, CPH).

In Christine's case the housing association required that she cease hosting immediately. Having effectively moved in with her partner, this urged her to sell her co-op apartment. Consequently, the dwelling changed from being a space of tourist accommodation to re-entering the housing stock for permanent residents.

Conclusion

Throughout this article, I have made the claim that changes in socio-institutional frameworks are not solely occurring through changes in formal legislation. I have focused on Airbnb hosting to explore how socio-institutional contexts are being remade and challenged through the continuous framings enacted by hosts. I argue that we should not solely explore the strategic attempts to influence policy, in the "control room" of "platform urbanism" (for excellent examples, see Söderström & Mermet, 2020; van Doorn, 2019), but we must equally address how everyday performances of individual agents work to (de)stabilize urban and economic forms. As such, this article can be seen in part as a contribution to the literature on the manner in which Airbnb changes our (usually) urban landscapes, as well as broader discussions on the heterogeneity of economies.

Through different strategies of navigating the socio-institutional frameworks pertaining to Airbnb, the article demonstrates not only how hosts navigate the uncertainty of performing in a novel economic constellation, but also how such performances inform and shape socio-institutional frameworks. As most of the strategies brought forward by hosts pertained to the novelty of Airbnb in a socio-institutional landscape not fully adapted, this article very much contributes to understandings of the performances of unstable economic forms. A key narrative brought forward by hosts was, nevertheless, a desire to end instability and achieve legitimacy in the economic system through more formal integration into legislative structures.

This instability appeared to be easing as Airbnb entered into multiple agreements with governments. In July 2019, automatic reporting of income was initiated in Denmark (Dandanell, 2019). In March 2020, the European Commission announced an agreement with Airbnb, Booking.com, Expedia Group and Tripadvisor, which is the first cross-national agreement on regularly sharing reliable data to "contribute to more complete statistics on tourist accommodation around Europe, allow public authorities to better understand the development of the collaborative economy and support evidence-based policies" (European Commission, 2020). This integrates Airbnb hosting into existing economic systems. Whereas these tendencies indicate integration into European national systems, such national integration is not yet occurring in the United States, where many guidelines are developed at the urban level. Here, New York and San Francisco are amongst the first US cities to roll out legislation challenging Airbnb hosting with attention to the impact on the housing market (Dolmetsch, 2018; Said, 2018).

Such developments add further to the geographical variation of hosting performances. Although the analysis I have shown examples of how performances vary based on a multitude of localised relationships. How some themes, like safety, are a central considerations in Philadelphia or how the prevalence in housing co-ops is creating a subsection of housing regulations to navigate within the Copenhagen context. Whether integration into national legislation will increase situated differences or offer some common reference point will depend on how national governments develop frameworks in the coming years. Whilst offering distinct insights into host performances, this research is not without limitations. A key limitation was the limited potential for comparing the sample of interviewees with the general host population within

Table 1. Key statistics for Philadelphia and Copenhagen 2017.

	Philadelphia	Copenhagen
Population	1,580,000	720,000
Active hosts	2083	10,790
Listings	4204	12,923
Hosts with only one listing	73%	94%
Percentage of listings run by multi-listing host	64%	22%
Listings for entire home	56%	81%

Sources: Airdna (2018a, 2018b); Copenhagen Municipality (2018); United States Census Bureau (2018).

each destination. As such, the insights produced in this document do not allow for generalized claims but could be seen as a solid knowledge base from which to pursue quantified knowledge. Additionally, expanding the research to other localities would not only add richness to the conclusions provided in this article, but also give more insight into geographical variations.

It has been claimed that Airbnb grew out of the financial crisis of the last decade. The company was founded in 2008 and often described as an attractive financial safety net (Allen, 2015). Whilst finishing this article, another crisis is shaping everyday lives around the planet, and the current pandemic might have equally important implications for Airbnb. This health crisis has laid bare the interrelational and constructed nature of economies as many industries, including the tourist sector, have found themselves at a standstill. Negotiations of the interwoven nature of public and private concerns are being exposed, as furloughing schemes in many countries have governments covering pay cheques from private companies and developing financial support packages for businesses.

Whilst planes and travellers are at a standstill, voices from cities highly affected by tourism are urging that we spend this time to reimagine a new, more sustainable, post-pandemic model (Robbins, 2020). The estimated value of Airbnb has fallen rapidly from $31 billion in 2017 to $18 billion by the end of April 2020, silencing, at least for the moment, speculations of Airbnb going public (Evans, 2020). Airbnb has laid off a quarter of its workforce (Collinson, 2020), and with bookings down between 80% and 90%, hosts will also be feeling financial consequences. What used to be a high-profit way of utilizing a dwelling has suddenly revealed itself to be a highly risky strategy for many hosts. In some cities, the housing stock has returned to the traditional rental market. The deputy mayor of Paris, Ian Brossat, has said: "We intend to take the opportunity to regain control … The city could buy up some of these apartments and return them to the traditional rental market" (Burgen et al., 2020). Such statements open the door for a new chapter. If municipal agents wish to "take control," it simultaneously opens up questions, not only about when and if tourism will return, but also how local authorities will employ this agency moving forward.

Notes

1. The vast majority of interviewees held at least a bachelor's degree or the equivalent, with only a couple of exceptions in each destination: 27.1% of Philadelphians over 25 have a bachelor's degree or higher (United States Census Bureau, 2018) compared to 52.8% of Copenhageners (Kommune, 2018)
2. Steve and a partner run a house with multiple listings, for both private and shared rooms.
3. Compared to 290,000 dwellings in total (Copenhagen Municipality, 2018).
4. Otherwise the tax-exempt amount is 11,000 DKK (1700 USD).
5. For renters and members of co-op housing associations, the tax-exempt amount was 2/3 of the annual rent for owners; it was 1.33% of the official value of the dwelling, with a minimum of 24,000 DKK (Skat.dk, 2017).
6. The vast majority of wage work is reported from employer to the tax authorities digitally; wageworkers check their tax return online and can make corrections and deductions the authorities have not registered.
7. The hosts explained this as ranging between 24,000 and upwards of 50,000 DKK (3600–7600 USD).
8. Minor changes have been made to conceal the placement of Anna's dwelling.
9. Thirty two percent of the Copenhagen housing stock was housing associations (Erhvervsstyrrelsen, 2018), where building is co-owned by inhabitants of the association who elects members onto the association's board.

Disclosure statement

No potential conflict of interest was reported by the authors.

ORCID

Mathilde Dissing Christensen (iD) http://orcid.org/0000-0001-6414-5979

References

Airdna. (2018a). *Copenhagen*. Retrieved April 23, 2018, from https://www.airdna.co/vacation-rental-data/app/dk/default/copenhagen/overview

Airdna. (2018b). *Philadelphia*. Retrieved April 23, 2018, from https://www.airdna.co/vacation-rental-data/app/us/pennsylvania/philadelphia/overview

Allen, J. (2015, January 20). Activists gather at NYC's City Hall to protest Airbnb. *USA TODAY*. https://www.usatoday.com/videos/news/2015/01/20/22062641/

Amin, A., & Thrift, N. (2007). Cultural-economy and cities. *Progress in Human Geography*, *31*(2), 143–161. https://doi.org/10.1177/0309132507075361

Andreotti, A., Anselmi, G., Eichhorn, T., Hoffmann, C. P., & Micheli, M. (2017). *Participation in the sharing economy*. Report form the EU H2020 Research Project Ps2Share: Participation, Privacy and Power in the Sharing Economy. Retrieved at: http//dx.doi.org/10.2139/ssrn.2061745

Botsman, R., & Rogers, R. (2010). *What's mine is yours; The rise of collaborative consumption*. Harper Collons Publisher.

Burgen, S., Henley, J., & Carroll, R. (2020, May9). Airbnb slump means Europe's cities can return to residents, say officials. *The Guardian*. https://www.theguardian.com/technology/2020/may/09/airbnb-slump-europe-cities-residents-barcelona-dublin

Butler, J. (1990). *Gender trouble: Feminism and the subversion of identity*. Routledge.

Butler, J. (2010). Performative agency. *Journal of Cultural Economy*, *3*(2), 147–161. https://doi.org/10.1080/17530350.2010.494117

Callon, M. (1998). *The laws of the markets*. Blackwell Publishers.

Callon, M. (2010). Performativity, Misfires and Politics. *Journal of Cultural Economy*, *3*(2), 163–169. https://doi.org/10.1080/17530350.2010.494119

Cansoy, M., & Schor, J. (2016). Who gets to share in the "sharing economy": Understanding the patterns of participation and [Unpublished Paper]. Boston College. https://pdfs.semanticscholar.org/ed92/5c002259d55482d16d9d3c0b7ccd2d38b9b5.pdf

Celata, F., & Romano, A. (2020). Overtourism and online short-term rental platforms in Italian cities. *Journal of Sustainable Tourism*, 1–20. https://doi.org/10.1080/09669582.2020.1788568

Cheng, M., Houge Mackenzie, S., & Degarege, G. A. (2020). Airbnb impacts on host communities in a tourism destination: An exploratory study of stakeholder perspectives in Queenstown, New Zealand. *Journal of Sustainable Tourism*, 1–19. https://doi.org/10.1080/09669582.2020.1802469

Cocola-Gant, A., & Gago, A. (2019). Airbnb, buy-to-let investment and tourism-driven displacement: A case study in Lisbon. *Environment and Planning A: Economy and Space*. 1–18. https://doi.org/10.1177/0308518X19869012

Collinson, P. (2020, May 6). Airbnb to make a quarter of its global workforce redundant. *The Guardian*. https://www.theguardian.com/technology/2020/may/06/airbnb-to-make-quarter-of-its-global-workforce-redundant

Colomb, C., & Novy, J. (2016). *Protest and resistance in the tourist city*. Routledge.

Copenhagen Municipality. (2018). Status på København 2018: Nøgletal for København. Retrieved September 12, 2018, from https://www.kk.dk/sites/default/files/status_paa_kbh_2018_aug.pdf

Dandanell, F. (2019, April 11). Airbnb og skatteminister i symbiose: Ny aftale udelukker professionel udlejning. *Berlingske*. https://www.berlingske.dk/virksomheder/airbnb-og-skatteminister-i-symbiose-ny-aftale-udelukker-professionel

Dolmetsch, C. (2018, October). Airbnb says New York City law seeking host records is 'murky.' *Bloomberg.Com*. https://www.bloomberg.com/news/articles/2018-10-05/airbnb-says-new-york-city-law-seeking-host-records-is-murky

Dredge, D. (2017). Policy and regulatory challenges in the tourism collaborative economy. In D. Dredge & S. Gyimóthy (Eds.), *Collaborative economy and tourism: Perspectives, politics, policies and prospects* (pp. 75–96). Springer.

Dredge, D., & Gyimóthy, S. (2015). The collaborative economy and tourism: Critical perspectives, questionable claims and silenced voices. *Tourism Recreation Research, 40*(3), 286–302. https://doi.org/10.1080/02508281.2015. 1086076

Edelman, B., Luca, M., Svirsky, D., Ayres, I., Katz, L., & Lang, K. (2017). Racial discrimination in the sharing economy: Evidence from a field experiment. *American Economic Journal: Applied Economics, 9*(2), 1–22. https://doi.org/10. 1257/app.20160213

Erhvervsstyrrelsen. (2018). Fakta om andelsboliger. Retrieved October 7, 2018, from https://erhvervsstyrelsen.dk/ fakta-om-andelsboliger

European Commission. (2020). Commission reaches agreement with collaborative economy platforms to publish key data on tourism accommodation. https://ec.europa.eu/growth/content/commission-reaches-agreement-collaborative-economy-platforms-publish-key-data-tourism_en

Evans, D. (2020, May 6). Airbnb's future is uncertain as it continues to struggle through its Covid-19 response. CNBC. https://www.cnbc.com/2020/05/06/can-airbnb-survive-the-coronavirus-pandemic.html

Farmaki, A., Stergiou, D., & Kaniadakis, A. (2019). Self-perceptions of Airbnb hosts' responsibility: A moral identity perspective. *Journal of Sustainable Tourism*, 1–21. https://doi.org/10.1080/09669582.2019.1707216

Francis, D. (2014, November 23). How Airbnb Makes Cities Less Safe. *New York Post*. https://nypost.com/2014/11/23/ how-airbnb-makes-cities-less-safe/

Frederiksberg Municipality. (2018). Prognose over Frederiksbergs Kommunes befolkning. Retrieved September 12, 2018, from https://www.frederiksberg.dk/sites/default/files/2018-04/Befolkningen_i_Frederiksberg_Kommune_ 2018.pdf

Gibson-Graham, J. K. (2008). Diverse economies: Performative practices for 'other worlds. *Progress in Human Geography, 32*(5), 613–632. https://doi.org/10.1177/0309132508090821

Gregson, N., & Rose, G. (2000). Taking Butler elsewhere: Performativities, spatialities and subjectivities. *Environment and Planning D: Society and Space, 18*(4), 433–452. https://doi.org/10.1068/d232

Gutiérrez, J., García-Palomares, J. C., Romanillos, G., & Salas-Olmedo, M. H. (2017). The eruption of Airbnb in tourist cities: Comparing spatial patterns of hotels and peer-to-peer accommodation in Barcelona. *Tourism Management, 62*, 278–291. https://doi.org/10.1016/j.tourman.2017.05.003

Guttentag, D. (2015). Airbnb: Disruptive innovation and the rise of an informal tourism accommodation sector. *Current Issues in Tourism, 18*(12), 1192–1217.

Guttentag, D. (2017). Regulating innovation in the collaborative economy: An examination of Airbnb's early legal issues. In D. Dredge & S. Gyimóthy (Eds.), *Collaborative economy and tourism: Perspectives, politics, policies and prospects* (pp. 97–128). Springer.

Haldrup, M. (2004). Laid back mobilities second home holidays in time and space. *Tourism Geographies, 6*(4), 434–454. https://doi.org/10.1080/1461668042000280228

Hansen, A. L., & Fabian, L. (2017, December 19). I vaerste fald kan Airbnb gøre folk hjemløse. *Berlingske*. https:// www.berlingske.dk/kommentatorer/i-vaerste-fald-kan-airbnb-goere-folk-hjemloese

Harris, J. (2018, February 12). Profiteers make a killing on Airbnb – and erode communities. *The Guardian*. https:// www.theguardian.com/commentisfree/2018/feb/12/profiteers-killing-airbnb-erode-communities

Horn, K., & Merante, M. (2017). Is home sharing driving up rents? Evidence from Airbnb in Boston. *Journal of Housing Economics, 38*, 14–24. https://doi.org/10.1016/j.jhe.2017.08.002

Ioannides, D., Röslmaier, M., & van der Zee, E. (2019). Airbnb as an instigator of 'tourism bubble' expansion in Utrecht's Lombok neighbourhood. *Tourism Geographies, 21*(5), 822–840. https://doi.org/10.1080/14616688.2018. 1454505

Knaus, K. (2020). At home with guests – discussing hosting on Airbnb through the lens of labour. *Applied Mobilities, 5*(1), 68–18. https://doi.org/10.1080/23800127.2018.1504600

Koch, R. (2020, September). Public, private, and the appeal to common good: Practices of justification in a peer-to-peer economy. *Transactions of the Institute of British Geographers, 45*(2), 392–314. https://doi.org/10.1111/tran. 12345

Kommune, K. (2018). Status på København 2018; Nøgletal for København. *Copenhagen*. https://www.kk.dk/sites/ default/files/status_paa_kbh_2018_aug.pdf

Larsen, J. (2019). Ordinary tourism and extraordinary everyday life: Re-thinking tourism and cities. In N. Stors, L. Stoltenberg, T. Frisch, & C. Sommer (Eds.), *Tourism and everyday life in the city*. Routledge.

Lee, D. (2016). How Airbnb short-term rentals exacerbate Los Angeles's affordable housing crisis: Analysis and policy recommendations. *Harvard Law & Policy Review, 10*(1), 229–253. http://search.proquest.com/docview/ 1769715296/

Leth, A. L., Olsen, M., Nielsen, C. M., & Vilsbøll, S. M. (2017, July 14). Airbnb gør flere københavnere til småspekulanter. *Politikken*. https://politiken.dk/indland/art6034774/Airbnb-gør-flere-københavnere-til-småspekulanter

Lofland, L. H. (1973). *A world of strangers: Order and action in urban public space*. Basic Books.

Lund, J. (2017, January 10). Tusindvis af Københavnske luksusboliger har aldrig haft en beboer tilmeldt. *Børsen*. https://borsen.dk/nyheder/penge/tusindvis-af-koebenhavns-luksusboliger-har-aldrig-haft-en-beboer-tilmeldt-4ib7k

Manjoo, F. (2018, August 29). 'Overtourism' Worries Europe. How Much Did Technology Help Get Us There? *New York Times*. https://www.nytimes.com/2018/08/29/technology/technology-overtourism-europe.html

Meged, J. W., & Christensen, M. D. (2017). Working within the Collaborative Tourist Economy: The complex crafting of work and meaning. In D. Dredge & S. Gyimóth (Eds.), *Collaborative economy and tourism perspectives, politics, policies and prospects*. Springer.

Mermet, A.-C. (2017). Airbnb and tourism gentrification: Critical insights from the exploratory analysis of the "Airbnb syndrome" in Reykjavik. In M. Gravari-Barbas & S. Guinand (Eds.), *Tourism and gentrification in contemporary metropolises: International perspectives* (pp. 52–74). Routledge.

Minca, C., & Roelofsen, M. (2019). Becoming Airbnbeings: On datafication and the quantified Self in tourism. *Tourism Geographies*, 1–22. https://doi.org/10.1080/14616688.2019.1686767

Muellerleile, C. (2013). Turning financial markets inside out: Polanyi, performativity and disembeddedness. *Environment and Planning A: Economy and Space*, *45*(7), 1625–1642. https://doi.org/10.1068/a45610

Polanyi, K. (1957). *The great transformation*. Beacon Press.

Poole, S. (2018, October 24). Airbnb can't go on unregulated – it does too much damage to citie. *The Guardian*. https://www.theguardian.com/commentisfree/2018/oct/24/airbnb-unregulated-damage-cities-barcelona-law-locals

Ravenelle, A. J. (2017). Sharing economy workers: Selling, not sharing. *Cambridge Journal of Regions, Economy and Society*, *10*(2), 281–295. https://doi.org/10.1093/cjres/rsw043

Regeringen (2018). Bred enighed om mere attraktive skattevilkår for dele-økonomien og styr på skattebetalingen. Retrieved May 20, 2018, from https://www.skm.dk/aktuelt/presse-nyheder/pressemeddelelser/bred-enighed-om-mere-attraktive-skattevilkaar-og-styr-paa-skattebetalingen-i-deleoekonomien/

Richardson, L. (2015). Performing the sharing economy. *Geoforum*, *67*, 121–129. https://doi.org/10.1016/j.geoforum.2015.11.004

Robbins, N. (2020, June). The trampling of Venice shows why tourism must change after Covid-19. *The Guardian*. https://www.theguardian.com/commentisfree/2020/jun/19/venice-tourism-covid-19-coronavirus-green-tourism

Roelofsen, M. (2018). Performing "home" in the sharing economies of tourism: The Airbnb experience in Sofia, Bulgaria. *Fennia - International Journal of Geography*, *196*(1), 24–42. https://doi.org/10.11143/fennia.66259

Said, C. (2018, January). Airbnb listings in San Francisco plunge by half. *San Francisco Chronicle*. https://www.sfchronicle.com/business/article/Airbnb-listings-in-San-Francisco-plunge-by-half-12502075.php

Simmel, G. ([1903] 1950). The metropolis and mental life. In K. Wolff (Ed.), *The Sociology of Georg Simmel*. Free Press.

Skat.dk. (2017). *Skat; Du udlejer et vaerelse eller en bolig du selv bor i*. https://skat.dk/skat.aspx?oid=2234798

Söderström, O., & Mermet, A.-C. (2020). When Airbnb sits in the control room: Platform urbanism as actually existing smart urbanism in Reykjavík. *Frontiers in Sustainable Cities*, *2*(May), 1–7. https://doi.org/10.3389/frsc.2020.00015

Srnicek, N. (2017). *Platform capitalism*. Polity.

Stergiou, D. P., & Farmaki, A. (2020). Resident perceptions of the impacts of P2P accommodation: Implications for neighbourhoods. *International Journal of Hospitality Management*, *91*(March), 102411. https://doi.org/10.1016/j.ijhm.2019.102411

Tonkiss, F. (2003). The ethics of indifference community and solitude in the city. *International Journal of Cultural Studies*, *6*(3), 297–311.

United States Census Bureau. (2018). QuickFacts: Philadephia City Pennsylvania. Retrieved September 12, 2018, from https://www.census.gov/quickfacts/philadelphiacitypennsylvania

van Doorn, N. (2019). A new institution on the block: On platform urbanism and Airbnb citizenship. *New Media and Society*, 1–19. https://doi.org/10.1177/1461444819884377

Varma, A., Jukic, N., Pestek, A., Shultz, C. J., & Nestorov, S. (2016). Airbnb: Exciting innovation or passing fad? *Tourism Management Perspectives*, *20*, 228–237. https://doi.org/10.1016/j.tmp.2016.09.002

Visit Copenhagen. (2017). The Latest Development in Bednights. Retrieved December 21, 2018, from https://www.visitcopenhagen.dk/sites/default/files/asp/visitcopenhagen/Corporate/PDF-filer/Overnatningstal/december_2017__greater_copenhagen.pdf

Visit Philadelphia. (2018). 2018 Annual Report. https://www.visitphilly.com/visit-philadelphia-annual-report/

Wachsmuth, D., & Weisler, A. (2018). Airbnb and the rent gap: Gentrification through the sharing economy. *Environment and Planning A: Economy and Space*, *50*(6), 1147–1170. https://doi.org/10.1177/0308518X18778038

Winberg, M. (2018). Why your Philly Airbnb won't get shut down. Retrieved September 5, 2018, from https://billypenn.com/2018/06/29/why-your-philly-airbnb-wont-get-shut-down/

Zelizer, V. A. (1994). *Pricing the priceless child: The changing social value of children*. Princeton University Press.

Zervas, G., Proserpio, D., & Byers, J. W. (2017). The rise of the sharing economy: Estimating the impact of Airbnb on the hotel industry. *Journal of Marketing Research*, *54*(5), 687–705. https://doi.org/10.1509/jmr.15.0204

Self-perceptions of Airbnb hosts' responsibility: a moral identity perspective

Anna Farmaki (iD), Dimitrios Stergiou and Antonios Kaniadakis

ABSTRACT

Responsible host conduct has emerged as important in regulating the peer-to-peer accommodation phenomenon. Utilising moral identity theory, this paper explores how hosts draw on their own perceptions of morality and responsibility to inform hosting practice. Through a qualitative research approach, the study reveals a variance of host practices that are not necessarily reflective of the perceived moral identity of hosts. In particular, the paper exposes the moral questions that hosts need to answer at different phases of the peer-to-peer transaction and, especially, if and how they enact certain aspects of their moral identity to guide their behaviour. The study offers a typology of Airbnb hosts' (im)moral behaviour, which may be of theoretical and practical value to academics and policymakers alike.

Introduction

Peer-to-peer (P2P) sharing activities have become popular within the accommodation sector, where online platforms enable individuals to easily convert their properties into short-term rentals (Belk, 2014). Whilst there are numerous P2P accommodation networks, Airbnb is recognised as one of the world's most successful (Volgger, Taplin, & Pforr, 2019). Since 2008 when it was first established, Airbnb has expanded to include more than 200 million members in over 191 countries (Airbnb, 2018), warranting its title as "a global *tour de force* in the tourist fabric of numerous places" (Ioannides, Röslmaier, & van der Zee, 2018:2). The growth of Airbnb is unsurprising considering the several socio-economic benefits it may provide to both hosts and guests (Ikkala & Lampinen, 2015). For instance, it has been suggested to offer a more authentic tourist experience (Bucher, Fieseler, Fleck, & Lutz, 2018; Lalicic & Weismayer, 2017; Palauskaite et al., 2017; Mody, Hanks, & Dogru, 2019; Shuqair, Pinto, & Mattila, 2019) that facilitates 'a home away from home' feeling (Zhu, Cheng, Wang, Ma, & Jiang, 2019). Similarly, it allows hosts to earn additional income by utilising idle property (Lutz & Newlands, 2018).

Nonetheless, the rapid growth of Airbnb has yielded concerns in relation to its effects on the hotel sector, local housing markets and local communities (Hadjibaba & Dolnicar, 2017; Mody, Hanks, et al., 2019; Stergiou & Farmaki, 2019). There is evidence of tourist overcrowding in central areas as a result of Airbnb growth, which has reportedly contributed to the touristification processes that transform urban space and, consequently, negatively impact the lives of residents

(Farmaki, Christou, & Saveriades, 2020; Ioannides et al., 2018). Much of the negative impacts of Airbnb have been attributed to the illegal operation of many Airbnb rentals (Gottlieb, 2013) and the management of multiple listings by 'professionals' such as real estate companies (Stergiou & Farmaki, 2019). For instance, studies report an increasing number of landlords who are evicting tenants in order to vacate units for use as short-term rentals (Stergiou & Farmaki, 2019). Similarly, many Airbnb hosts seem to operate Airbnb rentals illegally with their 'free rider' attitude being encouraged by the platform's absence of accommodation taxes (Guttentag, 2015). In addition, the absence of a regulatory framework in P2P accommodation has fuelled concerns over the potential discriminatory behaviour of hosts (Cheng & Foley, 2018; Farmaki & Kladou, 2019) as well as unethical acts illustrating disclosure of information to guests (i.e., installing hidden cameras in rented properties).

Consequently, calls for the strengthening of regulatory controls on Airbnb-type accommodation have intensified over the years (Edelman & Geradin, 2015; Gurran & Phibbs, 2017). In fact, anti-tourism marches are increasing in cities that are highly impacted by overtourism, to which Airbnb's growth contributes (Nieuwland & van Melik, 2018). Airbnb has been accused of reinforcing a nightmarish form of neo-liberalism that contributes to the creation of unregulated marketplaces (Martin, 2016) and the deception of customers by capturing and controlling user data (Srnicek, 2017), a phenomenon referred to as 'platform capitalism'. Even so, attempts to control the growth of Airbnb have insofar been largely unsuccessful due to the varying regulatory structures among cities (Grimmer, Vorobjovas-Pinta, & Massey, 2019) and the difficulty of regulating an online platform (Edelman & Geradin, 2015). According to Espinosa (2016), overlooking the innovative aspects of Airbnb and treating it as a traditional industry player limits the ability of formulating a feasible regulatory framework.

Within this context, the role of Airbnb in mitigating negative impacts by setting rules and ensuring users of the platform enforce them was highlighted (Cheng & Foyle, 2018). Equally, the responsible conduct of hosts as co-facilitators of P2P transactions has been emphasised (Farmaki & Kaniadakis, 2018). Airbnb hosts seem to emerge as a "community of practice" with the aim to share knowledge, experience and also set boundaries between what might be understood as responsible hosting behaviour (Farmaki & Kaniadakis, 2018). As such, hosts' perceptions of morality and responsibility become relevant. Nonetheless, it remains a challenging task to monitor the compliance of hosts to regulations (Nieuwland & van Melik, 2018). According to Sundararajan (2014), the concept of P2P sharing platforms may imply co-creation yet does not necessarily elicit a framework in which responsibility is equally shared. In this regard, it has been argued that individual regulation is better suited to govern Airbnb (Jonas, 2015). As Cohen and Sundararajan (2015) asserted, self-regulation may alleviate regulatory challenges that can otherwise impede the innovation elicited by the opportunities offered through P2P exchanges. Evidently, the responsible conduct of Airbnb hosts is key in the efforts to regulate the growing phenomenon.

Surprisingly, pertinent research has virtually ignored host views of their role in mitigating the impacts of Airbnb. Against this background, this paper explores the perceptions of Airbnb hosts with regard to their moral responsibility in P2P transactions. We draw from moral identity theory to understand how Airbnb hosts' views on moral responsibility are generated and how their hosting practice is linked to personal motivation to act responsibly. More precisely, we analyse how hosts draw on their own perceptions of morality and responsibility to inform their practice and how such perceptions compel them to use their role as co-facilitators of the P2P transaction in consistency with their moral values. In so doing, the study offers insights that contribute to policymaking and the efforts to improve platform governance, especially with regard to the negative impacts of Airbnb's expansion on local communities. As such, the study is timely in highlighting how business models based on sharing activities (i.e., P2P accommodation platforms) can contribute to more sustainable infrastructure in tourist places (Cohen & Munoz, 2016).

Overall, the study makes valuable contributions to both tourism and moral identity literatures. First, the concept of moral identity has been scarcely examined in tourism studies; a surprising omission considering calls for greater emphasis on morality in tourism scholarship (i.e., Caton, 2012). Second, by drawing from service provider perceptions, we contribute to existing knowledge on moral identity where focus was primarily placed on guest perspectives (i.e., He & Harris, 2014). In addition, the study advances both the conceptualisation and operationalisation of moral identity by considering the complexity of its content in the setting of P2P accommodation that is underpinned by a commercial and social orientation. As such, the study contributes to management literature that has examined moral identity mostly in organisational settings and in relation to voluntary behaviours (e.g., Reed, Aquino, & Levy, 2007). Moreover, by focusing on both moral identity internationalisation and symbolisation, we contribute to moral identity research which has most often conducted empirical examinations of moral identity internationalisation (Mulder & Aquino, 2013). By examining Airbnb hosts' moral identity perceptions and how they are enacted in host practices along various stages of the P2P exchange, a better understanding is gained of how moral identity evolves in a socially mediated process.

Literature review

Moral identity

The term 'moral identity' has been defined as a "self-conception organised around a set of moral traits" (Aquino & Reed, 2002, p. 1424). In other words, if individuals feel that moral traits such as being altruistic, honest, friendly, caring, and fair are central for defining their sense of self, they have a strong moral identity. Thus, being a moral person may occupy different levels of centrality in peoples' self-identity (Reed, 2002). The strength of this association to the self is referred to as the "self-importance of moral identity" (Reed & Aquino, 2003, p. 1272); if a person's moral identity has high importance to their self-definition then the readiness with which that moral self-schema will affect moral judgements and behaviours is high and vice-versa (Hardy, Bhattacharjee, Reed, & Aquino, 2010). As Damon and Hart (1992) have aptly put it, people whose self-concept is organised around their moral beliefs are more likely to turn those beliefs into action.

   Evidently, it is the enduring association between an individual's self-concept and the mental representation of their moral character that links this construct to moral behaviours. Moral identity, therefore, emerges as an important source of moral functioning leading to greater congruence between one's moral principles and behaviours (Hardy et al., 2010). Given that the centrality of moral identity varies across individuals, it follows that individuals with a strong moral self-concept should be more likely to expend efforts to self-regulate their behaviour (Seeley & Gardner, 2003). As Power and Khmelkov (1998) argue, the relationship between a person's conception of their moral self and their behaviour is related to the need to maintain a consistent self-image associated with this moral self-schema. In a similar vein, Blasi (1993) states that moral action stems from the desire to act in ways that are consistent with one's ideals.

   The above conceptualisation of moral identity corresponds to Erikson's (1964) proposition than an identity comprises of two dominant characteristics: first, identity is rooted in the core of one's being and second it involves being true to oneself in action (Erikson, 1964). Accordingly, Aquino and Reed (2002) theorised that moral identity has a private and a public aspect labelled, respectively, as internalisation and symbolisation. Internalisation reflects the degree to which moral traits are central to the overall self-schema. Symbolisation reflects the degree to which these traits are manifested outwardly to others. Aquino and Reed (2002) proposed that people with a strong moral identity should strive to maintain consistency between conceptions of their moral self and their actions. However, situational and contextual cues may activate or suppress knowledge structures, including the moral self-conception, influencing the social information processing which is pertinent to moral behaviour.

From moral identity to moral responsibility in P2P accommodation

It is not adequate to decide what is morally good in a given situation; rather, individuals need to make decisions with regard to what moral good is required for their self (Walker, 2014). On this view, judgements of responsibility are the result of the integration of morality in one's sense of self, which extend moral identity to concrete action (Blasi, 1993). Moral responsibility, therefore, emerges as an attitudinal dynamic arising from within the self that directs one's concern to being responsive to the interests and needs of others (Wineberg, 2006). Accountability implies that a person answers for his/her actions rather than being merely held responsible for something. As such, accountability has been acknowledged as a mechanism through which societies may control the behaviour of their members (Beu & Buckley, 2001) such as through the imposition of penalties in the case of illegal or irresponsible activities. Even so, the concept does not necessarily reflect the intentions behind a specific action. Contrary, moral responsibility recognises that moral values are central to one's self, guiding his/her behaviour as one feels ethically responsible to other parties.

Generally, responsibility may be undertaken on an individual or collective level. Individual responsibility occurs when people actively take responsibility rather than passively being responsible (Linley & Matlby, 2009). Collective responsibility is concerned with people's collective accountability. Nonetheless, collective responsibility is difficult to establish (Kaufman, 2015), particularly when there is absence of a relevant legal framework. Within this context, the elements of attribution and diffusion of responsibility emerge. Specifically, people will assign responsibilities to themselves when there are no other social agents to take up moral responsibility or, alternatively, they will diffuse responsibilities to others, particularly when there are too many actors involved in an act and responsibility is not clearly assigned to individuals or its application is inhibited by external barriers (McGregor, 2017). Correspondingly, irresponsibility may be exhibited in people's conduct (Linley & Matlby, 2009). In this regard, capacity to act responsibly gains relevance as sometimes people might be constrained in their ability to act responsibly due to contextual factors (Middlemiss, 2010). A wide range of evidence has emerged indicating that stronger self-importance of moral identity may predict higher rates of responsible actions and less moral disengagement (Kennedy, Kray, & Ku, 2017).

Despite the important theoretical and empirical work on moral identity and responsibility, it remains largely overlooked within the context of the P2P accommodation. One notable exception to the lack of research on moral responsibility in P2P accommodation is found in the recent work of Dredge and Gyimóthy (2017), who uses the P2P accommodation sector as a context to excavate issues of moral responsibility. Dredge and Gyimóthy (2017) argues that moral responsibility requires responsiveness to impacts and negative externalities. However, actors in P2P accommodation have displayed differing willingness to act responsibly and their behaviour has often raised controversies on whether P2P platforms reflect the sharing economy philosophy (Farmaki & Kaniadakis, 2018). Dredge and Gyimóthy (2017) attributes instances of irresponsible behaviour to the dynamic and fluid organisational form of P2P accommodation, which is resistant to rule-bound approaches to defining and assigning responsibilities. In this context, the responsibilities of various actors can be diffused, resulting in lack of accountability or even avoidance. Dredge and Gyimóthy (2017) acknowledges that greater understanding of the ethical decisions and trade-offs in collaborative economy practices is needed, further commenting that there is a need for specific tools and frameworks.

This is the challenge to which this paper responds, by adopting a moral identity approach to enhance understandings of responsibility in P2P accommodation, with particular emphasis being placed on Airbnb host practices. While issues of trust and transparency were previously examined in relation to Airbnb, these were considered from a guest perspective (e.g., Ert, Fleischer, & Magen, 2016; Yang et al., 2019). As such, little is known of how moral judgements of hosts act as a source for the motivation to behave morally in P2P exchanges. To this end, we sought to: a) evaluate how moral responsibility is understood by Airbnb hosts in relation to their moral identity; and b) to examine how Airbnb hosts' perceptions of moral responsibility inform their hosting practice to perform the hospitality exchange. Specifically, we considered all stages of P2P transactions (pre-transaction, during the hospitality exchange and post-transaction) to understand the 'moral questions' that hosts need to address in each stage and, accordingly, *if* and *how* they enact certain aspects of their moral identity in doing so.

Methodology

Data collection and analysis followed a qualitative research approach. A qualitative approach to research was deemed more appropriate given the aim of the study, as it allowed the in-depth exploration of the complex constructs of host perceptions of moral identity and moral responsibility in relation to their hosting practice. Indeed, qualitative research methods may enable the provision of thick descriptions of people's voices and experiences that uncover new understandings of a phenomenon (Ezzy, 2002). In relation to our study, qualitative research allowed a greater understanding of issues pertinent to responsible host conduct by identifying the factors driving the behaviours and practices of Airbnb hosts.

Data collection was undertaken between November 2018 to February 2019. The sampling process was facilitated by the principal investigator's involvement in a relevant European COST Action, which allowed her access to Airbnb hosts across Europe through workshops, training schools and other events organised by the COST. Specifically, the investigator used the network of the Action to identify Airbnb hosts participating in COST events and, subsequently, invite them to participate in the research via email. In so doing, the researcher informed hosts of the purpose of the study as well as the way in which data would be used, ensuring their anonymity would be maintained. Purposive sampling was used to select Airbnb hosts who were deemed knowledgeable of the topic (Schutt, 2018). According to Robinson (2014), in qualitative studies researchers use their a-priori theoretical knowledge of the phenomenon under study and select individuals they believe are able to offer valuable insights. Hence, for our study, we took into consideration the demographic factors (e.g., backgrounds, age and gender) of the informants to ensure a diverse enough sample was included in the study as per Ritchie, Lewis, Nicholls, and Ormston (2014) suggestion. In other words, participants of both genders and various age groups were targeted across different locations in Europe whereas efforts were undertaken to ensure that hosts on different accommodation types were considered (i.e., shared rooms, entire homes). We opted to focus on European-based Airbnb hosts to ensure some form of consistency and uniformity regarding hosts views, particularly in light of the influence of the context (e.g., regulatory framework) on host activities. Data saturation was reached at 35 informants, the profile of which can be seen in Table 1.

Semi-structured interviews of about 45–60 minutes each were undertaken via skype in accordance to informants' date and time preference. All interviews were conducted in English, with the researcher ensuring that the interviewees understood each question asked before proceeding to the next one. In particular, the informants were asked a number of questions, starting from 'grand tour' questions (McCracken, 1988) that aimed to establish the profile of the informants (e.g., number of property listed) before proceeding with questions about host motives and views over moral identity and responsible hosting practices. For instance, the following questions were asked to set the background:

- *Why did you decide to become a host?*
- *Why did you choose to host on the Airbnb platform specifically?*
- *How important is hosting for you?*

Table 1. Profile of participants.

Gender	Age	City/country of hosting	Host status
Female	21	Famagusta, Cyprus	Entire property
Male	27	Pafos, Cyprus	Entire property
Male	34	London, UK	Sharing property
Male	38	Limassol, Cyprus	Multiple listings
Male	32	Montpellier, France	Entire property
Female	41	Bournemouth, UK	Sharing property
Female	38	Barcelona, Spain	Sharing property
Female	53	Amsterdam, Netherlands	Sharing property
Female	50	Scotland, UK	Sharing property
Female	30	Larnaka, Cyprus	Entire property
Male	49	Stockholm, Sweden	Sharing property
Female	42	Berlin, Germany	Sharing property
Male	29	Limassol, Cyprus	Entire property
Female	60	Limerick, Ireland	Sharing property
Female	42	Corfu, Greece	Entire property
Male	35	Budapest, Hungary	Multiple listings
Male	39	Copenhagen, Denmark	Sharing property
Female	55	Cornwall, UK	Entire property
Male	47	Pamplona, Spain	Sharing property
Female	36	Sardinia, Italy	Entire property
Male	43	Nicosia, Cyprus	Multiple listings
Male	45	Crete, Greece	Entire property
Female	42	Lesvos, Greece	Sharing property
Female	43	Newbury, UK	Sharing property
Male	32	Athens, Greece	Multiple listings
Female	31	Frankfurt, Germany	Sharing property
Male	33	Amsterdam, Netherlands	Entire property
Female	57	Famagusta, Cyprus	Entire property
Female	62	Antwerp, Belgium	Entire property
Male	40	Athens, Greece	Multiple listings
Male	38	Prague, Czech Republic	Multiple listings
Male	34	Tallinn, Estonia	Multiple listings
Female	54	Edinburg, Scotland	Entire property
Female	54	Famagusta, Cyprus	Entire property
Male	44	Rome, Italy	Sharing property

These questions allowed us to understand the background and motivation of hosts for engaging in the hosting practice and served as the basis for subsequent questions to be asked on their moral identity and responsibility as Airbnb hosts. For instance, in order to understand the meaning informants attributed to the concepts of 'morality' and 'responsibility' on a personal level and in relation to hosting, we asked:

- *Would you say morality is an important aspect that defines your character?*
- *Can you identify certain moral traits which you think are associated with your character?*
- *Which moral traits do you think an Airbnb host must have? How do these influence his/her hosting practice?*
- *What does 'responsibility' mean to you?*
- *How would you describe a responsible Airbnb host?*

Following, additional questions were asked to uncover informants' views over responsible hosting practices at different stages of the exchange, such as:

- *What practices do you undertake prior to the exchange to ensure you abide to responsible hosting conduct?*
- *What practices do you follow during the exchange to maximise responsible hosting conduct?*
- *What practices do you undertake following the exchange to ensure responsible hosting conduct?*
- *Are there any instances throughout the exchange where you exhibited irresponsible hosting behaviour? If so, why?*

- *In what ways does Airbnb provide a mechanism for enhancing responsible hosting conduct? Does it carry any responsibility itself?*
- *What responsibilities do you think guests have throughout the exchange?*

The questions asked were general and open with the aim of allowing the informants to elaborate on their perceptions and experiences (Patton, 2002). Specifically, the questions asked were used as exploratory themes with the informants being further probed where appropriate. Data were analysed thematically in order to identify key themes within the discussion (Braun & Clarke, 2006). Three researchers were responsible for the analysis of the data. First, the researchers read the interview transcripts and notes multiple times to familiarise with the data. Then, the transcripts were analysed more closely with the three researchers identifying key topics in a "theory-driven" manner (Braun & Clarke, 2006, p. 88). To maximise analytical integrity and ensure data validity, each researcher took on an initial round of open coding separately before converging the first set of findings in a process called triangulation. Flick (2000) posited that investigator triangulation is an effective method to balance subjective research interpretations due to the collective comparison of coding schemes. Hence, in this study researcher triangulation ensured that interviewees' perceptions of moral issues pertaining to their hosting practice are objectively interpreted. Subsequently, axial coding was undertaken whereby emerging topics were grouped into interrelated themes by copying, re-organising and comparing thematic categories whilst refining the data under each theme to identify sub-categories (Goulding, 1999). In this way, thematic categories are expanded and clarified. Last, selective coding was used to combine sub-categories with the themes initially identified; thereby, validating relationships, refining and further developing thematic categories (Strauss & Corbin, 1990) to enhance elaboration on key issues (Hennink, Hutter, & Bailey, 2010). For instance, during open coding the topic of 'motives' was identified; this was then refined and categorised according to 'social motives' and 'economic motives' before being related to the professionalism degree of hosts.

Findings

Motives for hosting on Airbnb

Initially, we sought to examine the motives of hosts in using Airbnb in order to understand the drivers and background for engaging in hosting. As Krettenauer and Casey (2015, p. 175) noted, "moral identities differ in underlying motivations and goal orientations". Accordingly, an understanding of hosting motives may deepen knowledge on the motivation of hosts to act responsibly in relation to their practice. Economic opportunities were the most predominant driver identified by most hosts, although it appeared to carry varying degrees of importance for informants. Nearly half of the informants explained that hosting on Airbnb presents a way to earn additional income that allows them to cover personal expenses or subsidise indulgent consumption. For others, Airbnb offers the opportunity of a temporary salary given unexpected personal circumstances (i.e., unemployment). In some cases, the platform emerged as a space of enterprise whereby hosting has become a professional activity. As an informant commented [male, 40, Greece], "*I manage more than 50 properties and make a good living from this*". Within this context, informants argued that Airbnb, "*being the market leader*" [male, 38, Czech Republic] of P2P accommodation networks, presents greater economic opportunities than other platforms, which command higher commission fees or are less popular.

Equally, several informants acknowledged social benefits as key motivators for hosting on P2P accommodation, commenting on the ease of access to Airbnb. In the words of a host [female, 54, Scotland], "*there are no prerequisites, everyone can join the platform*". Specifically, informants highlighted the socialising opportunities offered by the platform, which they distinguished from competing ones on the grounds that "*Airbnb is about meeting people ... it's different to* booking.com" [male, 43, Cyprus], clarifying that "*hosting on Airbnb is like hosting friends, not customers*" [female, 42, Greece]. Another informant [female, 53, Netherlands] agreed, stating that "*Airbnb is an inspiring way [to live ... you meet all kinds of people from all over the world*". In this regard, the co-habiting option was identified as a marker reinforcing the social benefits of Airbnb, by reflecting hosts' moral principles of helping others. As a host [female, 60, Ireland] aptly put it, "*it's not about the money ... it's about the people you get to help*". Indeed, informants said that the 'sharing practice' entails willingness to "*extend a helping hand to those who might need a home away from home*" [female, 53, Netherlands]. Within this context, several informants commented on the ability to personalise listings on Airbnb, which allows hosts to "*see reviews of guests, understand who they are and what the purpose of their visit is*" [female, 31, Germany], thus offering additional security and trust with regard to the P2P transaction.

As discussion moved on, it became evident that there are different types of Airbnb hosts depending on whether economic or social motives dominate their decision to host on the platform and on how closely they interact with their guests. On the one hand, there are co-habiting hosts, who engage in P2P accommodation mostly for social reasons and actively interact with guests as they share their space with them. Likewise, there are hosts who rent their entire property on an ad-hoc basis yet manage this themselves and, in most cases, maintain some level of interaction with guests. These informants, upon reflection, identified themselves as 'non-professionals'. On the other hand, there were hosts who manage single or multiple listings either on their own or through another entity (e.g., co-host, professional company). For these informants the hosting activity presents an important source of income while, in some cases, a primary one. Unsurprisingly, these hosts self-identified as 'professional hosts'. Therefore, it appears that hosts may be categorised into professionals and non-professionals. Arguably, different hosting motives may signify varying motivation to act responsibly in relation to the hosting practice. To this end, we sought to evaluate the perceived importance of hosts' morality before examining how perceptions of moral identity may generate host judgements of moral responsibility.

Airbnb hosts' moral identity and responsibility perceptions

All of the informants, regardless of their self-assigned professionalism, acknowledged that having high morals was a central aspect of their character, attributing high importance to moral traits such as "being caring and thoughtful of others", "being fair when dealing with others", "maintaining courtesy and transparency in transactions" and "being helpful". Informants argued that such traits are important for hosting practice as they "*provide the framework in which P2P transactions take place*" [female, 55, UK] and "*reflect good hospitality practices*" [female, 42, Greece]. In this regard, we asked informants to elaborate on their judgements of moral responsibility and, specifically, describe what responsibility means for them. The majority of hosts reflected on personal values and ethos, making the following comments:

> Responsibility has to do with a person's character and way of life.
>
> [male, 34, Estonia]

> It is different for every person as it has to do with personal ethics, how one interprets things in life or deals with specific situations and people.
>
> [male, 40, Greece]

Within this context, informants related responsibility with "*accountability towards others*" [female, 38, Spain], "*respect for other cultures and different people*" [male, 47, Spain] and "*keeping your word and doing what it is expected to do*" [male, 38, Czech Republic]. In particular, several informants highlighted the importance of "*dutiful actions ... that we [people] need to take ownership for*" [female, 43, UK], stressing the importance of consequences as a result of (ir)responsible

Table 2. Moral responsibilities of Airbnb hosts.

Practices	Moral responsibilities	
	Internalisation	*Symbolisation*
Pre-transaction		
Developing platform presence	• Be transparent with property	• Adhere to platform rules on narrative
Selecting guests	description	and illustrations used to promote the
	• Be inclusive; not discriminate	listing (i.e. content and photos)
	• Be responsive to guest requests	• Obey platform anti-discrimination policy
During hospitality exchange		
Providing services to guests	• Be polite and hospitable	• Provide a clean and functional space
Managing expectations	• Be reachable, accessible	• Ensure the safety of guests (e.g.
Negotiating boundaries with guests	• Be thoughtful of neighbours	fire detector)
Maintaining good relations	• Be transparent	• Offer additional services (i.e.
with neighbours		cooking breakfast)
		• Offer contact details or information
		• Communicate property rules to guests
		• Set rules for respecting neighbours'
		peacefulness
		• Set boundaries to protect privacy
		of guests
Post-transaction		
Adhering to national laws	• Be honest	• Pay taxes
Reviewing guests	• Be transparent	• Offer truthful reviews
Supporting the community	• Be polite	• Rate cordially
	• Be considerate	• Support Airbnb community through
	• Be a team-player	exchange of knowledge

*Internationalisation refers to host perceptions of what their moral responsibilities should be.
**Symbolisation refers to the practices (actual behaviour) that hosts undertake.

behaviour. As such, informants explained that responsible conduct is illustrated by people's obedience to laws and adherence to obligations as a member of the wider society.

Following, we turned our attention to perceptions of moral responsibility in relation to hosting on Airbnb. Specifically, almost half of the informants suggested that "*a responsible host will be a responsible citizen*" [female, 43, UK]. In other words, hosts argued that responsible hosting practice implies that Airbnb hosts are generally dutiful members of the society. Such thoughts were mostly prevalent among non-professional hosts. Even so, the rest of the informants and mostly professionals pointed towards a distinction between a person's responsible behaviour and his/her hosting practice, arguing that "*being an Airbnb host is just one role of many that hosts have to play*" [male, 32, Greece]. Specifically, informants did not regard hosting practice as necessarily related to the degree of responsibility a person exhibits in their professional or personal life. Neither did informants thought hosting practice to be indicative of the morality of the host. Such views were surprising considering that all of the informants identified morality as a central aspect of their character and sense of self. Hence, we sought to understand how hosts adopt aspects of moral identity in their hosting practice and, subsequently, how they externalise their self-perceptions of moral responsibility through relevant activities. In doing so, we asked informants to elaborate on specific moral responsibilities as they become relevant at different stages of the P2P hospitality exchange. A summary of Airbnb hosts' moral responsibilities as emerging from the interviews is provided in Table 2, with host practices being explained in detail in the following section.

Airbnb host practices

Pre-transaction phase

Prior the transaction, both professional and non-professional hosts identified platform-related practices as a key activity, including developing and communicating their property descriptions and screening potential guests' profile in order to evaluate their suitability before accepting booking requests. Informants suggested that when undertaking these practices, the issues of transparency and inclusivity emerge as relevant to moral identity, guiding their activities accordingly. *"If you say your property is 100 square metres then it should be 100 square metres"* said a host [male, 45, Greece] commenting on the need for honesty in communicating the offering. Within this context, informants highlighted the freedom to personalise listings as a benefit of Airbnb, which further elevates the importance of *"transparency as a mechanism for good host conduct"* [female, 30, Cyprus]. As a host [female, 36, Sardinia] put it, *"there are cases where hosts exaggerate and give false representations of the property"*. In this regard, the role of the platform was emphasised as providing guidance to hosts, especially to non-professional ones. Indeed, several informants argued that they seek advice from the platform itself when developing the property descriptions. *"You need to agree to the rules of the platform to register, in other words hosts need to provide a fire detector and extinguishers, toiletries and so on"* explained an informant [male, 45, Cyprus]. In this regard, the support of online host groups was mentioned as influential on host practices, particularly for less experienced, non-professional hosts. Professional hosts with multiple listings were more inclined to use appealing visual narratives that convey *"the offering of experiences than simply list the things that the property has"* [male, 37, Czech Republic] in order to maximise their business. For these hosts, transparency emerged as an important business practice that may lead to positive word-of-mouth and higher guest satisfaction.

Additionally, informants pointed to the anti-discrimination policy of Airbnb as a restrictive factor on their hosting practice, arguing that greater flexibility is required in guest selection. Such views were strongly expressed by non-professional hosts. As a host commented:

> You can attribute bad behaviours on specific parameters such as nationality or age … for example, I don't accept booking requests from large groups of young, British men as they usually get drank and make noise.
>
> [male, 33, Netherlands]

In some extreme cases, cultural stereotyping was reflected in informants' explanations. For example, a host [male, 27, Cyprus] said he declines requests from potential guests from specific countries or religions. Other hosts, especially co-habiting ones, suggested that they should have the freedom to select who stays in their properties due to safety concerns. The following extracts reflect relevant concerns of hosts.

> It is not clear what ensues if something happens to the guest in the property … so I avoid bookings from old people.
>
> [male,45, Greece]

> I am a single mother of two girls, I accept only women in my house but with Airbnb's changing policy I feel I am being punished for being selective.
>
> [female, 41, UK]

Indeed, more than half of the informants commented on the platform's introduction of the 'superhost' badge that limits hosts' ability to reject or cancel bookings. As a host [female, 43, UK] stated *"if you cancel a reservation for whatever reason, you can't be a superhost for a year"*. Concerns over Airbnb's policy were expressed particularly by non-professional hosts whether co-habitation exists or not; for these informants, the superhost badge represents a significant booster on their bookings as well as an affirmation of their *"good hosting"*. Contrary, professional hosts with multiple listings tend to *"accept all bookings as this is good business"* [male, 38, Czech Republic]. Informants suggested that as non-professional hosts, there is *"inability to meet some guests' expectations … it's about what I can provide as a host"* [female, 43, UK]. In fact, nearly all of the informants discussed the increasing demands of guests, who *"think hosts are available 24/ 7"* [male, 40, Greece]. *"Some guests think that Airbnb properties are like hotels but it's about sharing"* argued another host [male, 47, Spain]. For non-professionals and especially co-habiting hosts, guest rejection is not equated to discrimination. As an informant [male, 47, Spain] explained, *"I reject on a regular basis. But rejecting guests is not the same as discrimination"*.

Within this context, nearly all of the informants identified the platform as a driver of guest expectations. As a host said:

> Airbnb is becoming increasingly professionalised. Its guidelines are pointing towards a standardisation of service which is comparable to hotels but the hotel sector is regulated ... having less flexibility to select guests means that hosts are exposed.

[male, 39, Denmark]

In this regard, non-professional informants explained that initiatives such as Airbnb Plus, used to categorise 'quality' properties, are adding pressure on their hosting practice which is nonetheless being applied within an unregulated context. While informants acknowledged that *"hotels don't have the luxury to screen guests"* [male, 33, Netherlands] contrary to Airbnb hosts who may go over reviews and guest ratings, they did emphasise the regulated framework in which hotels operate, which is insofar absent in P2P accommodation. An informant [male, 40, Greece] argued *"Airbnb started as the foundation of the sharing economy. Now, it has turned into a business-oriented company yet it is located in this grey area where there are laws but there is no enforcement of laws"*. Such views were equally shared by professional and non-professional hosts.

During hospitality exchange phase

Moving on, we asked informants to describe the hosting practice during the hospitality exchange phase, that is after booking request was accepted. *"Being hospitable is common sense"* argued an informant [female, 53, Netherlands] whereas another host [female, 60, Ireland] added that *"if you treat your guests like you treat your friends then you cannot go wrong"*. For nearly all of the informants, acts of hospitableness and courtesy were key elements of the service provision although these were expressed varyingly. For instance, some co-habiting hosts suggested that they may offer additional services to their guests such as *"cook breakfast for them or do pick-ups from the airport"* [female, 60, Ireland] while others argued that they are either unable or unwilling to offer such services. As an informant explained:

> I treat my guests like I treat my flatmates to manage expectations, so I expect them to do the dishes and cook their own food.

[female, 38, Spain]

In this regard, informants stated that they not only outline property rules on the platform but also explicitly articulate them to guests either verbally on a one-to-one basis or by leaving an information booklet in the property. In any case, all of the hosts irrespective of their degree of professionalism acknowledged that they are responsible for providing a safe, clean, functional environment to their guests and ensure that service provision matches their listing description in order to *"build trust with guests"* [female, 60, Ireland]. Indeed, transparency and trust emerged as an important moral aspect of hosting practice, particularly for co-habiting hosts. In the words of an informant:

> You hear stories of hosts putting up cameras in the properties to monitor guests but this is unethical ... we open up our home to strangers but they also need to trust us.

[female, 43, UK]

Moreover, being organised and maintaining communication with the guest before arrival at the property were also acknowledged as key elements of being a responsible host. As an informant [female, 31, Germany] put it, *"I need to be reachable for my guests in case something happens"*. Indeed, several hosts argued that they provide booklets with contact details and relevant tourist information to guests. Such services seem to be comparable to professional hotel standards; nonetheless, findings reveal that they are evident in the practices of both professional and non-professional hosts. In this context, informants argued that guests too have responsibilities towards the hosts. For instance, informants stated that guests need to respect the property rules, ensure they will not cause damage to the property and respect the neighbours as well as the privacy of the host, particularly in case of co-habitation. As an informant [female, 60, Ireland] put it, *"guests need to be thoughtful of the host. For example, if they are going to arrive late, they need to inform the host accordingly"*. As such, various incidents were described by hosts as indicative of guests' poor conduct. The text below acts as an exemplar of such incidents:

> I was sitting in the living room, chatting with a guest when he suddenly took the remote control and changed the TV channel. But I was watching a programme. I thought … hang on, this is my TV, my living room!

> [female, 43, UK]

Another informant [female, 53, Netherlands] described how one guest smoked inside the property despite the 'no smoking' warning and when confronted he simply carried on, stating that he was smoking a pipe and not a cigarette. As such, hosts and especially non-professional ones suggested that *"only Airbnb can regulate the irresponsible behaviours of guests and hosts … by setting standards"* [female, 43, UK]. Nonetheless, as hosts pointed to the *"guest-first approach"* advocated by Airbnb's changing policies, they described themselves as *"hostages of the platform"* [male, 27, Cyprus] unable to overpower guests who might in turn give them bad reviews.

Other incidents were mentioned with respect to guests' misconduct and/or disturbing behaviour against neighbours. Arguing that respect to neighbours is a reflection of civilian responsibility, hosts suggested that maintaining good neighbourly relations is an important host practice, particularly for non-professional hosts.

> I have to be a responsible Airbnb host for my neighbours … I generally try to avoid inflicting harm on others. I don't want to benefit myself but damage others in the process of doing so.

> [female, 44, Italy]

> I have to see my neighbours everyday, so I don't want any problems with them.

> [male, 34, UK]

In this context, some hosts highlighted the role of co-hosts on influencing neighbour relations. *"I gave the management of my property to a co-host but since then I've been getting complaints from my neighbours and started to receive bad reviews from guests"* [female, 38, Spain]. As such, informants stated that they warn guests to behave responsibly within the property and in communal areas of apartment building out of respect for neighbours. Even so, informants suggested that the degree to which such measures are successful vary, further reinforcing the need for guest selection.

Post-transaction phase

At the post-transaction phase, the majority of informants (both professionals and non-professionals) saw their practice as extending towards adherence to relevant laws, providing reviews for guests and supporting the Airbnb community such as through offering of information to fellow hosts on online social groups. For instance, in their dealings with the platform and the Airbnb society, most informants emphasised the importance of politeness when conducting reviews, honesty and transparency as well as being considerate so as to offer truthful information about others (guests) and to others (other hosts); thus, contributing to the Airbnb community. These values were correspondingly manifested through their active participation in host groups where, non-professional hosts in particular, exchange knowledge and information on hosting practices. Such channels represent the self-organising tactics of professional and non-professional hosts. In the words of an informant [male, 33, Netherlands] *"we got an accountant, a lawyer and we sought the knowledge of more experienced hosts from San Francisco"*. As Airbnb hosts are beginning to acquire a 'professional identity', informants engaging in P2P transactions for professional reasons expressed a desire for greater regulation in order to safeguard their hosting practice as well as obtain a legitimate stance. Such views are regarded as prevalent by informants in the current P2P accommodation context where guests appear to gain power. *"Some guests might give bad reviews out of spite because the host told them off for doing something they shouldn't"* explained an informant [female, 42, Germany]. In this regard, the importance of reading the general profile of users was highlighted, with hosts suggesting that the platform should consider the potential inciteful behaviour of guests and its effect on host ratings. Indeed, as one professional host [male, 40, Greece] put it, some guests attempt to 'punish' the host by giving bad reviews or breaking and stealing objects from the property as *"a last act of showing customer power"*. The informants implied that guest misconduct elicits negative criticism for Airbnb and highlighted the need for hosts to remain *"responsible for the Airbnb community otherwise it will gain a bad name"* [male, 47, Spain].

Arguably, the most recurrent theme dominating discussion on post-transaction practices was payment of taxes. Although half of the informants suggested they pay taxes as this is the *"right thing to do"*, the rest stated otherwise. Specifically, most professional hosts admitted to following the law on tax payment as this is a reflection of good business practice. Contrary, many non-professional and especially co-habiting hosts said they avoid declaring Airbnb revenue. In justifying such actions, informants stated that they don't make a lot of money and, hence, it would be *"unfair to pay taxes when the revenue is so small"* [male, 44, Italy]. Indeed, some co-habiting hosts argued that in certain European countries hosts renting a room in their property and making less than a specific amount per year are exempted from tax payment. Even so, several non-professional hosts commented that avoidance of tax payment is morally permissible as *"others avoid paying taxes too"* [male, 32, France]. Evidently, a form of irresponsible behaviour traverses as a norm in situations where there is collective irresponsibility of Airbnb hosts.

Within this context, both professional and non-professional hosts pointed to the role of the platform on minimising negative socio-economic impacts. As a host [male, 33, Netherlands] commented, *"Airbnb needs to create value for everyone … currently, it is disadvantaging hosts. You can't operate at the scale and not take up your share of responsibility"*. In this regard, informants suggested that Airbnb should collect tax from hosts. *"If the company could provide this service to hosts, it would solve many problems"* said an informant [female, 38, Spain]. Informants also commented on the pressures being placed on local housing markets as a result of the growth and professionalisation of Airbnb as well as the illegal operation of many Airbnb rentals. Even though many non-professional hosts were particularly concerned over such impacts, several professional hosts did not envisage these consequences as pertinent to their hosting practice, commenting that *"hosts cannot be accountable for all the problems in the society and economy"* [male, 32, Greece]. Rather, informants stated that the platform *"needs to be held accountable not only towards the guests or hosts but to all the parties involved, as its growth is affecting everyone from the hoteliers to residents"* [female, 36, Italy]. The words of an informant sum up the feelings of both professional and non-professional hosts:

> As Airbnb grows, its effects get bigger on housing, prices, crime, deviant behaviour of hosts and guests … they can't be exempted from the responsibility they have to users, the authorities and the society … we [hosts] are only a piece of the puzzle.
>
> [male, 39, Denmark]

These dynamics are evident in Figure 1, which shows the role of the platform in shaping the application of host and guest responsibilities.

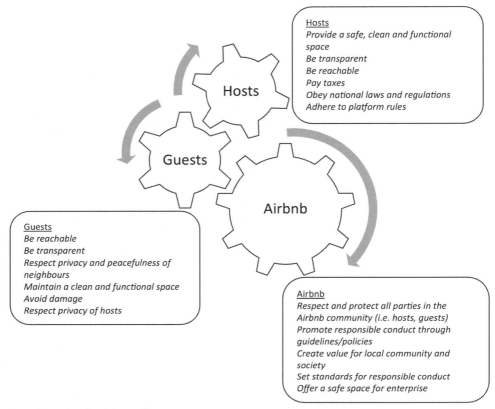

Figure 1. Perceived responsibilities of key actors.

Discussion

Study findings reveal that Airbnb hosts regard moral traits as central to their sense of self. In this context, hosts expressed the need for responsible behaviour, manifested by efforts to *"contribute to the community"* or *"abide by local rules"*; thus, adhering to perceptions of a dutiful citizenship (Powell, 2012). Hosts' moral identity seemed, in principle, to motivate their moral functioning; indeed, to be morally responsible one has to follow through in moral action (Blasi, 1993). Nonetheless, in relation to their hosting practice, there were hosts who distinguished between responsible citizenship and responsible host conduct, arguing that being an Airbnb host is just one role of many that one is called to play and, as such, not necessarily indicative of a person's morality. This fits well with the concept of moral identity centrality (Reed, 2002), in that some hosts assigned what they perceived as their moral identity a central role in their hosting practices while others saw their moral identity as completely separate to these. While prior studies identify moral identity centrality as an influencing factor on the moral disengagement of certain unethical behaviour (e.g., He & Harris, 2014), our study findings suggest that individuals' moral identity centrality varies in accordance to specific roles acquired in different contexts. For some informants, then, their moral self-concept (internalisation) did not necessarily self-regulate their behaviour as hosts (symbolisation).

In addition, findings indicate a variance in hosts' (ir)responsible behaviour across the different stages of P2P transactions (Table 2), with informants' motive and approach to hosting and their perceptions of moral responsibility emerging as key influencing factors on host practice heterogeneity. For instance, there were informants who see themselves as 'professional hosts', renting one or multiple listings systematically with the purpose of gaining a primary source of income as previously reported (e.g., Lutz & Newlands, 2018). Likewise, there were informants who self-identified as 'non-professional Airbnb hosts', sharing a room in their property or renting out the entire property on an ad-hoc basis to supplement their income and/or for socialising reasons. These informants emerge as 'social entrepreneurs' who are mostly interested in life experiences (Farmaki et al., 2020; Stabrowski, 2017). In fact, a theme which recurred throughout the interviews was that hosts have varying degrees of professionalism; in other words, they differ with regard to the degree of expertise and commitment they bring to their role as hosts on the platform. Within this context, professional and non-professional hosts expressed varying practices and, as such, heterogeneous responsible behaviours. Indeed, previous studies highlighted the illegal operation of many Airbnb rentals and the emergence of professional hosts as the root to the problems caused by Airbnb's expansion (e.g., Gottlieb, 2013; Guttentag, 2015; Stergiou & Farmaki, 2019).

While both professional and non-professional hosts offer services comparative to hotels as previously reported (Dann et al., 2019; Guttentag & Smith, 2017), the way hosts express 'hospitableness' differs. For example, some co-habiting hosts provide more services than others (i.e., cook breakfast); contrary, other informants perceive their hosting responsibilities as having certain boundaries. Although such discrepancies in hosting practices were more evident among non-professional hosts, for hosts self-identifying as 'professionals' a standardised service comparable to traditional hospitality emerged as a key aim, representing good business practice (Farmaki et al., 2020) that facilitates trust-building and enhances their reputation in line with prior research (e.g., Ert et al., 2016; Yang et al., 2019). Similarly, variance was noted among professional and non-professional hosts in terms of responsible behaviour extending to other parties beyond the guest. For instance, non-professional hosts expressed concerns over the potential impacts of their hosting practice on their neighbours, whom they interact with regularly. Indeed, past studies identify neighbours as a significant stakeholder group that needs to be considered in the regulation of the P2P accommodation phenomenon (Stergiou & Farmaki, 2019). Contrary, as our findings reveal, for 'professional' hosts a responsible hosting behaviour represents appropriate professional practice, mostly seen as a means for business maximisation rather than emanating from moral values. Evidently, the moral identity of Airbnb hosts emerges as an important factor directing their behaviour and, in turn, determining the intensity of impacts resulting from the growth of the platform and which threatens the sustainability of places (Ioannides et al., 2018).

Even so, the extent to which professional and non-professional hosts assume responsibility for their actions varies as perceptions of moral responsibility differ, exemplifying accordingly the various degrees of moral identity centrality in informants' hosting practices. As such, professional and non-professional hosts alike appear to justify irresponsible acts (Linley & Matlby, 2009) highlighting the context of P2P transactions as influential on their ability to exercise hosting practices responsibly (Middlemiss, 2010). Indeed, two factors appear to contribute to their reasoning. First, a similar irresponsible action being followed by other hosts (i.e., avoidance of tax payment); such form of irresponsible behaviour traverses as a norm because of the collective behaviour of Airbnb hosts that seems to reinforce their moral disengagement (Kennedy et al., 2017). In such cases, the moral identity of hosts is woven together with the actions of relevant others, which serve as the backdrop of their own decision on what is morally acceptable in this situation. Second, the lack and inconsistency of a regulatory framework on P2P accommodation seems to exacerbate irresponsible acts of hosts especially when the likelihood of being detected is minimal (Park, Kwak, & Lee, 2019). Specifically, findings identify hosts who attempt to self-regulate their practice in an effort to attribute responsibility to themselves. As collective responsibility is difficult to establish (Kaufman, 2015) particularly where there is absence of a formal regulatory framework as in the case of P2P accommodation (Rauch & Schleicher, 2015), individuals tend to either assign responsibility to themselves or diffuse responsibility to others (McGregor, 2017). Host views express an embedded assumption that hosts are not accountable for their irresponsible actions that arise due to the conditions that exist within the P2P context including the illegal activity of many Airbnb rentals (Gottlieb, 2013; Guttentag, 2015). In this regard, some

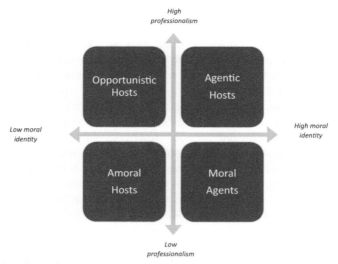

Figure 2. Typology of (im)moral Airbnb hosts.

hosts tend to diffuse responsibility to the platform or even to guests whom they regard as equally responsible.

This study concludes that there are various ways in which hosts draw on their moral identity to guide their practice. To be able to start comprehending and articulating the complexities of the relationship between moral identity and responsible host conduct, we found it necessary to devise a mechanism that would allow us to develop understandings of the variety of ways in which moral identity affects hosting practice. To this end, we offer a typology (Figure 2) of Airbnb hosts linking their understanding of moral identity as a self-assigned construct guiding their behaviour with the level of what we call here 'professionalism' in hosting practice, namely their approach to hosting as shaped by the primary motive to engage in P2P transactions (i.e., economic or social) and the degree of commitment and hospitality expertise they bring to their role as hosts. In other words, different types of hosts seem to exist in relation to whether their hosting practice reflects high or low moral identity and in accordance to their categorisation as high professionals (e.g., managing multiple listings for economic benefits) or low professionalism (e.g., sharing property for socio-economic benefits). Specifically, the typology illustrates a spectrum of Airbnb hosts: (a) those emerging as *moral agents* in P2P accommodation viewing their hosting practice as an extension of their moral self, with their hosting practice not being driven by economic reasons but a desire to help others in need, (b) *agentic hosts* who have a practical view in terms of their morality that seems to define their professional identity by safeguarding their reputation and so engage in self-regulating tactics (i.e., consulting accountants), (c) *opportunistic hosts* who are hosting professionally and define their practice according to economic interests, thus conform only to the minimum requirements of the law (e.g., paying taxes) as a means of protecting their professional resources and d) *amoral hosts* who justify immoral behaviour in the context of situational factors present in the external environment including the lack of a regulatory framework on P2P accommodation and/or in relation to peers' irresponsible behaviour.

Conclusions

This study aimed to explore the perceptions of Airbnb hosts with regard to their moral responsibility in P2P transactions. By drawing from moral identity theory, we sought to understand how Airbnb host views on moral responsibility are generated and how their hosting practice is linked to personal motivation to act responsibly. Given the growing concerns voiced by scholars with regard to the effects of Airbnb (i.e., Ioannides et al., 2018; Stergiou & Farmaki, 2019) which seem to be largely driven by the unscrupulous behaviour of hosts and threatening the sustainability of places (Martin, 2016), this study is a timely addition to the expanding literature on P2P accommodation. Although past studies have considered issues pertinent to trust and transparency in P2P practice (e.g., Ert et al., 2016; Yang et al., 2019), little is known of how hosts are motivated to behave morally throughout the different stages of the P2P exchange. This study responds to this gap and attempts to shed light on the 'moral questions' that hosts need to address in each stage and, accordingly, how they enact certain aspects of their moral identity in their hosting practice.

As the preceding discussion illustrated, hosting in P2P accommodation settings is fraught with moral issues. On the one hand, this study identified several examples of moral actions that hosts undertake to enhance transparency, hospitality provision and trust-building in line with past studies (Farmaki et al., 2020; Moon et al., 2019). On the other hand, there are morally irresponsible behaviours emerging that can take many forms such as tax avoidance, guest discrimination and providing misleading property information among others. Such behaviours were identified by researchers as a matter of concern requiring the regulation of the Airbnb phenomenon as they inevitably impact the socio-economic fabric of local communities (i.e., Gurran & Phibbs, 2017); further contributing to the negative effects emanating from overcrowding and the touristification of places (Ioannides et al., 2018) that result from the growth of illegal or professional operation of Airbnb rentals (Gottlieb, 2013; Stergiou & Farmaki, 2019). Indeed, as the study has shown, Airbnb hosts emerge as a 'community of practice' (Farmaki & Kaniadakis, 2018) and, thus, their potentially irresponsible behaviour becomes a norm, acting as a justifiable principle guiding the behaviour of their peers. Nonetheless, as this study has shown, there are various ways in which Airbnb hosts draw on their moral identity to inform their hosting practice, often according to the context in which they operate, wherein the absence of regulation reinforces moral disengagement (Kennedy et al., 2017). In order to capture the complexity of moral identity within P2P accommodation, this study identifies and illustrates in Figure 2 four types of hosts that exhibit different behaviours in accordance to their degree of professionalism and moral identity levels.

The typology, thus, makes a two-fold contribution to existing knowledge. First, it can be understood as an analytical tool that allows scholars to identify hosting behaviour, articulate causal relations, devise new research questions and design research within P2P accommodation. The typology enhances understanding of host behaviour as a response to certain moral responsibilities, as these emerge out of the different stages of the P2P exchange. In other words, hosts interpret their hosting practice as a set of certain responsibilities that either have a direct internal link to specific moral traits or are associated with broader social and community values. Subsequently, their hosting practice is drawn according to what would be the response to relevant moral questions. Each response, then, could be categorised and understood in the moral identity-professionalism matrix of the host typology. Secondly, it may be conceptualised as a diagnostic and reflective tool for hosts or those considering of becoming hosts. The typology may allow hosts to reflect on their own approach to hosting and understand their levels of moral engagement into their P2P activity, suggesting a self-reflective understanding of the self as host. Specifically, as hosts' identity switches between them being property owners and/or hospitality professionals and entrepreneurs, the typology may allow them to draw a personal strategy and decide where the boundaries between morality and hosting would lie. In other words, the typology can be seen as an action template for Airbnb hosting, one that takes into consideration the moral aspects of the practice. This is relevant given the diverse hosting approaches characterising P2P accommodation and associated effects on local communities and economies (Farmaki et al., 2020).

The typology also carries significant practical implications. Our findings suggest that while moral identity does act as a self-regulatory mechanism in inhibiting unethical host practices, the effect of this self-regulation may be rendered less potent by contextual factors. Considering the growth of P2P accommodation and the potential socio-economic impacts it yields at the local, regional and national levels, self-regulation presents an inadequate mechanism for monitoring the sector.

Accordingly, regulatory efforts should first consider the variance among P2P accommodation hosts and not treat them as a homogeneous group. Although categorising different types of hosts is not an easy task, as some may shift from one type to another over time, it is necessary to align regulatory controls to specific host categories to ensure maximum benefit for the parties involved. For instance, hosts may be categorised with regard to the degree of 'professionalism' they carry in their hosting approach and be regulated accordingly in terms of taxation and occupancy among others. Additionally, regulation should be targeted not only to hosts but also to other actors involved in the P2P transaction including guests, neighbours and the platform itself. As this study betrays, the dynamics among relevant stakeholders are to a great extent influential on hosts' assumed ability to carry out their practice responsibly. In particular, regulatory efforts should focus on eliminating those influences that motivate hosts to act irresponsibly.

Alternatively, policies may be directed at invoking a desired "ideal citizenship" (Haber & Levi-Faur, 2018, p. 242), encouraging moral host behaviour. In the political sphere, citizenship represents "a relation between the individual and the community, a membership status which contains a package of rights, duties and obligations" (Faulks, 2000, p. 13). Building on this conceptualisation, the equivalent of political citizenship in the P2P accommodation sphere would relate to a set of rights and values based on a strong moral element of the individual host as a participant in P2P activities. As such, Airbnb may incorporate relevant features in its platform to reward and encourage morally responsible host conduct. Such policies might include a badge comparable to the 'superhost' one that Airbnb already offers. Likewise, the platform might adopt a social responsibility strategy equivalent to the corporate social responsibility strategies of organisations in order to promote responsible host and guest behaviour that contributes to the sustainability of destinations. Regardless, such efforts should aim to develop a culture that upholds the broader community's moral values rather than simply those of personal aspirations and business ideals.

To conclude, this study identified both morally responsible and irresponsible acts of Airbnb hosts which indicate that P2P accommodation offers a fruitful landscape for further examination of the interplay between moral identity and hosting practices. Ultimately, articulating a fuller understanding of the role of moral identity and responsibility in P2P accommodation contexts will require the development of a comprehensive framework relating to *when* and *how* moral identity will exhibit self-regulatory potency to act responsibly. By making a case that responsible host conduct varies as a function of hosts' professionalism and self-perceived moral identity, we have taken a step towards this direction. Investigations aimed at mapping out what situational factors have the greatest potential to influence the relationship between hosts' moral identity and moral behaviour are needed to build on this initial effort. Moreover, there is a need to understand how guests perceive moral identity aspects in P2P transactions. We hope that the ideas presented in this study can provide researchers with an impetus to investigate these and other questions associated with (im)morality in the P2P accommodation context.

Disclosure statement

No potential conflict of interest was reported by the authors.

ORCID

Anna Farmaki (iD) http://orcid.org/0000-0002-9996-5632

References

Airbnb. (2018). Airbnb fast facts. Retrieved from https://press.atairbnb.com/app/uploads/2017/08/4-Million-Listings-Announcement-1.pdf

Aquino, K., & Reed, A. I. I. (2002). The self-importance of moral identity. *Journal of Personality and Social Psychology, 83*(6), 1423–1440. doi:10.1037/0022-3514.83.6.1423

Belk, R. (2014). You are what you can access: Sharing and collaborative consumption online. *Journal of Business Research, 67*(8), 1595–1600. doi:10.1016/j.jbusres.2013.10.001

Beu, D., & Buckley, M. R. (2001). The hypothesized relationship between accountability and ethical behavior. *Journal of Business Ethics, 34*(1), 57–73. doi:10.1023/A:1011957832141

Blasi, A. (1993). The development of identity: Some implications for moral functioning. In G. G. Noam & T. E. Wren (Eds.), *The moral self* (pp. 99–122). Cambridge, MA: The MIT Press.

Braun, V., & Clarke, V. (2006). Using thematic analysis in psychology. *Qualitative Research in Psychology, 3*(2), 77–101. doi:10.1191/1478088706qp063oa

Bucher, E., Fieseler, C., Fleck, M., & Lutz, C. (2018). Authenticity and the sharing economy. *Academy of Management Discoveries, 4*(3), 294–313. doi:10.5465/amd.2016.0161

Caton, K. (2012). Taking the moral turn in tourism studies. *Annals of Tourism Research, 39*(4), 1906–1928. doi:10.1016/j.annals.2012.05.021

Cheng, M., & Foley, C. (2018). The sharing economy and digital discrimination: The case of Airbnb. *International Journal of Hospitality Management, 70*, 95–98. doi:10.1016/j.ijhm.2017.11.002

Cohen, B., & Munoz, P. (2016). Sharing cities and sustainable consumption and production: Towards an integrated framework. *Journal of Cleaner Production, 134*, 87–97. doi:10.1016/j.jclepro.2015.07.133

Cohen, M., & Sundararajan, A. (2015). Self-regulation and innovation in the peer-to-peer sharing economy. *University Chicago Legal Review Dialogue, 82*(1), 116–119.

Damon, W., & Hart, D. (1992). Self-understanding and its role in social and moral development. In M. Bornstein & M. E. Lamb (Eds.), *Developmental psychology: An advanced handbook* (3rd ed., pp. 421–464). Hillsdale, NJ: Erlbaum.

Dann, D., Teubner, T. & Weinhardt, C. (2019). Poster child and guinea pig – insights from a structured literature review on Airbnb. *International Journal of Contemporary Hospitality Management, 31*(1), 427–473.

Dredge, D., & Gyimóthy, S. (Eds.). (2017). *Collaborative Economy and Tourism: Perspectives, Politics, Policies and Prospects.* Cham: Springer.

Edelman, B. G., & Geradin, D. (2015). Efficiencies and regulatory shortcuts: How should we regulate companies like Airbnb and Uber. *Stanford Technological Law Review, 19*(2), 293–297.

Erikson, E. H. (1964). *Insight and Responsibility.* New York, NY: Norton.

Ert, E., Fleischer, A., & Magen, N. (2016). Trust and reputation in the sharing economy: The role of personal photos in Airbnb. *Tourism Management, 55*, 62–73. doi:10.1016/j.tourman.2016.01.013

Espinosa, T. P. (2016). The cost of sharing and the common law: How to address the negative externalities of home-sharing. *Chapman University Law Review, 19*(2), 597–601.

Ezzy, D. (2002). *Qualitative Analysis: Practice and Innovation.* London: Routledge.

Farmaki, A., Christou, P., & Saveriades, A. (2020). A Lefebvrian analysis of Airbnb space. *Annals of Tourism Research, 80*, 102806. ahead-of-print. doi:10.1016/j.annals.2019.102806

Farmaki, A., & Kaniadakis, A. (2018). Responsibility in the sharing economy. In *Proceedings of the 28th CAUTHE conference* (pp. 553–556). Newcastle Business School, The University of Newcastle, Callaghan, Australia.

Faulks, K. (2000). *Citizenship.* London: Routledge.

Flick, U. (2000). An introduction to qualitative research. *European Journal of Information Systems, 9*(2), 127–127.

Gottlieb, C. (2013). Residential short-term rentals: Should local governments regulate the 'industry'? *Planning & Environmental Law, 65*(2), 4–9. doi:10.1080/15480755.2013.766496

Goulding, C. (1999). *Grounded theory: Some reflections on paradigm, procedures and misconceptions.* Working paper series, WP006/99, Wolverhampton: University of Wolverhampton.

Grimmer, L., Vorobjovas-Pinta, O., & Massey, M. (2019). Regulating, then deregulating Airbnb: The unique case of Tasmania (Australia). *Annals of Tourism Research, 75*, 304–307. doi:10.1016/j.annals.2019.01.012

Gurran, N., & Phibbs, P. (2017). When tourists move in: How should urban planners respond to Airbnb? *Journal of the American Planning Association, 83*(1), 80–92. doi:10.1080/01944363.2016.1249011

Guttentag, D. (2015). Airbnb: Disruptive innovation and the rise of an informal tourism accommodation sector. *Current Issues in Tourism, 18*(12), 1192–1217. doi:10.1080/13683500.2013.827159

Guttentag, D. A. & Smith, S. L. (2017). Assessing Airbnb as a disruptive innovation relative to hotels: Substitution and comparative performance expectations. *International Journal of Hospitality Management, 64*, 1–10.

Haber, H., & Levi-Faur, D. (2018). The financialization of European Union citizenship: An alternative to democratic empowerment. In D. Levi-Faur & F. van Warden (Eds.), *Democratic empowerment in the European Union* (pp. 239–268). Cheltenham: Edward Elgar.

Hajibaba, H., & Dolnicar, S. (2017). Substitutable by peer-to-peer accommodation networks? *Annals of Tourism Research, 66*, 185–188. doi:10.1016/j.annals.2017.05.013

Hardy, S. A., Bhattacharjee, A., Reed, A. I. I., & Aquino, K. (2010). Moral identity and psychological distance: The case of adolescent parental socialization. *Journal of Adolescence, 33*(1), 111–123. doi:10.1016/j.adolescence.2009.04.008

He, H., & Harris, L. (2014). Moral disengagement of hotel guest negative WOM: Moral identity centrality, moral awareness, and anger. *Annals of Tourism Research, 45*, 132–151. doi:10.1016/j.annals.2013.10.002

Hennink, M., Hutter, I., & Bailey, A. (2010). *Qualitative research methods*. London: Sage.

Ikkala, T., & Lampinen, A. (2015, February). Monetizing network hospitality: Hospitality and sociability in the context of Airbnb. In *Proceedings of the 18th ACM conference on computer supported cooperative work & social computing,*Vancouver, BC, Canada. (pp. 1033–1044). ACM. doi:10.1145/2675133.2675274

Ioannides, D., Röslmaier, M., & van der Zee, E. (2018). Airbnb as an instigator of 'tourism bubble' expansion in Utrecht's Lombok neighbourhood. *Tourism Geographies, 21*(5), 822–840. doi:10.1080/14616688.2018.1454505

Jonas, A. (2015). Share and share dislike: The rise of Uber and Airbnb and how New York City should play nice. *Journal of Law & Policy, 24*(1), 205–215.

Kaufman, B. (2015). Theorising determinants of employee voice: An integrative model across disciplines and levels of analysis. *Human Resource Management Journal, 25*(1), 19–40. doi:10.1111/1748-8583.12056

Kennedy, J. A., Kray, L. J., & Ku, G. (2017). A social-cognitive approach to understanding gender differences in negotiator ethics: The role of moral identity. *Organizational Behavior and Human Decision Processes, 138*, 28–44. doi: 10.1016/j.obhdp.2016.11.003

Krettenauer, T., & Casey, V. (2015). Moral identity development and positive moral emotions: Differences involving authentic and hubristic pride. *Identity, 15*(3), 173–187. doi:10.1080/15283488.2015.1023441

Lalicic, L., & Weismayer, C. (2017). The role of authenticity in Airbnb experiences. In Schegg, R. & Stangl, B. (Eds.), *Information and communication technologies in tourism 2017* (pp. 781–794). Cham: Springer.

Linley, P. A., & Maltby, J. (2009). Personal responsibility. In: S. J. Lopez (Ed.), *The encyclopedia of positive psychology* (pp. 685–689). Boston, MA: Blackwell Publishing.

Lutz, C., & Newlands, G. (2018). Consumer segmentation within the sharing economy: The case of Airbnb. *Journal of Business Research, 88*, 187–196. doi:10.1016/j.jbusres.2018.03.019

Martin, C. J. (2016). The sharing economy: A pathway to sustainability or a nightmarish form of neoliberal capitalism? *Ecological Economics, 121*, 149–159. doi:10.1016/j.ecolecon.2015.11.027

McCracken, G. (1988). *The long interview* (Vol. 13). London: Sage Publications.

McGregor, S. L. (2017). Consumer perceptions of responsibility. In: G. Emilien, R. Weitkunat, & F. Lüdicke (Eds.), *Consumer perception of product risks and benefits* (pp. 567–596). Springer: Cham.

Middlemiss, L. (2010). Reframing individual responsibility for sustainable consumption: Lessons from environmental justice and ecological citizenship. *Environmental Values, 19*(2), 147–167. doi:10.3197/096327110X12699420220518

Mody, M., Hanks, L., & Dogru, T. (2019). Parallel pathways to brand loyalty: Mapping the consequences of authentic consumption experiences for hotels and Airbnb. *Tourism Management, 74*, 65–80. doi:10.1016/j.tourman.2019.02.013

Mody, M., Suess, C., & Dogru, T. (2019). Not in my backyard? Is the anti-Airbnb discourse truly warranted? *Annals of Tourism Research, 74*, 198–203. doi:10.1016/j.annals.2018.05.004

Moon, H., Miao, L., Hanks, L. & Line, N. D. (2019). Peer-to-peer interactions: Perspectives of Airbnb guests and hosts. *International Journal of Hospitality Management, 77*, 405–414.

Mulder, L. B., & Aquino, K. (2013). The role of moral identity in the aftermath of dishonesty. *Organizational Behavior and Human Decision Processes, 121*(2), 219–230. doi:10.1016/j.obhdp.2013.03.005

Nieuwland, S., & van Melik, R. (2018). Regulating Airbnb: How cities deal with perceived negative externalities of short-term rentals. *Current Issues in Tourism*, 1–15. doi:10.1080/13683500.2018.1504899

Park, S. K., Kwak, K. T., & Lee, B. G. (2019). Policy compliance and deterrence mechanism in the sharing economy. *Internet Research, 29*(5), 1124–1148. doi:10.1108/INTR-03-2018-0098

Patton, M. Q. (2002). *Qualitative research and evaluation methods*. London: Sage Publications.

Paulauskaite, D., Powell, R., Coca-Stefaniak, J. A., & Morrison, A. M. (2017). Living like a local: Authentic tourism experiences and the sharing economy. *International Journal of Tourism Research, 19*(6), 619–628. doi:10.1002/jtr.2134

Power, F. C., & Khmelkov, V. T. (1998). Character development and self-esteem: Psychological foundations and educational implications. *International Journal of Educational Research, 27*(7), 539–551. doi:10.1016/S0883-0355(97)00053-0

Powel, F. (2012). Think globally, act locally: sustainable communities, modernity and development. *GeoJournal, 77*(2), 141–152.

Rauch, D. E., & Schleicher, D. (2015). Like Uber, but for local government law: The future of local regulation of the sharing economy. *Ohio State Law Journal, 76*, 901.

Reed, A. I. I. (2002). Social identity as a useful perspective self-concept-based consumer research. *Psychology and Marketing, 19*(3), 235–266. doi:10.1002/mar.10011

Reed, I. I., & Aquino, K. F. (2003). Moral identity and the expanding circle of moral regard toward out-groups. *Journal of Personality and Social Psychology, 84*(6), 1270–1286.

Reed, A., Aquino, K., & Levy, E. (2007). Moral identity and judgments of charitable behaviors. *Journal of Marketing, 71*(1), 178–193. doi:10.1509/jmkg.71.1.178

Ritchie, J., Lewis, J., Nicholls, C. M., & Ormston, R. (2014). *Qualitative Research Practice* (4th ed.). Los Angeles, CA: Sage.

Robinson, O. C. (2014). Sampling in interview-based qualitative research: A theoretical and practical guide. *Qualitative Research in Psychology, 11*(1), 25–41. doi:10.1080/14780887.2013.801543

Schutt, R. K. (2018). *Investigating the social world: The process and practice of research*. London: Sage Publications.

Seeley, E. A., & Gardner, W. L. (2003). The "selfless" and self-regulation: The role of chronic other-orientation in averting self-regulatory depletion. *Self and Identity, 2*(2), 103–117. doi:10.1080/15298860309034

Shuqair, S., Pinto, D. C., & Mattila, A. S. (2019). Benefits of authenticity: Post-failure loyalty in the sharing economy. *Annals of Tourism Research, 78*, 102741. doi:10.1016/j.annals.2019.06.008

Srnicek, N. (2017). *Platform capitalism*. Cambridge: John Wiley & Sons.

Stabrowski, F. (2017). People as businesses': Airbnb and urban micro-entrepreneurialism in New York City. *Cambridge Journal of Regions, Economy and Society, 10*(2), 327–347. doi:10.1093/cjres/rsx004

Stergiou, D. P., & Farmaki, A. (2019). Resident perceptions of the impacts of P2P accommodation: Implications for neighbourhoods. *International Journal of Hospitality Management*, 102411. doi:10.1016/j.ijhm.2019.102411

Strauss, A., & Corbin, J. (1990). *Basics of qualitative research: Grounded theory procedures and techniques*. Newbury Park, CA: Sage.

Sundararajan, A. (2014). Peer-to-peer businesses and the sharing (collaborative) economy: Overview, economic effects and regulatory issues. Written testimony for the hearing titled The Power of Connection: Peer-to-peer businesses.

Volgger, M., Taplin, R., & Pforr, C. (2019). The evolution of 'Airbnb-tourism': Demand-side dynamics around international use of peer-to-peer accommodation in Australia. *Annals of Tourism Research, 75*, 322–337. doi:10.1016/j.annals.2019.02.007

Walker, L. J. (2014). Moral personality, motivation, and identity. In: M. Killen & J. G. Smetana (Eds.), *Handbook of moral development* (pp. 497–519). New York, NY: Psychology Press.

Wineberg, T. W. (2006). *Enacting an ethic of pedagogical vocation: Pursuing moral formation in responding to the call of sacrifice, membership, craft, memory, & imagination* (Doctoral dissertation). Faculty of Education, Simon Fraser University, Burnaby, Canada.

Yang, S. B., Lee, K., Lee, H., & Koo, C. (2019). In Airbnb we trust: Understanding consumers' self-attachment building mechanisms in the sharing economy. *International Journal of Hospitality Management, 83*, 198–209.

Zhu, Y., Cheng, M., Wang, J., Ma, L., & Jiang, R. (2019). The construction of home feeling by Airbnb guests in the sharing economy: A semantics perspective. *Annals of Tourism Research, 75*, 308–321. doi:10.1016/j.annals.2018.12.013

The social practices of hosting P2P social dining events: insights for sustainable tourism

Anna Davies, Agnese Cretella, Ferne Edwards and Brigida Marovelli

ABSTRACT

In many ways, the expansion of commercial for-profit, P2P social dining platforms has mirrored those within mobility and accommodation sectors. However its dynamics and impacts have received less consideration to date, with a notable paucity of attention to the hosts of social dining events. The aim of this paper is to address this research lacuna. Through its exploration of the social dining platforms VizEat in Athens and Eatwith in Barcelona, this paper identifies, analyses and compares the social practices of hosts around their social dining events in two key tourist destinations in Europe. Data is gathered through multiple methods from participating in and observing social dining events in each city to interviews with key stakeholders in the P2P social dining process (such as hosts, platform employees and ambassadors). The research reveals how dynamic rules, tools, skills and understandings shape and reshape the performance of hosting social dining events. It exposes tensions and ongoing negotiations between hosts and guests regarding matters of authenticity and privacy, an uneven risk burden between hosts and platforms with regards liability and scant regard for matters of sustainability. As a result there is little alignment between P2P social dining and the goals of sustainable tourism.

Introduction

Digital platforms have become an increasingly familiar means of enjoying, acquiring or exchanging goods, services and experiences in the 21st Century. Indeed, the shift to platform-based trading has been depicted as a "third great economic revolution" (Munger, 2018, p. 391), both in the way that the businesses are organised and with respect to who is involved in the various stages of production and consumption. As this Special Issue highlights, these changes have already been identified as disruptive with respect to mobility (e.g. Uber and other ride sharing apps) and short-term accommodation (e.g. Airbnb and other similar short-term letting sites), with impacts and governance challenges of such peer-to-peer (P2P) service platforms increasingly well-documented, if not resolved (Davies et al., 2017). However, examination of P2P platforms within the food sector has been less forensic (Davies, 2019), with specific consideration of P2P social dining still in its infancy and dominated by the experiences of guests (Corigliano & Bricchi, 2018; Ketter, 2019).

P2P social dining involves meal-based experiences advertised through an online platform as a means for hosts and guests (including tourists) to connect and socialize over food and drinks. While existing tourism research has documented the value which tourists place on experiencing a domestic setting with locals (Bell, 2015), and benefits which might flow to hosts (Wang, 2007), the practices and impacts of P2P social dining from a hosts' perspective are largely unknown. In response, the aim of this paper is to identify, analyse and compare the social practices of hosting exhibited at P2P social dining events in Athens and Barcelona.

Providing a novel comparative contribution to the literature, this paper examines the rules, tools, skills and understandings that shape hosting practices (Davies et al., 2014) as a precursor to considering the sustainability credentials of P2P social dining. Existing research on the social practices of eating together is examined, before focusing on P2P social dining studies specifically. Highlighting gaps in exsting literature, and drawing insights from tourism research exploring sustainable livelihoods, we consider the opportunities and challenges for establishing the sustainability impacts of P2P social dining. The methodological approach adopted is then outlined, with Athens and Barcelona contextualised and illustrative case studies of P2P social dining events in both cities presented. Finally, key insights from the empirical data are outlined including a prospective agenda for further extending analysis of the sustainability of P2P social dining platforms.

Social practices, social dining and the challenges of sustainability in P2P

Social practices are embodied, routinized human activities which are mediated by a combination of objects, tools and technologies and artefacts (e.g. the material stuff involved in the social practices), and performed in the context of symbolic meanings, ideas and aspirations, as well as skills and understandings (e.g. competencies) (Davies et al., 2014; Shove et al., 2012; Warde, 2016). Practices are also shaped by rules, including social rules and formal legislation, such that while they might be experienced individually they are always socially constituted. Due to this social constitution, practices are dynamic, changing as the rules, tools, skills and understandings involved evolve. We adopt this social practice oriented framework – based on a rules, tools, skills and understandings format – to explore hosts experiences of P2P social dining in Athens and Barcelona.

In the case of social dining, the emergence of platform economies brought new technologies and tools, and by association new opportunities and possibilities, to shape symbolic meanings and aspirations around what it means to share food with others. Certainly social dining, as with eating more broadly, is currently practiced as a matter of convention rather than through authoritative regulation (Janta & Christou, 2019). Although, as will be outlined later in this paper, while P2P social dining might be performed in ways which make regulatory responsibilities opaque, the means and mechanisms of performance do in fact come under the purview of state organisations and regulatory agencies. At the same time, the skills and understandings of what it means to engage in social dining, as both host and guest, will also evolve as access to, and experience of, such platforms expands. P2P Social dining is then a recursive process, where the repetition of ICT-mediated social dining events establishes new ways of doing things, involving new standards and rules. In this paper, our analysis of social dining is informed by the parameters of social practice's theoretical framework as it usefully contests individualist explanations of behaviour, permitting a focus on practical activities and helping to compare the performance of P2P social dining across locations, in this case Athens and Barcelona.

P2P social dining

P2P social dining experiences bear some common characteristics with other forms of commercial platform-based exchange, particularly in the accommodation sector. Social dining often takes place in people's homes, thus blurring traditional boundaries between domestic and income generating spaces, and they use similar systems of reputational rating as a means to generate systems of trust between all parties. There are also some similarities between the expectations of hospitability from paying guests generated through short-term letting platforms and those who enter the home of a host to enjoy a meal. However, social dining experiences focus primarily on goods that are physically consumed, raising the levels of intimacy involved in the experience. As vital matter, the food consumed at the social dining events also has a limited window of edibility, which brings unique temporal risks to the P2P exchanges (Davies, 2012a; Weymes & Davies, 2019).

Research has begun to explore the characteristics and motivations of those who seek social dining opportunities (Corigliano & Bricchi, 2018). Both quantitative (Ketter, 2019) and qualitative studies (Privitera, 2016) conclude that social dining guests are consumers "looking for the commodification of the sharing economy into a trendy, authentic and social consumption experience" (Ketter, 2019, p. 1072). Both also find that guests stress the importance of intimate social interaction and the added (albeit unpredictable) benefits that may be generated through social dining compared with restaurant experiences. For guests, conviviality and commensality (Mortara & Fragapane, 2018), alongside the evocation of an authentic geographical sense of place through food, are key motivators. The food consumed in social dining settings, as with other studies of collective feasts, becomes more than mere sustenance and transforms itself into an immaterial "cultural artefact" (Everett & Aitchison, 2008, p. 151). This has been discussed by interrogators of culinary tourism (Bell, 2015) as a mechanism to build and exchange cultural capital, with tourists hoping to penetrate further inside cultures, learning about food history, production and everyday food practices. As such, tourists engaging in social dining engage in a form of networked relational tourism (Marques & Matos, 2020), emphasising interpersonal relationships, interactions and exchanges for participants mediated through the platform.

While few studies have explored the impacts of P2P social dining on hosts in settings which are both commercialised and domesticated, there are clear parallels with analyses of travel homestays (e.g. McIntosh et al., 2011). This literature expresses concern that the commercialisation of domestic spaces compromises the ability of hosts to be their authentic selves (Wang, 2007). Certainly, further understanding is needed with regards to how hosts in commercial P2P social dining settings create "complex hybrids that convey competing conceptions of home and work, inclusion and privacy, domestic hospitableness and commercial hospitality" (Di Domenico & Lynch, 2007, p. 336). Potential sustainability issues of homebased P2P social dining in terms of its impacts on social structures, income diversification and environmental resource consumption are addressed in the following sub-section.

Sustainability of P2P platform economies: insights from sustainable tourism

For tourism to be sustainable, economic, environmental and social impacts must all be considered (Xu et al., 2020). However, establishing impact across these arenas is not always straightforward, not least because it relies on access to appropriate metrics and data (Mackenzie & Davies, 2019). In the P2P sector to date, most studies have focused on one dimension of sustainability rather than conducting comprehensive sustainability impact analyses. For example, in the P2P accommodation sector, which perhaps has most synergies with P2P social dining, one study found Airbnb to be more ecologically sustainable when compared with traditional tourist accommodation due to its lower level of resource use and waste generation (Midgett et al., 2017). In another case, P2P accommodation sharing was found to be financially beneficial for consumers in some contexts as it introduced greater competition into the marketplace, lowering hotel room pricing (Zervas et al., 2017). Research in the US also identifies spin-off benefits for overall employment in the hospitality, tourism, and leisure industries (Dogru et al., 2020). However these benefits can also create challenges. It is clear that increased short-term letting in cities, for example, has produced negative social externalities, such as rising rents, overcrowded city centres and displacement of local communities, leading to reactions from residents and regulators aimed at reducing these impacts (von Briel & Dolnicar, 2020).

While sustainability analyses of P2P social dining have not yet occurred, studies of sustainable culinary tourism (Alonso et al., 2018) and sustainable livelihoods analyses of homestays (Anand et al., 2012) provide some preliminary insights and important synergies with the social practice framing utilised in this paper. Livelihoods include the capabilities, assets (including both material and social resources) and activities required to create a means for living. Capabilities map on to social practice's notion of skills, while assets incorporate both the notion of understandings (social resources) and tools (material resources). Under the livelihoods framework, sustainable livelihoods will be achieved through access to, and protection and enhancement of, these livelihood capabilities, assets and activities (Scoones, 1998). Central to the framework is attention to a range of formal and informal organisational and institutional factors that influence sustainable livelihood outcomes. We consider these factors in our social practice reading as rules (which can be social or legal). A sustainable livelihood is then defined as one that "can cope with and recover from stresses and shocks, maintain or enhance its capabilities and assets, while not undermining the natural resource base" (Chambers & Conway, 1992 cited by Tao & Wall, 2009, p. 91). Being people-centred, a sustainable livelihood through tourism "should not be the driver of community lifestyle if this direction overrides local community needs" (Wu & Pearce, 2014, p. 444), with Wu and Pearce (2014) also flagging the impact of sporadic and complementary income from tourism on the sustainability of livelihoods. This paper explores the relevance of these insights for establishing the practice and sustainability potential of hosting P2P social dining events through in-depth examination of P2P hosting experiences in two cities. The methodological underpinnings of this research are outlined in the following section.

Methods

One field researcher resided in each of the two case study cities – Athens and Barcelona – immersing themselves in P2P social dining, exploring the online spaces of social dining platforms, interviewing key stakeholders and engaging in dining events as guests. These two cities were selected for comparison because they are both member states of the European Union and therefore have similar overarching governance frameworks as a result. Both are key tourist destinations in their respective countries and both had active hosts on P2P social dining platforms at the time of the research. Initially, all procedural guidance, reviews, events and hosts profiles on the platforms were examined and a user profile was set up in order to book social dining events. Social dining events were then selected at a variety of price points to experience the range of events being offered. The research essentially followed the process of social dining from start to finish, tracing the dining experience from the online booking stage, to attending the meal, making fieldnotes, posting a review, viewing others' posts, and interviewing key stakeholders to hear their reflections on those hosts from the company's perspective. In this paper, data from engagements with Eatwith in Barcelona and VizEat in Athens are presented as illustrative cases. VizEat, founded in Paris by Camille Rumani and Jean Michel Petit in 2014 (now operating under the name Eatwith following its acquisition of that USA-based competitor business in 2017) operates in more than 130 countries. VizEat has raised multiple millions of dollars from financial backers and acquired other competitors including GrubClub (in 2018) and Cookening (in 2015). Eatwith, initially a US company headquartered in San Francisco, was established in 2012. It had hosts in more than 50 countries at the time of its acquisition by VizEat in 2017. VizEat's acquisition of Eatwith was seen as a means to expand its global profile by connecting its global tourism partners with Eatwith's active hosts. Rather than being a pure P2P exchange platform, VizEat also uses tourism agents to provide block bookings for hosts.

The research on Eatwith in Barcelona occurred between March and June 2017, prior to VizEat's takeover of Eatwith in September 2017. There were approximately sixty active hosts on the platform in Barcelona at the time, although around two hundred hosts had been approved. While the website appeared to offer numerous events, many were the same event run by the same host repeated weekly. In Barcelona, the researcher attended events described as: Catalan traditional; international cuisine; and "demo" meals (where new hosts menus and events are vetted by the platform's Country Manager). Interviews with Eatwith hosts and the Eatwith Country Manager were conducted, recorded and transcribed, and four social dining events were attended where the researcher engaged with all participants and created field notes.

In Athens the research took place over a period of seven months from April 2017 to October 2017 during which time the platform was only emerging as an active space for social dining. Initially the platform indicated there were 17 hosts listing events in Athens, ten of which were already providing tourist services in the city, such as gourmet walking tours and culinary schools, six marketed themselves as private hosts and one was registered as a food company that provides work experience for migrants and refugees. Only one host, the food company, provided an alternative to Greek traditional food. This company served food from the culinary traditions of the migrants and refugees who it worked with. Applications to participate in events offered by all six private hosts were made. However, only one host answered within the stated 48 hours limit set by the platform and so the other five applications were cancelled. The one host who did respond provided direct connections to the other five private hosts and in total six dinners were attended. Interviews with all hosts were conducted after social dining events. Two Ambassadors for VizEat who were promoting the platform in Athens, were also interviewed.

In both cities the interview transcripts and fieldnotes from engagements and experiences were transcribed and entered into NVivo, a qualitative analysis software package, and then coded to a suite of nodes relating to the practice of social dining. This included identifying data related to the tools of social dining such as hosts' domestic settings and access to ICT, as well as the material dimensions of their offerings (i.e. the food itself). Nodes relating to skills and understandings include data from questions around the motivations and experiences of hosts, while the rules component of the social practice involves data relating to both social norms and regulatory legislation. Unique identifiers are provided for quotes from interviews and for data from each social dining event which was attended. This identifier details the nature of the participant (e.g. Host, Country Manager, Researcher), the location (Athens or Barcelona) and interview or social dining event number. Pseudonyms are used throughout the paper.

P2P social dining platforms: hosting experiences in Barcelona and Athens

The similar operational procedures of VizEat in Athens and Eatwith in Barcelona open up possibilities for comparative research, particularly as both cities also have tourism as a key economic activity and were negatively impacted by the economic recession that took hold globally post-2008. Nonetheless they also exhibit unique characteristics. This section presents a summary of the cities contexts and two illustrative social dining events, which exemplify the rules, tools, skills and understandings that underpin them from the hosts' perspective.

Barcelona

Barcelona is Spain's second largest city and one of the most densely populated European city-regions (Area Metropolitana de Barcelona, 2019). Following the economic crash of 2008, Barcelona has continued to suffer from unemployment and economic austerity along with the rest of Spain. Economic precarity has fostered the creation of diverse economies, including social and solidarity activities that go beyond typical capitalist approaches (Ajuntament de Barcelona ND). However, until the COVID 19 lockdown in early 2020, unemployment was typically lower in Barcelona than other areas, with a buoyant tourist economy partly responsible for this. In 2019, Barcelona was the 33rd most visited city worldwide and 8th in Europe (Yasmeen, 2019). Within the tourist industry, gastronomic and culinary attractions such as food markets (e.g. La Boqueria), high profile restaurants (e.g. El Bulli, El Celler de Can Roca) and its world famous chefs (Ferrán Adriá, Joan Roca) have contributed to Barcelona and Catalonia being noted as one of the top culinary destinations in the world. This booming tourist industry is, however, placing pressure on residents' quality of life and leading to anti-tourist protests and movements (Hughes, 2018). Fieldwork took place during the uprising of the Catalan Independence Movement where increased protests and demonstrations were experienced across Barcelona and Catalonia.

High-end Catalan cuisine with Eatwith

The meal is highly anticipated – numerous reminders for the upcoming event are sent with supporting directions. On arrival we find our hosts' (Marta and Anna) apartment is a hidden gem with clean polished surfaces, a well-set table, and tasteful paintings and ornaments on display. All elements of the apartment are impressive – a clean, open-plan, well-organised kitchen with modern gadgetry. To add to the performance, the final touches of meal preparation are conducted by the host in front of guests. As the Country Manager stated, "it's an amazing space. I just wanted to live there. I'm like, 'you can go to my house, I go to your house!'." Guests take photos to capture their experience, the apartment and each other.

Marta and Anna are friendly, polite and welcoming, and able to converse comfortably in English. A seat is offered and a drink placed in your hand while other guests arrive. The hosts are middle-aged and middle-class, they have travelled extensively, understand tourists' needs and desires, and offer small talk about the city and themselves as an introduction to the meal. They explain how they find pleasure in cooking and are keen to see where this economic opportunity takes them. The income they receive from Eatwith events is complementary to their main employment currently, but they are exploring possibilities for transitioning from amateur host to professional chef. P2P social dining is a testbed for them. As Marta explains, "I love cooking anyway, so … I became hooked! And, you know, like one hundred and fifty people later already I'm still doing dinners."

The positive reputation of the hosts means they rarely have an empty seat at their table, despite the event being priced at the higher end of the Eatwith spectrum. To ensure maximum capacity they also offer this meal on other social dining platforms, including VizEat and Trip Advisor. Guests on this occasion include a young Canadian couple on their honeymoon who could not afford to experience such high quality food in restaurants and a cluster of American couples seeking more personal insights of Spain. According to the Country Manager, most of the guests to this event are middle income or higher with an interest in culture and "they always love to have a different experience. They don't feel like tourist people." Many guests become repeat customers. Indeed, the young honeymooners had attended this event three times in total.

Marta and Anna use highly-valued, organic Catalan ingredients sourced that morning from the local, fresh food market. Guests mentioned "Michelin Star" elements of the social dining experience in terms of the quality of ingredients, the presentation of the food and the hosting. As this meal has a high price compared to average restaurant choices in Barcelona it places the offering firmly in the wealthy international tourist bracket and too expensive for many Barcelona natives. During the meal, each dish is carefully described, where it comes from, its history, and how it is prepared. As Marta said:

> We don't just serve a menu. We talk to them [the guests] and we show them our culture or our costumes … and every time we give tips for restaurants, to go out to the places that aren't very touristic, because they don't want to be part of the maze of tourist people.

Non-national cuisine dining event with Eatwith

While many events advertised during the research focused on expensive Catalan cuisine as described above, there were also menu offerings from beyond the region and Spanish cuisine more broadly. This meets demand for diverse food events from both travellers and locals. As the Country Manager for Eatwith explains:

> In some other countries, for example, Israel, it's basically only locals. I mean, others such as Paris it's only foreigners. So it's like a pretty special case [in Barcelona] that we have like half of it of foreigners and half of it of locals, and I think that it is because we have a very diverse offering.

One "meal from elsewhere" offered by Eatwith Barcelona is a Palestinian Feast by Adela who is in her mid-thirties, initially from Palestine, but well-travelled. Her profile on Eatwith reads: "I used to work as a journalist back home, then as an information consultant in an asylum seekers reception centre in Norway, and now I am working in Booking.Com."

The meal consisted of affordable ingredients served at a much lower price point than the high-end Catalan cuisine event. The host prepared a very full table carrying a multitude of dishes, and the Country Manager explained, "She's making the food of her mum and she's making huge amounts of it." Adela describes this meal on the Eatwith website as follows:

> [The] Middle east is like most Mediterranean regions, food is a huge part of our culture. I used to help both my grandma and my mum in the kitchen and I got all these small secrets which made their dishes ... Due to the fact that I am living in Barcelona where I have the same climate which offers the same kind of fresh veggies, tasty fish and meat, I thought that this is the perfect chance to start serving traditional, healthy, tasty food made with love and enough time, served and presented in a modern way ...

Adela's place is a shared, rented apartment. It is like going home to eat, where the dining space feels intimate and where the kitchen is tucked away and used, rather than put on display. It was described by the Country Manager as "not the most beautiful apartment." The homely feel creates an urge to help carry dishes to and from the table, yet being a paying guest creates the expectation of "staying put" to be served. While the food is enjoyable, it is the personal stories behind the meal that make the evening special. Explanations of the meanings, methods and ingredients bring diners together in a unique and unexpected way. The meal attracts a very mixed international crowd from multiple locations and the menu sparks conversations that are sometimes quite political and charged, departing from the "polite" dinner conversations experienced in other social dining settings.

Adela also welcomes her own friends to events, creating even more diverse social gatherings. At this event a Syrian guest arrived later in the evening, when cultural alcoholic beverages were offered beyond the set menu. The conversations continued to flow. Music was put on and the dining room transformed into a dance floor until the early hours of the morning. When the guests finally left, many exclaimed how much they would like to hang out together in Barcelona again and phone numbers were exchanged.

In terms of authenticity, this meal certainly provided direct experience of food from the hosts' life. The experience was like being at the table of a friend or family member, where conversations rise and fall, and the meal satiates mind, soul and body. Due to setting, the food and the hosting, social connections developed over the meal. The experience felt both "at home" and "social," rather than being only a commercial exchange.

Athens

Athens is the capital and largest city of Greece. It, along with the rest of Greece, was deeply impacted by the 2008 financial crisis and during the data collection period unemployment levels remained the highest in Europe, with youth employment in Greece peaking at 44% in 2017 (OECD, 2018). In response to the financial crisis, Athens, like Barcelona, has witnessed a flourishing of social and solidarity economy practices (Rakopoulos, 2014), with some of these focused specifically on supporting refugees and people seeking asylum. In 2018 alone, the number of asylum applications in Greece increased by 14%, reaching 65,000 (OECD, 2019), many of whom arrive in Athens. At the time of the research Athens was re-establishing itself as a tourist destination (Panas et al., 2017).

Greek cuisine dining experience with VizEat

During the research period, all except one host on the VizEat platform in Athens offered a Greek dining experience, with baked aubergine (moussaka), spinach pies (spanakopita), and the wide variety of appetizers that are commonly shared at a beginning of a Greek meal (mezedes). Anna's meal was no exception. A highly educated woman in her late thirties, Anna welcomed us into a sleek minimalist flat in Kolonaki, an affluent area of central Athens. Guests were invited into her cosy dining room, which was separate from the small modern kitchen. There was no table cloth, but colourful placemats underneath the serving platters at the centre of the table. Anna's menu consisted of six mezedes, a main course and wine. The price, €46 per person, was high when compared with mainstream restaurant meals in Athens' at the time, where it was possible to eat well at a mezedepoleio – an informal restaurant serving mezedes – for about half the cost.

However, social dining is more than the food itself. Guests attend in order to have access to the way locals live, cook and share a meal. As Anna highlights below, she found that guests really want to meet a local and converse over food:

> The motivation is not the dinner, definitely. It's the communication with the locals. To sit down, not only have dinner – because they can have it everywhere – it's to exchange views with the locals. […] I wanted to use my love for food but to share it with other people and spread our culture, the Greek culinary culture to the world.

However, it is not that the hosts were without cooking skills. Anna, for instance, attended culinary school and the choice of dishes she prepared for dinner mirrored her knowledge of Greek traditions. She explained the history and the provenance of each dish, such as fried sardines savoro with vinegar, rosemary and onion, which dates back to the Venetian domination in the Aegean. Anna also takes pride in offering seasonal mezedes, pinpointing that during the summer, zucchini fritters served with tzatziki had to be part of the menu. Anna was highly skilled cook with a passion for the Greek culinary culture but she explained that the commitment to hosting entails considerable planning, shopping and preparation. It took a lot of effort to be a "good host":

> You should be very inviting, full of energy, because people are coming over; to start a conversation. For me, I have to say, I'm not the most extroverted person, so when I do this kind of home-dining … it takes a lot of energy […] you try to be as enthusiastic as possible because this is the reason why people come over to your house.

Anna was not only familiar with ICT, but also with P2P technologies which made the transition to becoming a VizEat host smooth. She was already familiar and comfortable with the concept of "stranger sharing" that P2P interactions generate. Anna was optimistic that technology would provide new ways for connecting people beyond their usual social networks, although she explains that hosting strangers had challenged her understanding of the rules of hospitality. For example, interest in the financial crisis and its economic and social consequences meant guests sometimes asked personal questions about how much hosts earned or how much they paid in rent.

On occasion, the regulatory rules of social dining were flagged by hosts as a matter of concern, particularly regarding hosts' liability for food safety, hygiene certification and taxation with respect to their VizEat activities. At the time of research these issues were a grey area for legislation in Greece. As Anna noted, navigating such greyness was something familiar to many in Greece:

I don't feel a hundred percent safe, to be honest, although VizEat says that they are covered by an insurance company, by Lloyds. But at the local level I don't think I'm covered. [...] Everybody's asking. But in Greece people are a bit used to trying to find the ways to go to get around it.

Non-national cuisine dining experience with VizEat

In Athens, the only non-Greek social dining experience offered during the fieldwork was "Homemade African Dishes" for €22 and it was a listed as being offered by a collective of chefs. The first request by the researcher to attend the African meal via VizEat was not answered within 48 hours, so the app automatically rejected it. After a few failed attempts, they wrote back apologising for not having answered and communicating that they would liaise with the chefs to establish their availability. A date was agreed via email and the platform was used only for paying the dinner fee for the researcher and their Greek research assistant. The day before the event the researcher received an email explaining that it would be more a party than a sit-down dinner, with the promise that many of the chefs would cook their own specialities and there would be music. All exchanges were with the collective's founder John, who managed the events and the online presence.

The dinner party was hosted on the rooftop of an apartment block, close to Nosotros, a reclaimed shared urban space in the buzzing heart of Exarcheia, a radical neighbourhood of Athens associated with anarchist groups. At the main entrance there was a buzzer with John's name and a shabby steep staircase that led up to John's apartment, where all doors were open and a Senegalese man indicated to continue straight to the rooftop. The poorly lit rooftop was arranged in a simple and minimal way, a plastic table and chairs for people to sit around, most of which were already taken by the chefs and their friends and families. A large wooden table served the buffet and a smaller one served as the bar where all the disposable plastic tableware was placed. Most of the food was pre-cooked and had already been placed on the buffet. Two barbecues were being used around which many men were busy grilling meat and fish. Arabic music was playing from a cell phone connected to a mini Hi-Fi, with power supplied from John's apartment with extension cords. The lighting was poor, with just a few lamps and scattered tealights meaning it was hard to move around the space comfortably, especially not knowing its layout and with cables running up from John's apartment.

As John confirmed, only the researcher and her assistant were paying guests. Nevertheless no one welcomed them on arrival, and they felt they were the uninvited ones at a private party. The researchers stood awkwardly between the buffet and the charcoal barbecues, facing the round table, and trying to make a connection with the people already conversing near the buffet. John finally introduced himself by offering some home-brewed beer. However, this first interaction was short, because the men around the barbecue called him to help. There was a sense of improvisation in the event. It did not seem that the group would usually organize this type of events for tourists or travelers. The atmosphere was extremely informal, as many guests seemed to know each other and were surrounded by their kids, roaming around freely and playing loudly around other guests.

When kebabs and octopus were brought to the table, people gathered around the buffet and started eating. The researchers were not invited to dig in and after waiting for others to finish helping themselves, they managed to get a plate of what was left on the buffet, meaning pies with rice, minced meat and nuts, a salad with lettuce, cucumber and parsley served without dressing, and a cold dry lasagna. Later, desserts like baklava, dates stuffed with pistachio and coconut, and cookies stuffed with walnuts were brought in by a Syrian woman. They were the most delicious part of the dinner and the researcher approached the lady, who spoke neither English nor Greek. Her son helped with the translation and explained that she made them at home. One Senegalese chef apologized because he had been unable to prepare any food for the event, having spent the day busy with a catering job. He also explained that every two weeks, they organised a free supper club where chefs can improve their skills trying out new recipes. They saw this event as one of those rather than a dinner party with guests. The price of the ticket was €22, but the researchers ate very little.

Before leaving, the researcher approached John to say goodbye. He said that the collective's use of the platform was sporadic, because they prefer to take on large scale catering jobs which make more sense financially. Nonetheless, he was proud of the food on offer and remarked that it would not be financially sustainable to host dinner for that price. John also explained that the collective is registered as a food company, which was founded in 2015 motivated by the realisation that many newcomers were arriving in Greece with a strong culinary expertise but without the skills and certification necessary to run a food business. It was imagined as a means to provide job opportunities and food education for unemployed chefs, migrants or refugees. John was also skilled technologically, managing the IT aspect of the collective, using tools such as Trello and Excel, in order to manage the workload smoothly. Their aim was to provide steady salaries to a core group, but at the time of the research everyone was paid whenever a catering job was secured.

Comparing practices

The illustrative examples of hosted events outlined above provide an initial picture of the hosts perspectives on social dining, specifically identifying the opportunities and challenges generated by the events they host. While each host has a unique life history, a number of broad and common themes emerged. First and foremost, all private hosts took pleasure in cooking and sharing their culinary cultures and life experiences with others. The private hosts interviewed also had similar levels of education (e.g. high levels of education), socio-economic status (e.g. middle-class), digital technology skills and experience of other places and cultures (e.g. well-travelled). They recognised the importance of understanding the needs and desires of their guests, and all spoke good English. Other similarities revolved around the hosts common experiences of post-recession austerity, which made the economic opportunities that P2P social dining offered attractive. Although hosts appreciated the extra income gained from organising events, they all acknowledged that it was currently not sustainable as a full-time occupation. This was primarily because of the unpredictability in P2P guest requests and the seasonality of tourism, but also because of the physical and mental effort it takes to host regularly and successfully.

There were some differences between the cases examined. In Barcelona, Eatwith was well-established, while VizEat was at an early stage in Athens. While the researcher could attend a meal as an individual in Barcelona, in Athens the researcher needed to join an established tourist group to access the social dinners. Hosts' embeddedness in tourism also varied across the two platforms and cities. The hosts interviewed in Athens were already involved in tourism, where VizEat further promoted a range of activities tailored for tourist groups, such as pie making classes or market food tours. After VizEat bought Eatwith in September 2017, the company model changed to reflect the experience in Athens rather than Barcelona. There were also differences between the cities with respect to the types of food and service provided. This is more than the obvious material differences between Greek and Catalan cuisine and refers to the different types of events offered in the two cities. In the Athens events, the food was proudly home cooked, exemplifying simple, tasty and hearty fare. In Barcelona, the social dining events were more diverse both in preparation and presentation.

There were differences too in terms of technology and user experience of the P2P platform. With Eatwith in Barcelona all communication relating to the dining experience between guests and hosts was done through the platform, while in Athens and VizEat the platform was used only for the initial contact and for payment. All other communications were moved to non-platform mechanisms such as email or WhatsApp. This promoted more intimacy between host and guest as personal phone numbers had to be exchanged.

With respect to hospitality, dining experiences in both cities raised questions about how to act and interact during social dining events. This was particularly challenging during meals on the lower end of the price spectrum where homeliness was often emphasised in hosting styles and simple, tasty cooking is provided. The contrasts between the two social dining events in Barcelona illustrate this well. During social dining events in Athens the issues of developing socially acceptable practices for both host and guests related more to issues of boundary setting. Guests often expected access to personal spaces and information; looking inside fridges or asking the host how much hosts earnt. There were also more concerns around privacy expressed in Athens, perhaps because the hosts were less experienced than those in Barcelona, but also because they had experienced challenging behaviour with guests publicly posting photos of hosts and their homes on social media without asking permission. Strategies to manage matters of privacy were developed by hosts themselves or through networks the hosts created.

Sustainability and the social practices of hosting

Building on the insights gained from hosts' perspectives on P2P social dining, in this section we reflect on the rules and tools, skills and understandings that shaped hosts' performance of social dining activities in different settings. We conclude by consolidating the sustainability implications of these insights and provide a prospective agenda for future work at the intersection of P2P social dining platforms, tourism and sustainability.

The rules and tools of social dining

It has already been established that social practices of eating are replete with all kinds of social rules (see Warde, 2016) and social dining is no exception, even if these rules are in a constant state of negotiation. However, despite the tight regulations around land use and food safety in the realm of P2P food sharing (Davies et al., 2019), few hosts volunteered information about regulatory rules or other formal checks and balances governing their activities either during interviews or dining events. When prompted to discuss these rules, hosts largely said they trusted the platform to manage any regulatory requirements and risks if they were to arise. At the time of research there had been no cause for exploring whether this trust was justified or not.

However, trust issues have long been a point of contention for platform economies generally (Molz, 2014). A key way that P2P platforms, including VizEat and Eatwith, have addressed trust has been through online reputational rankings. Digital reputations become currency, even capital, in online platforms. On the VizEat and Eatwith platform, you could explore hosts' profiles, you could contact hosts through the platform and you could read reviews left by past guests (either on the platform or on TripAdvisor, a partner of Eatwith). However, the ranking is one-way; it only makes visible guests reviews of hosts and does not allow hosts to also review guests.

Beyond the procedural vetting process for hosts, both platforms state that they hold insurance for hosts and guests. This provision was acknowledged by interviewees, although there was little understanding of the parameters of that insurance. Indeed, in interviews neither Country Managers nor hosts were able to say what and who would be covered in the event of an issue at a social dining event. Ultimately, the bulk of responsibility falls on the guests and hosts to find out what local regulations might be in place in relation to food safety, taxation and liability more broadly. Such uneven allocation of responsibility between hosts and platforms has been identified as problematic in other P2P sectors (Woodcock & Graham, 2019), with calls for stronger standards for those who labour through them.

The tools employed by social dining hosts include their homes, kitchens, toilet facilities, storage and preparation devices, utensils and the very food itself. P2P social dining reflects a networked kind of hospitality (Molz, 2014) in which ICT enables strangers to connect online and arrange offline encounters. The P2P platform provides no material supports for the acquisition of tools for delivering P2P social dining. Neither do they make allowances for differential access to digital devices and technological skills for engaging with them (addressed below). It is unsurprising then to find that those who were able to participate in P2P social dining were those who were already well-equipped with technological resources and material possessions that enable them to host dining events in an acceptable fashion for the platform. It is only available as a livelihood strategy for those with existing resources. So while the platforms offer additional and complementary income diversification opportunities, these are not accessible to everyone equally. As such it cannot be argued that P2P social dining provides an accessible option to achieve sustainable livelihoods in the absence of foundational material resources.

Skills and understandings of P2P social dining

While there were multiple reasons why people became social dining hosts in both cities, there was also some commonality, with hosts citing the career development and up-skilling opportunities that cooking at home for paying guests provided. Social dining events offered hosts the space to design and test new dishes in their homes and to learn new sets of cooking and hosting skills in the process without great financial burden and risk. However, while some hosts saw social dining as a way to get themselves "restaurant ready," others saw it as a means to get away from the busy, high-pressurised restaurant environment whilst still earning an income from cooking. Despite the existence of multiple motivations, a key driver for becoming a host was to generate income. As with other "sellers" on P2P platforms, such as car sharing drivers (Peticca-Harris et al., 2020), the social dining platform provided a means to generate this income while avoiding a large capital investment and significant bureaucracy. Yet none of the hosts' interviewed in this research used social dining as their only source of income, despite prices for the immersive experiences on offer being higher than many mid-price restaurants in central areas of both cities. This premium price also elevated expectations of guests at social dining experiences, which brings its own set of challenges.

As existing studies have already established (Corigliano & Bricchi, 2018; Ketter, 2019; Privitera, 2016), many guests are attracted to social dining to escape the commercial spaces of restaurants and experience authentic homecooked food, even if the food they are served is of restaurant quality and commercially priced. In the case of P2P social dining these culinary adventures take place in domestic spaces, and therefore create unparalleled moments of intimacy (Gyimóthy, 2016). Indeed, the Eatwith platform states that "discovery begins at home" and that social dining offers the opportunity to "eat something the way locals enjoy it." As with other P2P sectors (see Moon et al., 2019), hosts from both Athens and Barcelona were drawn to the interactions and social capital that social dining generates, describing the unexpected and positive social interactions they experienced through hosting. However, in both cities the curiosity of some guests about hosts lives and livelihoods was felt to be intrusive and there were several instances where hosts felt guests had overstepped the mark in terms of personal questioning, the publishing of photographs without permission or the exploration of personal spaces, such as fridges. Agreeing boundaries of hospitability and privacy is not a straightforward matter when social dining is based on a commercial transaction in a domestic setting as different economies of worth come together (Boltanski & Thevenot, 2006). In our research, hosts articulated uncertainties about how best to navigate the line between being hospitable and open to contextualising the immersive and authentic experience that guests are seeking, while maintaining a degree of privacy and their own personal security.

Sustainability and social dining

We found that the P2P social dining platforms examined in this paper claim to bring opportunities for economic diversification, social interaction and cultural enrichment, but environmental benefits were not mentioned and neither made an explicit claim that their operations contribute towards more sustainable development. Benefits were often framed in an individualistic fashion, to those directly involved in the P2P exchanges, and make no reference to the broader, indirect (and potentially negative) impacts that P2P sharing can have on neighbourhoods, communities and cities.

Following, Verbeek and Mommaas (2008), the benefit of adopting a social practice framing, as we have in this paper, is that it permits analyses to move away from such individualism, connecting organisational and technological (rules and tools) issues with behavioural concerns (skills and understandings) in particular places. Of course, none of this means that a sustainability impact analysis cannot be undertaken of P2P social dining providing suitable data and metrics can be identified. Building on the work of Hunter (2002), existing tools such as touristic ecological footprint analysis could, for example, be applied to understand the demands of P2P social dining on the biosphere with the ecological footprint of a social dining event across its entire life-cycle calculated. However, issues of power, politics and regulatory responsibility would not be captured in such analyses despite being central to sustainable development in the P2P and tourism sector (Scheyvens, 2011). It is also possible to analyse the sustainability of P2P social dining at a municipal (Torres-Delgado & Lopez Palomeque, 2014) or local level (Alfaro Navarro et al., 2020) provided indicator sets are sensitive to the practices of P2P social dining that might go undetected if their work is not visible on municipal balance sheets. However, online tools do exist which have been designed to capture the sustainability aspects of ICT-mediated food sharing initiatives (see Mackenzie & Davies, 2019), which could be utilised by the P2P platforms to identify and communicate their sustainability impacts more transparently. However, it would need modification to establish whether P2P social dining provides a sustainable livelihood for individual hosts.

Conclusion

This paper reveals how dynamic rules, tools, skills and understandings shape and reshape the performance of hosting commercial P2P social dining events. It exposes tensions and ongoing negotiations between hosts and guests regarding matters of authenticity and privacy, an uneven risk burden between hosts and platforms with regards liability, and scant regard for matters of sustainability. As a result there is, to date, little alignment between P2P social dining and the goals of sustainable tourism. Nonetheless, P2P platform-mediated social dining in both Athens and Barcelona does provide alternative opportunities to eat beyond mainstream restaurants through novel experiences of eating together with strangers in the home of a resident. While the scale of P2P social dining remains small compared to incumbent industries in the sector (e.g. restaurants, cafes etc.), it nonetheless offers paying "guests" unparalleled access into the domestic spaces and livelihoods of hosts.

Following Warde (2016), to create a clear picture of the social practice and performance of P2P social dining requires consideration of diverse and often cross-cultural understandings and norms, of procedures and tools, and of routines and conventions. However, the wider governance infrastructure of legal requirements around risk and responsibility are, at best, only a vague feature of those negotiations currently. Drawing on Molz (2013), we suggest such platform-based social dining companies are leaving governance primarily to morals. This is not unusual in the P2P platform economy sector, with Del Romero Renau (2018) and Davies (2019) also flagging unresolved matters of fiscal and other regulation with respect to ICT-mediated sharing.

The commercial P2P social dining exemplified in this paper does not follow a set of deliberate rules, rather hosts and guests respond to situations based on previous experiences and by implementing procedures they hope are suitable. In the absence of assistance from platforms, participants are feeling their way through new forms of interaction and exchange. These experimental interactions can be problematic. Some hosts struggled with the tensions they experienced from the monetisation of their domestic spaces which blurred the boundaries of public and private spaces, work-life balances, and the performance of domestic hospitableness and commercial hospitality. Without doubt, P2P social dining companies benefit from heightened access to legal advice and expertise when compared to hosts and guests, yet the burden of compliance with local regulatory frameworks remains with the hosts. In the absence of any major incident during P2P social dining events to date, hosts involved in this research were not overly concerned about this uneven power geometry but the risk remains.

There is certainly scope for the P2P social dining platforms considered in this paper to make more explicit efforts to consider the sustainability impacts of their operations. This could be done by: providing sustainability guidelines for hosts and guests; encouraging the use of local organic food produce; supporting the sustainable use of energy and water in the preparation for, and delivery of, a social dining event; supporting hosts to navigate positive socio-cultural interactions and economic shocks; and signing up to global principles for fair work in the platform economy (Woodcock & Graham, 2019). Ultimately, mechanisms to conduct sustainability impact assessment of P2P social dining need to be developed in order to ascertain whether they offer a sustainable livelihood to the host and whether they contribute to the sustainability of tourism within localities more broadly. Data from P2P social dining platforms will be required to do this comprehensively, which may be difficult to access given matters of commercial confidentiality.

To fully grasp the international landscape and sustainability impacts of P2P social dining, the delimited and exploratory research on which this paper is based requires extension. As an emergent arena of activity, further research is required to estabish whether the configuration of hosting experiences identified in Athens and Barcelona is replicated across time, in different places and in relation to other non-commercial models of social dining (Davies, 2012b; Edwards & Davies, 2018). Recognising the diversity of P2P social dining, it would be particularly productive to compare the experiences of hosts on multinational commercial platforms, as examined in this paper, with those which adopt different not-for-profit or social enterprise business models. We recommend a global horizon scanning study and classification of P2P social dining platforms according to the goals and business models adopted, as well as the development of a bespoke P2P social dining sustainability impact assessment tool.

Disclosure statement

No potential conflict of interest was reported by the authors.

Funding

The research on which this paper is based was supported by the European Research Council under Grant Number 646883.

References

Alfaro Navarro, J., Andres Martinez, M., & Mondejar Jimenez, J. (2020). An approach to measuring sustainable tourism at the local level in Europe. *Current Issues in Tourism, 23*(4), 423–437.

Ajuntament de Barcelona (ND). Social and solidarity economy. Retrieved May 17, 2020, from https://ajuntament.barcelona.cat/economia-social-solidaria/en/what-Social-and-Solidarity-Economy

Alonso, A. D., Kok, S., & O'Brien, S. (2018). Sustainable culinary tourism and Cevicherias: A stakeholder and social practice approach. *Journal of Sustainable Tourism, 26*(5), 812–831.

Anand, A., Chandan, P., & Singh, R. B. (2012). Homestays at Korzok: Supplementing rural livelihoods and supporting green tourism in the Indian Himalayas. *Mountain Research and Development, 32*(2), 126–136.

Area Metropolitana de Barcelona. (2019). The Metropolitan Area of Barcelona. Retrieved January 16, 2019, from http://www.amb.cat/en/web/area-metropolitana/coneixer-l-area-metropolitana/poblacio

Bell, C. (2015). Tourists infiltrating authentic domestic space at Balinese home cooking schools. *Tourist Studies, 15*(1), 86–100.

Boltanski, L., & Thevenot, L. (2006). *On justification: Economies of worth.* Princeton University Press: Princeton.

Chambers, R., & Conway, G. (1992). *Sustainable rural livelihoods: Practical concepts for the 21st century,* IDS Discussion Paper 296. Brighton.

Corigliano, M. A., & Bricchi, S. (2018). Are social eating events a tool to experience the authentic food and wine culture of a place? In N. Bellini, C. Clergeau, & O. Etcheverria (Eds.), *Gastronomy and local development: The quality of products, places and experiences.* (pp. 245–261). Routledge.

Davies, A. R. (2012a). Geography and the matter of waste mobilities. *Transactions of the Institute of British Geographers, 37*(2), 191–196.

Davies, A. R. (2012b). *Enterprising communities: Grassroots sustainability innovations.* Emerald Publishing.

Davies, A. R. (2019). *Urban food sharing: Rules, tools and networks.* Policy Press.

Davies, A. R., Franck, V., & Cretella, A. (2019). Food sharing initiatives and food democracy: Practice and policy in three European cities. *Politics and Governance, 7*(4), 8–20.

Davies, A. R., Fahy, F., & Rau, H. (2014). *Challenging consumption: Pathways to a more sustainable future.* London.

Davies, A. R., Gray, M., Donald, B., & Knox-Hayes, J. (2017). Sharing economies: Moving beyond binaries in a digital age. *Cambridge Journal of Regions, Economy and Society, 10*(2), 209–230.

Del Romero Renau, L. (2018). Touristification, sharing economies and the new geography of urban conflicts. *Urban Science, 2*(4), 104. https://doi.org/10.3390/urbansci2040104

Di Domenico, M., & Lynch, P. A. (2007). Host/guest encounters in the commercial home. *Leisure Studies, 26*(3), 321–338.

Dogru, T., Makarand, M., Suess, C., McGinley, S., & Line, N. (2020). The Airbnb paradox: Positive employment effects in the hospitality industry. *Tourism Management, 77,* 104001. https://doi.org/10.1016/j.tourman.2019.104001.

Edwards, F., & Davies, A. R. (2018). Connective consumptions: Mapping Melbourne's food sharing ecosystem. *Urban Policy and Research, 36*(4), 476–495.

Everett, S., & Aitchison, C. (2008). The role of food tourism in sustaining regional identity: A case study of Cornwall, South West England. *Journal of Sustainable Tourism, 16*(2), 150–167.

Gyimóthy, S. (2016). Dinner sharing: casual hospitality in the collaborative economy. In C. Lashley (Ed.), *The Routledge handbook of hospitality studies* (pp. 115–126). Routledge.

Hunter, C. (2002). Sustainable tourism and the touristic ecological footprint. *Environment, Development and Sustainability, 4*(1), 7–20. https://doi.org/10.1023/A:1016336125627

Hughes, N. (2018). 'Tourists go home': Anti-tourism industry protest in Barcelona. *Social Movement Studies, 17*(4), 471–477.

Janta, H., & Christou, A. (2019). Hosting as social practice: Gendered insights into contemporary tourism mobilities. *Annals of Tourism Research, 74,* 167–176.

Ketter, E. (2019). Eating with EatWith: Analysing tourism-sharing economy consumers. *Current Issues in Tourism, 22*(9), 1062–1075.

Mackenzie, S. G., & Davies, A. R. (2019). SHARE IT: Co-designing a sustainability impact assessment framework for urban food sharing initiatives. *Environmental Impact Assessment Review, 79,* 106300. https://doi.org/10.1016/j.eiar.2019.106300

Marques, L., & Matos, B. G. (2020). Network relationality in the tourism experience: Staging sociality in homestays. *Current Issues in Tourism, 23*(9), 1113–1153.

McIntosh, A. J., Lynch, P., & Sweeney, M. (2011). "My home is my castle" defiance of the commercial homestay host in tourism. *Journal of Travel Research, 50*(5), 509–519.

Midgett, C., Bendickson, J. S., Muldoon, J., & Solomon, S. J. (2017). The sharing economy and sustainability: A case for AirBnB. *Small Business Institute® Journal, 13*(2), 51–71.

Molz, J. G. (2013). Social networking technologies and the moral economy of alternative tourism: The case of couchsurfing.org. *Annals of Tourism Research, 43*, 210–230.

Molz, J. G. (2014). Toward a network hospitality. *First Monday, 19*(3), 1-16. https://doi.org/10.5210/fm.v19i3.4824

Moon, H., Miao, L., Hanks, L., & Line, N. (2019). P2P interactions: Perspectives of Airbnb guests and hosts. *International Journal of Hospitality Management, 77*, 405–414.

Mortara, A., & Fragapane, S. (2018). Vieni a mangiare da me? Un'analisi esplorativa del fenomeno del social eating. *Sociologia Della Comunicazione, 55*(55), 71–86.

Munger, M. C. (2018). *Tomorrow 3.0: Transaction costs and the sharing economy.* Cambridge University Press.

OECD. (2018). *Regions and Cities at a Glance 2018.* OECD.

OECD. (2019). *International Migration Outlook 2019.* OECD.

Panas, G., Heliades, G., Halkiopoulos, C., Togias, P. D., Tsavalia, D., & Bougioura, A. (2017). Evaluation of Athens as a city break destination: Tourist perspective explored via data mining techniques. In V. Katsoni, A. Upadhya, & A. Stratigea (Eds.), *Tourism, culture and heritage in a smart economy* (pp. 85–103). Springer.

Peticca-Harris, A., deGama, N., & Ravishankar, M. (2020). Postcapitalist precarious work and those in the 'drivers' seat: Exploring the motivations and lived experiences of Uber drivers in Canada. *Organization, 27*(1), 36–59.

Privitera, D. (2016). *Describing the collaborative economy: Forms of food sharing initiatives.* Proceedings 2016 International Conference Economic Science for Rural Development, No 43, LLU ESAF. 21-22 April 2016, pp. 92–98.

Rakopoulos, T. (2014). The crisis seen from below, within, and against: From solidarity economy to food distribution cooperatives in Greece. *Dialectical Anthropology, 38*(2), 189–207.

Scheyvens, R. (2011). The challenge of sustainable tourism development in the Maldives: Understanding the social and political dimensions of sustainability. *Asia Pacific Viewpoint, 52*(2), 148–164.

Scoones, I. (1998). Sustainable rural livelihoods: A framework for analysis. *IDS Working Paper 72.* https://www.ids.ac.uk/publications/sustainable-rural-livelihoods-a-framework-for-analysis/

Shove, E., Watson, M., & Pantzer, M. (2012). *The dynamics of social practice: Everyday life and how it changes.* Sage.

Tao, T., & Wall, G. (2009). Tourism as a sustainable livelihood strategy. *Tourism Management, 30*(1), 90–98.

Torres-Delgado, A., & Lopez Palomeque, F. (2014). Measuring sustainable tourism at the municipal level. *Annals of Tourism Research, 49*, 122–137.

Verbeek, D., & Mommaas, H. (2008). Transitions to sustainable tourism mobility: The social practices approach. *Journal of Sustainable Tourism, 16*(6), 629–644.

von Briel, D., & Dolnicar, S. (2020). The evolution of Airbnb regulation – An International Longitudinal Investigation 2008-2020. *SocArXiv, March 12.* https://doi.org/doi:10.31235/osf.io/t4nqs

Wang, Y. (2007). Customized authenticity begins at home. *Annals of Tourism Research, 34*(3), 789–804.

Warde, A. (2016). *The practice of eating.* Wiley.

Weymes, M., & Davies, A. R. (2019). Re]Valuing Surplus: Transitions, technologies and tensions in redistributing prepared food in San Francisco. *Geoforum, 99*, 160–169.

Woodcock, J., & Graham, M. (2019). *The gig economy: A critical introduction.* Polity.

Wu, M.-Y., & Pearce, P. L. (2014). Host tourism aspirations as a point of departure for the sustainable livelihoods approach. *Journal of Sustainable Tourism, 22*(3), 440–460.

Xu, Z., Chau, S. N., Chen, X., Zhang, J., Li, Y., Dietz, T., Wang, J., Winkler, J. A., Fan, F., Huang, B., Li, S., Wu, S., Herzberger, A., Tang, Y., Hong, D., Li, Y., & Liu, J. (2020). Assessing progress towards sustainable development over space and time. *Nature, 577*(7788), 74–78. https://doi.org/10.1038/s41586-019-1846-3

Yasmeen, R. (2019). *Top 100 city destinations 2019.* Euromonitor International.

Zervas, G., Proserpio, D., & Byers, J. W. (2017). The rise of the sharing economy: Estimating the impact of Airbnb on the hotel industry. *Journal of Marketing Research, 54*(5), 687–705.

Overtourism and online short-term rental platforms in Italian cities

Filippo Celata and Antonello Romano

ABSTRACT
Although Italian cities have undergone several waves of touristification, concerns about overtourism have only recently become widespread. In the article, we suggest that the diffusion of short-term rental platforms is not merely a concomitant factor, but is crucial to understanding the how and where of contemporary overtourism. To this end we apply a fractal methodology to identify, map and compare those parts of the city that are most affected, and measure the pressure short-term rentals have on city centres as places of residence. By allowing the conversion of residential apartments into tourist accommodation, we argue, short term rentals contribute to the displacement of residents more directly than a generic process of gentrification or touristification. Second, platforms such as Airbnb not only contribute to increasing the accommodation capacity of urban areas, but radically change the morphology of the tourist city. The growing concerns about overtourism are not due to the rising number of tourists per se, but to their increasing penetration into the residential city. We suggest, therefore, that to conceive of overtourism merely as overcrowding is not only inadequate but counterproductive. Even though the depopulation of city centres is difficult to reverse, the coronavirus emergency is an opportunity to plan a different city where tourism coexists with other urban uses and functions.

Introduction

In recent years overtourism has been on the agenda of various cities worldwide. The term has been used in Google searches since 2006; it became a hashtag on Twitter in 2012 and was first discussed in an article on the travel industry site Skift.com in 2016. Since then the term has gained increasing popularity: a simple search on Google Scholar for the keyword "overtourism" returns approximately 400 papers in 2019 and 150 in 2018, while the same search in 2017 returned only 12 results (Goodwin, 2017). The term "tourismphobia" is also recent; it first appeared in 2008 and since then has been widely used to label, or rather stigmatize anti-tourism protests. These protests have been observed in many European cities (Barcelona, Venice, Palma de Mallorca, Paris, Dubrovnik, Berlin, Bologna, Reykjavik, and others), and elsewhere (Koens et al., 2018). Anti-tourism movements have also flourished in recent years (Colomb & Novy, 2016; Hughes, 2018). Some may argue that these concerns belong to the past, given that the coronavirus emergency has practically halted tourism flows worldwide. However, the epidemic may change mass tourism more or less permanently, but will not stop it indefinitely. However, many of the effects overtourism produced are difficult to reverse, as we will discuss further in the paper.

Despite the relevance of the issue and its effects, there is still lack of conceptual clarity about what overtourism is, how contemporary concerns about it differ from earlier worries, what are its causes and consequences and, consequently, how it should be investigated and managed. In this paper, we first provide a review of current conceptualizations in order to highlight the specificities of contemporary concerns about overtourism, and how previous research has attempted to define, measure and monitor the pressure tourism is exerting on cities. In particular, we discuss the crucial role played by the spread of digital accommodation platforms, which sparked a huge and uncontrolled expansion in cities' accommodation capacity with the potential to impact housing availability and affordability, displace permanent residents, and transform the social ecology of the most affected urban neighbourhoods. The article focuses upon Airbnb.com, given that it is the most widely-used short-term rental platform in Italy, and based on the idea that such diffusion is an important part of the problem. The hypothesis is that short-term rentals do not merely contribute to increasing the accommodation capacity of urban areas, but radically change the morphology of the tourist city and, consequently, the relationships between residents and visitors.

On this basis, we develop a methodology aimed at identifying and mapping sub-municipal areas that are most affected by overtourism, and apply this methodology to the most touristified metropolitan cities in Italy – Venice, Florence, Rome, Naples, Palermo, and Bologna. The aim is to provide comparable evidence about the incidence and impact of short-term rentals upon the liveability of city centres, and their contribution to the depopulation of the urban core.

The case study cities have been identified based on the number of short-term rentals listed on the accommodation platform Airbnb.com (Picascia et al., 2017). All of these cities have seen a proliferation of initiatives and social movements denouncing the effects of overtourism and short-term rentals, in particular in terms of housing availability for residents or students.[1] Hotel associations have criticized short-term rentals as a form of unfair competition, given their unregulated status.[2] These views are often countered by those who argue instead that short-term rentals represent a precious source of (extra) income and urban regeneration. Concerns from local public authorities have initially been limited to attempts to avoid excessive tourism congestion, to "educate" or "discipline" tourists, or to limit their access to certain parts of the city. Mayors in some of those cities (Florence, Venice, Rome) have, for example, issued ordinances that ban tourists from consuming meals in public spaces or sitting on monuments. The Mayor of Florence announced in 2017 that he would have church steps watered to prevent tourists from sitting there. In Venice, entry gates were set up to regulate access to the city centre, so that they can be closed when the number of accesses exceeds a certain threshold (the gates were removed shortly afterwards as they were never used). The same has been attempted around specific attractions, like Fontana di Trevi in Rome, which tourists are invited to visit quickly. Visitors entering Venice have recently been asked to pay an entry ticket that ranges from 3 to 10 euros depending on the degree of congestion in each period, with the exception of tourists staying in local accommodation facilities and other categories of city users. Several local associations and (anti-tourism) social movements have protested vehemently against these measures, which they judge counter-productive. What those associations criticize is the transformation of cities into some sort of theme park: access gates and entry tickets cannot but promote and accelerate such process. It is clear, however, that current approaches are far from constituting an appropriate and definitive management of overtourism, which is not simply an issue of overcrowding, as we will discuss in the next sections.

With regard to the widely debated issue of short-term rentals and digital accommodation platforms, none of those cities have taken any formal steps, but some of them (Bologna and Firenze) have declared very recently their intention to introduce specific regulations and even to "stop" the conversion of residential dwellings into lodgings for tourists. Proposals have been made, moreover, to change existing regional and national laws in order to provide cities with some tools for monitoring and regulating short-term rentals, which are currently very weak, for example by introducing an ad-hoc licence. Moreover, national authorities have attempted to limit tax evasion and tax avoidance, with limited success. The paper aims both to contribute to existing research and to put forward a more appropriate system for management of overtourism and of its effects.

The how and where of platform-mediated overtourism

Although the term has gained popularity only very recently, concerns about overtourism are by no means new. In tourism research, the topic has been discussed at least since the early seventies (Capocchi et al. 2019; Wall, 2020). For example, an index for measuring residents' "irritation" towards tourists was proposed by Doxey in 1975. Within Butler's well-known theory of the Tourism Area Life Cycle, the "consolidation" stage is described as the moment when the number of visitors exceeds that of permanent residents (1980). According to Butler, this situation can easily lead to stagnation and decline, as well as causing "opposition and discontent among permanent residents, particularly those not involved in the tourist industry in any way, and result in some deprivation and restrictions upon their activities" (Butler, 1980, p. 8). More recent definitions of overtourism are basically similar, except that the emphasis is more on residents' discontent and perceptions, rather than overcrowding per se (Butler, 2019).[3]

The first difference with respect to previous concerns about overtourism is indeed this "discontent". Concerns and protests about the negative effects of excessive tourism are today particularly widespread (Milano et al., 2019) whereas previously they were more limited (Dodds and Butler, 2019). The second difference is that concerns about overtourism arise today mainly in big cities. The question we must ask therefore is: why? The easiest answer is that tourism is simply growing too much and that this growth is particularly concentrated in cities. This view has been advanced by a recent UNWTO report on the topic (2018), and is common in the burgeoning literature about overtourism (Capocchi et al., 2019; Dodds and Butler, 2019; Oklevik et al., 2019; Sequera & Nofre, 2018). However, this is just part of the answer since the *how* of this growth is, in our view, at least equally important. In this regard, we believe that the role of digital accommodation platforms is crucial for understanding contemporary overtourism. The diffusion of "network hospitality" or platform-mediated short-term rentals is in fact often mentioned as a concomitant factor in the literature about overtourism (Bouchon & Rauscher, 2019; Dodds and Butler, 2019; Goodwin, 2017), but it is rarely the main focus of the analysis.

One hypothesis that we wish to explore further in this paper is that platforms such as Airbnb have not only hugely increased the accommodation capacity of many destinations, they have also changed substantially the morphology of the tourist city, which "plays an important role in the sentiment of contested spaces between residents and visitors" (Bouchon & Rauscher, 2019, p. 14). Inhabitants, it has been argued, feel increasingly alienated from their own city which they feel has been appropriated by tourists (Diaz-Parra & Jover, 2020).

Evidence about the spatial effects of accommodation platforms is indeed ambivalent (for a review, see Guttentag, 2019). Short-term rentals, it has been shown, are causing both the overtouristification of already highly touristified city centres (Alizadeh et al., 2018; Arias Sans & Quaglieri Domínguez, 2016; Benítez-Aurioles, 2018; Picascia et al., 2017) and the invasion and gentrification of non-touristic neighbourhoods (Cocola-Gant, 2016; Ioannides et al., 2019; Wachsmuth & Weisler, 2018). This apparent ambivalence can easily be solved by assuming that short-term rentals are much more diffused and widespread all over the cities' central and near-central areas than hotels and traditional accommodation facilities (Celata, 2017; Gutiérrez et al., 2017; Gyòdi, 2017). The rising concerns about overtourism may therefore be due not to the growing number of tourists per se, but to their growing penetration into the residential city, closer to where the inhabitants live.

Moreover, the diffusion of short-term rentals may have a much more direct effect on the socio-spatial ecology of city centres than a "standard" gentrification process (Jover & Díaz-Parra, 2019; Sequera & Nofre, 2018) and even than touristification in general, whose effects are mainly indirect. By allowing the conversion of thousands of residential apartments into tourist lodgings, short-term rentals immediately cause a substantial decrease in the housing stock available for long-term residents and contribute directly to the depopulation of city centres, as we will show.

Another difference with respect to previous debates about overtourism, as already mentioned, is in the typology of destination that is today more exposed (Bouchon & Rauscher, 2019; Butler, 2019; Phi, 2019; Wall 2020). Traditionally, concerns about the number of tourists exceeding an acceptable threshold have been raised with regard to, for example, natural parks and areas of ecological importance, small islands, specific tourist sites, or "resort cities" where "a major part of the area's economy will be tied to tourism" (Butler, 1980, p. 8). Since today overtourism predominantly affects big cities, the conceptual and empirical lens through which we observe and eventually react to over-touristification must change.

For example, based on previous experiments in destinations affected by overcrowding, the application of "carrying capacity" or "the limits of acceptable change" methods is frequently suggested (Bouchon & Rauscher, 2019; Capocchi et al., 2019; Dodds and Butler, 2019; Goodwin, 2017; Koens et al. 2018; Milano et al., 2019; Papathanassis, 2017; Peeters et al., 2018; Phi, 2019; UNWTO, 2018) . A wealth of "urban carrying capacity" assessment methods exists (Wei et al., 2015), and these have been applied to determine the maximum amount of tourism allowable in, for example, Venice (Bertocchi et al., 2020). The option attracted several criticisms (Koens et al., 2018; Saarinen, 2006; Wall, 2019, 2020). The measurement of the maximum acceptable number of tourists may be based on the physical capacity of, e.g. accommodation facilities, public transport or the waste treatment system (Bertocchi et al., 2020). However, touristification can cause irreversible and detrimental effects, as well as raising concerns and protests from the local population, much before such an extreme threshold and the city's complete saturation is reached. Contemporary overtourism is not, moreover, simply due to congestion or overcrowding; the concern is about how touristification affects and interacts with the social fabric of the city, and what the consequences are for residents. At the same time, to measure carrying capacity based on residents' perceptions or socio-cultural variables is problematic, equivocal, and potentially flawed, as long as what is an "acceptable" pressure is based on a complicated and debateable aggregation of individual preferences (Seidl & Tisdell, 1999). Additionally, the relationship between the density and degree of touristification and the "acceptable change" it induces is not linear (Wall, 2019). And what should we do once we know that the number of tourists is excessive? Such a view implicitly calls for an approach based on limiting tourist numbers, which is not only problematic, but also far from being a proper management of the causes and consequences of overtourism in an urban context (Phi, 2019), as mentioned in the introduction. Moreover, cities have a much more diversified social and economic base with respect to those over-specialized destinations that have been traditionally affected by tourism congestion. The issue is therefore not merely overcrowding, but how touristification relates to – and potentially conflicts with – other urban functions, and how it contributes together with a wealth of other factors and processes to urban change. Finally, as long as the destinations that are the most affected by contemporary overtourism are big metropolitan areas, the issue is not "how much" but "where" overtourism is in the urban area (UNWTO, 2018).

In the following sections, we will provide evidence about some of the issues mentioned above, issues that, in our view, are crucial for understanding the how and where of contemporary overtourism.

Data and methodology

The analysis presented below provides first, the identification of those areas in the city that are affected by overtourism and, secondly, some evidence about the socio-spatial impact of platform-mediated touristification. The methodology and measurements are aimed at providing comparable evidence across some of the main Italian tourism cities: Bologna, Florence, Naples, Palermo, Rome, and Venice. The study is based on data scraped from Airbnb.com in 2019 by Insideairbnb.com, microdata from official statistics (ISTAT), Municipal statistics and Openstreetmap geodata.

We first identify within the six cities the area that may be defined as the "tourist city", based on a common method, and using the location of Airbnb listings. In particular, we apply a fractal methodology (Jiang & Miao, 2015) in order to make the different cities comparable or, more precisely, to avoid the so-called modifiable area unit problem (MAUP). The analysis presented in the paper is in fact applied to various urban areas that range from medium-sized cities such as Venice (260,000 inhabitants) to big metropolitan areas such as Rome (2.9 million inhabitants). In order to properly compare those cities, their different sizes as well as their different internal structures should be taken carefully into account. Figure 1 enables us to appreciate such variation: the city's "skyline" is composed of bars whose height is proportional to the ratio of the city's housing stock that is for rent on Airbnb.com per each census tract. Bars are coloured based on the percentage of entire homes over total listings. Tall blue bars, in short, indicate areas in the city where not only are there more Airbnb listings, but where the impact on the availability

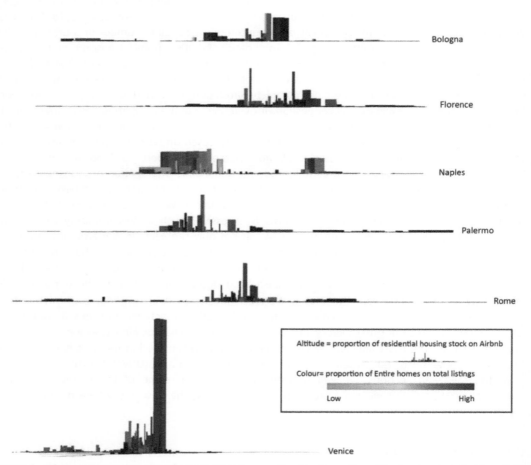

Figure 1. Airbnbscapes in Italian cities. The bars' height is proportional to the portion of the housing stock that is available for rent on Airbnb.com per census tract. The bars' colour is the proportion of "entire homes" out of total Airbnb listings. Data sources: Insideairbnb, ISTAT.

of housing for permanent residents is higher, an issue that we will discuss in greater detail below. At this stage, the figure is useful to provide some sort of 3D visualization of the pervasive but non-homogeneous distribution of short-term rentals over the urban space, and to outline a preliminary taxonomy of the tourist city's morphology. In Florence and Bologna the spatial pattern is concentrated in and more or the less equally distributed all over the city centre. Naples shows a multi-polar pattern. Venice is heavily polarized, while Palermo and Rome are both multi-polar and hierarchical.

The fractal methodology permits us to account for such variability by taking into account those areas where Airbnb listings are most concentrated, but also the overall structure of the (tourist) city, without adopting any predefined spatial partition. Previous analyses of the distribution and impact of short-term rentals are often affected by the MAUP. Such impact is in fact analysed sometimes at the city scale, e.g. based on municipal boundaries (Alizadeh et al., 2018; Wegmann & Jiao, 2017), sometimes on a sub-municipal scale using predefined divisions such as neighbourhoods or census tracts (Cocola-Gant, 2016; Gutiérrez et al., 2016; Wachsmuth & Weisler, 2018), and other times focussing on specific neighbourhoods (Cocola-Gant & Gago, 2019; Ioannides et al. 2019; Smith et al., 2018). Estimates are therefore affected by the scale and shape of the geographical divisions adopted, which is particularly problematic if we wish to compare cities or neighbourhoods. Municipal and sub-municipal boundaries are in fact not only very different in size and shape but also arbitrary, being imposed from the top down by public authorities. The actual extent of cities in more geographical/spatial terms is defined and delineated based on their physical morphology, for example in terms of the average distance between buildings. The same applies to the "tourist city": our methodological option is to identify these tourist cities based on the distance between Airbnb listings or, more precisely, based on the head/tail breaks rule. In detail, the approach "involves dividing things around an average into large and small, which respectively constitute the head and the tail of the rank-size plot" (Jiang, 2015, p.6). The process has four steps (Figure 2): we first calculated the Triangular irregular networks of Airbnb listings (A); we then measured the length of the interpolation edges (B), and (C) selected those whose length is below the median value, and those below the 75th centile. Finally, we created the fractal areas (D) by aggregating those high proximity features (point C) into single-part polygons. Figures 3–8 report the results: in orange the fractal area obtained by aggregating edges whose length is below the median, and in blue those below the 75th centile. In the analysis that follows, the "tourist city" corresponds to the fractal area with proximity of listings below the median value. The methodology allows us to obtain homogeneous and comparable spatial units, as well as to highlight the spatial structure of the tourist city, e.g. the extent to which it is more or less compact or, on the contrary, fragmented.

Using those spatial units, we calculated several indicators such as the extent of the tourist city, the concentration of Airbnb listings in this area, their growth rate, the ratio of short-term rentals on the residential housing stock, and the relation between their accommodation capacity and the resident population (Table 1).

Finally, we present and discuss the trends of population variation within and outside of the tourist city, and we then focus on some of those cities in order to provide further evidence about the association between the city centre's depopulation and the diffusion of short-term rentals, and about how the distribution of Airbnb listings in the city differs from that of hotels and registered accommodation facilities.

The spatiality and impact of platform-mediated overtourism

The fractal approach described in the previous section permits us, first, to obtain a comparable delimitation of the "tourist city" within the metropolitan areas that are the object of our analysis. The results are presented in Figures 3–8. These maps adopt the same geographical scale, and

A   B

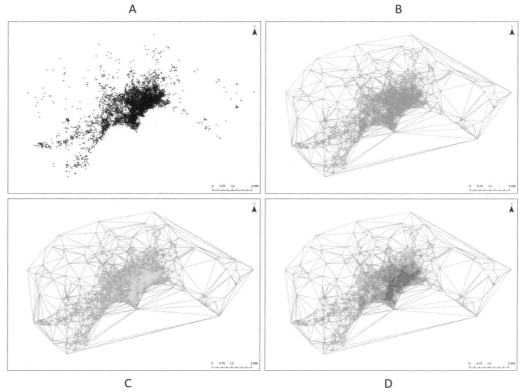

C   D

Figure 2. Fractal methodology to identify the tourist city: A) Airbnb listings (1 dot = 1 listing), B) interpolation edges between listings, C) selection of edges shorter than the median length, D) identification of the fractal area (in orange). Naples. Data source: Insideairbnb.com, 2019.

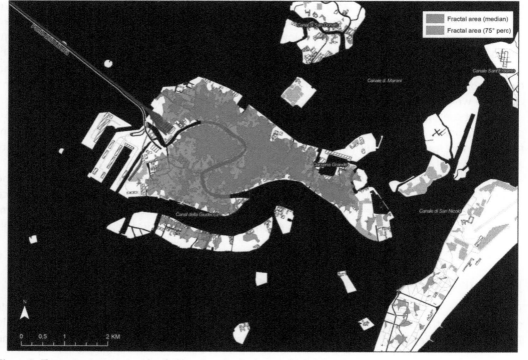

Figure 3. The tourist city in Venice, identified based on the distribution of Airbnb listings. Data source: insideairbnb.com, May 2019.

Figure 4. The tourist city in Bologna, identified based on the distribution of Airbnb listings. Data source: insideairbnb.com, May 2019.

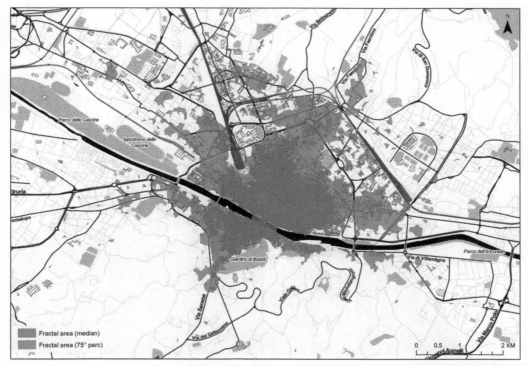

Figure 5. The tourist city in Florence, identified based on the distribution of Airbnb listings. Data source: insideairbnb.com, May 2019.

Figure 6. The tourist city in Rome, identified based on the distribution of Airbnb listings.
Data source: insideairbnb.com, May 2019.

Figure 7. The tourist city in Naples, identified based on the distribution of Airbnb listings.
Data source: insideairbnb.com, May 2019.

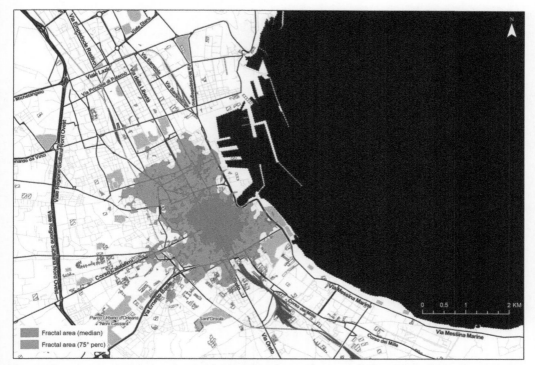

Figure 8. The tourist city in Palermo, identified based on the distribution of Airbnb listings. Data source: insideairbnb.com, May 2019.

show that the overall extension of the tourist city is more or less similar despite these cities having very different sizes and populations, with the exception of Rome, where the tourist city is bigger, and Bologna, where it is smaller and more fragmented.

As reported in Table 1, the "tourist city" is relatively small in terms of extent with respect to the entire municipality (2.2% of the municipal area in Florence, 1.5% in Venice, approximately 0.5% in the other cities), but also quite significant as it covers most of the city centre, and includes between one third and three quarters of the entire supply of Airbnb listings. The demand for those listings is even more heavily concentrated in this central area: the percentage of reviews obtained by central listings (which can be considered proportional to the number of guests) is always above the percentage of listings located in this area, with the single exception of Florence, due to the attractiveness of villas in less central areas for rent on Airbnb.

In terms of impact, as already mentioned, the most direct and worrying effect is the subtraction of housing units available for permanent residents, and their conversion into short-term rentals. In order to assess this, we calculate the ratio between the entire residential housing stock in the census tracts that have their centroid in the "tourist city", and the number of entire apartments for rent on Airbnb.com in the same area. The ratio ranges from 11% (Naples) to 30% (Florence and Bologna). Census data is only available for 2011; however, in the "tourist city" the housing stock is relatively stable, given that the area includes heavily regulated historic neighbourhoods.[4]

It should be noted that in most Italian cities the availability of rentals is very limited, as the great majority of families live in homes they own. The conversion of residential apartments into short-term rentals impacts therefore, in particular, upon the already small proportion of the housing stock which is available for long-term rentals. To measure such pressure, we compare the number of entire apartments listed on Airbnb with the number of families renting in the

Table 1. Tourist city's extent and incidence of Airbnb listings in Bologna, Florence, Naples, Palermo, Rome, Venice. Data source: Insideairbnb.com, Istat.

City	Fractal area / Tourist city (km²)	Percentage of Airbnb listings in the fractal area	Percentage of Airbnb reviews in the fractal area	Density of Airbnb listings in the fractal area (per Km2)	Yearly growth rate (%) of listings within the fractal area (2018-2019)	Ratio between entire homes on Airbnb and the total residential housing stock in the fractal area	Ratio between entire homes on Airbnb and the number of families residing in rented apartments in the fractal area	Ratio between the accommodation capacity of Airbnb listings and the resident population in the fractal area
Bologna	0.25	34%	41%	5632	+288%	32.4%	136.8%	99.7%
Florence	2.3	77%	70%	3599	+39%	29.1%	149.5%	118.5%
Naples	1.76	64%	71%	2823	+84%	10.9%	30.3%	34.8%
Palermo	0.93	54%	71%	3266	+91%	25.0%	85.7%	95.2%
Rome	5.78	62%	74%	3300	+57%	17.0%	118.4%	75.9%
Venice	2.01	73%	75%	2986	+46%	21.8%	124.3%	86.0%

year 2011, i.e. before the Airbnb "invasion" began. In four of the six cities, the number of apart-ments listed on Airbnb in 2019 exceeds those rented to residents in 2011. The indicator is not meant as a ratio but simply, as already mentioned, as a proxy of pressure. In fact, not only rented apartments but also those occupied by their owners may have been converted into short-term rentals. The available data do not allow us to measure actual conversion rates. However, while the percentage of families living in owned apartments increased consistently over the past decades, the percentage of residential apartments for rent (to either tourists or res-idents) increased in Rome and Naples from 2012 to 2016, and more in the city centres (+5.5%) than in the whole city (+3%). This may be due to various factors. What the above-mentioned data show is that the growth of short-term rentals is probably one of those factors.

The ratio of tourists to the permanent population is also a potential indicator of (over)touristi-fication and of the pressure short-term rentals exert on city centres as places of residence. We therefore compared the entire accommodation capacity of Airbnb listings with the number of residents in 2011: with the single exception of Naples, such ratio is always close to or even above (in the case of Florence) 100%. Obviously, the resident population may have changed since 2011, as we discuss below. It is also unlikely that the total accommodation capacity of Airbnb listings is permanently and completely occupied by tourists. On the other hand, we only considered Airbnb listings. When tourists staying in hotels or in accommodation facilities adver-tised through other digital platforms are added, these numbers increase substantially.

Short-term rentals and the depopulation of city centres

How are such numbers and trends actually impacting the liveability of cities? The primary and most visible impact is upon the resident population of city centres. Figures 9, 10 and 11 show population trends within and outside the "tourist city", i.e. those neighbourhoods that corres-pond more closely to the fractal areas identified in Figures 3–8.

In Rome, the central and most touristified part of the city is indeed depopulating fast (Figure 9), in particular since 2010, and especially after 2014: in four years, the two most touristified neighbourhoods – the zone labelled "historical centre" and Trastevere – have lost approximately one third of their inhabitants. In Venice (Figure 10), the municipal population is also more or less stable overall, while the number of residents in the historic city is decreasing. Unlike in the case

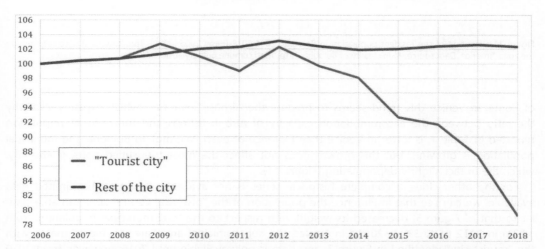

Figure 9. Variation of the resident population in Rome, 2006-2018 (Base: 2006 = 100). The tourist city's neighbourhoods are those that fall almost completely within the fractal area (Figure 5): Centro Storico, Trastevere, Esquilino, XX Settembre, Prati and Eroi. Data source: Municipality of Rome (https://www.comune.roma.it/web/it/roma-statistica-popolazione.page).

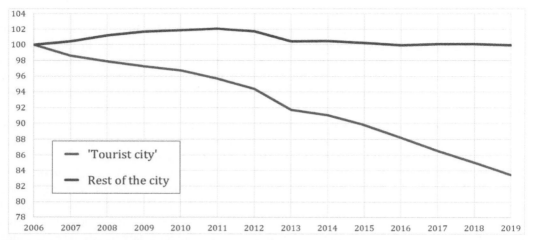

Figure 10. Variation of the resident population in Venice, 2006-2018 (Base: 2006 = 100). The tourist city corresponds to the zone "centro storico", i.e. the main central islands (neighbourhoods: S.Marco-Castello-S.Elena-Cannaregio and Dorsoduro-S.Polo-S.Croce-Giudecca). Data source: Municipality of Venice (https://www.comune.venezia.it/it/content/serie-storiche).

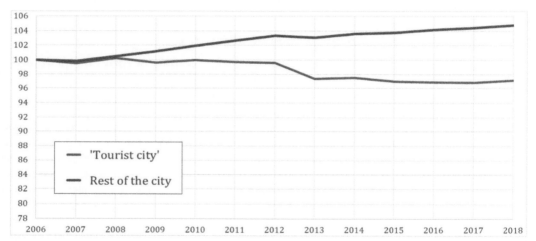

Figure 11. Variation of the resident population in Bologna, 2006-2018 (Base: 2006 = 100). The "tourist city" corresponds to the zone "Irnerio". Data source: Municipality of Bologna (http://dati.comune.bologna.it/node/1033).

of Rome, in Venice this trend seems to predate the Airbnb "invasion" (which explains also why the ratio between the accommodation capacity of Airbnb listings and the resident population reported in Table 1, is lower in Venice than Florence or even Palermo). In Bologna, the municipal population is growing, but this growth does not affect the most touristified parts of the city, which are in fact slightly depopulating (Figure 11).

For the other cities, a complete historical series is not available. Based on the limited data available, we can see that in Florence the population of the "historical centre" zone (an area similar to that of Figure 5) decreased its weight with respect to the total municipal population, from 18.2% in 2012 to 17.3% in 2018.[5] In Naples, the sub-municipal areas are too big to match with the "tourist city" identified in Figure 7, and data is only available until 2016; however, from 2010 to 2016, the resident population of the central area of the city shows a small decrease in absolute numbers, but not with respect to the rest of the city, as the whole urban population is decreasing.[6] In Palermo, the zone "circoscrizione 1" – which includes the "tourist city" identified in Figure 8, although it is bigger – the resident population decreased by 4.9% between 2012 and 2018, while the total urban population decreased by 4.25%.[7]

The depopulation of city centres is certainly not a new phenomenon. However, the population in the "tourist city" from 2001 to 2011 – i.e. before the "Airbnb invasion" – remained stable in Bologna (+0.2%), increased in Naples (+3.4%) and Palermo (+9.3%), and decreased in Florence (-4.5%). The population trend for the historic centre of Rome is reported in Figure 12, and it had been more or less stable since 1991. Venice (Figure 13) experienced the highest decrease between 2001 and 2011 (-10%), which is in any case lower with respect to both the previous five decades, and the most recent one (-15% from 2009 to 2019).

In order to assess to what extent depopulation is associated with the spread of short-term rentals, we calculated the Pearson correlation between the variation of the resident population in each of the 155 neighbourhoods of Rome ("zone urbanistiche") and in the 12 neighbourhoods of Venice ("quartieri"), with several measures of the concentration of Airbnb listings in those neighbourhoods. As shown in Table 2, the correlations are always significant, above a 99% confidence level, and also quite high. The highest correlation is, not surprisingly, with the number of entire apartments for rent on Airbnb. The same correlation for the 18 neighbourhoods of Bologna is significant (the correlation is -0.585, significant at the 0.05 level) only if the variation of the population is calculated from 2012, and if two low-income but central zones (Bolognina

Figure 12. Resident population in the historic centre of Rome, 1901-2011.
Source: Sonnino et al., 2011 (1901-1991 data) and Istat (2001-2011 data)

Figure 13. Resident population in the historic centre of Venice, 1901-2011.
Source: Municipality of Venice

Table 2. Pearson correlation between the resident population variation in the neighbourhoods of Rome (2014-2018) and Venice (2014-2019), and the concentration and variation of Airbnb listings.

	Number of Airbnb listings, 2019	Number of entire apartments for rent on Airbnb, 2019	Cumulate number of Airbnb listings reviews, 2019	Absolute difference in the number of Airbnb listings, 2016-2019
Rome	−,616**	−,699**	−,629**	−,648**
Venice	−,862**	−,897**	−,857**	−,834**

** Correlation is significant at the 0.01 level (2-tailed). Data source: Insideairbnb, Municipality of Rome, Municipality of Venice.

Table 3. Average distance between the resident population and the closest accommodation facility in Rome.

	Entire Municipality	"Tourist city"
Hotels and similar	649.5 mt	279.2 mt
Airbnb listings	136.7 mt	10.5 mt
Non-hotel registered accommodation facilities	351.1 mt	51.1 mt

Data source: Insideairbnb, Municipality of Rome, ISTAT.

and Marconi) where both the number of residents and of Airbnb listings have grown in the last years are eliminated.

Finally, in order to assess how the morphology of the tourist city is changing due to the expansion of short-term rentals, we calculated the average distance between the resident population and the closest accommodation facility, which measures how "close" tourists are to where residents live. Table 3 shows that this distance is substantially lower for Airbnb listings with respect not only to hotels and similar, which are obviously fewer in number, bigger and consequently more concentrated, but also with respect to registered accommodation facilities such as bed & breakfasts or "formal" rooms and apartments for rent to tourists. Such "closeness" is relatively even higher in the central area we defined as the "tourist city" than in the entire municipality.[8]

Discussion and conclusions

Although Italian cities have undergone several waves of touristification, concerns about overtourism are very recent. The hypothesis explored in this article is that the growth of digital short-term rental platforms is not merely a concomitant factor contributing to an excessive growth in the number of tourists, but crucial for understanding how such growth is distributed in the city and, consequently, how it impacts upon city centres as living spaces.

Accommodation platforms such as Airbnb produce two primary effects. First, platform-mediated touristification radically changes the most affected neighbourhoods, producing more direct and immediate effects compared to a generic process of gentrification (Jover & Díaz-Parra, 2019; Sequera & Nofre, 2018) or of touristification in general. As mentioned in Section 2, gentrification causes resident displacement mainly indirectly, by driving up rents and prices. Indeed, several studies demonstrate how the spread of short-term rentals influences the cost of rents and real estate values (for a review, see Guttentag, 2019). The conversion of residential units into short-term rentals, however, reduces the housing stock that is available for permanent residents directly and immediately, without even having to assume or to demonstrate any impact on the cost of housing.[9] The impact is dramatic in those parts of the city where the concentration of short-term rentals exceeds a certain threshold.

In the article, we applied a methodological approach to identify those parts of the city that are more greatly affected. Such an ad-hoc delimitation was also aimed at obtaining comparable evidence for cities with very different sizes and structures. In those "tourist cities", short-term rentals listed on Airbnb.com occupy a substantial portion of the total residential housing stock;

their number in the majority of cases exceeds the number of long-term rentals; and their capacity is close to or above that of apartments occupied by residents.

We showed, moreover, that the resident population of those city centres is decreasing. Such depopulation may indeed have many causes, not limited to touristification. Population may decrease because residential dwellings are converted into short-term rentals, or because of the indirect effects touristification has on, for example, the commercial fabric, congestion, noise, etc., but also due to unrelated factors such as ageing, decreasing occupancy rates, the conversion of residential units into office space, or other factors. The depopulation of city centres is also a much older process, but it had slowed considerably before the last decade, even if it had not stopped completely. It goes beyond the scope of the paper to demonstrate any direct causality between the spread of digital accommodation platforms and population de-growth. Intuitively, however, in Rome in particular, there is a clear temporal coincidence between the depopulation of the city centre and not touristification in general, but platform-mediated touristification, which started in around 2013. As a confirmation of this, the correlation between population de-growth and the growth in Airbnb listings, in Rome and Venice, is high and significant: those areas in the city where the resident population decreases the most are also the areas with the highest concentration and the fastest growth of Airbnb listings. The available data does not permit us to test the same correlation for the other cities.

The analysis has also some limitations. The evidence presented in the paper is in fact mainly indirect, although consistent with our hypothesis. The numbers are in any case impressive. The conversion of thousands of residential apartments into short-term rentals cannot but contribute to the depopulation of city centres where the housing stock is stable, if not decreasing. However, future research should confirm the validity of our hypothesis and findings, based both on direct evidence and longitudinal micro-data to be obtained through, for example, an ad-hoc survey of residential apartments and their actual usage through the years, or more recent secondary data and more robust analytical techniques that permit testing for casual relationships, or through a comparison with less touristy cities.

A second hypothesis we explored in the paper is that short-term rentals penetrate the residential city much more deeply than hotels or other more traditional accommodation types. In terms of spatial pattern, the fractal methodology whose results are reported in Figures 3-8 outlines a very compact and dense "tourist city" that covers more or less homogenously a substantial proportion of the city centre. The only exception is Bologna, where the growth of Airbnb listings is more recent and less widespread, i.e. more clustered in specific locations. The assessment of the average distance between places of residence and tourism accommodation in Rome confirms the extent to which Airbnb brings tourists "closer" to where people live (see also Gutiérrez et al., 2017; Gyòdi, 2017). The distribution of short-term rentals, in other words, is pervasive and invades central or near-central zones that were more marginal during previous waves of touristification.

By allowing its guests to "live like a local", short-term rental platforms cause visitors and inhabitants to make use more often of the same spaces, infrastructure and services, causing discontent in the resident population (Bouchon & Rauscher, 2019). The perceived impact of these transformations goes well beyond the areas of the city that are more heavily affected. These changes affect in fact predominantly a central and relatively small part of the urban area, but one which is crucial for both the material life of the city and for its inhabitants' sense of belonging to the city. Permanent residents, consequently, are both physically displaced from the urban centre and feeling increasingly alienated from their own city (Diaz-Parra & Jover, 2020).

It is not surprising, then, that most of the discontent about overtourism is today addressed to Airbnb and short-term rental platforms, rather than against tourism per se. Slogans such as "go to hotels" are indeed common in protests and campaigns against overtourism; those slogans are implicitly calling for a more segregated tourist city in which inhabitans and visitors are more functionally and physically separated.

The problem of overtourism is, therefore, not simply the growth or overcrowding of tourists (Butler, 2019), but their increasing penetration into the residential city. The case of Italian cities confirms moreover that the relationship between the degree of tourism congestion and the effects it causes in terms of residents' perceptions and reactions is not linear (Wall, 2019). For example, our analysis shows that in Bologna the incidence of short-term rentals is much lower than in the other cities, and no significant correlation with the variation of the resident population has been found. Bologna has, however, seen some of the strongest protests against short-term rentals and the city was the first to declare its will to stop any further increase in Airbnb listings, especially because they are severely limiting the availability of apartments for rent to students.[10] In Palermo, on the contrary, impact indicators are much higher, similar to Venice or Florence, but overtourism has only recently induced some reactions from residents and local social movements.[11]

In this framework, approaches to the management of overtourism based on limiting tourists' access to and use of the city are useless, as these do not address the root causes nor the more worrying effects of touristification. Those approaches even risk being counterproductive, as they contribute to the "museumification" of city centres and increase the alienation of inhabitants from such an important part of the city. Instead, based on our hypothesis and findings, appropriate regulation of short-term rentals could make a difference. The problem is that the same elements that cause platform-mediated touristification to be so pervasive and impactful prevent adequate governance of the short-term rentals market. Since lodgings advertised through platforms such as Airbnb are predominantly residential apartments, they are not subject to ad-hoc planning regulations, and the instruments available to monitor and regulate the phenomenon are very weak if not non-existent (Ferreri & Sanyal, 2018; Gurran & Phibbs, 2017). Even more pressing and more challenging is the need to guarantee that the urban centres of big tourist cities remain lively and liveable for both visitors and inhabitants, through for example (social) housing policies, rental support or urban planning more generally.

The coronavirus emergency has thrown us, at least temporarily, into a different world. At the time of writing, lockdown measures have been implemented in many countries worldwide that have radically reduced movement and activities. The impact of those measures upon tourist destinations and especially upon the centres of historic cities has been particularly dramatic.[12] Local authorities are therefore now desperately looking for alternatives, while some short-term rentals are being converted into longer-term ones (Celata, 2020). The emptiness that the lockdown created in tourist cities' centres may eventually be filled again by tourists, or by a return of residents, or both. It is also a matter of what kind of policies will be adopted after the emergency. To outline those policy options in detail goes beyond the scope of the paper. The crisis is having a terrible impact, but it is also making the problem evident and providing an opportunity to prepare for a different future. Our cities, we believe, are perfectly capable of again hosting masses of tourists, but only if we take this opportunity to understand how these numbers can be made compatible with other urban uses and functions.

Notes

1. See, for example, the manifesto of the SET network, "Sud Europa di fronte alla Turistizzazione", which many Italian cities signed up to: https://setfirenze.noblogs.org/post/2019/02/13/founding-manifesto-of-set-network/.
2. See for example the report "Tourism and the shadow economy" published by Federalberghi, the main Italian association of hotels: http://www.federalberghi.it/UploadFile/2018/09/turismo%20e%20shadow%20economy%20-%20edizione%20settembre%202018.pdf.
3. The UNWTO defines overtourism as "the impact of tourism on a destination, or parts thereof, that excessively influences perceived quality of life of citizens and/or quality of visitors experiences in a negative way" (2018, p. 4). The Responsible Tourism Partnership (Goodwin, 2017) defines overtourism as "destinations where hosts or guests, locals or visitors, feel that there are too many visitors and that the quality of life in the area or the quality of the experience has deteriorated unacceptably" (p. 1). According to a report commissioned by the

European Parliament, "overtourism describes the situation in which the impact of tourism, at certain times and in certain locations, exceeds physical, ecological, social, economic, psychological, and/or political capacity thresholds" (Peeters et al. 2018, p. 22).

4. Census data shows that from 2001 to 2011 the number of apartments in residential buildings has indeed decreased in Venice (-9%), Bologna (-3%), Florence (-16%) and Rome (-8%), probably due to their conversion into office space, and increased only slightly in Naples (+2%) and Palermo (+6%) (dati.istat.it). More recent data shows moreover that the average surface of residential apartments in the historic centres of Rome and Naples didn't change from 2012 to 2016 (https://www.agenziaentrate.gov.it/portale/web/guest/agenzia/agenzia-comunica/prodotti-editoriali/pubblicazioni-cartografia_catasto_mercato_immobiliare/immobili-in-italia); we can therefore exclude that the number of these apartments increased due to their subdivision into smaller units.

5. Data accessed at http://dati.toscana.it, February 7th 2020.

6. Data accessed at http://www.comune.napoli.it/flex/cm/pages/ServeBLOB.php/L/IT/IDPagina/34362, February 7th 2020.

7. Data accessed at https://opendata.comune.palermo.it, February 7th 2020.

8. It is worth noting that in Rome the average distance to the three 'top' attractions (the Colosseum, the Pantheon and Fontana di Trevi), which measures how 'conveniently' located tourists are in the city, is higher for tourists staying in hotels (4.6 km) than for those staying in Airbnb listings (3.6 km), when calculated for the entire municipality. This result is in line with the evidence provided by Gutiérrez et al. (2016). However, when the same indicator is calculated only for the 'tourist city', i.e. for a more central area, the opposite is true: Airbnb guests are relatively more distant from the three top attractions (2 km) than tourists staying in hotels (1.5 km).

9. In most Italian cities, real estate values have decreased in the last years because of the economic recession. Between 2012 and 2016 the average value per square metre of a residential apartment decreased by -27% in Bologna, -20% in Naples, -15% in Rome, -11% in Florence and -1.2% in Venice (https://www.agenziaentrate.gov.it/portale/web/guest/agenzia/agenzia-comunica/prodotti-editoriali/pubblicazioni-cartografia_catasto_mercato_immobiliare/immobili-in-italia).

10. https://bologna.repubblica.it/cronaca/2019/11/13/news/case_bologna_il_sindaco_in_arrivo_un_freno_ad_airbnb-240978631/

11. https://www.facebook.com/turistificazionepalermo/.

12. During the lockdown in Italy, the population of historic cities' centres decreased up to 70-80%, similarly to sky resorts: https://www.nocodegeography.com/big-data/spostamenti-popolazione-ai-tempi-del-coronavirus/

Disclosure statement

No potential conflict of interest was reported by the author(s).

Acknowledgments

We thank Massimiliano Crisci (IRPPS-CNR), Patrizia Veclani (Osservatorio civico indipendente sulla casa e sulla residenzialità, Venezia) and Grazia Galli (Pensare urbano, Firenze) for providing detailed population data, and the three anonymous referees for their constructive comments.

References

Alizadeh, T., Farid, R., & Sarkar, S. (2018). Towards understanding the socio-economic patterns of sharing economy in Australia: an investigation of Airbnb listings in Sydney and Melbourne metropolitan regions. *Urban Policy and Research*, *36*(4), 445–463. https://doi.org/10.1080/08111146.2018.1460269

Arias Sans, A., & Quaglieri Domínguez, A. (2016). Unravelling Airbnb: Urban Perspectives from Barcelona. In Russo A. P., Richards G. (Eds.), *Reinventing the Local in Tourism: Producing, Consuming and Negotiating Place. Channel View*. (pp. 209–228). Reinventing the Local in Tourism.

Benítez-Aurioles, B. (2018). The role of distance in the peer-to-peer market for tourist accommodation. *Tourism Economics*, *24*(3), 237–250. https://doi.org/10.1177/1354816617726211

Bertocchi, D., Camatti, N., Giove, S., & van der Borg, J. (2020). Venice and Overtourism: Simulating Sustainable Development Scenarios through a Tourism Carrying Capacity Model. *Sustainability*, *12*(2), 512. https://doi.org/10.3390/su12020512

Bouchon, F., & Rauscher, M. (2019). Cities and tourism, a love and hate story; towards a conceptual framework for urban overtourism management. *International Journal of Tourism Cities*, *5*(4), 598–619. https://doi.org/10.1108/IJTC-06-2019-0080

Butler, R. W. (1980). The concept of a tourist area cycle of evolution: implications for management of resources. *The Canadian Geographer/Le Géographe Canadien*, *24*(1), 5–12. https://doi.org/10.1111/j.1541-0064.1980.tb00970.x

Butler, R. W. (2019). Tourism carrying capacity research: a perspective article. *Tourism Review*, *75*(1), 207–211. https://doi.org/10.1108/TR-05-2019-0194

Capocchi, A., Vallone, C., Pierotti, M., & Amaduzzi, A. (2019). Overtourism: A literature review to assess implications and future perspectives. *Sustainability*, *11*(12), 3303. https://doi.org/10.3390/su11123303

Celata, F. (2017). La airbnbificazione delle città: gli effetti a Roma tra centro e periferia. Working paper. https://web.uniroma1.it/memotef/sites/default/files/Celata_Airbnbificazione_Roma_2017_0.pdf.

Celata, F. (2020). Come cambieranno le città degli affitti brevi e di Airbnb dopo la pandemia. Che-fare.com. https://www.che-fare.com/celata-citta-affitti-piattaforme-pandemia/

Cocola-Gant, A. (2016). Holiday rentals: The new gentrification battlefront. *Sociological Research Online*, *21*(3), 112–119. https://doi.org/10.5153/sro.4071

Cocola-Gant, A., & Gago, A. (2019). Airbnb, buy-to-let investment and tourism-driven displacement: A case study in Lisbon. *Environment and Planning A: Economy and Space*, *0*(0) 1–18 https://doi.org/10.1177/0308518X19869012

Colomb, C., & Novy, J. (2016). *Protest and resistance in the tourist city*. Routledge. https://doi.org/10.4324/9781315719306

Diaz-Parra, I., & Jover, J. (2020). Overtourism, place alienation and the right to the city: insights from the historic centre of Seville, Spain. *Journal of Sustainable Tourism*, online first.DOI: 10.1080/09669582.2020.1717504

Dodds, R., & Butler, R. (Eds.). (2019). *Overtourism: Issues, realities and solutions*. De Gruyter Oldenbourg. https://doi.org/10.1515/9783110607369

Doxey, G. (1975). A Causation Theory of Visitor–Resident Irritants: Methodology and Research Inferences. In *The Travel Research Association Conference* (Vol. 6, pp.195–198). The Travel Research Association.

Ferreri, M., & Sanyal, R. (2018). Platform economies and urban planning: Airbnb and regulated deregulation in London. *Urban Studies*, *55*(15), 3353–3368. https://doi.org/10.1177/0042098017751982

Goodwin, H. (2017). The challenge of overtourism. Responsible Tourism Partnership Working Paper 4, October 2017.

Gurran, N., & Phibbs, P. (2017). When tourists move in: how should urban planners respond to Airbnb? *Journal of the American Planning Association*, *83*(1), 80–92. https://doi.org/10.1080/01944363.2016.1249011

Gutiérrez, J., García-Palomares, J. C., Romanillos, G., & Salas-Olmedo, M. H. (2017). The eruption of Airbnb in tourist cities: Comparing spatial patterns of hotels and peer-to-peer accommodation in Barcelona. *Tourism Management*, *62*, 278–291. https://doi.org/10.1016/j.tourman.2017.05.003

Guttentag, D. (2019). Progress on Airbnb: a literature review. *Journal of Hospitality and Tourism Technology*, *10*(4), 814–844. https://doi.org/10.1108/JHTT-08-2018-0075

Gyòdi, K. (2017). Airbnb and the hotel industry in Warsaw: an example of the sharing economy?. *Central European Economic Journal*, *2*, 23–34. https://doi.org/10.1515/ceej-2017-0007

Hughes, N. (2018). Tourists go home': anti-tourism industry protest in Barcelona. *Social Movement Studies*, *17*(4), 471–477. https://doi.org/10.1080/14742837.2018.1468244

Ioannides, D., Röslmaier, M., & Van der Zee, E. (2019). Airbnb as an instigator of 'tourism bubble' expansion in Utrecht's Lombok neighbourhood. *Tourism Geographies*, *21*(5), 822–840. https://doi.org/10.1080/14616688.2018.1454505

Jiang, B. (2015). The fractal nature of maps and mapping. *International Journal of Geographical Information Science*, *29*(1), 159–174. https://doi.org/10.1080/13658816.2014.953165

Jiang, B., & Miao, Y. (2015). The evolution of natural cities from the perspective of location-based social media. *The Professional Geographer*, *67*(2), 295–306. https://doi.org/10.1080/00330124.2014.968886

Jover, J., & Díaz-Parra, I. (2019). Gentrification, transnational gentrification and touristification in Seville, Spain. *Urban Studies*. online first. https://doi.org/10.1177/0042098019857585

Koens, K., Postma, A., & Papp, B. (2018). Is overtourism overused? Understanding the impact of tourism in a city context. *Sustainability*, *10*(12), 4384. https://doi.org/10.3390/su10124384

Milano, C., Novelli, M., & Cheer, J. M. (2019). Overtourism and degrowth: a social movements perspective. *Journal of Sustainable Tourism*, *27*(12), 1857–1875. https://doi.org/10.1080/09669582.2019.1650054

Oklevik, O., Gössling, S., Hall, C. M., Jacobsen, J. K., Grøtte, I., & McCabe, S. (2019). Overtourism, optimisation, and destination performance indicators: A case study of activities in Fjord Norway. *Journal of Sustainable Tourism*, *27*(12), 1804–1824. https://doi.org/10.1080/09669582.2018.1533020

Papathanassis, A. (2017). Over-tourism and anti-tourist sentiment: An exploratory analysis and discussion. *Ovidius" University Annals, Economic Sciences Series*, *XVII*(2), 288–293. https://EconPapers.repec.org/RePEc:ovi:oviste:v:xvii:y:2017:i:2:p:288-293.

Peeters, P., Gössling, S., Klijs, J., Milano, C., Novelli, M., Dijkmans, C., Mitas, O. (2018). Overtourism: Impact and possible policy responses, Research for TRAN Committee. European Parliament, Brussels, Belgium. http://www.europarl.europa.eu/thinktank/en/document.html?reference=IPOL_STU(2018)629184.

Phi, G. T. (2019). Framing overtourism: a critical news media analysis. *Current Issues in Tourism*, 1–5. https://doi.org/10.1080/13683500.2019.1618249

Picascia, S., Romano, A., & Teobaldi, M. (2017). *The* airification of cities: making sense of the impact of peer to peer short term letting on urban functions and economy. In Proceedings of the Annual Congress of the Association of European Schools of Planning, Lisbon. (pp. 2212–2223). ISBN: 978-989-99801-3-6.

Saarinen, J. (2006). Traditions of sustainability in tourism studies. *Annals of Tourism Research*, *33*(4), 1121–1140. https://doi.org/10.1016/j.annals.2006.06.007

Seidl, I., & Tisdell, C. A. (1999). Carrying capacity reconsidered: from Malthus' population theory to cultural carrying capacity. *Ecological Economics*, *31*(3), 395–408. https://doi.org/10.1016/S0921-8009(99)00063-4

Sequera, J., & Nofre, J. (2018). Shaken, not stirred: New debates on touristification and the limits of gentrification. *City*, *22*(5-6), 843–855. https://doi.org/10.1080/13604813.2018.1548819

Smith, M. K., Egedy, T., Csizmady, A., Jancsik, A., Olt, G., & Michalkó, G. (2018). Non-planning and tourism consumption in Budapest's inner city. *Tourism Geographies*, *20*(3), 524–548. https://doi.org/10.1080/14616688.2017.1387809

Sonnino, E., Bertino, S., Casacchia, O., Crisci, M., D'Orio, G., & Rosati, R. (2011). *Popolazione e previsioni demografiche nei municipi di Roma Capitale. Dinamiche attuali e prospettive fino al 2024.*, Gangemi.

UNWTO (2018). *Overtourism'? Understanding and managing urban tourism growth beyond perceptions*. UNWTO. https://doi.org/10.18111/9789284420070

Wachsmuth, D., & Weisler, A. (2018). Airbnb and the rent gap: Gentrification through the sharing economy. *Environment and Planning A: Economy and Space*, *50*(6), 1147–1170. https://doi.org/10.1177/0308518X18778038

Wall, G. (2019). *Perspectives on the environment and overtourism*. In R. Dodds & R. Butler (Eds.), *Overtourism* (pp. 27–45). De Gruyter Oldenbourg.

Wall, G. (2020). From carrying capacity to overtourism: a perspective article. *Tourism Review*, *75*(1), 212–215. ahead of print. https://doi.org/10.1108/TR-08-2019-0356

Wegmann, J., & Jiao, J. (2017). Taming Airbnb: Toward guiding principles for local regulation of urban vacation rentals based on empirical results from five US cities. *Land Use Policy*, *69*, 494–501. https://doi.org/10.1016/j.landusepol.2017.09.025

Wei, Y., Huang, C., Lam, P. T., & Yuan, Z. (2015). Sustainable urban development: A review on urban carrying capacity assessment. *Habitat International*, *46*, 64–71. https://doi.org/10.1016/j.habitatint.2014.10.015

Venice as a *short-term city*: between global trends and local lock-ins

Giacomo-Maria Salerno (iD) and Antonio Paolo Russo (iD)

ABSTRACT

This paper examines the ongoing transition of Venice towards a *short-term city*, posited as an urban form which accommodates the dwelling practices of temporary populations as tourists, at the expenses of a stable resident population. This shift is approached through the conceptual framework of resilience, which is also explored in its political and discursive dimensions. At the base of the emergence of a short-term city, we analyse the redistributive impacts of short-term rentals mediated by digital platforms and their influence on the housing market, but also the related entrenchments of a local policy agenda supporting the resilience of the industry itself above that of the city as a living organism. After illustrating the development of the hospitality sector in the city fabric over the last four decades and presenting the historical challenges that Venice has been facing in regard to its capacity to retain a stable population, we seek to unravel the debate on 'the future of Venice', which confronts local and global agents defending a 'conservationist' approach for Venice as an ineluctably tourist city, with social actors who claim for the defence of residence – and therefore for a ban on STR – as a necessary condition for a socially resilient alternative.

Introduction

The rise of 'platform capitalism' (Srnicek, 2017) and its articulation in the hospitality sector as platform-mediated short-term rentals (henceforth: STR) may well be the last critical nudge for Venice towards a destiny of city without residents, or, as we propose in this paper, a *short-term city*. One of the most attractive destinations worldwide, and iconized in the popular global imagery well before the XX century (Davis & Marvin, 2004), Venice has grown increasingly dependent on tourism at least since the late 1970s, when the proliferation of hotels and tourist services started to flank the progressive loss of economic functions, with regulations and policy regimes eventually adapting and favouring such changes. While the increased orientation towards the visitor economy and the progressive intensification of the use of space by visitors (Indovina, 1988) has gone hand-in-hand with processes of displacement of the resident population, marking a steady erosion of the city's social mass (Costa & Martinotti, 2003; De Rita, 1993; Fregolent & Vettoretto, 2017; Minoia, 2017; Russo, 2002a), the uptake of the housing market by

STR since the early 2010 has driven the domain of tourist commodification to an unprecedented scale.

For decades, the debate on the 'future of Venice' has been prominent in society and institutions at state, regional and local level. Yet the policies implemented have mainly been in the realm of physical conservation, and in 2020 the future of Venice as a living city looks dimmer than ever. Submerged by tourism and simultaneously becoming more vulnerable and dependent by the day, the question as to whether it will also remain attractive, and at what cost for a resident population, has been risen by several scholars (e.g. Seraphin et al., 2018), but also by the public opinion locally and globally. This reflection becomes even more relevant in the wake of the abrupt downsizing of tourism activity provoked by COVID-19. Contrasting with the bleak figures on losses in the tourism sector (13,2 million visitors, 3 billion Euros of turnover and 26,000 jobs lost with respect to 2019), commentators have been surprisingly reporting the momentary relief from tourism pressure that has been enjoyed by the Venetian population during the first part of the high season of 2020 (Momigliano, 2020). This paradoxical situation has revamped the debate on the future of Venice and its tourism, and is also likely to shape the post-COVID debate, when, as in other places, advocates of full recovery and the global agencies that will push in that direction will be faced with mounting arguments in favour of reforms towards greater resilience (Gössling et al., 2021).

Venice has been noted as an early – and epitomic – case of what has recently come to be called 'overtourism' (Milano et al., 2019a), denoting not only a strong and increasing tourism pressure on destination spaces, but most significantly the magnitude of its environmental and social effects, the most remarkable of which are possibly the unaffordability of housing for residents and for the very workers of the tourism industry. Such issues have been noted in Venice for a very long time (at least since the seminal report COSES 1979), and Venice has frequently been described as 'worst case scenario' in the tourism planning literature. Yet it could be argued that the situation of Venice realigns with many other overtouristed cities where the 'touristification of housing', through the conversion of a substantial part of the city's residential stock to short-term vacational rentals, is considered a critical factor of acceleration and extension of the disruptions produced by tourism. The burgeoning literature on the impacts of STR hints at the shrinking of affordable housing supply, the rise of rents, and the associated interrelated processes of capital concentration and exclusion and displacement (Barron et al., 2017; Celata et al., 2017; Cocola-Gant & Gago, 2019; Lee, 2016; Wachsmuth et al., 2017; Wachsmuth & Weisler, 2018). All this is happening in Venice, only at a possibly grander scale and in the context of a six-decade struggle for its very survival in an extremely delicate ecosystem – fragile, expensive, and increasingly marginal from a political, economic and cultural perspective.

The scholarly and societal debate on Venice's overtourism has been focusing on other – certainly relevant – aspects, such as the endogenous transformation of the tourist marketplace towards low quality (Caserta & Russo, 2002), the impacts of cruise tourism (Vianello, 2016), or the regional scale of tourism activity and the differential and interrelated impacts of overnight stayers and excursionists (Costa & Van Der Borg, 1988; Russo, 2002b). Yet the degree at which STR have been taking over Venice's housing market calls for a fresh examination of the effects that this is having on the city – and may have in the long run – and of the opposing positions in the debate on whether this form of accommodation should be regulated, how, and of the alternative visions on the future of Venice as a city with a resident population. In this sense, the peculiarity of Venice's territorial conformation, in which the modern urban expansion of the city remains physically separated from the insular historical (and tourist) core, requires a specific understanding of how the intersection between a long-standing tourist saturation and the new frontiers of platform capitalism represented by STR could lead to the risk of collapse of the city's capacity of social reproduction, envisaging the emergence of what could be called a *short-term city*.

In this paper, we are introducing this term as an analytical dimension of urban change which may tie into the resilience debate. By short-term city we denote an urban form that is not any-more anchored to - and dependent on – a resident population: it reorients to the transits and dwelling practices of a *transient* population like short term-visitors, while the mass of the *stable* population shrinks. The case of Venice provides insights on how these two dynamics may be interrelated, looking at historical lock-ins as well at causal relations. In this sense, we posit the emergence of the short-term city as a specific effect of overtourism, based on a housing market increasingly geared on the practices and affordabilities of a population of transient dwellers. Ultimately, we seek to contribute to the wider debate on *place resilience* taking in the dimension of tourism mobilities and temporary uses. Are short-term cities resilient? Or are these two charac-teristics inherently in opposition? How can this question be framed in the scholarly debate on place resilience, sustainable tourism and overtourism, and how does the case of Venice pre-sented here illuminate on such issues?

Place resilience, a concept derived from disaster studies and challenging the approach based on sustainability in the analysis of the transformation of socio-economic systems (Mehmood, 2016; Vale & Campanella, 2005), seems particularly adequate in providing a conceptual frame-work of reference for the short-term city, even more so in pandemic times. Beyond the efforts to emancipate resilience from emergency planning towards a progressive and evolutionary perspec-tive (Davoudi et al., 2012), shock situations as the Covid-19 outbreak may highlight to a greater extent the unsustainability inscribed in the pre-disaster conditions. Moreover, a resilience frame-work could be a better way to embrace the political dimension of place transformations: firstly, because resilience studies are progressively turning from the bounce-back-ability of the exam-ined system to its capacity of 'bouncing forward' to a more sustainable state (Shaw, 2012), ques-tioning and challenging the "profound inequality" on which the previous state was built upon (Vale, 2014); secondly, because the hegemonic struggle between different groups for the defin-ition of resilience criteria (Paidakaki & Moulaert, 2017a, 2017b) nuances a 'politics of resilience', in which it is key to unravel implicit answers to questions such as "who counts as 'the city'? (And who decides who counts as 'the city'?)" (Vale, 2014, p. 197), or "resilience for whom and against what?" (ibid, p. 191).

This approach paves the way to a transformative use of the resilience concept, disentangling it from a dominant neoliberal semantisation and reframing it in a *right to the city* perspective (Meriläinen et al., 2020), as *subversive resilience* (Grove, 2013). In the specific field of tourism stud-ies, the concept of resilience has largely focused on the capacity of recovery of the tourism industry in the aftermath of catastrophic events (Lew, 2014). Our interest in place resilience refers, instead, to the capacity of the urban organism that is a tourist destination to reproduce itself socially, while evolving towards conditions of spatial and social justice. This, we claim, is at stake in the context of the tourist monoculture in which Venice seems trapped (Salerno, 2020), an overspecialisation that - as we argue in this paper – extends critically to housing as key resource for social reproduction. It has indeed been shown that resilience is threatened "within social systems that are dependent on a single ecosystem or single resource" (Adger, 2000, p. 350), and in this regard Venetian tourist monoculture is no exception (Cristiano & Gonella, 2020). Moreover, hazardous resource dependency is not the only reason for which touristification could be seen as a threat to resilience, if the latter is not understood within a neo-liberal framework but comprehends justice as one of its key features (Davoudi et al., 2012). Economic and demo-graphic aspects such as uneven distributional effects in terms of income or population displace-ment processes, could be interpreted *per se* as indicators of the lack or breakdown of resilience (Adger, 2000), even in the absence of catastrophic events.

The structure and methodology of this paper is inductive, seeking to build new general know-ledge from existing empirical evidence. Thus, we first introduce the main coordinates of the debate on the 'future of Venice' and its evolution as an overtouristed destination. We focus on the recent evidence on the reconfiguration of the Venetian real estate market triggered by the rise of STR, examining their 'exceptional' character in relation to previous trends. Although we mostly use secondary sources and data, we interrogate the literature to make sense of such trends and propose an original interpretation. We then discuss the politics underlying the different stages in the construction of Venice as a short-term city, looking at the different positionings and discourses deployed along such evolution, gathered from media pieces and public statements. In the last section, we refer back to the debate on place resilience and (sustainable) destination development, proposing that the case of Venice and its evolution as a short-term city could be considered a 'template' of how overtourism can pose a serious threat to place resilience, and insisting on the existence of alternatives that should orient policy initiatives at different scales. We also engage critically with the Tourism Carrying Capacity analytical approach to set targets for sustainable tourism – but possibly ignoring resilience – and propose instead a 'subversive resilience' policy approach with a key focus on housing use regulations and economic diversification.

The 'tourist destiny' of Venice: from iconisation to socio-spatial stratification

The enmeshment and signification of Venice with its tourism is obviously not new. Already in the 19th century, several classical authors would define Venice as a "visitable past" (James, 1888, p. 31), a place that "scarcely exists any more as a city at all; [a place] that exists only as a battered peep-show and bazaar" (James, 1909, p. 12), "half fairy-tale and half tourist trap" (Mann, 1912, p. 45). The re-production of Venice as *tourist attraction* has been a longstanding process rooted both in the peculiar characteristics of the city (Davis & Marvin, 2004; Salerno, 2020) and in the modern history of urban transformations, marked by dynamics of implosion/explosion and heritagization (Choay, 1996; Lefebvre, 1970). This process may represent an early example of iconisation or Disneyfication of an historical landscape (Cosgrove, 1982), to be tracked down at least to the Romantic period (Bettini, 1978).

The acceleration of the tourist nature of the city could however be situated in the 20th century, when Venice started its modern expansion into the mainland, while the insular historical city (henceforth: HC) became the object of strict conservation intended to preserve its value and maintain its main functions as an international pole of arts, culture and entertainment (Fregolent & Vettoretto, 2017). Indeed, during the last 60 years, Venice's HC has been going through an articulate process of population restructuring by which "poor and low-middle classes [had] no other choice than to move out of the city centre, and possibly become daily commuters involved in *servient* economies exploiting the city landscape" (Minoia, 2017, p. 263). Since the construction of the industrial settlement of Marghera in 1917, the population of the Venetian mainland has been growing steadily, while the population of the HC shrunk to less than a third compared to the post-war period (see left axis of Figure 1, in lines). This evolution nuances a "spatially separated urban society", in which the working and middle classes flee with jobs to the mainland, while insular Venice remains mainly a site of residence for upper class rentiers (Fregolent & Vettoretto, 2017, pp. 83–84). Since the 1960s, this relentless process of depopulation has been tagged in Venetian chronicles as 'the exodus' (Zanardi, 2020), one of the key issues of the so-called "Problem of Venice" (Comune di Venezia, 1964).

At the same time, tourist activity in the city increased constantly (see right axis of Figure 1, in columns). Zannini (2014) identifies two main phases of tourism growth in Venice in the 20th century: the former, from the post-war period to the 1980s, consists of an élite market developing into proper mass tourism (with a constant growth of arrivals from a total 1,669,000 in 1952 to the 4,389,000 of 1992). The latter stage – from the 1990s to present days – is characterized by the rise of global 'postmodern' tourism trends, by national and local easing on urban regulations, and by the simultaneous decline of Marghera's industrial strength. In this stage, the growth curve undergoes a further surge (Barbiani & Zanon, 2004), reaching the most recent official

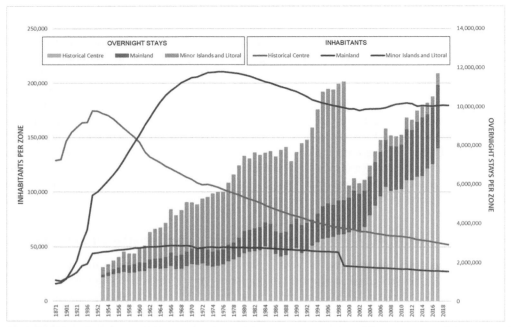

Figure 1. Evolution of inhabitants (1871–2019) and overnight stays (1953–2017) in different sections of the Municipality of Venice.[1]

estimation of around 28 million visitors a year (30 million for Lanapoppi, 2015), an 80% of which are day visitors, a trend which is "decisively upwards" (Van Der Borg, 2017, p. 15). This quantity of visitors pouring into the city yields an average visitors-per-resident/day ratio of more than 1.5, or, in other words, "500 visitors per year for each resident of the 750 hectares of the historical urban fabric" (Fabbri et al., 2020, p. 41).

Venice's everyday scenario, then, goes far beyond the Tourist Carrying Capacity (henceforth: TCC) threshold identified by Costa and Van Der Borg (1988), who fixed in 20,750 visitors per day the maximum tolerance of Venice's services, subdivided into 13,000 overnight stays and less than 8,000 day visits, for a total of around 7.5 million yearly presences in the HC. That limit that was surpassed for two thirds of the days in the year then, and it is widely surpassed almost any day of the year today, when daily presences of visitors average around 80,000. The TCC approach has conceptual and empirical limitations as a target for a resilient city, as will be discussed below. However, this situation can certainly be defined as an over- or hyper-tourism scenario, which Costa and Martinotti (2003, p. 61) identified in socio-demographic terms as one in which the use of the city by visitors exceeds that of residents, defining it as a site of predominant tourist consumption. This definition of a hyper-tourist city is echoed by that given, with a more elastic formulation, by D'Eramo, who argues that the threshold that "separates a tourist city from a city that also lives on tourism" is the one that marks the passage from a situation in which "tourists benefit from services and facilities designed for residents", and one in which "residents are forced to use services designed for tourists" (D'Eramo 2017, p. 72).

From this point of view, the situation of Venice would seem to swing dangerously on the edge of the "transition phase" (ibid.) from a proper urban organism to a wholly *touristified* space. Referring back to the resilience literature, continuous incremental change has brought the city to the brink of a qualitative shift (Lew, 2014) after which it is no longer perceived by a part of its residents as belonging to them, but more as "a simulacrum of an inhabitable space that no longer exists" (De Rita, 1993). This argument reflects the debate on the loss of sense of place (Davidson & Lees, 2010) for the local community when space adapts to other uses and market forces. This is particularly evident in relation to commercial activities, which are radically reorienting their offer and image to the transient visitor demand (Gheno, 2016; Russo, 2002a) to the detriment of proximity commerce, a process encouraged by national liberalization laws (the so called Bersani law of 2006). The earnings required to cover the costs of renting and running a shop in the HC make it impossible to cater for the everyday necessities of the few remaining inhabitants (Scheppe et al. 2009). The whole economic fabric of the city then faces a metamorphic wave by which "every store that sell stationery, hardware, groceries and the like, is being converted into a uniform space offering fake Murano glass or imitations of Carnival masks" (ibid, p. 290). This further reduces the opportunities and affordability of everyday routines for residents, whose 'reaction tactics' range from drawing increasingly out of the most congested areas (Quinn, 2007) to abandon the city altogether, reproducing the 'exodus'.

To summarize, Venice could be considered a school case for overtourism, in which the presence of visitors "invades, suffocates and distorts the physical city and overturns the very life of its inhabitants" (Fabbri et al., 2020, p. 41). In the next section, we will then discuss how the impact of platform capitalism on Venetian housing market has strongly worsened an already deteriorated situation.

From the 'hotelisation' of the city to the touristification of housing

To reconstruct the role that the affirmation of short-term rentals as dwelling modality in in Venice may have played in the emergence of the short-term city, we will situate these trends against the broader dynamics of the hospitality sector and of the housing market.

At the turn of the XX century, Venice already hosted a substantial number of hotels and boarding houses (Bernardello, 2002; Zannini, 2002). As the data on overnight stays presented in the previous section suggest, the supply of accommodation has been growing steadily during the post-war expansion and the consolidation of Venice as a mass-tourism destination since the 1970s. This growth has gone through different stages. Until the end of the 1990s, planning regulations on land uses and hospitality prevented expanding the supply in the hotel sector beyond a limit of 11,000 bedplaces, while housing rentals for short periods, or for rooms, were strictly regulated. In 1997, an amendment to the planning regulations for the HC gave way to a substantial number of conversions from residential to tourist use; in the same period, the cap on hotel bedplaces offered in the HC was progressively released. In the verge of a few years, the supply increased by 30% in the HC, reaching in 2003 the number of 16,650 beds in hotels and 2,500 new bedplaces in 'other forms of accommodation' (Barbiani & Zanon, 2004, p. 9). Yet these figures are quite small compared with the most recent ones: in the first decade of the 2000s, the number of establishments was tripled, introducing around 10,000 new bedplaces in the market; the main driver of this growth is the non-hotel sector, whose establishments multiplied by 10 in 8 years (COSES 2009a, p. 47). This extraordinary expansion reflects a new global trend in the hospitality industry, in which the non-hotel sector has been taking advantage of deregulation policies and of the extension of internet as a commercialisation channel.

Even before the appearance of STR, the housing market was already strongly bent on Venice's tourist appeal. In 2007, one of three houses was bought by a foreigner. The attractiveness of real estate for international buyers, collecting second homes as prestige acquisitions used for a few weekends a year, ties the Venetian housing market to global rather than local trends, dominated by corporate agents, with prices that rarely drop (Scheppe et al. 2009). Furthermore, especially after the austerity turn in European policy, a consistent share of the property owned by the public sector, including buildings of historical value and popular housing, started being liquidated on the private market to meet the financial needs of local, regional and state institutions, and are frequently re-functionalized into tourist facilities as hotels and restaurants (Salerno, 2019). This process occurs both in the HC and in the lagoon, where minor islands

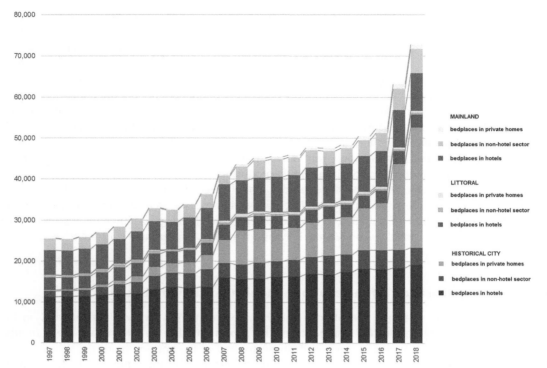

Figure 2. Evolution of accommodation supply in different sections of the Muncipality of Venice and by typology. Source: Alice Corona for OCIO (2020b) on data provided by Regione Veneto – Ufficio Statistica.

seems to have no other perspective of salvation from abandonment than being transformed into luxury resorts (Salerno, 2015). Those complementary elements, then, further illustrates how the ever-increasing tourism pressure reinforces the recursive loops by which touristification keeps growing towards monoculture (Cristiano & Gonella, 2020) and urban rent "become the key driver of the local economy" (Fabbri et al., 2020, p.44).

The emergence and affirmation of STR platforms like Airbnb took these trends to the next level (see Figure 2). After a first period of introduction of the platforms (2010–2015), the growth of non-hotel supply accelerated, leading to the boom of the very last years. It is estimated by OCIO – a recently founded "grassroots civic watchdog on housing" – that between 2016 and 2018, 18,600 new tourist bedplaces have appeared in the HC, equalling the growth of the previous 15 years; in 2017 alone, the non-hotel supply registered a growth of 44.2% (57.4% in the HC), while the hotel sector increased of only 3% (2% in the HC) (OCIO 2020a, p. 210). The main role in this unprecedented expansion of supply has been played by platform-mediated STR, whose success is also significantly outcompeting other traditional forms of complementary accommodation, such as official B&B and guesthouses, reduced to 9,400 of the total 33,496 non-hotel bedplaces (OCIO 2020b). This process is also accompanied by a sort of "hotelization" of STR themselves, to be intended as the tendency to list each unit in a building on Airbnb and "thereby creating 'cottage hotels'" (Lee, 2016, p. 230), whose appearance in Venice has draw the attention both of independent grassroots organizations (OCIO 2020c) and law enforcements (Fullin, 2020).

The most recent official data published by Comune di Venezia (2017) indicate a total amount of 63,217 beds available in the entire municipality: 30,715 beds in hotels and 32,502 in other forms of accommodation, such as B&B, guesthouses, rooms-to-let and above all apartments in STR regime. Of this total, the vast majority (43,685) are located in the HC (excluding minor islands), including 18,384 hotel beds and 25,301 beds in other forms of accommodation. This scenario is constantly shifting: in February 2020, just before the COVID lockdown, the record was

tourist bedplaces per resident

0.0
0.1
0.5
1.0
5.0
10.0
20.0

Figure 3. Bedplaces in all types of accommodation per inhabitant in Venice's census zones. Source: elaboration by Alice Corona on data provided by Population Register of the City of Venice and accommodation data included in the GeoIDS portal of the City of Venice. Population and bedplaces data refer to June 24, 2020.

of 77,810 bedplaces spread over the entire municipal territory, of which 49,295 in the HC (the 63%, including the 76% of the total number of bedplaces in STR), almost as many as its constantly declining 52,000 residents (OCIO 2020b). This concentration is not surprising, being the HC the traditional core of tourist supply; what actually does catch the attention is the distribution between accommodation types: 2017 marks the first year in which the supply in the non-hotel sector exceeded that of the hotel sector, which, just 20 years earlier, represented the 85% of the total. Moreover, besides the traditional anti-Airbnb public stance of the hotel industry, cases of hoteliers recurring to apartments in STR regime in order to extend their accommodation capacity have been registered (RESET, 2015), even if it is hard to evaluate the numeric significance of the phenomenon due to the unavailability of reliable data on the connection between management and property.

A closer look at the available data, such as in Corona's (2019) work for the independent research platform InsideAirbnb, reveals that in August 2019, 8,907 listings in Venice were advertised on Airbnb, three quarters of which consisted of an entire home or apartment, a growth of 14% over the previous year/month. The spatial distribution of the listings follows that of the overall accommodation supply, with a 76% of the total located in the HC. Corona estimates that the 12% of the housing units in the HC is on offer in Airbnb; the share of this supply that is occupied for more than 60 nights a year, the 46% of all listings, is likely to be removed from the residential market thoroughly. This equates to 3,338 homes in the HC alone. If we put together these different estimates of STR and the hotel data, almost a half of the geography of the HC thus experiences a tourist bedplace-per-inhabitant ratio of at least 1:1 (with areas where this ratio is even higher, up to 51,020 and more bedplaces per inhabitant). With very few low-intensity areas – also comprehensive of non-residential, monumental or infrastructural landcover – the high-intensity zones cover almost the totality of the HC, sketching a geography of what we call the *short-term city* (Figure 3).

Another recent work nuances an even more problematic scenario than that depicted by Corona: using data directly offered by Airbnb itself, De Marchi (2019) calculates a global incidence of Airbnb listings on the housing stock of the HC ranging from 11% to 16%. Airbnb however is not the only STR platform, and considering the supply of platforms such as Homeaway

(3,876, of which 98% entire apartments), Housetrip (1,754 and 96% namely) and Booking.com (2,700 and 83% namely), the incidence of STR prior to the COVID-19 crisis could be even stronger, as – according to the data sourcing agency AirDNA – the offer of those platforms is not completely overlapping with that of Airbnb.

Referring to Zannini's periodization of tourist development quoted above, it could be argued that the current situation may represent a *third phase*, inaugurated by the affirmation of platform capitalism. The boom of STR registered in 2016-2018 could be due in part to a measurement glitch, as more efficient control tools implemented by the administration in order to increase tax revenues may have resulted in the surfacing of a consistent amount of previously 'invisible' rental activity. However, it seems legitimate to affirm that the opening of the housing market to platform-mediated STR has enlarged the domain of tourist commodification to an unprecedented scale, boosting Venice's overtourism situation to a higher level of criticality and posing new fundamental challenges to the city.

Debunking the debate: distributional effects and impacts of STR on the housing market

The 'future of Venice' has been the object of intense debate in the last decades, locally and nationally, but also at international level given the universal historical and artistic value attributed to Venice. In spite of the countless statements, agreements, and publications promoting at least a mitigation of Venice's depopulation trends and environmental degradation, no effective solution to Venice's destiny as a tourist monoculture is in view, even if there seems to be today a certain agreement among social actors that the tourism trends presented in the previous section condemn the city to a bleak future. Yet the social and political landscape has changed radically in the last years, possibly also a sign of the increasing irrelevance of the HC as constituency and of the extreme dependence on tourism of the whole municipality, if not the whole Veneto region. The political turnover in 2015 – confirmed in 2020 – has represented a breakthrough shift for the concerns of the municipal administration. Until then, Venetian policy, which caters for a dynamic city that extends far beyond its insular historical limits, had always kept a close eye on the 'future of Venice' intended as preservation of the HC. However, most policy efforts to retain residents and jobs have met more failures than achievements.

As if this incapacity to revert trends had reached the state of entropy, the new administration has settled on simply monitoring visitor flows and cashing in tourist expenditure. A remarkable example of this new orientation has been the leeway given to the construction of a large stock of new budget accommodation establishments in the Venetian mainland. This might represent an affordable alternative for visitors that would come as excursionists and pay hotel taxes elsewhere; however, in the absence of any regulation on STR, is further enlarging the daily pressure on the HC, exacerbating the boundary – functional and semiotic – between the insular short-term destination and its periphery as 'sleeping quarters'. At the same time, statements of the new major against the residents of the HC who complain about excessive tourism pressure, have brought to light the how the interests of the mainland and of the HC are diverging also in policy discourses (Tantucci, 2016, 2018).

As a counterpart to this subtle 'turn' in policy, a new generation of social movements has taken the struggles for the protection of the lagoon and housing affordability – which characterised grassroots activism in the 1970s and 1980s – to a new level, achieving support even among middle classes and patrimonialistic institutions (Visentin & Bertocchi, 2019). Their campaigns focus on tourism growth as the cornerstone of the many disruptions that threatens the social and environmental survival of the city, directly questioning the 'tourist destiny' of Venice as antithetical to a liveable and lived city. Their analyses and campaigns are aligned with those of the expanding international activist movements against touristification (Milano et al., 2019b), to which local collectives have contributed since the foundation of the SET Network – Southern Europe against Touristification (Borelli, 2019; Gainsforth, 2019; Pardo & Gómez, 2019). Their main claims concern housing rights, the transformation of local commerce, the saturation of public space and transports, precarious employment and environmental issues related to the relentless growth of tourism and of the monocultural specialisation of urban destinations (SET 2018).

Many other actors at different scales are also involved in this debate, and most notably the extractive conglomerate that groups global actors like 'platform capitalism' organisations, small investors, large financial corporations, transport companies like cruise companies, and their local filières. Thus, the 'future of Venice' is now more than ever a discursive battleground. This debate has taken on many derivatives. Although we focus in this paper on the effects of STR on population dynamics, the policy implications of this debate go beyond the strict topic of housing use regulations, as they invest more broadly the struggle between rent extraction and urban resilience, of which housing is a key element and stress test (Paidakaki & Moulaert, 2017a, 2017b).

Sharing rhetorics and distributional effects

There is no unanimity on the fact that the trends presented in the previous section represent an actual problem, in Venice or in any other city where the expansion of STR in recent years has substantially transformed the tourism landscape. The digital platforms themselves as Airbnb, from their side, have settled on a redistributive rhetoric, part of their peculiar strategy to deface mounting critiques to the role they are attributed as agents of gentrification and neighbourhood change, proposing instead a socially responsible corporate image through the mobilization of the hosts (Gainsforth, 2019; Sans & Quaglieri Domínguez, 2016). In the specific case of Venice, the company actively intervened in the local political debate by positioning itself as an advocate of sustainable tourism, first of all adhering to the City Council's campaign #EnjoyRespectVenezia with the production and diffusion of a video entitled "Live like a local in Venice", providing nothing more than basic information on the city's accessibility and instructions for waste recycle. In its 'Healthy travel and healthy destinations' report the company also affirmed that in Venice

> crowding has become such an issue that the Mayor has considered limiting access mainly to overnight travellers, with prominent publications listing the city as a place to not visit in 2018. But with Airbnb, local hosts are actively promoting less-trafficked routes and local shops to their overnight guests, helping City Hall in its efforts to attract healthy, sustainable tourism. (Airbnb, 2018, p. 22)

These and other claims, as the fact that Airbnb spreads tourism off the beaten track to the advantage of lower-class areas that are neglected by the mainstream visitor economy, can be debunked with hard data proceeding from a variety of mostly case-study based (see for instance Gutiérrez et al. 2017 or Arias Sans & Quaglieri Domínguez, 2016); our contribution here will be to bring out some evidence for the case of Venice.

More specifically on the topic of the distributional effects, Airbnb's public discourse insists on the fact that unlike corporate hotel chains, hosts on Airbnb keep up to 97% of the posted price to themselves. Hence, a dollar spent on the platform would be the one producing more benefits for the local economy, compared to the 14–36% of "chain travel dollars." They also claim that the "cruise line accommodations are the worst offenders in this exercise," with mostly no positive impact on the host community (Airbnb, 2018, pp. 10–12). However, the redistributive role of the STR platforms is increasingly contested. Not only the owners of valuable assets turn their homes into capital assets to earn rents, and such valuable consumer goods are typically concentrated in a small group of well-off people; but also, the marketplace for such valuable goods is very dynamic and getting concentrated in the hands of multi-proprietors, with a growing share of rental properties acquired by corporations or even rentiers following 'buy to rent' strategies (Cocola-Gant & Gago, 2019).

Table 1. Estimation of rents from different rental profiles and contracts. Source: De Marchi 2019, p. 231).

Rental type	Cannaregio neighbourhood	Castello neighbourhood
STR – typical host	750€	661€
STR – entrepreneurial host	1,117€	1,503€
STR – hotelier host	1,475€	1,968€
Residential contract (3 + 2)	941€	923€
Residential contract (4 + 4)	804€	804€

In the case of the Venetian market, the top 5% hosts by number of listings own the 30% of the total number of listings, and the top 5% hosts by estimated revenue accumulate the 35% of the total revenue stream generated by Airbnb listings in Venice (Corona, 2019). The pretended redistributive effect of the platform is then to be intended as significantly uneven, sharpening the already existing unbalance between tenants, who by definition have no real estate assets to rely on, and landlords: "it takes money to make money", as "with Airbnb, earning requires coming to the market with valuable assets" (Schor, 2017, p. 31). This uneven distribution is in line with the overall situation of the Italian Airbnb market, comparatively analysed in 2017 by Picascia et al. (2017) who look at Gini inequality indexes comparing the distribution of STR property and income distribution. Their study suggests the supposed benefits of the platforms are appropriated very disproportionately by a small number of users. In Venice, like in other 10 of 13 cities included in that study, the growth of the supply of STR has been paralleled by increasing income inequality, from a Gini index of 57 in 2015 to 60 in 2016.

Therefore, the famous Airbnb dollar does not equally land on the local economy, as the revenues are strongly unbalanced towards the top of the pyramid, and besides that they are getting increasingly concentrated in corporate hands. A closer insight on uneven distributional effects of STR in Venice has indeed been recently provided by De Marchi (2019), who compares the revenues of locating a housing unit in the residential or in the tourist market, under different scenarios in relation to the type of contract for the residential rent (formulas defined by the Italian law for the length of rental contracts, such as 3 + 2 years and 4 + 4 years, have different taxation levels) and to the average occupancy rate of tourist rentals. In this second case, three cases have been identified: the so-called "typical host" situation, that of an occasional tourist use with a relatively modest occupation rate (between 15% and 23% days/year); the entrepreneurial host, with an occupancy rate averaging 53%; and the hotelier host, with an occupancy around 70%.

The result of this exercise illustrates that revenues in general are superior with tourist rentals, yet, playing around parameters of costs and taxation schemes, tourist rentals are more advantageous than residential ones only when occupancy levels are superior to 50% (De Marchi, 2019, p. 231). Taking as examples two popular and densely populated neighbourhoods, Castello and Cannaregio, the related estimations offer the results shown in Table 1.

Thus, tourist rentals in both areas are more competitive only at higher occupancy rates, providing a further explanation of why just the 27% of the hosts are non-commercial ('typical') and why, owning the 20% of the property on offer, they make only the 4% of the total revenue generated through platform listings (Corona, 2019). In short, market dynamics push for a professionalization of STR and its management in order to maximize revenues, and this applies also to the case in which there has been an investment to start STR activity. De Marchi (2019, p. 234) calculates that an entrepreneurial tourist location almost halves the amount of time necessary to recover a mortgage investment (in the example of the Castello neighbourhood, 23 years for entrepreneurial hosts, 17 years hotelier hosts, and an average of 40 years for a residential rent), and he clarifies that this is a prudential estimation. Moreover, investments that would be deterred by a high inflationary pressure would otherwise become attainable and may be larger in the case of properties with Airbnb-potential (Aalbers, 2019, p. 6).

This pressure towards professionalization exacerbates the already relevant crowding-out effects, pricing out both the non-commercial host and the resident, and fostering concentration of STR management and property. First of all, the small landlord, who was promised great revenues, is likely to face the choice between becoming a professional entrepreneurial host, or be driven out of the STR market by better performing competitors. Pushing an occasional host to maximize occupancy means that the management of reservation, check-in operations, cleanings and laundry is likely to be outsourced, fostering concentration of management in multi-listing commercial hosts, as noted in much recent research on this topic (e.g. Gil & Sequera, 2020). By doing so, the dynamics of this marketplace pushes towards a situation in which hosts tend to become multi-proprietors, managing something that, rather than 'home sharing', appears to be a distributed hotel network, with rooms decentralized throughout the city, as in Venice, where 27% of the hosts control 63% of the listings (Corona, 2019); a trend not limited to whole apartments but also to room rentals, which in public discourse remains a practice more adherent to the genuine meaning of home-sharing (Quaglieri-Domínguez et al., 2020). Thus, we can identify a sort of second-level crowding-out effect: either the occasional host crowds out a resident by converting a residential unit in a *de facto* hotel, or he gets crowded out by more professionalised competitors who can further concentrate property through acquisition investments. As suggested for instance by Frenken and Schor (2017) or Yrigoy (2019), these trends uncover questions of class (already well-off home owners will profit most) but also the overarching power of mobile dwelling, determining an uneven negotiation for home – a 'mooring' device – at the cost of 'stable' populations (López-Gay et al., 2020).

Price escalation and crowding-out

Obviously, the related impacts of STR on the residential housing market are equally unmentioned by the platform campaigns. Several studies conducted in different territorial contexts (Cocola-Gant & Gago, 2019, García-López et al., 2020; Lee, 2016; Wachsmuth et al., 2017; Wachsmuth & Weisler, 2018) highlight how the housing market becomes increasingly unaffordable to long-term residents under the pull of STR. As a growing number of housing units is subtracted from residential market and converted to tourism use, long-term tenants are increasingly crowded out, as they are "no longer bidding against the local residential rent price, but instead against the extra profit that STRs can bring" (Lee, 2016, p. 238). Besides, housing market exclusion in high-intensity STR areas (such as most historical cores in European urban destinations) is also related to non-economic factors, as the conflicts arising to the mixed tourist and residential uses of buildings and surrounding public spaces, or the erosion of the support systems for everyday life such as gentrifying commercial supply or social networks (López-Gay et al., 2020). So the tendency towards "hotelization" and realization of "cottage hotels" is reinforced by a snowball effect as the conversion of residential units to STR increase the displacement pressure on other tenants (Cocola-Gant & Gago, 2019), further reducing the housing supply and the overall resilience of the housing system in a loop of "self-destroying feedbacks" (Cristiano & Gonella, 2020, p. 10).

Yet, in Venice as elsewhere, these critiques to the 'airbnbization' of cities are not universally recognized. For example, De Marchi argues that the incidence of STR in the housing stock replicates cadastral surveys on empty dwellings, nuancing a potential positive impact of *sharing accommodation* on the use of idle residential spaces (De Marchi, 2019, p. 229). In fact, Venice counted around 10% of empty housing units before the rise of STR, a percentage – the highest among all Italian regional capitals – that is easily explained by the very high maintenance costs. Hence, STR allegedly had the effect of 'filling the voids' in a strongly under-utilised urban fabric, providing an incentive for valorising property otherwise not rehabilitated. More in general, agents who benefit from the visitor economy (like ABBAV, the association of hosts and property managers) deny the correlation between growth or STR and depopulation by claiming that the exodus began long before the rise of non-hotel accommodations or the more recent affirmation of platform hospitality. In their view, STR are a virtuous way not only to valorise and maintain idle assets (i.e. abandoned or empty residential units) but also to create 'local' jobs to sustain the city economy (Dianese, 2020). To make this position more explicit, ABBAV hijacked in 2019 a slogan of the Venetian social movements, *"mi no vado via"* ("I will not leave") by reformulating it in "anca mi no vado via" ("I will not leave either"), suggesting that tourism rentals were allowing more Venetian residents to stay put in front of a strong gentrification pressure. For their part, grassroots movements contested these claims as unprovable and misleading (OCIO 2019), and several arguments can be moved against the proprietors assertions.

For instance, there is little doubt that the depopulation of Venice started well before the appearance of STR platforms, but it could be argued that if the same exodus is related to more complex urban dynamics occurred during the 20th century (zoning policies, suburbanization, new housing standards, demographics), the tourist specialization of the city is definitely part of those dynamics. While a proper examination of the relation between the growing tourist arrivals in the city and population loss of the HC (COSES 2009a) came to the conclusion that there was no direct causation, apparently supporting ABBAV's thesis, this study did not have the chance to consider the impact of STR after 2010 and the related challenges on housing affordability. Besides, it recognized that it remains to be questioned "how much of this property stock would have remained unused without tourism (or at more accessible market prices)" (ibid, 50); thirdly, it acknowledged that "the part of the real estate stock intended for residential use 'freed' by the resident population (...) was promptly reused for contested purposes (ibid.). Hence, if tourist reconversions, in a first stage, could have effectively just 'filled the voids', they may have become a hindrance to residential uses in a later stage when STR were came to be boosted by platform intermediation and professionalised through a concentration of property. In the first place, by making the available stock for medium- or long-term rents scarcer, and thus raising its cost (Lee, 2016; Yrigoy, 2019); secondly, by favouring evictions, as argued by Fava (2018) and targeted by grassroots social movements through denounce and direct action (Ghiglione, 2018; Rossi, 2018).

The emerging problem of crowding out of residents specifically due to the competition with STR, noted by De Marchi (2019) in his albeit prudent work, is also expanding to another segment of the market which presented in the past large speculative opportunities for landlords, such as student accommodation. This represents an additional threat for the social reproduction of the city. The student population at the two local universities, of which 8,000 (15% of which were foreigners) were estimated to reside in the city during their studies (COSES, 2009b), has been identified as an antidote to the specialisation towards the low-end of tourism market and to ageing and depopulation processes (Russo & Arias Sans, 2009). After a period dating approximately from the mid-1990s in which the opening of new student residences in the HC and housing renewal programs were starting to attract a younger population of 'cultural consumers' to reside in the city and to retain a sizable share of people formed in Venice, evidence shows that the 4-10% increase in rental prices registered in 2017 and the intensification of tourism pressure through STR has started to force young people to the mainland (Fava, 2018), as they would do before the 1990s, when the strongly regulated room rental market was unaffordable for many. Once considered themselves gentrifiers, now students are being gentrified out of the city – but with much direr consequences in terms of the social fabric of the city, as skilled human capital loses any chance to 'make roots' and turn into social capital that will keep the city alive in the future.

A last important impact of STR on the housing market concerns the buying and selling dynamics. As we have seen, inoccupancy is a strong feature of Venetian housing stock, where "to the amount of unused units (19%) a likewise quantity of houses occupied by non-residents must be added, thus releasing about 40% of housings from conditions of ordinary residential dwelling" (Fava, 2018). Nevertheless, in the context of STR the notion of emptiness is not immediate nor neutral, being possible that some of this empty units are relocated in the tourist market, a possibility that the emergence of platform STR has widely facilitated. If, for example, "a person were to buy a second home and rent it out to tourists permanently, that constitutes running a commercial lodging site, such as a B&B or hotel" (Frenken & Schor, 2017, p. 5), filling the voids of residents with temporary visitors. As it can be seen by real estate market reports, just "a 26.5% of home are bought for a first-home residential purpose, while respectively 26% and 29% are destined to investment and second home" (Fava, 2018). The Engel and Völkers (2019) market report states that the high demand from international buyers

ensures stability in the growth of the Venetian real estate market. The international customers who decide to buy a house in Venice make up about 70% of sales. (...) With a percentage of around 75%, the market is characterized by customers who buy second homes to be used for investments, guaranteeing an excellent economic income often deriving from tourist rentals (8-10% gross). (Engel & Völkers, 2019, p. 18)

If on the other hand "only a quarter of buyers decide to buy a residential property in Venice for private use" (ibidem), it becomes clear that the new possibilities offered by the STR is also changing the second homes market, opening these traditional luxury acquisitions to the opportunity of a quick return on investment. Thanks to these new opportunities, corporations and individual investors increasingly use cities like Venice "as 'safe deposit box', a place to store their excess capital safely" (Aalbers, 2019, p. 6), giving place to a sort of generalized *flat grabbing*.

To conclude this section, the data presented here should support the claims that also in the Venetian case platform-mediated STR leads to "negative externalities in neighbourhoods and to shortages and rising prices in the long-term housing rental market", as recognized also by a report from the Joint Research Centre of the European Commission (Codagnone et al., 2016, p. 34). Despite the platform's attempts to be recognized as a positive actor in enhancing destinations sustainability, and the efforts of agents at multiple scales, from small-scale investors to corporate speculators and their local professional filières offering services to STR. advocating for this model, its growth is menacing the social fabric of cities, and Venice is no exception. To put it short, as Inside Airbnb's founder wrote, "Airbnb claim they are disrupting the hotel industry, when they are really disrupting the housing market" (Cox, 2017, p. 11).

Final reflections and recommendations

The trends presented in the above sections, involving material and socioeconomic transformations of the city, may be interpreted as a third phase of its tourism development trajectory, the ongoing realization of a short-term city. This new phase may be interpreted as closely associated with the higher gear that the structural changes of the contemporary globalized economy and rent extraction strategies have imposed on urban dynamics worldwide, and specifically transnational gentrification and the real estate market restructuring driven by now forms of dwelling 'on the move' (López-Gay et al., 2020; Sequera & Nofre, 2018; Sigler & Wachsmuth, 2016). Venice, as an international pole of attraction for leisure, culture and tourism activities, proved to be particularly exposed to this processes, with Airbnb and other STR platforms playing a key role in it, as they shift "the 'highest and best use' of residential housing" to tourist functions in order to realise rent gaps (Wachsmuth & Weisler, 2018, p. 7). The geographical configuration of the city, where the physical separation of its insular tourist core from the productive socioeconomic landscape of the mainland accentuates a social stratification, is arguably a further element to explain the dimensions of this drift.

However, our presentation has highlighted that the case Venice offers insights for reflection also in terms of its 'capacity to respond' as part of a resilience strategy, showing that the socioeconomic changes it has been exposed to for a long time also have been paralleled by fundamental shifts in its political and discursive landscape. In fact, the current Venetian policy debate on overtourism seems outdated and the policies implemented or being discussed totally inadequate to tackle the global drivers that are pushing Venetians out of their city. The current municipal administration is apparently not taking such threats seriously. While its management approach combines a very basic promotion strategy with rhetoric claims on urban decorum, reflected by the #EnjoyRespectVenezia campaign, other measures – like the continuously postponed adoption of the so-called 'access contribution' (an entry fee to the city, which should put a brake especially on 'bite and run' visits and levy some extra resources for conservation), or the much less ambitious 'revolving doors' access system occasionally put up to divert and spread out the incoming crowds, hardly address any of the challenges related to the residential market and the crowding out of locals. These policy attempts have also been noted to be very problematic in terms of equity and implementation costs (Salerno, 2018), let alone producing a dangerous semantic shift in the common perception of Venice from living urban entity to tourist compound, whose access can be controlled and charged for (see Arias Sans & Russo, 2016, for an analogue critique).

This approach and the narrative of it that is aired through the media, rather than distancing from the TCC concept (as proposed by Fabbri et al., 2020) seems to look at it from a merely technical perspective, without considering the broader social sustainability and resilience implications. In this sense, the operationalisation of the TCC from a socioeconomic perspective (as in Costa & Van Der Borg, 1988), whose target function is to maximize tourist revenues, controls for the negative externalities just inasmuch as they produce diseconomies for the tourist industry itself. It is then unsurprising that the consensus, hegemonic at least since the 1990s, that "what should be avoided at all costs is putting an explicit cap on the development of tourist accommodation, as Amsterdam and Barcelona are currently considering" (Van Der Borg et al., 2020, p. 13), is not at odds with the TCC policy target. It is claimed that capping or regulating supply in the HC would just "boost excursionism", seen as the worst performing mode of visiting the city; for the same reason "also the introduction of a tax on overnight stays (...) should be reconsidered. A tax on all the movements to and from the HC should take its place" (ibidem), sustaining by this means the model of a theme-park oriented urbanism, in which the access to the city is subject to pricing regulations.

Indeed, it can be noted that Van Der Borg himself in recent works has revised upwards the TCC threshold to 14 million (Van Der Borg, 2017) and again to 19 million visitors per year (Van Der Borg et al., 2020), taking in the calculus the extension of the local accommodation supply. These upwards revisions of the carrying capacity threshold, in a moment in which almost all social actors agree on the fact that the housing crisis threatens the very future of residence in the city, cast more than a doubt on the very aptness on the TCC framework to function as a policy target for a resilient city. This very author, in fact, claims that the TCC threshold is "a quantitative formulation of the original problem of how many tourists a destination can bear without compromising the quality of the tourist experience" (Van Der Borg et al., 2020). In a nutshell, it takes into account just the resilience of the tourist industry and not that of the urban organism, whose possibilities for conservation and reproduction (Russo, 2002a) are highly questionable in such conditions.

Based on the evidence presented in this paper, we believe that this conceptualisation of a 'sustainable tourist flow' and the related strategy (controlling for and taxing excursionism, but giving almost free rein to HC accommodation expansion as well as that of other visitor services such as mobility systems) would not necessarily alleviate overtourism, but definitely turn the city and its social and cultural complexity into a destination-product. Policies insisting on this model would align the definition of urban resilience to the specific resilience of its pro-tourism and pro-growth subjects, i.e. to the needs of what we identified as the extractive conglomerate. To increase the sustainability of the tourism sector and enhance the resilience of the overall urban organism, it should be at the contrary necessary to envision different strategies, with the aim of overcoming the dependency on tourist resource and promoting a "bounce forward" outside the monocultural model. Indeed, one of the necessary foundations of a complex city, sustaining any type of socioeconomic renaissance compensating the dependence on a low value-added and extractivist industry like tourism (or anyway the tourist model Venice has been drifting towards in the last five decades), is residence. And affordable housing, challenged by the rise of STR, is precisely the battlefront which – in spite of the efforts of local grassroots social movements – has received very little attention by the administration, possibly the reflection of a municipal constituency that due to the very dwindling of resident population in the HC is increasingly oriented to reaping short-term rents.

While a regulation project for STR of the national government is stalled from years, and the regional government (whose territory largely 'predates' over destination-Venice as highlighted for instance in Russo, 2002a) is not likely to enforce any hard regulation, in a city where a sizable part of its housing stock is currently on offer in short-term rental platforms it is unlikely that this very social mass will support such decision. Yet a regulation is considered urgent if there can be a 'future for Venice' beyond that of becoming a short-term city, even more so when its evident lack of resilience is being proved by the ongoing pandemic crisis. Indeed, the economic slump provoked by the prolonged absence of tourists could possibly affect the city's capacity of recovery in its entirety, as not just the rentiers see their profits curtailed, but the overall economic system is at a standstill. It is then predictable that the negative effects of the COVID crisis will primarily affect the lowest income strata of the population, exposing the already fragile social tissue of the city to unemployment and evictions, and thus further endangering its capacity of social reproduction. A new orientation in economic and social policy is therefore necessary as ever, in the face of the scenario presented by the most recent evolution of the socio-political situation, such as the surge in the acquisition of bankrupt tourist activities by shady investors (Trevisan, 2020) or the protests by affected sectors and their workers towards the enforcement of security measures, which resulted in Covid denial actions (Gasparon, 2020).

Besides the emergency measures needed to avoid social and economic collapse, putting a cap on STR, as suggested by Wachsmuth et al. (2017, p. 3) (with the following specifications: one host, one rental; no full-time, entire-home rentals; platforms responsible for enforcement) seems a reasonable first step for public policies that aim to recover acceptable levels of retention of a stable population in Venice. A proposal in this sense, comprehensive of an analysis of its legal feasibility, has indeed recently been developed by OCIO (2020d). Regulating STR should however be just a part of a more complex strategy meant to pull back the city from the "phase transition" (D'Eramo, 2017), and should be accompanied by a cap on hotel licenses at a metropolitan level, thus including at least the whole Municipality of Venice, and possibly addressing the whole regional territory (whose vast implications and problematics we leave for further research). Moreover, a de-marketing strategy should take place, and more resources – for instance the income from tourist taxes – dedicated to fundamental housing policies. Finally, in order to stimulate the local economy to get beyond the actual extractivist tourist model and foster the overall resilience of the urban organism, stronger investments in a more diversified economy are badly necessary, out of a sound diagnostic of the differential factors that would make Venice's HC an attractive location. If none of this will happen, it is likely that 'short-term city Venice' will become more and more real and irreversible.

Note

1. The sharp decline in overnight stays in the minor islands and littoral zone in the year 2000 is a statistical glitch due to the secession of a section of the littoral; since that year, the overnight stays at Cavallino are not counted anymore in municipal statistics.

Acknowledgments

The authors wish to thank Alice Corona for the precious help on data collection and for the realisation of Figure 3.

Funding

Ministero dell'Istruzione, dell'Università e della Ricerca (MIUR), PRIN 2017EWXN2F; Spanish Ministry of Economy, Industry and Competitiveness (POLITUR project. CSO2017-82156-R), AEI/FEDER, and Department of Research and Universities of the Catalan Government (2017SGR22).

ORCID

Giacomo-Maria Salerno (iD) http://orcid.org/0000-0001-5697-4830
Antonio Paolo Russo (iD) http://orcid.org/0000-0001-8768-246X

Bibliography

Aalbers, M. B. (2019). Introduction to the forum: From third to fifth-wave gentrification. *Tijdschrift Voor Economische en Sociale Geografie*, *110*(1), 1–11. https://doi.org/10.1111/tesg.12332

Adger, W. N. (2000). Social and ecological resilience: Are they related? *Progress in Human Geography*, *24*(3), 347–364. https://doi.org/10.1191/030913200701540465

Airbnb. (2018). *Healthy Travel and Healthy Destinations report*, web content: https://news.airbnb.com/wp-content/uploads/sites/4/2018/05/Healthy-Travel-and-Healthy-Destinations.pdf

Arias Sans, A., & Quaglieri Domínguez, A. (2016). Unravelling Airbnb: Urban perspectives from Barcelona. In G. Richards and A. P. Russo (Eds.), *Reinventing the local in tourism. Producing, consuming and negotiating place* (pp. 209–227). Channel View.

Arias Sans, A., & Russo, A. P. (2016). The right to Gaudí. What can we learn from the commoning of Park Güell, Barcelona?. In C. Colomb & J. Novy (Eds.), *Protest and resistance in the tourist city* (pp. 247–263). Routledge.

Barron, K., Kung, E., & Proserpio, D. (2017). *The sharing economy and housing affordability: Evidence from Airbnb*. SSRN Scholarly Paper ID 3006832. Social Science Research Network, web content: https://papers.ssrn.com/abstract=3006832.

Barbiani, E., & Zanon, G. (2004). (Eds.). *Condizioni di competitività delle strutture ricettive del Comune di Venezia e della regione turistica*. COSES - Consorzio per la Ricerca e la Formazione.

Bettini, S. (1978). *Venezia. Nascita di una città*. Electa.

Bernardello, A. (2002). Iniziative economiche, accumulazione e investimenti di capitale (1830-1866). *Storia di Venezia. L'Ottocento*, vol. II, 567–601. Istituto della Enciclopedia Italiana Treccani.

Borelli, C. (2019). Overtourism e diritto alla città: il caso di Venezia. *Il granello di sabbia*, *40*, 37–41. Attac Italia

Caserta, S., & Russo, A. P. (2002). More means worse. Asymmetric information, spatial displacement and sustainable heritage tourism. *Journal of Cultural Economics*, *26*(4), 245–260. https://doi.org/10.1023/A:1019905923457

Choay, F. (1996). *L'allegoria del patrimonio*. Officina Edizioni.

Celata, F., Sanna, V. S., & De Luca, S. (2017). *La "Airbnbificazione" Delle Città: Gli Effetti a Roma Tra Centro e Periferia*. Università di Roma La Sapienza. Dipartimento MEMOTEF.

Cocola-Gant, A., & Gago, A. (2019). Airbnb, buy-to-let investment and tourism-driven displacement: A case study in Lisbon. *Environment and Planning A: Economy and Space*, 1–18. doi:10.1177/0308518X19869012.

Codagnone, C., Biagi, F., & Abadie, F. (2016). *The passions and the interests: Unpacking the 'sharing economy'*. Institute for Prospective Technological Studies, JRC Science for Policy Report, European Commission.

Comune di Venezia. (1964). *Atti del Convegno internazionale Il problema di Venezia: Venezia, 4-7 ottobre 1962*. Fondazione Giorgio Cini.

Comune di Venezia. (2017). *Annuario del turismo 2017*. Assessorato al Turismo.

Corona, A. (2019). *Venezia. Inside Airbnb Infokit*, 2019-08-12, web content: http://insideairbnb.com/venice/report.html

Consorzio per la Ricerca e la Formazione (COSES). (1979). *Il turismo a Venezia*. Venezia.

Consorzio per la Ricerca e la Formazione (COSES). (2009a). *Rapporto 141.0 Turismo sostenibile a Venezia*, web content: http://archive.comune.venezia.it/flex/cm/pages/ServeAttachment.php/L/IT/D/D.fe155294363b8b944ed1/P/BLOB:ID=28868

Consorzio per la Ricerca e la Formazione (COSES). (2009b). *Documento 1106.0 Città e università: il nodo delle residenze studentesche*. http://coses.comune.venezia.it/download/Doc1106.pdf.

Cosgrove, D. (1982). The myth and the stones of Venice: An historical geography of a symbolic landscape. *Journal of Historical Geography*, *8*(2), 145–169. https://doi.org/10.1016/0305-7488(82)90004-4

Costa, N., & Martinotti, G. (2003). Sociological theories of tourism and regulation theory. In L. M. Hoffman, S. S. Feinstein, e D. R. Judd (a cura di). *Cities and visitors. Regulating People, markets and city space*. Op. cit.

Costa, P., & Van Der Borg, J. (1988). Un modello lineare per la programmazione del turismo. Sulla capacità massima di accoglienza turistica del Centro Storico di Venezia. *Coses Informazioni"*, *32, 33*, 21–26.

Cox, M. (2017). *Inside [the data of] Airbnb*. The Devices of Tourism, Lo Squaderno 45, September 2017.

Cristiano, S., & Gonella, F. (2020). Kill Venice': A systems thinking conceptualisation of urban life, economy, and resilience in tourist cities. *Humanities and Social Sciences Communications*, *7*(1), 1–13. https://doi.org/10.1057/s41599-020-00640-6

D'Eramo, M. (2017). *Il selfie del mondo. Indagine sull'età del turismo*. Feltrinelli.

Davidson, M., & Lees, L. (2010). New-build gentrification: Its histories, trajectories, and critical geographies. *Population, Space and Place*, *16*(5), 395–411. https://doi.org/10.1002/psp.584

Davis, R., & Marvin, G. (2004). *Venice, the tourist maze. A cultural critique of the world's most touristed city*. University of California Press.

Davoudi, S., Shaw, K., Haider, L. J., Quinlan, A. E., Peterson, G. D., Wilkinson, C., Fünfgeld, H., McEvoy, D., Porter, L., & Davoudi, S. (2012). Resilience: A bridging concept or a dead end? *Planning Theory & Practice, 13*(2), 299–333. https://doi.org/10.1080/14649357.2012.677124

De Marchi, D. (2019). Le Venezie turistiche. In *Quattro Venezie per un Nordest. Rapporto su Venezia Civitas Metropolitana 2019*. Marsilio.

De Rita, G. (1993). *Una Città Speciale: Rapporto su Venezia*. Marsilio.

Dianese, M. (2020). *"Bastonata" in arrivo per chi ha più case a Venezia e le affitta ai turisti*, Il Gazzettino 11/02/2020, web content: https://www.ilgazzettino.it/nordest/venezia/affitto_casa_vacanza_venezia_cosa_cambia-5044005.html

Engel & Völkers. (2019). Market Report Venezia 2019, web content: https://issuu.com/engelvoelkers_italia/docs/market_report_2019_venezia

Fabbri, G., Migliorini, F., & Tattara, G. (2020). *Venezia, il dossier UNESCO e una città allo sbando*. 2nd ed. Libreria Editrice Cafoscarina.

Fava, F. (2018). *Vuoti di normalità. Evoluzioni della casa veneziana nell'era del turismo globale*. Engramma, 155, April 2018.

Fregolent, L., & Vettoretto, L. (2017). Genesis of a fluid metropolitan space. In A. Balducci, V. Fedeli, and F. Curci, (Eds.), *Post-metropolitan territories: Looking for a new urbanity*. Taylor & Francis.

Frenken, K., & Schor, J. B. (2017). Putting the sharing economy into perspective. In *A research agenda for sustainable consumption governance*. Edward Elgar Publishing.

Fullin, M. (2020). *Ostelli e finti hotel in pieno centro: scattano i controlli di vigili e finanzieri*, Il Gazzettino. https://www.ilgazzettino.it/nordest/venezia/hotel_abusivi_centro_storico_finannza-4992046.html

Gainsforth, S. (2019). *Airbnb città merce. Storie di resistenza alla gentrification digitale*. DeriveApprodi.

García-López, M. À., Jofre-Monseny, J., Martínez-Mazza, R., & Segú, M. (2020). Do short-term rental platforms affect housing markets? Evidence from Airbnb in Barcelona. *Journal of Urban Economics, 119*, 103278. https://doi.org/10.1016/j.jue.2020.103278

Gasparon, M. (2020). Protesta contro Dpcm e chiusure: «Via le mascherine», caos a Venezia, Il Gazzettino. https://www.ilgazzettino.it/nordest/venezia/dpcm_protesta_senza_mascherine_cosa_e_successo-5565477.html

Gheno, M. (2016). Anamnesi dell'abbandono. In L. Fregolent, M. Gheno, e F. Ferronato (Eds.), *Laboratorio Venezia*. Università IUAV di Venezia.

Ghiglione, G. (2018). *Occupy Venice: 'We are the alternative to the death of the city'*, Guardian Cities. https://www.theguardian.com/cities/2018/sep/13/occupy-venice-alternative-to-death-of-city-activists-tourism

Gil, J., & Sequera, J. (2020). The professionalization of Airbnb in Madrid: Far from a collaborative economy. *Current Issues in Tourism*, 1–20. https://doi.org/10.1080/13683500.2020.1757628

Gössling, S., Scott, D., & Hall, C. M. (2021). Pandemics, tourism and global change: A rapid assessment of COVID-19. *Journal of Sustainable Tourism, 29*(1), 1–20. https://doi.org/10.1080/09669582.2020.1758708

Grove, K. (2013). Hidden transcripts of resilience: power and politics in Jamaican disaster management. *Resilience, 1*(3), 193–209. https://doi.org/10.1080/21693293.2013.825463

Gutiérrez, J., García-Palomares, J. C., Romanillos, G., & Salas-Olmedo, M. H. (2017). The eruption of Airbnb in tourist cities: Comparing spatial patterns of hotels and peer-to-peer accommodation in Barcelona. *Tourism Management, 62*, 278–291.

Indovina, F. (1988). Turisti, Pendolari, Residenti. *COSES Informazioni, 32/33*, 27–36.

James, H. (1888). *The aspern papers*. Reprint. Penguin. 1986.

James, H. (1909). *Italian Hours*. Reprint. Penguin. 1995.

Lanapoppi, P. (2015). *Caro turista*. Corte del Fontego.

Lee, D. (2016). How Airbnb short-term rentals exacerbate Los Angeles's affordable housing crisis: Analysis and policy recommendations. *Harv. L. & Pol'y Rev, 10* (2016), 229.

Lefebvre, H. (1970). *La révolution urbaine*. Gallimard.

Lew, A. A. (2014). Scale, change and resilience in community tourism planning. *Tourism Geographies, 16*(1), 14–22. https://doi.org/10.1080/14616688.2013.864325

López-Gay, A., Cocola-Gant, A., & Russo, A. P. (2020). Urban tourism and population change: Gentrification in the age of mobilities. *Population Space and Place*. https://doi.org/10.1002/psp.2380

Mann, T. (1912). *Tod in Venedig*. Translated. Death in Dover Publications. 1995.

Mehmood, A. (2016). Of resilient places: planning for urban resilience. *European Planning Studies, 24*(2), 407–419. https://doi.org/10.1080/09654313.2015.1082980

Meriläinen, E. S., Fougère, M., & Piotrowicz, W. (2020). Refocusing urban disaster governance on marginalised urban people through right to the city. *Environmental Hazards, 19*(2), 187–208. https://doi.org/10.1080/17477891.2019.1682492

Milano, C., Novelli, M. & Cheer, J. (Eds.). (2019a). *Overtourism: Excesses, discontents and measures in travel and tourism*. CABI.

Milano, C., Novelli, M., & Cheer, J. M. (2019b). Overtourism and degrowth: a social movements perspective. *Journal of Sustainable Tourism*, *27*(12), 1857–1875. https://doi.org/10.1080/09669582.2019.1650054

Minoia, P. (2017). Venice reshaped? Tourist gentrification and sense of place. In N. Bellini & C. Pasquinelli (Eds.), *Tourism in the city: Towards an integrative agenda on urban tourism*. Springer International Publishing.

Momigliano, A. (2020). Venice tourism may never be the same. It could be better. The New York Times (3 July 2020). https://www.nytimes.com/2020/07/02/travel/venice-coronavirus-tourism.html.

Osservatorio Civico sulla Casa e sulla Residenzialità (OCIO). (2019). *Fact-Checking: Affitti turistici: favoriscono o ostacolano la residenza? Alcune considerazioni*. Available at: https://ocio-venezia.it/fact-checking/locazioni%20turistiche/abbav/2019/12/04/abbav/

Osservatorio Civico sulla Casa e sulla Residenzialità (OCIO). (2020a). *Abitare la città. Politiche della residenza ai tempi del turismo*. In G. Fabbri, F. Migliorini, & G. Tattara, (Eds.), *Venezia. Il dossier unesco e una città allo sbando.*, cit.

Osservatorio Civico sulla Casa e sulla Residenzialità (OCIO). (2020b). *Gli squilibri del turismo veneziano*, web content: https://ocio-venezia.it/pagine/affittanze-dati/

Osservatorio Civico sulla Casa e sulla Residenzialità (OCIO). (2020c). *Campo San Zan Degolà a Santa Croce (Venezia): un luogo dimenticato dalla calca … ma non dagli speculatori* (ed. Corona, A.). https://medium.com/ocio-venezia/campo-san-zan-degolà-a-santa-croce-venezia-un-luogo-dimenticato-dalla-calca-ma-non-dagli-5ad3c73fbb49

Osservatorio Civico sulla Casa e sulla Residenzialità (OCIO). (2020d). Regolamentare le locazioni turistiche è possibile, oltre che necessario. https://medium.com/ocio-venezia/regolamentare-le-locazioni-turistiche-è-possibile-oltre-che-necessario-b5742d2dded2

Paidakaki, A., & Moulaert, F. (2017a). Does the post-disaster resilient city really exist? A critical analysis of the heterogeneous transformative capacities of housing reconstruction'resilience cells. *International Journal of Disaster Resilience in the Built Environment*, *8*(3), 275–291. https://doi.org/10.1108/IJDRBE-10-2015-0052

Paidakaki, A., & Moulaert, F. (2017b). Disaster resilience into which direction(s)? Competing discursive and material practices in Post-Katrina New Orleans. *Housing, Theory and Society*, *35*(4), 1–454. https://doi.org/10.1080/14036096.2017.1308434

Pardo, D., & Gómez, R. (2019). Southern Europe as an anti-tourism political space. In E. Cañada (Ed.), *Tourism in the geopolitics of the Mediterranean* (no. 9, pp. 86–91). Alba Sud. Contrast Reports Serie.

Picascia, S., Romano, A., Teobaldi, M. (2017). The airification of cities: Making sense of the impact of peer to peer short term letting on urban functions and economy. *Proceedings of the Annual Congress of the Association of European Schools of Planning*, 11-14/07/2017. Lisbon.

Quaglieri-Domínguez, A., Arias Sans, A., & Russo, A. P. (2020). Home sharing, city selling. Insights from the airbnbzation of Barcelona. *City*, (forthcoming).

Quinn, B. (2007). Performing tourism Venetian residents in focus. *Annals of Tourism Research*, *34*(2), 458–476. https://doi.org/10.1016/j.annals.2006.11.002

RESET. (2015). *Affitti turistici a Venezia – Una economia da far emergere e regolamentare*, Reset Venezia. https://reset-venezia.it/2015/08/23/affitti-turistici-a-venezia-una-economia-da-far-emergere-e-regolamentare/

Rossi, R. (2018). *Elderly woman with a sick son to be evicted to make way for tourist rental – but Venetian citizens block the way*, Campaign for a living Venice. https://campaignforalivingvenice.org/2018/07/21/elderly-woman-with-a-sick-son-to-be-evicted-to-make-way-for-tourist-rental-but-venetian-citizens-block-the-way/

Russo, A. P. (2002a). *The sustainable development of the heritage city and its region. Analysis, policy, governance* [Thela Thesis] ISBN: 90-5170-670-7.

Russo, A. P. (2002b). The vicious circle of tourism development in heritage cities. *Annals of Tourism Research*, *29*(1), 165–182. https://doi.org/10.1016/S0160-7383(01)00029-9

Russo, A. P., & Arias Sans, A. (2009). Student communities and landscapes of creativity: How Venice—The world's most touristed city'—is changing. *European Urban and Regional Studies*, *16*(2), 161–175.

Salerno, G. M. (2015). Ritorno alla Laguna. L'esperienza dell'associazione "Poveglia per Tutti" come esempio di ritessitura urbana. In C. Cellamare & E. Scandurra (Eds.), *Pratiche insorgenti e riappropriazione della città*. SdT edizioni.

Salerno, G. M. (2018). *Oltre i tornelli*, Rivista Il Mulino, web content: https://www.rivistailmulino.it/news/newsitem/index/Item/News:NEWS_ITEM:4400

Salerno, G. M. (2019). *Gondole d'acciaio sulla Laguna*. Luoghi Comuni 1, 1, Castelvecchi

Salerno, G. M. (2020). *Per una critica dell'economia turistica. Venezia tra museificazione e mercificazione*. Quodlibet.

Scheppe, W, & the IUAV Class on Politics of Representation (2009). *Migropolis: Venice/Atlas of a global situation*. Hatje Cantz.

Schor, J. B. (2017). Does the sharing economy increase inequality within the eighty percent? findings from a qualitative study of platform providers. *Cambridge Journal of Regions, Economy and Society*, *10*(2):263–279. https://doi.org/10.1093/cjres/rsw047

Sequera, J., & Nofre, J. (2018). Shaken, not stirred: New debates on touristification and the limits of gentrification. *City*, *22*(5-6), 843–855. https://doi.org/10.1080/13604813.2018.1548819

Seraphin, H., Sheeran, P., & Pilato, M. (2018). Over-tourism and the fall of Venice as a destination. *Journal of Destination Marketing & Management*, *9*, 374–376.

Southern Europe against Touristification (SET). (2018). *Manifesto*. http://www.iut.nu/wp-content/uploads/2018/08/RED-SET-Manifesto-Inglès.pdf

Shaw, K. (2012). The rise of the resilient local authority? *Local Government Studies, 38*(3), 281–300. https://doi.org/10.1080/03003930.2011.642869

Sigler, T., & Wachsmuth, D. (2016). Transnational gentrification: Globalisation and neighbourhood change in Panama's Casco Antiguo. *Urban Studies, 53*(4), 705–722. https://doi.org/10.1177/0042098014568070

Srnicek, N. (2017). *Platform capitalism*. John Wiley & Sons.

Tantucci, E. (2016). *"Il futuro è a Mestre? Brugnaro tradisce Venezia"*. La Nuova Venezia, 31/05/2016. https://nuovavenezia.gelocal.it/venezia/cronaca/2016/05/31/news/il-futuro-e-a-mestre-brugnaro-tradisce-venezia-1.13574126

Tantucci, E. (2018). *Caos di Carnevale, Brugnaro: "Andatevene in campagna"*. La Nuova Venezia, 29/01/2018. https://nuovavenezia.gelocal.it/venezia/cronaca/2018/01/30/news/il-controcanto-di-brugnaro-1.16411171

Trevisan, E. (2020). *Negozi e hotel, mezza Venezia in vendita. E gli albanesi se la stanno comprando*, Il Gazzettino, 27/09/2020. Available at: https://www.ilgazzettino.it/nordest/venezia/vendita_case_prezzi_asta_albanesi_comprano_venezia-5490203.html

Vale, L. J. (2014). The politics of resilient cities: whose resilience and whose city? *Building Research & Information, 42*(2), 191–201. https://doi.org/10.1080/09613218.2014.850602

Vale, L. J., & Campanella, T. J. (2005). *The resilient city: How modern cities recover from disaster*. Oxford University Press.

Van Der Borg, J. (2017). Sustainable tourism in Venice: What lessons for other fragile cities on water? In Caroli, R., & Soriani, S. (Eds.), *Fragile and resilient cities on water: Perspectives from Venice and Tokyo*. Cambridge Scholars Publishing.

Van Der Borg, J., Bertocchi, D., Camatti, N., & Giove, S. (2020). Venice and overtourism: Simulating sustainable development scenarios through a tourism carrying capacity model. *Sustainability, 12*(2), 512.

Vianello, M. (2016). The No Grandi Navi campaign: protests against cruise tourism in Venice. In *Protest and resistance in the tourist city* (pp. 185–204). Routledge.

Visentin, F., & Bertocchi, D. (2019). *Venice: An analysis of tourism excesses in an overtourism icon*. In C. Milano, M. Novelli, & J. Cheer (Eds.).

Wachsmuth, D., Kerrigan, D., Chaney, D., & Shillolo, A. (2017). *Short-Term Cities: Airbnb's Impact on Canadian Housing Markets*. A Report from the Urban Politics and Governance Research Group. School of Urban Planning, McGill University, web content: https://davidwachsmuth.com/airbnbreport/.

Wachsmuth, D., & Weisler, A. (2018). Airbnb and the rent gap: Gentrification through the sharing economy. *Environment and Planning A. 50*(6), 1147–1170.

Yrigoy, I. (2019). Rent gap reloaded: Airbnb and the shift from residential to touristic rental housing in the Palma Old Quarter in Mallorca, Spain. *Urban Studies, 56*(13), 2709–2726. https://doi.org/10.1177/0042098018803261

Zanardi, C. (2020). *La bonifica umana. Venezia dall'esodo al turismo*. Unicopli.

Zannini, A. (2002). La costruzione della città turistica. In *Storia di Venezia. L'Ottocento* (vol. II, pp. 1123–1149). Istituto della Enciclopedia Italiana Treccani.

Zannini, A. (2014). Il turismo a Venezia dal secondo dopoguerra ad oggi. *Laboratoire Italien*, (15), 191–199. https://doi.org/10.4000/laboratoireitalien.848

Whose right to the city? An analysis of the mediatized politics of place surrounding *alojamento local* issues in Lisbon and Porto

Kate Torkington (iD) and Filipa Perdigão Ribeiro (iD)

ABSTRACT

In view of the proliferation of *alojamento local* (short-term vacation rentals) in the major Portuguese cities of Lisbon and Porto, along with the recent transformation of the historic city centre neighbourhoods, this study explores the mediatized politics of place by analysing data sets resulting from different, but interconnected, discursive practices. At the level of governance, we examine how legislation has enabled and facilitated this transformation. We then explore the media coverage of the issues surrounding these recent changes. Finally, we focus on individual and collective stakeholder voices by analysing the various rights claims and arguments found in social media communication channels. Framing our analysis initially in Lefebvre's concept of 'the right to the city', often invoked as an argument for the promotion of justice, inclusion and sustainability in the face of urbanisation policies, we argue that a 'rights *in* the city' approach is better suited to gaining insight into the multiple tensions and conflicts brought about through the interlinking processes of regeneration, gentrification and touristification that affect neighbourhoods with high proportions of short-term rental accommodation, and conclude that there are many rights claimants within a seemingly unified group of stakeholders, invoking rights claims which are sometimes overlapping, but often conflicting.

Introduction

Short-term urban vacation rentals have witnessed staggering levels of growth in major cities around the world in recent years. Whilst the demand for and expansion of this type of tourist accommodation in cities is leading to the revitalisation of certain urban areas, it is also clear that there is a direct association in many urban neighbourhoods between an excessive supply of short-term vacation rentals and processes of tourism-driven gentrification, as well as leading to situations of 'overtourism' (González-Pérez, 2020; Ioannides et al., 2019; Peeters et al., 2018). This then puts into question both the sustainability of residential zones in city centres and the future sustainability of tourism in urban spaces, until recently generally considered as one of the more 'sustainable' economic growth strategies for cities (Koens et al., 2018). This is certainly the case in the two major Portuguese cities, Lisbon and Porto, which are the focus of this study. Following the downturn of the global economic crisis, both these cities have recently seen massive increases in both tourist numbers and peer-to-peer (e.g. Airbnb) listings. Mendes (2016) has described the tourist gentrification currently being witnessed in Lisbon as the transformation of the *bairros populares* (traditional, working-class inner-city neighbourhoods) into places of tourism-led consumption and where new types of accommodation and entertainment are replacing the residential and traditional commercial functions and leading to a population exodus. These neighbourhoods are therefore the focus of increasing 'touristification', driven in large part by the "Airbnb-ization" which is "allowing the cobbled streets [of Lisbon] (…) to become a Disneyland for Creative tourists" (Muzergues, 2020, p. 22).

Online platforms such as Airbnb, which have facilitated the exponential growth of short-term tourism rentals were, until very recently, widely regarded as "the most emblematic manifestation of the 'sharing economy'" (Oskam, 2019, p. 7). The sharing economy was initially seen not only as a 'disruptive innovation' (Guttentag, 2015) in the traditional accommodation market, but also as a positive development in the trend towards a more sustainable type of tourism (Dredge & Gyimóthy, 2015), with proponents flagging its potential for positive environmental, economic and social contributions and benefits (Gössling & Hall, 2019). However, others have been questioning the extent to which it can and will ultimately lead to a more equitable and sustainable development of tourism (Leung et al., 2019; Martin, 2016). It is by now becoming clear that the majority of practices of such platforms are not complying with any real definition of 'sharing', and in many instances - such as the case of 'multi-listers' who offer multiple units for rental - can even be said to be in opposition to the essential principles of 'sharing'(Oskam, 2019, p. 14).

In some cities, the emerging social problems associated with the concentration of large numbers of short-term vacation rentals are leading to restrictive measures being taken. In the case of Portugal, the possibility of placing restrictions on the licencing of short-term rental units has recently been put in place by new legislation, passed in August 2018, giving Municipal Councils the power to designate geographical 'areas of contention' within their municipalities, where restrictions on vacation rental accommodation (known in Portugal as *'Alojamento Local' (local accommodation)* or simply 'AL') can then be enforced. Lisbon Municipal Council immediately identified 'areas of contention' in the historic central district, setting the parameter used to define these areas at 25% or more of housing stock being used as AL. In fact, in some of these neighbourhoods, short-term rentals were already thought to occupy over 40% of housing stock. In November 2018, shortly after the legislation came into effect, Airbnb listed over 3,000 properties in the historic centre of Lisbon, of which 87.7% were 'entire homes/apartments', and 77% belonged to multi-listers (*Inside Airbnb*, 2018). The situation in the historic centre of Porto, the second largest Portuguese city, is similar, although the Municipal Council of Porto has yet to designate any 'areas of contention'.

However, support for the legislation and its apparent aim to restrict the unchecked growth of AL in Lisbon and Porto has been by no means consensual. A range of different stakeholders, with sometimes competing and sometimes overlapping interests and rights claims, can be identified. Thus, the spread of Airbnb-type accommodation becomes entangled in the politics of place, in which different social actors seek to establish their own 'place frame' - or social construction of space - in order to assert and legitimise their own interests and rights claims, or to dismantle and delegitimize the claims of others.

With this context in mind, our study explores the politics of place from a discursive perspective, at distinct but interconnected levels, by analysing data from different mediated, public discursive practices. We chose to focus on this type of discourse (rather than, say, research interviews) because public discourse, as part of the public sphere (Habermas, 1962 [1994]), is a crucial part of participatory democracy, albeit certainly not of equal access to all (Modan, 2007, p. 331). It can be argued, then, that the politics of place are in large measure negotiated and enacted through different forms of public discourse at interacting levels. At the level of governance, we first examine briefly how legislation has enabled the transformation of historic residential neighbourhoods through (often conflicting) processes of rehabilitation, regeneration, and gentrification. We then explore the recent media coverage of these processes, which is particularly focused on the reporting of the new AL legislation and its impacts, and finally, we focus on individual and collective voices by analysing the various positions and tensions found in public posts and comments in online digital news media and social media channels. In this way, we aim to unpack some of the process of the mediatization of the politics of place, broadly understood as a social change process driven by the increasing importance and influence of media channels, including social media (Strömback & Esser, 2014).

We frame our analysis in the theoretical concept of 'the right to the city', originally formulated by Lefebvre (1968 [1970]) and increasingly invoked in recent years as an argument for the promotion of justice, inclusion and sustainability in the face of urbanisation policies and processes governed by the exchange value of real estate. Following Pierce et al. (2016), however, we seek to extend this framework analytically by applying an approach that these authors designated as rights *in* places. As such, the research questions that guided the study are related to the uncovering of the different perspectives on the recent proliferation of short-term vacation rentals in the major Portuguese cities by asking: who are the different stakeholders (or, more specifically, 'rights claimants') involved; what are their rights claims and goals; and what are the relationships among them. We also explore the place-frames that are articulated, either explicitly or implicitly, in order to advance particular rights claims and/or dismantle the claims of others.

The right to the city/rights in the city and the politics of place

Since the phrase was first coined in the writings of the French philosopher Henri Lefebvre in the late 1960s, the 'right to the city' has become a widely-used, 'fashionable' slogan (De Souza, 2010) or a "rallying cry" (Attoh, 2011, p. 678), in many cities around the world where social groups feel they are being in some respect disenfranchised, or where highly-charged issues of urban justice and the erosion of long-standing rights are at stake (Borja, 2011; Mayer, 2009).

As proposed by Lefebvre, the right to the city is not simply the right to what already exists in urban spaces, but a right to *transform* the city, to make it a better place to live in. In his book *Le Droit à la Ville (The Right to the City)*, Lefebvre (1968) discussed the negative impacts of the capitalist economy on cities, arguing that the commodification of cities serves only the interest of capital accumulation (Marcuse, 2009; Mathinet, 2011), and making the case for a more just society based on urban occupancy and, importantly, participation, which is necessarily divorced from land ownership (Pierce et al., 2016). Lefebvre (1996, p. 158) saw the right to the city as being "like a cry and a demand", with the cry coming from present need, and the demand from future aspirations (Marcuse, 2009). The context in which Lefebvre wrote involved campaigns to stop the destruction of 'traditional' neighbourhoods in Paris by the encroaching and dehumanising high-rise tower blocks (Harvey, 2008). Ultimately, as Purcell (2014, p. 150) points out, Lefebvre conceived of the right to the city not as users "claiming more access to and control over the existing capitalist city, a bigger slice of the existing pie", but rather as a movement aiming to "go beyond the existing city, to cultivate the urban so that it can grow and spread". For Lefebvre, then, 'the urban' referred to "a society beyond capitalism, one characterized by meaningful engagement among inhabitants embedded in a web of social connections"; in other words, a 'possible world' for the future (*ibid.*: 151).

The right to the city is still, as Marcuse (2009, p. 189) observes, "an immediately understandable and intuitively compelling slogan", despite the fact that it is, at the same time, "a theoretically complex and provocative formulation and that nowadays, its invocation comes from a variety of distinct social groups with differing ideological stances and a wide range of causes (Schmid, 2012), leading to inevitable differences as to what the right to the city entails. However, there seems to be a general agreement that the overall goal is to promote justice, sustainability and inclusion in cities, and that this involves prioritizing the use-value of urban space over its exchange value (Purcell, 2014). Since it has become commonplace in cities that the exchange value of real estate determines how it is used, the idea of the right to the city has come to be understood as a struggle over conflicting rights between city-users and inhabitants on the one hand, and property owners and developers on the other (*ibid.*).

Besides being invoked by social movements and organisations, the idea of the right to the city is also increasingly featuring in urban policy debates as well as in academic discussions. The original formulation of the concept by Lefebvre has subsequently been developed by theorists such as Harvey (2008), Marcuse (2009) and Attoh (2011) to situate it in the context of globalisation and neoliberalism, which has contributed to the global spread and 'discursive success' of the concept (Domaradzska, 2018). Although for some, it is a right primarily ascribed to the impoverished, deprived, exploited and discontented (Marcuse, 2009) and the working classes (e.g. Soja, 2010), many scholars foreground the notion of the collective right to the democratic, participatory management of urban resources (e.g. Harvey, 2008; McCann, 2002; Purcell, 2003; cf. also Busa, 2009), thus reflecting Lefebvre's original proposal for an alternative to the primacy of property rights.

The struggles in cities around the world resulting from the profit-oriented logic of 'property development' - the increasing privatisation of space and services, processes of gentrification, an ever-increasing gap between the wealthy urban elite and the poor, and a lack of affordable housing in city centres - are becoming progressively more visible through discursive practices that report or opine on them. Moreover, there is now an additional dimension of tourism-driven gentrification in city centres, where tourism plays a vital role in developing possibilities for leisure and entertainment that contribute to the attractiveness of central urban areas to an increasingly young, cosmopolitan crowd (Cocola-Gant, 2018). The concept of the right to the city therefore seems to serve well as a framework for unpacking the urban politics underlying the short-term vacation rentals issue that has become so prominent in many city neighbourhoods which traditionally have been residential and are now becoming simultaneously 'touristified' and gentrified, as is the case in many central neighbourhoods in Lisbon and Porto.

However, despite its obvious appeal as motivating discourse, the notion of the right to the city is not without its limitations. Besides the criticism often put forward that it is too 'utopian' to be of practical use (Purcell, 2014), the main analytical problem is its universalist tendencies, which tend to group urban inhabitants together as an "amorphous entity" (Mayer, 2009, p. 368), whilst it is clear that in the 21st century the social relations and social identities that characterise urban settings are far more complex and go beyond social class. Marcuse (2011) has argued that the usefulness of the right to the city banner is rooted in the bringing together of diverse rights claims and claimants into one unified movement with a common 'enemy', thus serving as a unifying discourse for different groups of city-users with distinct ideological and identity positionings. However, this is also problematic, in that many urban issues are not always clear-cut enough to be able to identify common enemies.

Such collective approaches may therefore, according to Pierce et al. (2016, p. 80), "obscure ongoing processes of negotiation between various *competing rights claims* and overlapping, *simultaneous claimants*" (original emphasis). These authors therefore argue for an approach which is able to take into account the "multiple, overlapping, fractured and contentious, constantly (re)negotiated" (*ibid.*) nature of contemporary urban rights and the socio-political processes in which they are invoked, or contested. This approach is better called 'rights in places', to underscore both the plurality of rights claims and claimants, and the versions of place(s) that they are seeking to construct or defend. Drawing on Massey's (1994; 2005) relational conception of place, which highlights the on-going negotiations among overlapping discursive representations of places, it is argued that when different stakeholders (both individuals and collectives) are in contestation, they articulate different place-frames (Martin, 2003; 2013) to argue for different rights to/in places. Following Goffman (1974), the idea of 'framing' refers to the way in which social actors organise and make sense of their experiences in the social world. A place-frame is thus considered to be a shared representation of a place toward specific ends, based on material experience of the place and drawing on a set of goals, values and beliefs, and which is articulated through discourse (Martin, 2003). The discursive practice of place-framing, then, involves positioning a particular representation of place towards social and/or political ends (Pierce et al., 2011).

In this way, the concept of place-framing fits within the view of the politics of place taken by this research. We see the politics of place as encompassing: (1) the ways in which social (power) relations and social hierarchies are both constituted and legitimated (or contested, or marginalised) through 'representations' (Rose, 1994); (2) the ways in which community members, or stakeholders, create and contest versions and visions of localities (neighbourhoods) and how discursive constructions of both place and of personal identity are key elements in struggles over rights to spatial resources and authority over which kinds of practices or activities are permissible in particular localities (Modan, 2007); (3) a relational politics of place that combines both the "politics of propinquity" (in everyday negotiations of local spatial relations and diversity) and the "politics of connectivity", which necessarily reaches out to other places and also brings in people, and investments, from the 'outside' (Amin, 2004, p. 38); and (4) the fact that the ubiquity of both mass media and new (social) media mean that the political arena is increasingly mediatized (Thimm et al., 2014).

In short, the politics of place refers to how individuals and groups engage in meaning-making processes – or 'place-making' processes – through both discursive and other forms of spatialised social practices.

Methodology and data

We situate this research in critical discourse studies (CDS), which take a problem-oriented, interdisciplinary and qualitatively-driven methodological approach, characterized by an interest in demystifying ideologies and power relations through discourse analysis (Wodak & Meyer, 2016). Discourse is seen as a social practice, which simultaneously shapes and is shaped by other social practices (Unger et al., 2016). Both discourse and discursive practices therefore need to be examined within the socio-political contexts in which they are embedded, and as such, discourse analysis should take into account the interactions among the macro-, meso- and micro-levels of practice which mediate the dialectical relationship between social structures and individual agency.

Our data consist of texts arising from three distinct, but interconnected, types of discursive practices in the public sphere. Firstly, at governance level, after a brief description of how legislation and public policies have had profound effects on the historic central neighbourhoods of the two major Portuguese cities, opening them up to processes of gentrification, we examined recent (2018) legislation which has provided a national legal framework for short-term vacation rentals (AL) in Portugal, as well as empowering local government agents with the responsibility for licencing, monitoring and regulating this type of tourist accommodation.

Secondly, we draw on a corpus of media texts from a variety of Portuguese digital news sources from the period immediately before and after the enactment of this recent AL legislation (i.e. published online during the year 2018). The texts were collected in two ways; firstly by a Google search online using the key words 'alojamento local' (local accommodation) at the end of December 2018, selecting particularly texts which had comments posted by readers, and secondly by adding any texts which were shared on the Facebook pages used for the social media analysis (see below), and whose main topic was alojamento local. A total of 60 texts were eventually selected, having verified their relevance to the study, from 18 different sources (see Table 1).[1] Besides news items, informative articles and in-depth feature reports, a number of opinion pieces, were collected.

Table 1. Digital news media texts collected.

Media site/Genre	News/ Information	Feature/ In-depth report	Opinion piece	Total texts
Diário de Notícias	4	1	2	7
Dinheiro Vivo	3			3
ECO- Economia online	1		1	2
Expresso	2			2
Idealista	1			1
Jornal de Madeira			1	1
Jornal de Notícias	3	1		4
Jornal de Negócios	4		4	8
NIT	1			1
Observador	1		5	6
O Corvo		3		3
O Jornal Económico			1	1
Público	4	5	5	14
Sábado	1			1
Sapo24	3			3
Sol			1	1
TSF	1			1
Visão	1			1
Total	30	10	20	60

The third type of textual data can be categorised as social media communication (SMC). We consider SMC to be conducted on any electronic platform where users can co-produce content, perform interpersonal and mass communication simultaneously or separately, and have access to see and respond to institutionally- or user-generated texts (KhosraviNik, 2017). As a new communicative paradigm, SMC has entailed a break from the traditional, unidirectional linear flow of mass media content from powerful producers to relatively passive and powerless consumers, since it potentially enables a more participatory, interactive and co-creative means of production and dissemination of content (KhosraviNik, 2019; KhosraviNik & Unger, 2016).

For the purposes of this study, we collected texts which appeared either in comment threads following the digital texts used in the corpus of news media texts, or as posts or comments on Facebook pages, selected according to the following criteria: a) based in Portugal; b) 'Community' pages that are open to the public (i.e. not 'closed' groups); c) with posts and/or comments relating to AL issues; and d) with a relatively large number of 'followers'. Four pages corresponding to these parameters were selected, which are briefly described below, using the information on their social media profile available at the time of the study.

Alojamento Local – Esclarecimentos (Local Accommodation – Clarifications) has a Community page aimed at owner-operators of AL in Portugal. At the time of the study, around 4700 people were following the Facebook page.[2] According to information available on the page, the aim of the group is to "promote the sharing and joining of efforts around common priorities, with a view to encouraging a collaborative and sharing economy (…) and supporting those who host tourists by providing clarifications and information exchange and encouraging community participation".[3]

Morar em Lisboa (Living in Lisbon) considers itself to be a 'citizens' platform' whose main aim, according to its Community page (created in January 2017 and with around 4800 Facebook followers at the time of the study), is "to defend a living, participatory city that belongs to everyone". In an Open Letter published on the Facebook profile, it is made clear that the issue of the right to decent and affordable housing for all is at the heart of the movement. It is argued that housing in Lisbon has become "a privilege of the few and an almost inaccessible right for Portuguese families in general", due to "gentrification associated with and accelerated by (…) the greater intensification of tourism and accommodation for tourism purposes that Lisbon is experiencing".

O Porto não se vende (Porto is not for sale) is a similar social movement, based in the city of Porto. Its Community page was originally created as *Turismo Precário* (Precarious Tourism) in

Table 2. Social media communication data.

		No. of Comments
Digital news media	60 articles	395
Social media	155 posts	535
Total		**930**

December 2016, changing its name to the current one in August 2017. It had around 3000 fol-lowers at the time of the study. It also considers itself to be an advocate for participatory democ-racy, at the same time as defending the rights of people in the lower income brackets who are being pushed "towards the periphery of the city, with the centre becoming progressively elitist", as a direct result of gentrification processes.

Direito à Cidade (Right to the City) is a social movement based in the city of Porto. Its Facebook page was created in November 2017. At the time of the study, it had around 2200 fol-lowers. In comparison to the other social movement pages under study, it has very little informa-tion about its origins and aims, except to rally around the slogan of *"Mais Habitação, Não à Especulação!"* (More Housing, No to Speculation!).

From these Facebook pages, we collected posts which made some mention of AL and the comment threads attached to these posts in 2018. The total number of comments collected from both the digital news media and the social media pages is shown in Table 2 below.

Analysis of media and social media texts

From an initial reading of the corpus of media texts, we firstly noted the contextual information given relating to the AL situation in the cities under study and categorised this information into topics. We then sought to identify the different stakeholders involved, with a particular focus on: 1) who are the different rights claimants? 2) what are the relationships among them? 3) what are their goals? 4) which rights claims are invoked (explicitly or implicitly)?

The next stage of the analysis involved exploring social media communication (SMC), firstly by revisiting the four questions outlined above and then by investigating how SMC is used to discursively invoke and promote individual and/or collective rights claims, to attempt to enrol others in support for social action to this end, and to dismantle and/or deny the right claims of other actors. Finally, we sought to unpack how the rights claims involve competing place-frames, and the consequences of this in terms of the current politics of place in Lisbon and Porto.

Post-1974 legislation affecting the Portuguese inner-cities

Before examining the recent *Alojamento Local* legislation and its potential effects, we deemed it necessary to briefly summarise the legislation which has opened up the potential for gentrifica-tion processes. Over the past decades, Lisbon and Porto have witnessed a range of national and local government measures and programmes aimed at rehabilitating the historic central neigh-bourhoods, particularly in terms of housing and basic infrastructures. Before the democratic revo-lution of 1974, restoring built heritage in cities had been limited to monuments and buildings of historic national interest (Mendes, 2013). By the mid-1970s, the so-called 'fixed-rent laws' of Salazar's *Estado Novo* regime[4] which had kept extremely low residential rents from increasing since the 1950s (Balsas, 2007) meant that many of the ancient residential tenement buildings in the city centres were falling into serious disrepair as landlords refused to renovate, or even prop-erly maintain, buildings from which they received very little income.

The first national programmes aimed at providing financial incentives and aid to repair, recu-perate and improve both state- and privately-owned city centre housing dated from 1976[5] and 1985.[6] The discourse underpinning these early initiatives was clearly geared towards preserving the social fabric of the neighbourhoods (Mendes, 2013). Throughout the 1990s and into the turn of the century, various extensions of these programmes continued with a two-fold focus; both aiming to recuperate old buildings and to increase the supply of affordable rented housing for the lower income groups that had traditionally inhabited these areas (*ibid.*).

The success of these programmes was limited, however. Much of the rehabilitation work carried out was no more than a partial facelift, especially since the housing stock in these areas was characterised by small rooms, no bathroom, no lifts or garages, and therefore not considered 'suitable' for modern lifestyles (Balsas, 2007). The population exodus away from the city centres towards newly-built, affordable housing in the peripheries continued, and the number of empty, uninhabited buildings in bad states of disrepair hardly seemed to decrease. At the time of the 2001 national population census, it was found that over 60% of buildings in Lisbon needed repair work, with 5% being seriously dilapidated (Mendes, 2013). This paved the way for a new law in 2004,[7] which opened up the possibility of public-private partnerships by allowing local governments to form 'Urban Rehabilitation Companies', responsible for attracting investment and with executive powers for policy making and decisions. In this way, the hitherto publicly-governed rehabilitation processes were in effect handed over to the logic of market-oriented, private investment 'regeneration' projects, and the rapid gentrification processes of the city centres began. The new discourse of 'regeneration', or 'renovation' - the preferred term in Portugal, according to Balsas (2007) - hinged more on the need to re-populate these areas, by attracting 'new' residents, and the construction of modern, global, vibrant city centres (Tulumello, 2016).

At the same time, legislation (initially from 2006) began to remove the rent control mechanisms which were still in place in Lisbon and Porto, despite having been phased out in the rest of the country several decades previously (Lestegás, 2019).This process gained a further boost from legislation in 2012 which further liberalised the housing market, imposed as a condition of the IMF-EC-European Bank bailout for Portugal at the height of the economic crisis (Tulumello, 2019). Whilst the 2006 law enabled rental contracts of between 5 and 30 years, and also allowed landlords to update the rent, the 2012 law allowed leases of just 6 months, effectively leading to an increase in the number of tenants being forced to move out of their buildings due to non-renewal of rental contracts or sudden and unaffordable rises in rent.

Alojamento local (AL) legislation in Portugal

In Portugal, short-term vacation rentals are covered by recent legislation relating to *Alojamento Local* (AL). This is a category of tourist accommodation which has formally existed only since 2008, covering a range of accommodation types - privately-owned rooms, apartments and houses, as well as small guesthouses or hostels - which were seen to be previously operating outside the 'official' categories of tourist accommodation in Portugal. Until then, privately-owned rented accommodation had generally been disparagingly referred to within the tourism industry and governance as 'illegal' accommodation, or 'parallel beds', but had been long tolerated in tourist regions (such as the Algarve) as a means for people to supplement their income.

In 2014, a new law was created to give 'autonomy' to AL, separating it from the legislation governing other types of tourist accommodation. The preamble to this law[8] explains that privately-owned apartments are "a type of accommodation found more and more frequently in the world tourism market (…) especially due to the advent of digital marketing", and therefore the new legislation is intended to "give an important margin of freedom" to those offering this type of service, whilst at the same time aiming "to impede the development of this activity in a context of tax evasion", which was widely supposed to be the case among many AL operators.

An AL unit is defined by the law as having a maximum capacity of 9 rooms and 30 guests. Landlords may own and operate up to 9 units in the same building. Units must be registered with the local municipal council, whose responsibility it is to issue a licence. This new legislation made it relatively easy and cheap to obtain a licence, and initially very low tax rates were set on the income obtained from operating an AL unit in order to encourage owners to legalise their unit(s).

It is important to note that most AL units in cities, like the majority of housing stock, are essentially apartments in buildings which have Condominium Associations composed of the apartment owners and which are responsible for the management and maintenance of the building and its communal spaces. To this end, annual condominium fees are set for each owner. In Lisbon and Porto, several widely publicised cases of Condominium Associations going to court to try to prevent individual owners from using their apartments as AL units were instrumental in the creation of new legislation, in 2018,[9] which crucially altered some aspects of the 2014 law.

Firstly, it extended the powers of municipal councils by introducing measures to "preserve the social fabric of neighbourhoods", thus discursively resonating with the early urban rehabilitation programmes noted above. Specifically, these measures entail the power to designate "areas of contention" where limits to the amount of AL units can be imposed. Secondly, it allowed for the possibility of objecting to "nuisance behaviour" emanating from AL units in a building which also contains residential apartments; the other residents can now oppose the AL licence, via the Condominium Association. Condominiums were also given the right to apply an additional quota on AL proprietors, to "cover the costs of the extra use of communal areas" of the building. Both of these aspects of the new legislation have been focal points for public debates centred on the rights, powers and privileges of various stakeholders. Before analysing this in more detail, we next explore the coverage of the AL situation in Lisbon and Porto, around the time of the new legislation, as reported in the media.

Media coverage of AL in Lisbon and Porto

This part of the analysis sought firstly to explore what kind of contextual information about the AL situation in Lisbon and Porto was being transmitted by the media in the period surrounding the passing of the new legislation, and secondly to identify possible rights claims and the claimants who were given voice either directly or indirectly via the media texts. It should be noted that the aim of this was not to conduct a comparative discourse analysis of the various different sources, but simply to ascertain what kind of information, arguments and opinions were being put into the public domain by the media coverage. This also provided the context for the next and most important stage of our analysis, which involved exploring how SMC texts invoke and promote, or contest, individual and/or collective rights claims.

The contextualisation of AL by the media texts can be categorised into four main topics: the increase in AL; the housing crisis; the regeneration of the city centres, and the legal issues surrounding AL.

Firstly, the massive increase in this type of tourist accommodation is flagged. According to one report, it has "more than quadrupled" since 2014. In Lisbon, AL is said by some sources to represent "around a third" of all tourist accommodation, and by others to represent closer to one half. One source notes that whilst there were only around 100 registered units in Lisbon in 2010, now there are over **15,000,** with 50% of these concentrated in five historic central neighbourhoods. These neighbourhoods are now said to have up to 40% of all available housing units given over to AL. Furthermore, 14 of the neighbourhoods which make up the downtown area of Lisbon are now said to have more AL users than residents (assuming that the AL units are fully occupied), with, in some cases, a ratio of somewhere between 200% and 400% more AL users to residents. In Porto, the situation is similar. One text reports on a study which found that the majority (over 70%) of the 6,198 officially registered AL units in the city were in the historic centre neighbourhoods. Since the majority of AL units are apartments, this means that over

5,000 apartments in the city centre are currently being used as tourist accommodation. In some neighbourhoods, the capacity for AL users has "overtaken the number of residents".

Whilst the numbers and figures differ slightly among the different sources and studies cited, excessive AL is seen as a driver of the dual processes of 'touristification' and 'gentrification', and the intense pressure on these neighbourhoods, particularly in terms of housing, is made clear. The in-depth articles and opinion pieces, in particular, highlight the growing housing crisis. One source argues that AL in the centre of Porto is "occupying apartments and buildings that could and should be made available for long-term housing". It is also noted that current tenants, particularly the elderly, are the victims of "harassment and threats" by landlords eager to remove them from their long-term residences. Another source laments the lack of stability for tenants and argues for the urgent need "to stop the voracity of real estate speculation which is killing Lisbon".

However, it is far from consensual in these media texts that AL is directly to blame for the exacerbation of the housing crisis which has seen many people evicted or forced from their homes. The fact that so many apartments in the historic city centre neighbourhoods were allowed to reach (and remain in) an extremely degraded state is most often blamed on bad urban planning and management policies, at both national and local governance levels, and going back several decades since the democratisation of Portuguese politics in the 1970s. It is noted in some texts that the population exodus from Lisbon city centre began in earnest in the 1980s, with around 30% of downtown housing units unoccupied by the beginning of the 21st century. The 2011 population census is quoted as revealing **185,000** empty housing units across the city, with only 20% of those available for renting at the time. The present electoral register for the city centre is cited as showing just 45% of the number of registered voters in the mid-1990s, bearing witness to a steady decline in permanent residence in this area. One source claims that around one third of the apartments currently used for AL in the historic central neighbourhoods of Lisbon were standing empty 10 years ago. Another source quotes the results of a study which found that 44% of AL owners said they were occupying spaces that had "previously been unoccupied". The argument that conversion into AL units has saved many buildings from abandonment and falling into ruin is often voiced, as is the role of AL in urban regeneration: one source notes "the extremely positive effect that local accommodation has brought by rehabilitating hundreds, or even thousands, of buildings that were degraded and unoccupied", whilst another argues that "if it's true that AL has taken some units out of the housing market, it is no less true that it has given many abandoned units back to the city, bringing new life to the neighbourhood, the street and the building".

The fourth main topic concerns the legal issues surrounding the explosion of short-term vacation rentals. Several articles published around the time of the legislation provide explanations of what will change, and what new rights, obligations and powers have been set out. Others serve to highlight the tensions among the different possible rights claims and indeed the different types of rights at stake, for example. This will be further explored in the following sections.

Stakeholders in AL identified in the media

The media coverage of AL in the cities of Lisbon and Porto makes it evident that there are a number of stakeholders with differing positionings regarding the AL situation and the recent (2018) legislation.

At the individual level, the rights claimants identified are primarily apartment owners and tenants. The apartment owners may or may not be AL operators, and may or may not reside in the apartment in question. There are clearly two types of AL owner-operator: on the one hand, there are those whose goal is to make extra income through renting part or the whole of their apartment to tourists, in some cases to be able to afford their own housing costs in the city. Indeed, in some cases, this may be the only source of income. In Portuguese, there is a specific nomination for these stakeholders which is often employed in the media texts: *'pequenos proprietários'*, or literally 'small owners'. The right claims invoked here are the right to own property, the right to do what one wants with one's property, and sometimes the right to live in a certain part of the city (which wouldn't be possible without the extra income from rentals). On the other hand, there are those who have taken an investment opportunity, which may have required significant financial outlay in the renovation of a building or part of a building. These owners (who may be individual operators, micro-companies or part of larger business operations) therefore claim the right to a return on their investment which has, as is often alleged, contributed to the general level of "improvement" of the neighbourhood and therefore to the common good.

At the same time, the right to equal treatment within a condominium building may be invoked. Many see the power invested in condominiums to determine higher fees for AL operators as unjust, since they claim that many apartment buildings have long had commercial businesses operating in them (for example, medical or dental clinics, legal practices, hairdressing salons, etc.) which pay the same fees as the residents. Collectively, AL owners and operators are represented by a not-for-profit Association (ALEP – Local Accommodation in Portugal), which has a vocal President who is often quoted in the media coverage, and a strong social media presence (see below).

Then there are the apartment owners (and tenants) who are not involved in AL practices themselves, but whose neighbours are operating AL units. These people may invoke the right to live in peace and safety, which they see as being put in jeopardy by the constant flows of strangers through the building, and their sometimes anti-social practices. Whereas this was once a primarily social right, it has now become somewhat more 'official' through the recent addition to the legislation discussed above. Collectively, these people may be represented by their condominium associations, and as noted above, the media cite several court rulings in this matter. Interestingly, the legal discussions surrounding these cases hinged on whether or not AL can be considered as *'habitação'* (housing), since in theory Portuguese law forbids the use of apartments in condominiums for any other purpose. Cases are cited where the ruling went in favour of those wishing to force the closure of an AL unit which was causing anti-social behaviour, whilst other ruled against this.

Finally, there are the tenants who have either been evicted or forced from their home by rental increases they can no longer afford or the termination of their contracts, as well as those who feel that they are at risk of this happening to them. It is reported that many landlords have taken advantage of the 2012 legislation which liberalised the housing market to either convert long-term rentals into the seemingly more profitable AL model, or to sell to private investors who intend to do this. These tenants are represented collectively by several social movements which have put the right to decent and affordable housing at the centre of their manifestos, notably *Direito à Cidade* (Right to the City), *O Porto não se Vende* (Porto is not for Sale), and *Morar em Lisboa* (Living in Lisbon). Although there is some coverage of these movements in the media texts, it is mainly through the social media channels that their voices are heard (see below).

As for public sector stakeholders, the most important rights and powers regarding AL have been handed to the Municipal Councils by national government. As already noted above, the Lisbon Municipal Council was quick to act on this, declaring two central districts as 'areas of contention'. This action provoked a lot of media and social media response; on the one hand, some AL owners complained of being "persecuted" and of having their rights curtailed. AL, it is argued, is being made a scapegoat for a problem that is rooted in other causes. It is also pointed out that collective entities such as the Lisbon Municipal Council and the Catholic Church own plenty of properties in the city that could be given over to social housing projects. On the other hand, those against the expansion of AL in the city bemoan the fact that not enough is being done to limit AL and that the actions of the City Hall are merely 'token gestures' which will have no obvious effect. In Porto, where the Municipal Council has yet to act in this matter, there have been vociferous demands from activists for drastic measures, including the complete "outlawing" of Airbnb.

In the following section, we further explore the tensions and discords among the various stake-holder positionings and rights claims by examining the voices heard through the social media communication channels outlined above. In the final section, we discuss the conflicting place-frames that emerge from the data, and examine the effect of this on contemporary urban politics of place.

Alojamento local *issues in social media communication*

Unsurprisingly, all the Community pages studied had a strong element of invoking collective rights and incentivising others to take action in support of these rights. The social movements *Morar em Lisboa*, *Direito à Cidade* and *O Porto não se vende* are all concerned with a perceived collective 'right to the city' of local people whose access to decent and affordable housing is under threat. These pages therefore promote and encourage participation in public events such as meetings, demonstrations, seminars, debates, book launches and fund raisers which are geared towards the social cause of housing, as well as providing links to public petitions, open letters and polls. Posts around these topics tend to be rallying calls for collective rights, signalled by the inclusive pronoun *we*, including the right to live in the city centres (particularly for those who were "born and raised" there), along with calls for the State to fulfil its corresponding duties in terms of providing adequate housing options, as the following extracts illustrate:

"We are here to say loud and clear that the inhabitants of Porto are in the streets, in the neighbourhoods, to fight for the right to live in Porto. Porto is not for sale. Full stop!"

"We need to denounce this scandal of *Portuenses* [people from Porto] being expelled from the city where they were born and raised to make room for foreign real estate speculators. The City of Porto belongs to the *Portuenses* and the people who work there. Tourists yes, but *Portuenses* Always! !!"

"It is up to the State to solve part of the housing problem. There are hundreds of vacant properties belonging to the State that are abandoned in the Greater Lisbon region. Why not renovate them and rent them to those who need them most? (…) The State is not fulfilling its duty and it is a pity that people in Portugal do not understand this."

In a similar fashion, the *AL-Esclarecimentos* page seeks to promote activities in defence of the collective right of citizens to operate AL units in the face of external threats from 'them', who seek to curtail this right (such as a public petition entitled "Don't Let Them Kill AL") as well as social get-togethers designed to enhance solidarity and information sharing amongst individual AL operators. Interestingly, in view of the accusations that AL is leading to forced evictions and increased rates of homelessness, this Community page strongly promotes a crowdfunding project initiated by the founder of *AL-Esclarecimentos*, aimed at helping homeless people.

However, also of interest to this study are the individual comments posted in response to the sharing of media articles, infographics and other texts which provide support for the various underlying rights claims and arguments, as well as the comments threads posted directly following the online publication of the articles used in our media corpus. It is here that the interactive aspect of SMC comes into play, and where the multiple and often conflicting rights claims become most visible.

A great deal of the comments are from individuals who make rights claims as AL operators. These claims tend to focus on the right to do what one wants with one's property, often framed in a discourse of freedom and Constitutional rights, and even suggesting that the renouncing of these rights will lead back to constraints suffered under Salazar's dictatorship:

"Well unfortunately, a ban on AL ban would run into a document called "The Constitution of the Portuguese Republic" since it means a restriction on private property and private enterprise".

"Since when can a person not manage his property as he sees fit? Will we be going back to a dictatorial regime where there is no freedom of action?"

On the other hand, such arguments are often countered by those who summon up the "Constitutional right of property" to defend the claim that condominium buildings are solely for the purpose of housing, and that AL does not comply with either the legal or the functional definition of 'housing':

> "the content of Decree-Law 128/2014 (29-August)[10] seriously contravenes the RIGHT OF PROPERTY of those who previously acquired a residential unit in a building whose Licence for Use (issued by the City Council) (...) determines that all the autonomous fractions of that building are "destined for HOUSING". Thus, Decree-Law 128/2014 (29-August) must be declared INCONSTITUTIONAL."

> "How ridiculous! Visiting is different from living. Does any entity recognise someone with a contract for one day as an inhabitant of that city or country? No."

> "Of course AL is not housing. It is a service, a business, a commercial activity. Or will you say that a hotel is also housing? The only way that AL differs from hotels is that it meets fewer criteria for cleanliness, safety, certifications and inspections, etc. In addition to the fact that many avoid paying tax ... "

Another frequent comments thread is around the issue of the right to supplement incomes via AL rentals. Many AL operators feel that they are being "unfairly attacked" or even "persecuted" for simply trying to "survive":

> "I have full respect for housing rights concerns. But I would be grateful if I was given the same respect for my livelihood, which is the result of my honest work."

> "Some people think this is the goose that lays the golden eggs, but for most of us, it's our way of surviving. We end up working long hours and do not save very much."

> "I have a friend who was unemployed for years, meanwhile she returned (in her 40s) to her mother's house and transformed the apartment where she lived and which she owns into AL and this is the only income she has (...) We are talking about survival and not about running a business. The persecution of AL does not take into account how many people survive thanks to it. "

Once again, the framing of such "persecution" as a throwback to the days of the restricted freedoms, harassment and intimidation of the Salazar regime is also present:

> "This looks like PIDE.[11] So a few hundred people have seen here a way of living or increasing their income, they bought an apartment, invested in remodeling it, opened a business, pay taxes and now are being persecuted like criminals??"

However, this type of argument is then offset by dismantling the rights claims of the few in favour of the 'common good' of "the majority of city dwellers", with the argument that AL is socially prejudicial and is "destroying" the city:

> "to talk about the rights of those who saved up "a little bit of money" and bought a "little house" to get "income" and now want to protect their "investment" (which is actually not in question, as they could always rent it out as permanent housing or sell it when the price is right!) from risk is simply ridiculous, as they are involved in an activity that is socially detrimental to the vast majority of city dwellers".

> "Housing is not just a business for a few people, it is first and foremost a resource that enables balanced and functional cities to exist. That enables the development of healthy communities. Because Lisbon or Porto are much more than houses. And it is not only homeowners who have the right to do whatever they want with the city, including destroying it".

Furthermore, many comments are targeted at condominium neighbours who operate AL units, or absentee landlords, invoking the right to live in "peace and privacy" and to defend one's home from "the daily insecurity" arising from the tourists/strangers who are "invading" their living space and causing both material and psychological damage with their anti-social behaviour:

> "It's about co-ownership of a building, but some owners are getting profits while the others are being harmed by frequent habitual damage [to common spaces in the building] as well as the insecurity and risks due to the presence of unknown strangers"

"These tourists come and go as they please, drink until dawn and couldn't care less about the buildings' common spaces"

Not everyone concurs with these arguments, however. Some AL operators see fit to counter-argue that AL guests are no worse than other types of neighbours:

"I can assure you that there are no more comings-and-goings in my AL apartment than in the neighbouring apartments - most of them illegally rented out to students."

"You're lucky not to have neighbours who arrive home every night drunk and shouting at their family. Tourists disturb, but neighbours don't????"

A related question that is discussed in the threads is whether condominium associations should have the right to prevent individual apartment owners from operating AL. From the perspective of actual or potential AL operators, this is usually framed in the argument that it is unfair, considering that there have long been other types of "commercial activities" operating in condominiums, as well as the fact that condominium associations do not generally have to approve tenants for long-term rentals:

"Do the condominiums have the right to decide whether or not there will be an AL in the building? I don't see why. Do they decide in the case of long-term rentals? Or if a commercial space changes business? Or if someone rents a parking space or storage rooms? Either they start authorizing everything or it doesn't make sense to me … "

Finally, there is some debate over the rights of landlords versus the rights of tenants, in view of the fact that the AL issue is said to be causing the forced "expulsion" of people from their city centre homes. Many commenters strongly defend the rights of property owners, or landlords, over those of tenants, firmly within a neoliberal capitalist framework of the right to property and free enterprise:

If you aren't the owner, how can you demand rights over the property?

The concept of a tenant is just that: a temporary occupation of someone else's property. The protectionist legislation towards tenants, at the expense of the landlords who have been forced to finance these policies since 1974, has resulted in the degradation of housing and a lack of investment, harming the cities, the country and even the tenants themselves, who have seen their homes fall into disrepair without being able to do anything about it.

I am sad for the elderly [residents who have been evicted], but I am also sad for the landlord who has been doing forced charity work for decades and decades, imagine that they were obliged to give 5 euros to each beggar they saw on the street, would you think it was fair? Many landlords lose hundreds and hundreds of euros every month because they are forced to do the charity that the State refuses to do.

To accuse the landlord of having no feelings is ridiculous. What obligation does a landlord have to be charitable? A contract is not based on sentiment, but on the interests of both parties, and not just the interests of one side. Those with no feelings are the public institutions which don't support underprivileged people, including tenants but also landlords who are impoverished due to Salazarian rent policies that are still being imposed by the left-wing troika.

Once again, we see here a discursive thread of the fear of a return to the politics and values of the Salazar regime, but this time the framing is that of the landlord as "impoverished" victim, obliged to be "charitable" towards tenants who have, according to this narrative, no rights claims since they have been living almost 'rent free' for many years, but who are also negatively affected by the policies of a democratic State which is accused of not carrying out its public duty to help the 'underprivileged' and, at the same time, as being 'protectionist' towards long-term tenants.

Emerging place-frames

Some dominant place-frames emerge from our data. Firstly, primarily in the media texts, the framing of Lisbon and Porto modern, cosmopolitan, fashionable but still "authentic" cities - with their "traditional" neighbourhoods. This combination of apparently conflicting frames has long been used to promote Portugal as a tourist destination (cf. Santos, 2004), but has recently taken on a new dimension as processes of tourism-driven gentrification of the city centre neighbourhoods mean that Lisbon and Porto easily rival any major European city and that tourists nowadays can easily find accommodation and 'live-like-a-local' in these 'authentic' neighbourhoods which were formerly residential areas to be 'gazed' upon. Governance stakeholders and legislators, keen to pursue policies of tourism-driven gentrification, have given private investors the opportunity to further reinforce that particular place-frame, by moving away from discourses and practices of "recuperating" the old neighbourhoods towards those of "regeneration", which aim at attracting new residents into these areas.

However, by doing that, they inevitably collide with the place-framing of local residents who invoke their social right to remain in the historic neighbourhoods. In this case, the underlying place-frame is the 'nostalgic' framing of traditional, village-like socio-geographical structures, where neighbours know one another, meet and socialise in the streets and public spaces, organise their own local festivities, and often work and send their children to school in the immediate vicinity. This framing is particularly reinforced by social activists and supporters of social movements, who are given voice in both the mass media and social media. Since these neighbourhoods have traditionally been inhabited by people in low-income brackets, this place-frame relies on a supply of affordable rented housing. An excess of Airbnb-type accommodation in these neighbourhoods would therefore seem wholly at odds with this framing, and this is made evident in some of the comments, which also point to overtourism and local saturation with the numbers of tourists, as well as putting the blame on local people who operate AL units:

> "Lisbon belongs to whom? No longer to those who were born there or who have always lived there. There are too many tourists."

> "Our city is progressively becoming less authentic and it has developed with flagrant disregard for its 'native' inhabitants. The city is dirtier, more expensive and more unjust".

> "They [tourists] are destroying our city, it no longer has soul, and even worse this tourism is of low quality all dirty and it is us who pay the bill for cleaning up the city. I can understand the foreign owners, who are just taking advantage of the situation, but I don't understand local owners."

Yet this place-frame is by no means shared by all the residents of the city centres. Some seek to dismantle the "romanticised" framing of the "typical neighbourhoods", constructing an alternative framing of an "old and falling down" and "ugly" city centre. One AL operator claims that what characterised Lisbon when she arrived in 1999 was "rot", arguing that AL is making a vital contribution to the modernisation of the city. "The houses [in Alfama] were very small and inadequate for families", and the general living conditions were "unhealthy". Moreover, the younger generation in particular are now claiming, under the umbrella of constitutional law, the right to own private property and to do as they please in and/or with it, including operating short-term tourist rentals to complement their income, or as an alternative to unemployment. Many of these young AL operators claim the right to a lifestyle that is flexible and entrepreneurial in spirit, and besides the economic benefits accrued, it allows them to extend their social capital by meeting and interacting with a whole new range of people, including tourists and temporary residents.

A further rights claim focuses on the collective right to enjoy public spaces in the form of a "clean and rehabilitated" city centre, free from drugs and petty crime, with modernised infrastructures and a greater element of choice in leisure and entertainment services. This, it is claimed, is one of the benefits that comes from a type of tourism that is focused on the type of tourists who want to (rather paradoxically) enjoy the "real" Portugal, and which ensures that Portuguese cities will not return to the bad state that they were in until recently. The juxtaposing framings of the 'old' and the 'new' cities are often found in the data:

> "The cities re-made themselves and attracted more- not less – inhabitants. They pulse with life and activity. And they brought the whole Country along with them".

"Well, in the centre of Porto 6 years ago I used to see ruin and poverty and I see today cleanliness, joy, diversification … AL has saved dead city centres."

"Lisbon was like a kind of Havana in Europe, with buildings that were run down, dirty, falling apart. Great improvements have been made. Where there were chicken coops, now we have swimming pools. The displacement of people to the peripheries has been happening for decades, the city was becoming deserted, it was in absolute decay"

For this reason, it is rare to find any voicing of 'anti-tourist' sentiments. Although it is often claimed that tourism-driven gentrification threatens the right "to stay put" of existing local communities, in our data it is fairly clear that tourists themselves are not being blamed for the housing crisis in the cities. Indeed, residents often claim to welcome the presence of foreign tourists; the arguments that 'everyone is a tourist' nowadays, as well as the notion that local lives are improved by tourism are often deployed:

"What's wrong with having tourists? Aren't they people just like anyone else, who abide by laws, stimulate the local economy and help to keep the city alive."

"I don't understand the complaints about 'serving' tourists – is it better to work in a factory?"

Finally, a more balanced framing is also voiced, which suggests a type of urban development that prioritises the right to the city for local residents, whilst simultaneously acknowledging the right to visit the city, and the right of the city to be visited:

"We are not against tourists. We want a city that can be visited, but which first and foremost can be lived in".

This echoes the question posed by a Human Rights researcher, who represents the *Porto is Not for Sale* movement, which neatly summarises the issue of how AL impacts on the right the city: "What proportion between tourist accommodation and housing allows everyone to live in and enjoy the city, and to share it with visitors?" (Barbiero, 2018). On a final note, however, it should be pointed out that the question of visitor/tourist rights in the city is barely touched upon or discussed in our data. This may well signal an underlying acceptance of both the universal 'right' to travel as a tourist which has taken root in contemporary free-market, neo-liberal capitalist society (Higgins-Desbiolles, 2010) and also the corresponding 'duty' of the Portuguese people to welcome tourists, since tourism is so strongly discursively framed as being a main 'driver' of the Portuguese economy (see, for example, WTTC., 2019).

Conclusions

This study highlights the multiplicities of place-making practices and the contentious nature of contemporary urban politics of place. The findings confirm the appropriateness of interpreting the multiple, disperse, overlapping, contested, and constantly (re)negotiated nature of contemporary urban rights discourses within a place-making framework that takes account of rights *in* place, wherein both individual and collective experiences, understandings, values and imaginings create different versions of the same place. As such, there is no clear, cohesive and universal 'cry and demand' for the right to the city, but rather an always ongoing and incomplete negotiation of rights (and privileges, duties, and powers) in places (Pierce et al., 2016) which can be identified in interacting discursive practices at different levels.

Moreover, it would appear that the social processes underlying these discourses are no longer entirely rooted in the traditional power struggles amongst well-defined contenders (e.g. defined by social class), or between property owners/developers and city-dwellers/city-users, but are in fact not only diffuse but also divisive. The various media and SMC platforms echo this discord, giving voice to a wide range of stakeholders, but also showing how some apparently similar stakeholders differ greatly as rights claimants. Property-owning neighbours are now pitted against each other, disputing rights claims to do with freedom of choice, property rights, employment rights and rights to prevent others from carrying out these activities. Given that some 'small' owners claim to be from the traditional working classes and are now seeking, through AL, a novel way out of the challenge of the spiralling cost of urban living and unemployment, we might well ask if they are facing the same 'enemy' as the tenants who face displacement from their homes due to encroaching gentrification, be it tourism-driven or not. and their various and often conflicting rights claims which underlie the arguments used to advance particular place-frames.

However, the fact that rights in the city are increasingly multifaceted and often conflicting among what might appear at first glance to be a unified group of stakeholders (i.e. 'local' residents) does not mean that the urban power structures do not continue to be unequal and unjust. It is clear that the major negative impact of the gentrification and touristification (or 'airbnb-ization) of the *bairros populares* of Lisbon and Porto is the rapidly worsening housing crisis in the city centres. In the face of increasing concern, and perhaps as a conciliatory move within a counter-frame of left-wing politics, the current national government has created the possibility for local government at municipal level to create 'areas of contention' as well as governance measures at the micro-local level in the form of granting more powers to condominium associations. This move is in apparent conflict with place-making from a neo-liberal economic and individualistic perspective, as it was designed to impose limits on the 'right' to operate an AL service or business and also to curb the real estate speculation associated with AL. However, the measures did not appear to have any immediate effect, especially in Porto, where the Municipal Council did not take up their newly-granted powers. It may well be, as argued by Mendes (2016), that what is required to ensure the balance between the right to housing and the development of tourism in city centres is more 'critical innovation' in local processes and practices of urban regeneration. Although this study has a very clear geographical and socio-political context, we would argue that there is a clear need for detailed, careful, contextualised studies of the local politics of place, on an ongoing basis, in cities across the world which are experiencing similar issues, to inform eventual policies and urban planning decisions. We also note that the limitations of the study, in terms of data collection, suggests that some stakeholders and their rights claims may be missing and therefore that further research using different and/or more exhaustive data collection methods could add further dimensions to an already complex situation.

As a final comment, it should be noted that this study was carried out in a context of over-tourism-related issues in Lisbon and Porto – a context which did not foresee any drop in tourist numbers in the near future and where the success of AL ventures therefore seemed secure and almost guaranteed. The sustainability of tourism, and AL, was seen as primarily threatened by *too much* tourism – a case perhaps of 'killing the golden goose that lays the golden eggs', as well as the obvious environmental and social pressures on the neighbourhoods in question. In the current context of the global COVID-19 pandemic which, almost overnight, led to a situation of *no* tourism, the AL sector and the socio-economic context in which it is embedded could not be more different. This seismic shift, which is affecting cities worldwide, serves to reinforce the shifting, relational nature of the politics of place, and the need for rapid and flexible solutions, rather than a reliance on sets of rights and powers that are non-negotiable.

Notes

1. It should be noted that this method of selection resulted in a corpus of texts which does not include every possible news source; indeed, it may be noticeable to those familiar with the Portuguese mediascape that certain high-profile titles are missing. One obvious example is the *Correio de Manhã* newspaper, a tabloid with a high circulation. This was not a deliberate exclusion, but simply reflects the lack of articles that corresponded to our selection criteria. It is also important to note that we are not performing a comparative analysis of the different news sources; the media texts were, for the purposes of this study, collected to identify what kind of information, arguments and opinions were being put into the public domain.

2. There is also a closed group linked to this page, currently with around 65 000 members.
3. All data excerpts in this paper have been translated into English from the Portuguese original by the authors of this paper.
4. The *Estado Novo* (New State) was the official name given to the dictatorship regime established in Portugal following the coup détat in 1926 and lasting until the democratic revolution of 1974. For much of this period, the regime was headed by António Salazar.
5. *Programa de Recuperação de Imóveis Degradados (Programme of Recuperation of Degraded Buildings).*
6. *Programa de Reabilitação Urbana (Urban Recuperation Programme).*
7. Law n° 104/2004, 7 May - Regime Jurídico Excepcional de Reabilitação Urbana de Zonas Históricas e de Áreas Críticas de Recuperação e Reconversão Urbanística (Exceptional Legal Regime for the Urban Rehabilitation of Historical Zones and Critical Urban Recovery and Re-conversion Areas).
8. Law n° 128/2014, 29 August
9. Law n°62/2018, 22 August
10. Law governing AL operation – see above.
11. PIDE were the notorious political police during the New State dictatorship, responsible for the repression of all forms of opposition to the regime.

Disclosure statement

No potential conflict of interest was reported by the authors.

ORCID

Kate Torkington (iD) http://orcid.org/0000-0001-9729-7872
Filipa Perdigão Ribeiro (iD) http://orcid.org/0000-0003-3267-7166

References

Amin, A. (2004). Regions unbound: Towards a new politics of place. *Geografiska Annaler, 86*(1), 33–44.
Attoh, K. A. (2011). What *kind* of right to the city? *Progress in Human Geography, 35*(5), 669–685.
Balsas, C. J. L. (2007). City centre revitalization in Portugal: A study of Lisbon and Porto. *Journal of Urban Design, 12*(2), 231–259.
Barbiero, A. (2018, October 20). Mapear o Alojamento Turístico: bastam alguns "cliques" e contas. *Público*, (online).
Borja, J. (2011). Democracy in search of the future city. In A. Sugranyes & C. Mathinet (Eds.), *Cities for all: Proposals and experiences towards the right to the city* (2nd ed., pp. 31–43). Habitat International Coalition.
Busa, A. (2009). The right to the city: The entitled and the excluded. *The Urban Re/Inventors Online Journal, 3* (09 November), 1–13. http://www.urbanreinventors.net/3/busa/busa-urbanreinventors.pdf
Cocola-Gant, A. (2018, February). O capitalismo imobiliário e a crise da habitação em Lisboa [Real estate capitalism and the housing crisis in Lisbon]. Le *Monde Diplomatique* (Portuguese edition).
De Souza, M. L. (2010). Which right to which city? In defence of political-strategic clarity. *Interface, 2*(1), 315–333.
Domaradzska, A. (2018). Urban social movements and the right to the city: An introduction to the special issue on urban mobilization. *Voluntas, 29*, 607–620.
Dredge, D., & Gyimóthy, S. (2015). The collaborative economy and tourism: Critical perspectives, questionable claims and silenced voices. *Tourism Recreation Research, 40*(3), 286–302.
Goffman, E. (1974). *Frame analysis: An essay on the organization of experience*. Harvard University Press.

González-Pérez, J. (2020). The dispute over tourist cities. Tourism gentrification in the historic Centre of Palma (Majorca, Spain). *Tourism Geographies, 22*(1), 171–191.https://doi.org/10.1080/14616688.2019.1586986

Gössling, S., & Hall, C. M. (2019). Sharing versus collaborative economy: How to align ICT developments and the SDGs in tourism? *Journal of Sustainable Tourism, 27*(1), 74–96. https://doi.org/10.1080/09669582.2018.1560455

Guttentag, D. (2015). Airbnb: Disruptive innovation and the rise of an informal tourism accommodation sector. *Current Issues in Tourism, 18*(12), 1192–1217.

Habermas, J. (1962 [1994]). *The structural transformation of the public sphere.* Polity Press.

Harvey, D. (2008). The right to the city. *New Left Review, 53,* 23–40.

Higgins-Desbiolles, F. (2010). The elusiveness of sustainability in tourism: The culture-ideology of consumerism and its implications. *Tourism and Hospitality Research, 10*(2), 116–129.

Inside Airbnb. (2018, November 19). *Detailed listings data for Lisbon.*

Ioannides, D., Röslmaier, M., & van der Zee, E. (2019). Airbnb as an instigator of 'tourism bubble' expansion in Utrecht's Lombok neighbourhood. *Tourism Geographies, 21*(5), 822–840.

KhosraviNik, M. (2017). Social Media Critical Discourse Studies (SM-CDS). In J. Flowerdew & J. Richardson (Eds.), *Handbook of critical discourse analysis* (pp. 582–596). Routledge.

KhosraviNik, M., & Unger, J. (2016). Critical discourse studies and social media: Power, resistance and critique in changing media ecologies. In R. Wodak & M. Meyer, *Methods of critical discourse studies* (3rd ed., pp. 205–233). Sage.

KhosraviNik, M. (2019, October 28). Populist digital media? Social media systems and the global populist right discourse. *Public Seminar.* https://publicseminar.org/2019/10/populist-digital-media-social-media-systems-and-the-global-populist-right-discourse/

Koens, K., Postma, A., & Papp, B. (2018). Is overtourism overused? Understanding the impact of tourism in a city context. Sustainability, *10*(12), 4384. https://doi.org/10.3390/su10124384

Lefebvre, H. (1968). *Le droit à la ville.* Anthropos.

Lefebvre, H. (1996 [1968]). The right to the city. In E. Kofman & E. Lebas (Transl. & Eds.), *Writings on cities* (pp. 147–159). Blackwell.

Lestegás, I. (2019). Lisbon after the crisis: From credit-fuelled suburbanization to tourist-driven gentrification. *International Journal of Urban and Regional Research, 43*(4), 705–723.

Leung, X. Y., Xue, L., & Wen, H. (2019). Framing the sharing economy: Toward a sustainable ecosystem. *Tourism Management, 71,* 44–53.

Marcuse, P. (2009). From critical urban theory to the right to the city. *City, 13* (2–3), 185–197.

Marcuse, P. (2011). Rights in cities and the right to the city? In A. Sugranyes & C. Mathinet (Eds.), *Cities for all: Proposals and experiences towards the right to the city* (2nd ed., pp. 89–100). Habitat International Coalition.

Martin, C. (2016). The sharing economy: A pathway to sustainability or a nightmarish form of neoliberal capitalism? *Ecological Economics, 121,* 149–159.

Martin, D. (2003). Place-framing' as place-making: Constituting a neighbourhood for organising and activism. *Annals of the Association of American Geographers, 93* (3), 730–750.

Martin, D. (2013). Place frames: Analysing practice and production of place in contentious politics. In W. Nicholls, B. Miller, & J. Beaumont (Eds.), *Spaces of contention: Spatialities and social movements* (pp. 85–99). Routledge.

Massey, D. (1994). *Space, place and gender.* Polity Press.

Massey, D. (2005). *For space.* Sage.

Mathinet, C. (2011). The right to the city: Keys to understanding the proposal for 'another city is possible'. In A. Sugranyes & C. Mathinet (Eds.), *Cities for all: Proposals and experiences towards the right to the city* (2nd ed., pp. 23–28). Habitat International Coalition.

Mayer, M. (2009). The 'right to the city' in the context of shifting mottos of urban social movements. City, *13*(2–3), 362–374.

McCann, E. (2002). Space, citizenship, and the right to the city: A brief overview. GeoJournal, *58*(2–3), 77–79.

Mendes, L. (2013). Public policies on urban rehabilitation and their effects on gentrification in Lisbon. *AGIR – Revista Interdisciplinar de Ciências Sociais e Humanas, 1*(5), 200–218.

Mendes, L. (2016). What can be done to resist or mitigate tourism gentrification in Lisbon? Some policy findings & recommendations. In M. Glaudemans & I. Marko (Eds.), *City making & tourism gentrification* (pp. 35–42). Stadslab.

Modan, G. G. (2007). *Turf wars: Discourse, diversity and the politics of place.* Blackwell Publishing.

Muzergues, T. (2020). *The great class shift: How social structures are redefining western politics.* Routledge.

Oskam, J. A. (2019). *The future of airbnb and the 'sharing economy'.: The collaborative consumption of our cities.* Channel View Publications.

Peeters, P., Gössling, S., Klijs, J., Milano, C., Novelli, M., Dijkmans, C., Eijgelaar, E., Hartman, S., Heslinga, J., Isaac, R., Mitas, O., Moretti, S., Nawijn, J., Papp, B., & Postma, A. (2018). *Research for TRAN Committee – Overtourism: Impact and possible policy responses.* European Parliament.

Pierce, J., Martin, D., & Murphy, J. (2011). Relational place-making: The networked politics of place. *Transactions of the Institute of British Geographers, 36*(1), 54–70.

Pierce, J., Williams, O., & Martin, D. (2016). Rights in places: An analytical extension of the right to the city. *Geoforum, 70*, 79–88.

Purcell, M. (2003). Citizenship and the right to the global city: Reimagining the capitalist world order. *International Journal of Urban and Regional Research, 27*(3), 564–590.

Purcell, M. (2014). Possible worlds: Henri Lefebvre and the right to the city. *Journal of Urban Affairs, 36*(1), 141–154.

Rose, G. (1994). The cultural politics of place: Local representation and oppositional discourse in two films. *Transactions of the Institute of British Geographers, 19*(1), 46–60.

Santos, C. A. (2004). Framing Portugal: Representational dynamics. *Annals of Tourism Research, 31*(1), 122–138. https://doi.org/10.1016/j.annals.2003.08.005

Schmid, C. (2012). Henri Lefebvre, the right to the city and the new metropolitan mainstream. In N. Brenner, P. Marcuse, & M. Mayer (Eds.), *Cities for people, not for profit: Critical urban theory and the right to the city* (pp. 42–62). Routledge.

Soja, E. (2010). *Seeking spatial justice*. University of Minnesota Press.

Strömbäck, J., & Esser, F. (2014). Mediatization of politics: Transforming democracies and reshaping politics. In K. Lundby (Ed.), *Mediatization of communication* (pp. 375–403). De Gruyter Mouton.

Thimm, C., Dang-Anh, M., & Einspänner, J. (2014). Mediatized politics - structures and strategies of discursive participation and online deliberation on Twitter. In A. Hepp & F. Krotz (Eds.), *Mediatized worlds: Culture and society in a media age* (pp. 253–270). Palgrave Macmillan.

Tulumello, S. (2016). Reconsidering neoliberal urban planning in times of crisis: Urban regeneration policy in a 'dense' space in Lisbon. *Urban Geography, 37*(1), 117–140. https://doi.org/10.1080/02723638.2015.1056605

Tulumello, S. (2019). Struggling against entrenched austerity from the housing crisis toward social movements for housing in post-crisis Lisbon and Portugal. In F. Othengrafen & K. Serraos (Eds.), *Urban resilience, changing economy and social trends* (pp. 61–80). Leibniz Universität Hannover.

Unger, J., Wodak, R., & KhosraviNik, M. (2016). Critical discourse studies and social media data. In D. Silverman (Ed.), *Qualitative research* (4th ed., pp. 277–293). SAGE.

Wodak, R., & Meyer, M. (2016). Critical discourse studies: History, agenda, theory and methodology. In R. Wodak & M. Meyer (Eds.), *Methods of critical discourse studies* (3rd ed., pp. 2–23).Sage.

WTTC. (2019, October 7). *Portugal records highest Travel & Tourism growth in the European Union*. https://wttc.org/News-Article/Portugal-records-highest-Travel&Tourism-growth-in-the-European-Union

Politicising platform-mediated tourism rentals in the digital sphere: Airbnb in Madrid and Barcelona

Julie Wilson ⓘ, Lluís Garay-Tamajon ⓘ and Soledad Morales-Perez ⓘ

ABSTRACT
Both short-term tourism rentals and the digital platforms that manage and mediate them have expanded enormously in recent years, against a backdrop of increasing platform urbanism and platform capitalism. This expansion triggers transformations that are contributing to acute negative externalities never envisaged within the original ethos and sustainability promises of the sharing economy. The severe knock-on effects of the unanticipated reconfiguration of economic and everyday life have met with a strong civic response, leading to a growing politicisation of platform-mediated rentals increasingly performed in the digital sphere. Numerous social movements have arisen in opposition to platforms such as Airbnb, while lobbyists and user collectives have also mobilised to defend their respective rights to 'home-share' and generate extra income, as the business becomes increasingly professionalised in large cities. Through the lens of the increasingly politicised and polemical impacts of the platform economy, this article analyses Twitter narratives and counter-narratives surrounding Airbnb-mediated rentals and their impact on Madrid and Barcelona. Findings show how narratives are choreographed by a range of actors and that narrative ecosystems emerge in the form of interconnected virtual relationship networks, often embedded in translocal assemblages.

Introduction

Digital platforms and the algorithms that underpin them are becoming increasingly and rapidly prominent in society and across space. Having first emerged just over a decade ago, collaborative platforms were initially seen to represent a sustainable form of peer-to-peer (P2P) exchanges. However, as the practices they mediate have taken on new and unexpected externalities with acute socio-spatial consequences, and as civil society reacts increasingly vocally, the evolving platform economy represents a major socio-economic and political challenge.

Short-term rentals (STRs) – a practice increasingly mediated by digital platforms – are especially controversial. The dual consequences of their rapid expansion are an unsustainable spread of tourism into residential neighbourhoods with little or no prior tourism trajectory and an intensification of negative impacts in already densely touristic areas. In parallel, platform-mediated STRs have become increasingly politicised, with what started out as seemingly innocuous platform-enabled sharing later evolving into a marked duality.

First, social protest and resistance movements have mobilised in opposition to collateral effects within a broader call to rethink cities' relationships with tourism mobilities. As the impacts and reach of platform-mediated STRs become clearer, protest and resistance collectives are increasingly voicing concerns online and offline (see, e.g. Hassanli et al., 2019 analysis of Airbnb in Sydney), particularly on Twitter, affording them a translocal voice with potentially global resonance.

Second, and receiving little academic attention to date, lobby groups and STR platform user collectives have mobilised to defend their rights, some in favour of participation in the platform economy and the 'right to share' as a means of subsistence on a more domestic level, and others with an increasingly professional profile (major capital investment funds and commercial intermediaries) lobbying at an advocacy level to protect and strengthen their position. Recent research suggests that politicisation of the platform economy is a key determinant in whether – and to what extent – platforms and the practices they mediate are regulated. The local context and type of actors that initially politicise the issue are also important determinants (Aguilera et al., 2019; Artoli, 2018).

Adopting a comparative approach, we posit two research questions:

a. How do digital narratives/counter-narratives that choreograph social media discourses surrounding Airbnb align with politicisation of the platform and the mediated STRs?
b. What relationship networks can be identified within Twitter narratives/counter-narratives and how do they politicise and polemicise Airbnb and STRs?

Two contrasting case studies (Madrid and Barcelona) were conducted, to allow interpretation of how each city's particular geographical context and socio-political relationship with Airbnb/STRs (a) influences digital narratives/counter-narratives around Airbnb on Twitter and (b) shapes the relationship networks producing and disseminating those narratives. The case studies are also useful in framing an analysis of Airbnb's mediating praxis, given that its own strategy has tended to vary considerably between cities. A further rationale for this spatial comparison is varying regulatory stances in relation to platform-mediated STRs and differing forms of (trans)local politicisation of tourism/platforms, social mobilisation and socio-political contexts.

The article is structured as follows: we review relevant literature on platforms, STRs, the 'Airbnb effect' and conceptual approaches to politicisation in terms of protest, resistance and lobby/advocacy pressures. We then describe the methodology and present and discuss our main findings. We finally outline the conclusions drawn from these findings and their implications.

Literature review

Platform urbanism: the reshaping of cities and the urban everyday

Whether platforms are defined as online ecosystems, digital matchmaking infrastructures or a means of sociotechnical connectivity, scholars are beginning to comprehend them in terms of how their increasing density can rapidly and profoundly reshape the dynamics of cities and their regulation – a form of platform urbanism (Barns, 2018, 2020). This development increasingly extends to the mediation of urban infrastructures and management processes, whereby platform practices permeate experiences of the urban everyday to the point that their 'mundane ubiquity' legitimises them and gives them leverage in the urban sphere (Aguilera et al., 2019; Söderström & Mermet, 2020).

Söderström and Mermet (2020) understand platform urbanism as the impact of digital platforms on the materiality, daily lives and governance of cities, with major platform companies increasingly wielding greater control over urban governance. Furthermore, via their shifting strategies and business models, platforms can, according to Barns (2020), reconfigure economic and social exchanges, urban governance and the data infrastructures that underpin the circulation of people, goods and information as key components of everyday life, to the point where

" … platform urbanism, enacted daily as we commute, transact, love, post, listen, tweet or chat, deeply implicates the everyday urban encounter" (Barns, 2018, online source). In relation to the widespread disruption caused by platforms, Barns also observes a recent "backlash against major global platforms, evidenced by burgeoning literatures on platform capitalism, the platform society, platform surveillance and platform governance, as well as regulatory attention towards the market power of platforms in their dominance of global data infrastructure" (2020, 1).

Given the rapid emergence of extractive, unicorn-tech platforms in recent years, with intermediaries controlling and profiting from most transactions (Gössling & Hall, 2019), platform capitalism has been much critiqued and aligned with neoliberal discourses (Cockayne, 2016; Srnicek, 2017), with critics tending to centre on major emerging socio-economic and spatial transformations (Barns, 2020; Belk, 2014; Gillespie, 2010; Leszczynski, 2020; Srnicek, 2017).

The emergence of STRs and their corresponding digital platforms arguably generate long-term impacts and broad societal implications for cities (Cócola-Gant & Gago, 2019), with large multinationals evidently lying at the opposite end of the spectrum to more sharing-oriented, cooperativist endeavours (Demailly & Novel, 2014; Scholz & Schneider, 2017). As Aguilera et al. (2019) remind us, the fact that such new forms of corporate 'digital capitalism' do not land homogeneously upon cities (particularly given the variable strategy often employed by STR platform intermediaries) suggests a need for comparative analyses of local processes of actor mobilisation, collective action and regulation of digital platforms.

While Airbnb may be a convenient poster child for platform capitalism in recent years, it is the upshot of its practices and their transformative impacts – the Airbnb effect – that has provoked the strongest reactions. Having disaggregated STRs from their mediating platforms and the platform actors, it is pertinent to discuss what is meant by the Airbnb effect. We adopt van der Zee (2016) definition which refers to the broad range of negative socio-spatial externalities of the platform's presence in major tourism destinations, where tourism-related tensions already run high and where a considerable share of the housing stock is removed from the long-term rental market to be offered as STRs (thus contributing to residential displacement, rent gaps and other negative externalities). While other authors have also used this terminological framing (Barron et al., 2020; Garay et al., 2020; Söderström & Mermet, 2020), Airbnb is not the only platform commercialising STRs.

This article focuses specifically on Airbnb for several reasons. As the largest and probably most visible unicorn-tech STR mediation platform, Airbnb has steadily gained transformative power over cities, politics and social relations. Söderström and Mermet (2020) underline this idea, arguing that uneven power balances, determined by control over code and data, exist between platform companies and local policymakers. Their argument in relation to platform urbanism applies specifically to Airbnb, as this platform is inconspicuously but deeply reshaping contemporary cities by cleverly bypassing existing regulatory frameworks crafted for the 'physical' and not the virtual world (Furukawa & Onuki, 2019).

Numerous socio-spatial studies of Airbnb listings have emerged in recent years (see the review by Morales et al., 2020), with several focusing on Madrid and Barcelona. Studies of Barcelona (Arias & Quaglieri-Domínguez, 2016; Cócola-Gant, 2016; Gutiérrez et al., 2017) illustrate how Airbnb listings are spatially demarcated between districts and neighbourhoods. Indeed, Gutiérrez et al. (2017), who examined spatial patterns of hotels and peer-to-peer accommodation listings, maintain that, due to platform-mediated STRs, new residential areas are being added to traditional areas experiencing strong tourism pressures along Barcelona's main tourism axis. As for Madrid, research shows a greater centrality in listing patterns, although studies have generally focused on STR impacts on specific neighbourhoods (Ardura Urquiaga et al., 2019; Barrado-Timón & Hidalgo-Giralt, 2019; Cabrerizo, 2016; Cabrerizo et al., 2017; Gil & Sequera, 2018, 2020; Roman, 2018; Sequera & Nofre, 2018b).

Far from its origins as a supposedly innocuous peer-based subculture facilitating space-sharing practices, Airbnb (and the STRs it mediates) represents a highly complex urban issue, with technology as a key dimensional factor. Indeed, beyond the mediated STRs, it is important to underline the transformative power of the platform itself, the impacts of displacement pressures, exclusionary displacements (Cócola-Gant, 2016), the removal of housing from long-term markets (Amore et al., 2020; Wachsmuth & Weisler, 2018) and the negative externalities (rising rents, socio-spatial and economic reconfiguration, loss of character) of neighbourhoods touristified by STRs, not to mention the platform's appropriation by commercial capital players and large-scale multi-hosters (Morales et al., 2020). These issues are arguably at the heart of both online and off-line politicisation of Airbnb and STRs.

Digital protest and resistance as a key dimension of a politicised and polemical platform economy

The digitalisation of socio-political conflict in relation to tourism arguably preceded Airbnb and STR politicisation by half a decade or so. Some studies suggest that the upsurge in tourism-related protest and resistance movements constituted a strong critical response to growing tourism pressures (Cabrerizo et al., 2017; Colomb & Novy, 2016; del Romero Renau, 2018; Milano & Mansilla, 2018; Paredes-Rodriguez & Spierings, 2020), whereby particular forms and effects of tourism are contested or deplored for their negative impacts. Technology and social media has played an increasingly important role in such protests, as has the increase in action research perspectives involving academic-activists. However, the major bones of contention for tourism-related protest movements did not generally extend to platform capitalism until more recently (post-2014), as researchers started to map the negative externalities of platforms in space and time and drew inferences regarding socio-spatial impacts.

More broadly, social protest has become firmly situated within new radical geographies of resistance (Keith & Pile, 2013), often initially rooted in localist agendas (Cañada, 2019; Garay et al., 2020), even though activist arenas are increasingly translocal or even global in scale. Given the global scalability afforded to local activism by technology and social networks, geographies of resistance are an increasingly (although not exclusively) digital concern. This notion dovetails with the idea of social movements as translocal assemblages (Della Porta & Diani, 1999; McFarlane, 2009): composites of place-based social movements exchanging ideas, knowledge, practices, materials and resources across sites.

Social networks such as Twitter have become global platforms for maximising exposure of all kinds (van Harperen et al., 2018). In response, there has been an increasing academic interest in social movements, digitally-networked activism, the pursuit of digitally-enabled social change (Castells, 2015; Gerbaudo, 2012) and latterly in relation platforms (see Ricart et al., 2020). Contemporary protest cultures that shape geographies of resistance (Keith & Pile, 2013) make extensive use of social media as a 'global digital frontstage' where they embed and project their activism (Gerbaudo & Treré, 2015). Such digital amplification of local-scale activism also corresponds to the idea of 'cloud protesting' (Milan, 2015), exacerbating the centrality of the individual's subjective and private experience in contemporary mobilisations.

As far as analysis of social media narratives goes, this article draws on studies using data from social media conversations, as a means of representing Airbnb narratives as a fundamental part of the platform's socio-technical assemblage (Calzada, 2018; de Landa, 2006; Latour, 2005). Twitter conversations are understood as determining and delimiting actor relationship networks and as mapping discursive deliberation of socio-political issues and the corresponding lobbying, protest and regulatory tones (Bakardjieva, 2015; Gerbaudo, 2012; Postill, 2018; Theocharis et al., 2015). This is not to argue that Twitter is the main narrative construction tool for civil society deliberation, lobbying and activism, nor that it is the primary sphere in which policy and regulation are negotiated. Rather, it increasingly plays a major role in both those processes and so is an ideal social network with which to map conversations surrounding platforms like Airbnb.

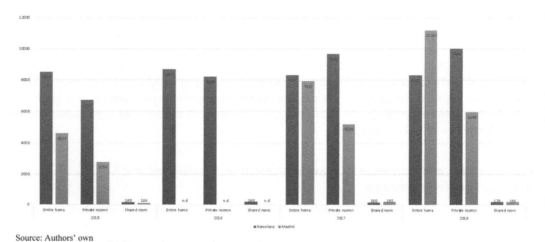

Source: Authors' own

Figure 1. Evolution of Airbnb listings by type in Barcelona and Madrid (2015-2018). Source: Authors' own.

Fuelled by offline public space polemic, Twitter has become a digital emotional conduit, not only in reinforcing offline divisiveness and polemic, but also in reconstructing a sense of togetherness among a spatially dispersed constituency and in facilitating digital gatherings (Bakardjieva, 2015; Theocharis et al., 2015).

Relationship networks tend to have no clear leadership; rather, leadership is present via decentralised and distributed relationships (Theocharis et al., 2015; Gerbaudo, 2012), although in a soft and emotional form – a 'dialogical' leadership captured in the concept of 'choreography'. Postill (2018) identified such choreographers or dialogical leaders as pro-democracy actors operating at the intersection of technology and politics. Choreographers, arguably at the top of George et al.'s (2019) hierarchy of digital activists, create and disseminate content to a mass following of activists or interested individuals (through 'clicktivism', i.e. garnering endorsement/support from 'followers' on social media).

Digital narrative/counter-narratives arguably play a primary role in mediating the transformative power wielded by Airbnb over city governments and in Airbnb becoming subject to stronger regulatory measures, or indeed striking a collaborative regulatory agreement with a local authority (or the EU, as seen in March 2020). As such, this article heeds Aguilera et al. (2019) call – to pay attention to the social struggles that make platform-mediated STRs a mainstream political issue in cities and that push governments to design public policies – by analysing the broader politicisation of the Airbnb effect in Madrid and Barcelona via digital narratives/counter-narratives.

Contextualising the Airbnb effect and the politicisation of platform-mediated STRs in Madrid and Barcelona

Barcelona and Madrid, the most prominent tourism cities in Spain and among the top ten cities worldwide for Airbnb listings, are a living illustration of the nature and paradoxes of the Airbnb effect in reshaping the urban fabric and associated place dynamics (Arias & Quaglieri-Domínguez, 2016; Gutiérrez et al., 2017; Lagonigro et al., 2020; Martínez-Caldentey et al., 2019; Molas, 2017, Morales et al., 2020; Tong & Gunter, 2020). Airbnb's market share is considerable; in 2017 it accounted for 13% of overnight stays in Barcelona and 10% in Madrid (Colliers International, 2018).

The evolution and characteristics of Airbnb supply in both cities (Figure 1) reflect an explosive emergence predominated by entire-home listings (although managed somewhat differently in each city). In Barcelona, a steep increase has been increasingly curtailed in terms of listing numbers but also by keeping entire-home rentals relatively under control; these increased by 3,099

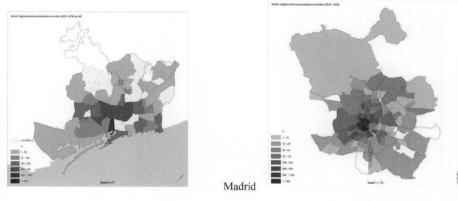

Barcelona   Madrid

Source: Authors' own

Figure 2. Evolution of Airbnb listings by city, 2015 to 2018. Source: Authors' own.

between 2015 and 2018, but only by 347 in 2019. Furthermore, while entire homes constituted the principal listing type in 2015, the situation has since reverted, following systematic removal of several thousand unlicensed entire-home listings by Airbnb in 2018 under orders from Barcelona City Council via the 2017 Special Tourist Accommodation Plan [PEUAT]. In Madrid, listings experienced exponential growth, doubling over that same period (9,866 listings, increasing by 4,001 in 2019) and mostly comprising entire-home listings.

As in several other cities (Adamiak, 2018; Amore et al., 2020; Ioannides et al., 2018; Quattrone et al., 2016), listings are generally concentrated in central areas, and more so in Madrid than in Barcelona (Figure 2), reflecting Airbnb's contribution to already uneven tourism development models and exacerbation of pre-existing tourism pressures. The neighbourhoods most susceptible to the Airbnb effect in Barcelona and Madrid are attractive areas for tourism and leisure and are also the traditional locations for tourism accommodation, as indicated by Gil and Sequera for Madrid (2018, 2020) and Morales et al. (2020) for Barcelona.

Airbnb host motivations vary considerably, from intercultural exchange and extra income generation to high financial returns and other diverse reasons for professional actors and multi-property owners. Multi-hosting (professional management/listing of two or more properties) is considered to be a broadly reliable measure of the formal commercial economy within Airbnb's platform model and its effects on touristification (Gil & Sequera, 2018; Gil & Sequera, 2020; Molas, 2017). Multi-hosting is often linked to property speculation and intensified housing pressures (Barron et al., 2017; Russo & Scarnato, 2018; Wachsmuth & Weisler, 2018; Yrigoy, 2019), as multi-hosts, whether agencies or large-scale investors managing 'hometel' properties, remove housing from the long-term residential market to offer them as STRs on Airbnb, reducing available housing stock, increasing long-term rents (Lee, 2016) and underpinning displacement effects (Cócola-Gant & Gago, 2019).

Table 1 illustrates how listings in each city are dominated by four categories of professionals and multi-hosts, and how Airbnb-mediated STRs for both entire homes/apartments and private rooms are currently controlled by few actors in Madrid and Barcelona. This business-to-peer dimension of Airbnb-mediated rentals has become consolidated over time, despite the implementation of new regulatory instruments. In Barcelona, hosts with more than 21 listings have increased notably and are also the most rapidly growing host contingent, while in Madrid, growth is distributed more homogeneously among all multi-host profiles.

Figure 3 shows how large-scale multi-hosting practices are concentrated in the same neighbourhoods as the highest overall concentrations of listings – a pattern seen most clearly in

Table 1. Distribution of Airbnb listings by host (2018)/evolution from 2015 to 2018, by city.

Range	Barcelona								Madrid							
	2018				2015 to 2018 evolution				2018				2015 to 2018 evolution			
	Listings	%	N. hosts	% of hosts	Listings	%	N. hosts	% of hosts	Listings	%	N. hosts	% of hosts	Listings	%	N. hosts	% of hosts
1 listing	6,999	37.8	6,999	72.56	941	−3,4	941	1.0	7,770	44.9	7,770	77.3	4,280	−2.0	4,280	−0.1
2 to 5 listings	5,829	31.5	2,295	23.79	346	−5,8	167	−1.4	5,001	28.9	1,943	19.3	2,697	−2.1	1,063	−0.2
6 to 20 listings	2,736	14.8	283	2.93	415	−1,0	34	0.0	2,673	15.4	291	2.9	1,538	0.2	169	0.2
more than 21 listings	2,940	15.9	69	0.72	2,091	10,1	43	0.4	1,868	10.8	45	0.4	1,350	3.8	32	0.2
Total	18,504	100	9,646	100	3,793		1,185		17,312	100	10,049	100	9,865		5,544	

Source: Author's own.

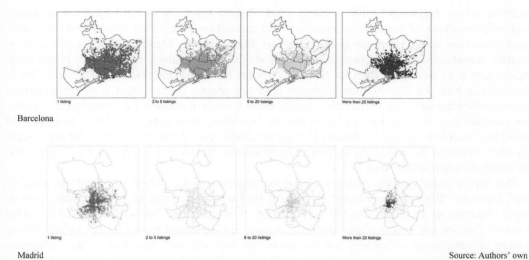

Barcelona

Madrid   Source: Authors' own

Figure 3. Spatial distribution of Airbnb multihosting in Barcelona and Madrid (2018). Source: Authors' own.

Madrid. In short, Airbnb supply in both cities is increasingly commercial, professionalised and controlled by a relatively small group of hosts. The lack of heterogeneity between districts underlines how platform capitalism can underpin uneven socio-spatial transformations.

This scenario has led to both city councils introducing regulations aimed at controlling the reach and impact of Airbnb-mediated STRs – although not to the same degree. Responses range from strong regulatory measures aimed at curbing or banning STRs to lighter or non-regulatory intervention (Artioli, 2018; Berkowitz & Souchaud, 2019). As Aguilera et al. (2019) argue, the difference is due not only to different structural political-economic conditions but also to pressures and negative civic reactions that have placed both tourism and platform-mediated STRs in the political spotlight. This notion underpins the logic of this article in terms of the influence exerted by civil society mobilisation on regulatory intervention, in the case of Barcelona and Madrid.

A new political map emerged in Spain after the local elections of May 2015 that was particularly disruptive in Madrid and Barcelona. In Barcelona, a coalition of left-wing political groups, civic movements and grassroots organisations (Barcelona en Comú, linked to the earlier 15 M movement and later to the Podemos party) entered the scene led by social activist Ada Colau; a similar grouping (Ahora Madrid) led by former lawyer Manuela Carmena took over in Madrid, breaking with local political monopolies (socialists in Barcelona and conservatives in Madrid). However, tourism and STRs have not merited the same attention in each city's political agenda. As Russo and Scarnato (2018) point out, Barcelona en Comú's 2015 election campaign was characterised by a strong critique of the previous administration's attitude to tourism development and a critical discourse repositioning tourism centrally within the urban agenda, in a 'right to the city' context (Colau, 2015). This climate for change represented a rejection of earlier neoliberal visions of the 'tourist city' (Russo and Scarnato, op cit.). In Ahora Madrid's 2015-2019 administration, tourism was not subject to intense political debate until towards the end of Carmena's term in office.

Barcelona City Council swiftly reinforced the regulatory approach to platform-mediated STRs, immediately halting the concession of any new licenses for accommodation establishments of any type while new measures were being devised. In January 2017, the aforementioned PEUAT was approved, establishing zero STR growth to avoid overconcentration and ensure a more balanced distribution. Barcelona City Council also fined both Airbnb and HomeAway €600,000 each in November 2016 for repeatedly, despite warnings, advertising unlicensed listings.

Madrid adopted a more laissez-faire regulatory response, avoiding direct penalties for unlicensed listings while designing a Special Accommodation Plan (PEH) to regulate tourist accommodation, approved tardily in March 2019. Despite relatively similar objectives (balanced land use, reduction of negative externalities and promotion of housing rights) and regulatory focus (limitation according to geographical areas) (Roman, 2018), Madrid's PEH was less restrictive than Barcelona's PEUAT (Ardura Urquiaga et al., 2019), as evident, for instance, in the maximum number of permitted days for STRs: 30 days for Barcelona and 90 days for Madrid. This is illustrative of how the STR situation in Madrid reflects a greater specialisation in whole properties disproportionately concentrated in the central district, while Barcelona has curtailed the explosive increase in listings and entire-home rentals. However, while both the PEUAT and the PEH aimed to curtail STRs in central districts (Ardura Urquiaga et al., 2019), their successful application has been hindered by disparities in geographical zoning criteria and a tardy reaction to professionalised supply/multi-hosting.

Also key to understanding evolving regulatory responses to the Airbnb effect are the relationships between different government levels and the relative strength of existing policy instruments (Aguilera et al., 2019). Madrid was marked by relative tensions and weak collaboration between the city and regional governments (powers are delegated to the former by the latter), centred on ideological differences and the confrontational approach favoured by the right-leaning Partido Popular regional government. Additionally, the PEH was broadly contested by the National Commission on Markets and Competition (CNMC), a public body overseeing the proper operation of markets in the interest of consumers and corporations (CNMC, 2018) – an issue still complicating implementation in 2020. Furthermore, the current Madrid City Council (a right-wing coalition partially supported by the extreme right resulting from the 2019 elections) has already made clear its intention to modify the PEH (Vargas, 2019).

Political-ideological differences also existed between Barcelona City Council and the centre-right Catalonian government, leading to subsequent modification of the original PEUAT. STRs (under the regional government's regulation on tourism accommodation), which fall into the tourist-use dwelling (HUT) category, are central to the evolving legal treatment of Airbnb listings in regional Catalonia (Morales et al., 2020); thus, large-scale professional operations and multi-hosting practices are regulated, but not room-sharing practices.

These different regulatory responses to the Airbnb effect help explain the rise of socio-political conflicts and the growing influence of organised social movements in local policy spheres. Barcelona and Madrid have both witnessed highly vocal social protest and resistance movements in opposition to tourism saturation and platform-mediated STRs, largely revolving around the contested use of urban space (public space, housing and local mobility) (Cabrerizo et al., 2017; Cócola-Gant, 2016; Cócola-Gant & Pardo, 2017; Gil & Sequera, 2018, 2020; Martínez-Caldentey et al., 2019; Milano & Mansilla, 2018; Molas, 2017).

As Sequera and Nofre (2018a) maintain (see also Pirillo Ramos & Mundet, 2020), in Barcelona the politicisation of tourism has been a highly organised process, addressed from two perspectives that are not mutually exclusive. Firstly, there is a performative protest perspective (reform movements contesting capitalism and globalisation while advocating new means of social, political and economic organisation, typified by an umbrella movement called the Neighbourhood Assembly for Sustainable Tourism (ABTS), reconfigured in 2019 as the Neighbourhood Assembly for Tourism Degrowth (ABDT). Secondly, there is a radical protest dimension (more revolutionary, and arising in Catalan far-left pro-independence movements, some linked to the Candidatura d'Unió Popular and Endavant's youth wing, Arran. These more radical movements are also highly performative (arguably more so than the former), with highly visible, impactful mediatic mobilisations, aimed at generating new discourses in relation to tourism that are closely aligned with anti-capitalist perspectives.

In Madrid, socio-political tourism conflicts were particularly intense in the Lavapiés neighbourhood, spearheaded by a local movement called Lavapiés ¿Dónde Vas? and rooted in countercultural and anti-capitalist rhetoric (Barrado-Timón & Hidalgo-Giralt, 2019). Their aim was to force Madrid City Council to paralyse or at least decelerate gentrification and touristification processes via stricter regulation (Ruano de la Fuente et al., 2019). While also performative in their activism, their international projection is arguably less than in Barcelona, while local government has not acknowledged the problematic issue of tourism saturation to the same extent. In fact, the 2017 Madrid City Council report on the hotel sector (using 2015 data) concluded that Madrid has not experienced similar levels of tourism saturation as cities like Barcelona (Ayuntamiento de Madrid, 2016); this controversial assumption was called out by several activists and journalists, e.g. Bravo (2017), who also called for the urgent regulation of platform-mediated STRs.

Both cases illustrate how grassroots social mobilisations contribute to the politicisation of platform-mediated STRs, reinforced not only by well-organised social movement structures and consistent tourism counter-narratives, but also via their particular use of discourse and methods of activism. One such method is an extensive reliance on social media (c.f. Garay et al., 2020), which open participative channels and increase influence on local policy. In fact, while Ada Colau's profile as a 'mayor for change' (Nel·lo, 2019) and her former leadership of the mortgage crisis platform, PAH, initially facilitated a direct line of dialogue between social movements and the city's governance structures (Blanco-Romero et al., 2018), increasingly differing opinions have emerged on both sides on how best to deal with issues like tourism saturation and (platform-mediated) STRs.

Methodology

This study is based on large-scale content and cluster analysis of digital narratives of Airbnb in Madrid and Barcelona. Undoubtedly one of the most popular mass communication platforms globally, Twitter, with over 800,000 searches and 65 million tweets daily, is considered to be influential in political debates and virtual activism (Puente et al., 2019) and often generates controversy. It is also important in terms of relationship network development, as it powers interpersonal communication and networking capabilities (Garay & Morales, 2020).

Within the comparative narrative analysis (after Riessman, 2008), of particular importance in terms of the politicisation of the Airbnb effect is the notion of counter-narrative, understood as "giving consideration to multiple layers of positioning" and possessing "fluidity of relational categories" (Bamberg & Andrews, 2004: ix). We understand counter-narratives as positions only making sense in relation to what they counter, generally, established and possibly hegemonic narratives (op cit). To ensure a balanced approach to unpacking digital narrative construction beyond the purely polemical dimensions of the Airbnb platform (as a complex socio-technical assemblage) and the Airbnb effect, we also interpreted mainstream, non-critical, lobbyist advocacy and also perceptibly neutral narrative content.

Twitter's Full-Archive Service API (application program interface) was used to obtain textual material making overt reference to the combinations Airbnb + Barcelona, and Airbnb + Madrid, disaggregated by quarter from January 2017 to September 2018. After removing bot-sent tweets, the sample contained 9,200 tweets for Madrid and 17,200 tweets for Barcelona (original tweets and replies but not retweets to avoid reiteration), including text, author (user id) and other variables such as language, number of replies, number of retweets and favourites.

Frequency analyses of words and hashtags and two cluster analyses were run on the resulting database of Airbnb + Madrid and Airbnb + Barcelona narrative content. For the words and hashtags (after manual removal of nonsensical words and connectors), we used QSR-NVivo to perform the frequency analysis, ordering words and hashtags by number of mentions. We used Gephi software to perform the cluster analyses via a modularity algorithm, so as to highlight words/ hashtags and users having the greatest number of interconnections between them. The first cluster analysis, aimed at mapping the relationship networks of conversation participants, included relationships established between users (by way of mutual replies) and specific mentions of other users. This combination of replies and mentions identified network relationships in which some users are protagonists according to the number of 'entries' they receive (replies and mentions by other users) or 'exits' (replies and mentions referencing other users). The second cluster analysis generated clusters of hashtags grouped concurrently within a single tweet.

Finally, this quantitative analysis was triangulated via a manual qualitative coding exercise (using NVivo), to interpret user profiles and the meaning/orientation of words and hashtags within the frequency and cluster analyses. To clarify our interpretations, where necessary, examples of illustrative tweets (translated by the authors) are provided.

Findings

Actors, interests and relationship networks within digital narratives mentioning Airbnb in Madrid and Barcelona

Analysis of different actors' narratives/counter-narratives within conversations shows the intervention of different actors and the differing intensities of the relationship networks that unite them. The most active/mentioned/replicated users in each conversation were analysed, in accordance with Aguilera et al. (2019), who highlighted six outstanding actors influencing recent debates around the regulation of STR platforms in Europe, albeit with different levels of intensity: professional STR operators, associations of hosts or home-sharers, the hotel industry, residents' associations or citizens' movements, sharing economy advocates and corporate platforms.

Airbnb hosts and guests (both global and Spanish/Catalan) engage in both the Barcelona and Madrid conversations, although not prominently. Their online role is mainly passive, although they play an important role in offline short-term regulatory debates in the Spanish/Catalan national and local political scenarios. While the presence of an Airbnb community manager (@sergiovinay, one-time head of public policy for Airbnb in Spain and Portugal) stands out, there is little deliberative engagement with other actors. This relatively passive attitude is also shown by the hotel industry, generally very active in other arenas but practically invisible in Twitter debates on Airbnb in Madrid and Barcelona.

Much more active is another group: users pertaining to professional organisations representing agencies, operators and marketing companies (@MVPInmobiliaria and @MkrSoluciones in Madrid, and @CPM_Int and @CPMICC in Barcelona), although their participation is largely apolitical; they basically position their listed properties and occasionally comment on more political (regulatory) aspects. In Madrid (and to a lesser extent Barcelona) there is an identifiable presence of actors representing new host or home-sharer associations (such as Iniciativaprovt, Iniciativa ProViviendasTurísticas), interested in avoiding regulation and defending the right to rent/share their home to generate additional income in difficult times. Another strong presence is residents' associations, more diffuse in Madrid, but much clearer in Barcelona, largely due to very active engagement by ABTS/ABDT (@AssBarrisTS), whose discourse focuses centrally on the right-to-housing issue, particularly through retweets of national/international media articles and critical opinions by highly vocal individual activists closely aligned with their own position.

Not so clear is the role of what Aguilera et al. (2019) term 'sharing economy intellectual advocates'; they are clearly marginal in the period analysed, although they may have previously been more active. However, what does stand out in both cities, but predominantly in Madrid, is the activity of intellectual activists advocating the anti-Airbnb counter-narrative (e.g. @Gil_JavierGil and @CGerardoPerla in Madrid and @indignindigente in Barcelona). Such users are typically writers/academics, digital freelance journalists and/or critical 'influencers', (re)producing critically-oriented content, mostly in relation to the impact on housing. This profile is in line with Gerbaudo's (2012) social media 'choreographers': rather than lead social movements on networks, they direct and shape the narratives of other participants ('dancers') in the conversation. The profile also aligns well with Postill's (2018) 'techpol nerds' concept, of pro-democracy agents from diverse backgrounds (computing, law, art, media and politics, referred to as 'clamp') that

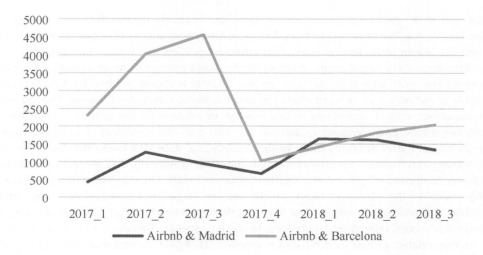

Source: Authors' own.

Figure 4. Volume of Tweets (original and replies) mentioning Airbnb + Madrid and Airbnb + Barcelona (2017-18). Source: Authors' own.

operate at the intersection of technology and politics. Another profile is especially prominent in Barcelona: digital publications with different orientations, although mostly critical (cronicaglobal, e24diari, Reporte24ES, Univers_Airbnb). This user profile, also performing a choreographer role, is particularly active in disseminating national/international news on the ongoing battle between Airbnb and city councils. The UK newspaper The Guardian is another clear example.

Focusing on the most replied-to users, another prominent actor appears, the mayor of Barcelona (@AdaColau) and her party (@BComuGlobal), whose Twitter posts on Airbnb draw both approval and criticism. Colau and her party defend actions implemented in relation to Airbnb-mediated STRs and hint at new control measures if Airbnb persists in circumventing rules. Among the most replied-to and mentioned users are protest collectives (@InquilinatoMad in Madrid and ABTS/ABDT in Barcelona), but also staunch defenders of the platform model (including Airbnb's own community arm/advocacy initiative, @AirbnbCitizen; see van Doorn, 2019; Minca & Roelofsen, 2019). This highlights the (albeit less prominent) engagement of actors from within Airbnb's own realm, who, beyond a simple marketing presence on Twitter, also shape deliberation on the platform's practices and impacts.

The actors and their interests congregate on Twitter to form relatively demarcated groups of interrelated actors (Figure 4), within which user clusters, indicated by colours, can be referred to as digital relationship networks. To a certain extent, albeit on a different scale, such narrative-driven networks could also be considered as socio-technical assemblages in themselves (Kitchin, 2017; García-Olivares, 2019). The actors, ideas and artefacts unite to constitute a deliberation sphere prior to social institutions formally engaging with these debates online and offline, via practices such as 'clicktivism' (see George & Leidner, 2019).

Such networks also have their own range of choreographers and dancers (Gerbaudo, 2012; Postill, 2018). In Madrid, the most important digital relationship network (green, comprising 22% of relationships, mentions and replies) is choreographed by Airbnb-related users, 'Airbnbeings' (Minca & Roelofsen, 2019) and individuals championing Airbnb's interests (destinations, STRs, listings) by projecting advocacy-oriented narratives favourable to Airbnb's own rhetoric, including internal/external marketing activity, perpetuating the platform's philosophy. The second network (red, 18%) is choreographed by critical counter-narratives from social movements and representatives of Madrid City Council, calling out the housing issue and signalling a need for increased regulation (with critical slogans prominent). The third network (yellow, 12%) is choreographed by digital and mass media users, whose narratives are relatively neutral and do not flag critical issues. Finally, the fourth network (blue, 7%) groups together users interested in business advances and the link to technological innovation (often hinging on the 'smart' concept).

In Barcelona, three broad digital relationship networks emerge from conversational exchanges (Figure 4). The most prominent network (brown, 21.24%) is choreographed by Airbnb promoters (particularly Airbnb's own content manager) and Barcelona City Council/mayor. Beyond Airbnb's own narratives, critical counter-narratives emerge in relation to the platform's practices, perceived hegemony and spiralling growth, along with calls for regulatory intervention featuring strongly critical hashtags (#unfairbnb, #tourismkillsthecity, #noensfaranfora [we won't be pushed out], #youarenotwelcome, #desmuntantAirbnb [unmasking Airbnb]). The second network (green, 16.36%) is composed of general and specialist tourism media. Once again, counter-narratives are starkly critical of the platform's rapid growth and the illegality of many of its listings (dubious subletting and unlicensed rentals). The final Barcelona network (violet, 12.23%) is choreographed by individuals both related and unrelated to Airbnb, specific Barcelona City Council members and tourism-related protest and resistance movements. Again, counter-narratives in this cluster are highly critical, as evident in the #decreixementurístic [tourism degrowth) hashtag.

In discussing the significance of these findings, it is clear that Airbnb generally abstains from dialoguing with activists regarding its practices and impacts. In Madrid, overt engagement is avoided, while in Barcelona certain narrative strands force engagement, at times in a relatively friendly tone. Airbnb generally avoids engaging directly in political debate (Niewland and van Melik, 2018) or having a transformative agenda, but rather adopts an additive strategy (variable between places and markets), aimed at sustaining quiet expansion and avoiding noisy, mediatic stand-offs (Uzunca et al., 2018; Uzunca & Borlenghi, 2019). This is surprising for a platform that aims at co-shaping the terms of current and future policy debates pertaining not just to home-sharing/STRs but also at accessing and influencing the very fabric of city life as a powerful biopolitical social regulator (Minca & Roelofsen, 2019; van Doorn, 2019); this, however, is arguably easier to achieve through their own (controllable) channels, such as their @Airbnbcitizen community. In Twitter's open and often rough deliberative waters, Airbnb's own narratives in relation to Barcelona and Madrid takes on the guise of a wolf in a sheep's clothing in some contexts and, in other contexts, of a compliant collaborator in purporting a willingness to remedy its often criticised 'sharing or trading' mindset. The intention of the platform and its beneficiaries appears to be to avoid – rather than actively mitigate – negative attention on Twitter and also, as Söderström and Mermet (2020, p. 4) observe, to stealthily bypass "existing regulatory frameworks that have been crafted for the 'physical' and not for the virtual world".

What lessons might be learned here, in terms of the significance of the online politicisation of Airbnb in the future? Airbnb's additive strategy – so variable between different socio-spatial and market contexts – has effects that are subtle and apparently innocuous in the first instance; this has meant that the accompanying digital geographies of resistance are also more difficult to mobilise on a large collective scale (being more diffuse and less targeted). However, it is surely only a matter of time before the amplification afforded by global digital frontstages such as Twitter elevate this conflict into the digital and offline mainstreams (via internationally-networked social movements or translocal resistance assemblages).

Content analysis: Twitter narratives/counter-narratives

Figure 5 shows that narrative content referring to Airbnb + Barcelona as tweeted in the first three quarters of 2017 was particularly high, and much higher than for Airbnb + Madrid, pointing to an important relationship between tweet intensity and debate surrounding the impacts of Airbnb, protest counter-narratives and calls for stronger regulation.

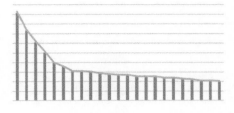 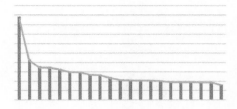

Airbnb+Madrid   **Airbnb+Barcelona**

Figure 5. Most tweeted words within Twitter conversations on Airbnb + Madrid and Airbnb + Barcelona (2017-2018); (Total number of tweets; original and replies). Source: Author's own.

In relation to Barcelona, four aspects converge in the marked peak in attention during this period, which merit further discussion. Firstly, by 2017 Airbnb had undergone three years of sustained growth and consolidation in the city (Garay et al., 2020), with increasingly visible impacts (Gutiérrez et al., 2017). Secondly, protest movements in opposition to unsustainable tourism were gaining momentum, particularly the ABTS/ABDT, created in 2015 and by 2017 already highly (inter)active on social media, especially Twitter. Thirdly, post-2015 the Barcelona en Comú administration opened up new political spaces, fostering increasingly strong links with neighbourhood movements, the anti-eviction platform PAH and collectives directly involved in anti-tourism mobilisations in the city, with STRs, Airbnb and PEUAT enforcement as their primary targets. Finally, Airbnb and its impacts were the subject of growing international interest, not only in translocal activism but also in the media. In the summer of 2017, digital media worldwide gave considerable coverage to the Airbnb effect in Barcelona, with myriad actors widely and actively recirculating related news on Twitter. Before the sharing economy's first decade was even over, critical voices had begun to proliferate (Slee, 2017; Srnicek, 2017). Airbnb was undoubtedly one of the most targeted platforms for its well-publicised drift towards platform capitalism, while Barcelona was a perfect laboratory for observing what could happen when Airbnb-mediated STRs expanded in an international destination already under pressure from tourism saturation and where the politicisation of the Airbnb effect was increasingly visible online and offline.

A clear example of the increasingly critical media attention was *The Guardian* article, titled "Barcelona cracks down on Airbnb rentals with illegal apartment squads" (Bergen, 2017), widely retweeted (from Barcelona and also globally) over the summer. The article described how, as rising rents continued to fuel rows over STRs and tourism, Barcelona City Council doubled its team of holiday-let inspectors. Airbnb itself was called out for its practices and impacts, but the emphasis was on the new regulatory approach and, ultimately, on the ongoing battle between opposing actors, with Airbnb's contribution to housing problems at its centre.

This intense media focus quickly shifted, as the high volume of tweets mentioning Airbnb + Barcelona fell off abruptly when attention on Barcelona largely centred on the mid-August terrorist attacks and the independence movement in Catalonia during autumn 2017. This is not to say that the topic of the Airbnb effect had ceased to be relevant, merely that other topics temporarily took precedence in tweets mentioning Barcelona. This flags up the importance of immediacy as a distinctive feature of Twitter, affecting how individuals and professional commentators deliberate online (Zeller and Hermida, 2015).

Returning to the Airbnb + Madrid findings; this combination was much less evident on Twitter during this period, for several reasons. Firstly, Airbnb listings in Madrid were less expansive spatially than in other cities, particularly since, after a period of steady growth, the explosion there occurred mainly after the analysed period. Second, although protest and resistance to Airbnb-mediated STRs and their impacts were already visible (Ardura Urquiaga et al., 2019; Cabrerizo,

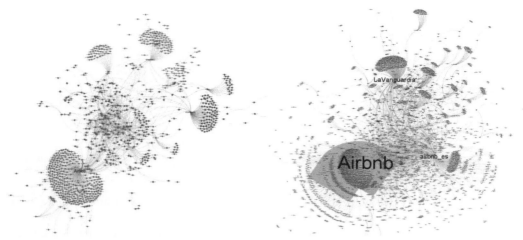

Figure 6. Twitter user ecosystem clusters and relationship networks within Twitter conversations on Airbnb + Madrid and Airbnb + Barcelona (2017-2018). Source: Author's own.

2016; Ruano de la Fuente et al., 2019; Sequera & Nofre, 2018b), in 2017 Madrid City Council (led by Ahora Madrid) adopted a stand-by stance as regards forcefully taking on Airbnb and similar platforms. Finally, and possibly even more decisive, is the fact that this incipient battle resonated less in the media, not least because the city is less dependent on international visitors than Barcelona (Madrid 55% vs. Barcelona 83% of the visitor total). The evolution of Airbnb + Madrid mentions was much steadier in this period, signalling that the Airbnb effect was not yet perceived as a major problem.

Analysis of the most tweeted words within the two Airbnb + conversations (Figure 6) shows how housing issues are indeed at their heart, with *pisos* (flats) mentioned the most in both cases, along with *viviendas* (housing) and *alquiler* (rent). Critical tones are also prominent in both conversations – mentions of *ilegal* in Barcelona and *problema* in Madrid – as seen in the following tweets:

- Madrid: *Airbnb and illegal apartments are driving the new property bubble that is growing at full speed in Madrid.*
- Barcelona: *One of the hundreds of cases of professional networks of illegal flats marketed by @airbnb was uncovered yesterday #Barcelona.*

Similarly, critical mentions of current economic and tourism models ('economy', 'tourism') appear prominently in both conversations, with the most-cited tweets referring to specific print media ('elconfidencial' or 'elpais' in Madrid and 'theguardian' and 'lavanguardia' in Barcelona), e.g.:

- Madrid: *@Airbnb Lavapiés is the neighbourhood in Madrid that loses the most population due to pressure from tourism. This is not tourism phobia.*
- Barcelona: *Is @Airbnb really to blame for #Barcelona's problem with mass #tourism? #rentals #hotels).*

Interesting findings also emerge from the thematic cluster analysis of hashtags, as coded manually by the authors. Hashtags for Madrid fell into three clusters: concepts broadly relating to tourism, marketing and commercialisation (45% of hashtags), logistical aspects of tourism (15%), and pro-Airbnb perspectives (often in direct response to criticism) and 'techie' (tech-related) concepts (6%). Hashtags for Barcelona were clustered in four groups: tourism marketing, holidays, etc. and also the collaborative economy, technology, start-ups, etc. (almost 45% of hashtags), major urban destinations in Europe and the USA and related aspects such as graffiti or urban art (15%), business-related hashtags (5%), and denouncements and criticisms (5%). Explicitly critical hashtags are secondary within both conversations, however. Only the fourth Barcelona cluster is oriented to direct criticism (e.g. #unfairbnb, #tourismkillsthecity), demands to recover public and private spaces (e.g. #noensfaranfora, #youarenotwelcome) and for tourism degrowth (#decreixementurístic). Furthermore, it is important to add that most hashtags originate in grassroots campaigns led by the ABTS/ABDT and the Federation of Barcelona Neighbourhood Associations (FAVB).

As regards the significance of the content analysis findings, it is important to highlight the weight of such critical terms within counter-narratives on the positive home-sharing rhetoric of Airbnb and its hosts and guests. Such criticism underlines a rejection of Airbnb's infiltration of daily neighbourhood life/appropriation of residential lifestyles and spaces for tourism ends; this issue can be situated within a wider antagonism towards tourism in digital protest spheres. This wider criticism is especially intense in Barcelona, amplified by media coverage and the window of opportunity opened following the 2015 elections, which had situated tourism as a contested issue.

This transposition of Airbnb effect debates to the mainstream political agenda is also played out during this period. Beyond pure denunciation of the platform's impacts in both cities, many tweets (especially retweets of digital press articles) clearly refer to current and potential intervention by local agents, and namechecking city councils in particular. Allusions to the measures initiated in these cities predominate, whether in the form of the threat of fines and limitations or the need for more inspections. Two examples illustrate:

- Madrid: *The @Madrid City Council has already asked @Airbnb to reduce the number of nights to 60 per year. For now, without success.*
- Barcelona: *Barcelona City Council fines Airbnb and HomeAway for announcing apartment rentals without a tourist license.*

Even considering that the overall volume of Airbnb + Barcelona narratives is much higher, the proportion of critical counter-narratives is greater than non-critical narratives for both cities (as coded by the authors). In both cases, appeals to local government pushing for stronger regulatory responses to keep Airbnb's practices under control are prominent, particularly in relation to the housing problem. Nevertheless, Barcelona seemed to have become globally emblematic of popular resistance to Airbnb-mediated STRs, capturing much national and especially international media attention. Additionally, although Madrid also had a strong activist movement and a council of the same political colours as Barcelona, both its regulatory context (opposition from the regional government and a city council reacting later) and a more incipient Airbnb listings scenario combined to ensure that Airbnb-mediated STRs received less attention (at least in terms of volume).

Within conversations, mutual mentions in a comparative or contrasting manner are frequent, with, for instance, Barcelona often cited as an example in the Airbnb + Madrid conversation of the need for greater regulatory intervention:

- Barcelona: *Barcelona doubles the number of Airbnb rentals in Madrid (and they are more expensive).*
- Madrid: *The problem of short-term rentals must be raised by local administrations, as is already the case in Barcelona, Palma and now in Madrid.*

Some of the mutual cross-references refer to a coalition of protest movements across 14 southern European cities, represented by a translocal resistance collective known as Southern European Cities against Touristification (SETnet), that aims at the acquisition of more information about the platform that would allow for greater monitoring and control. In interpreting these findings, we argue that activists and affected parties are thus situated centrally within a translocal resistance assemblage (Della Porta & Diani, 1999; McFarlane, 2009), with SETnet at its axis, collaboratively activist online in calling for Airbnb and STR regulation. This collective, networked pressure is clearly shifting the role of civil society participation in regulatory debates and its effects are not going unnoticed. Other European cities are also lobbying the EU on Airbnb data:

- Madrid/Barcelona: *Amsterdam, Barcelona, Madrid, Vienna, Paris, Reykjavík, Krakow and Brussels urge the European Commission to take action on Airbnb data.*

These findings imply that social media are helping to bridge the geographical contextual boundaries between places living with STRs, allowing geographies of resistance to thrive via digital protest networks as global frontstages (Gerbaudo & Treré, 2015; Treré, 2015) and virtual resistance communities. This represents a significant shift in the power axis of regulatory tendencies and perceived control over platform impacts, potentially providing local authorities with the strong mandate they needed to step in (Barns, 2018; 2020). The question remains, constituting an important topic for future research, as to whether this digital grassroots movement can challenge the slippery and contentious nature of Airbnb's additive strategy (Uzunca & Borlenghi, 2019), which, to date, has been beyond the reach and capacities of the public sector.

A final observation can be made as regards the significance of both series of findings (actors, interests and relationship networks and narrative content of digital narratives). In effect, they both point to the same emerging idea - that the locus of control in the likelihood of platform regulation is shifting, due to the increasing digital translocal assemblage surrounding protest and resistance towards platform impacts. In addition, both sets of findings imply that the digitally-networked projection on the part of those collectives aiming for change is key to their increasing influence in policy debates, via collaborative, digital amplification/'front-staging' of previously unconnected voices.

Conclusions

Many cities are still a long way from figuring out how to address platform-mediated STRs and the Airbnb effect. However, increasing our understanding of local contexts (underlying political contexts, institutional dynamics, local-specific 'landscapes' of protest and resistance and specific patterns of socio-spatial inequalities) is important for the deliberation and shaping of local and common responses to the Airbnb effect. Beyond the local aspect, understanding the socio-political struggles that surround platforms as translocal assemblages in themselves is an insightful means of framing a complex and ever-shifting situation in terms of its capacity to transcend local space and link to a wider sphere via social networks.

In terms of future research agendas, we maintain that understanding the underlying socio-political and institutional dynamics of the Airbnb effect in different urban (and non-urban) contexts is essential if the platform and the mediated STRs are to become inherently more sustainable. Also important is paying close attention to the online and offline (trans)local geographies of resistance that surround platforms, so as to gauge other narratives not captured through a purely digital approach. After Barns (2020), we argue that multi-disciplinary approaches to studying and understanding the challenges presented by platforms present in cities are much needed, along with more sophisticated conceptual frameworks.

Recognising and understanding Airbnb's corporate strategy is also important, so as to understand the different ways in which it is deployed by the platform itself in the different cities it enters. Furthermore, empirical research must be capable of capturing the perpetually shifting scenarios and regulatory responses surrounding the platform's ongoing relationship with cities. For example, in the wake of the COVID-19 pandemic, Barcelona's relationship with Airbnb is shifting once again (see Mumbrú, 2020) in that STR regulations will become much more restrictive, while the regional government has ceded responsibility for tourism rental licencing to

Barcelona City Council. The platform's adaptive and additive response to this and other shifts will shed light on likely future relationships between cities, STRs and the digital platforms that mediate STRs.

In the post-COVID-19 platform era (Pirone et al., 2020), regulators will need to acquire an in-depth understanding of the possibilities and limitations offered by platform initiatives, so as to provide answers that can feed into public policy and development strategies. Sustainability needs to become a central concern of the platform economy (Fuster-Morell et al., 2020; Gössling & Hall, 2019), particularly where socio-spatial impacts can be severe and potentially irreversible. As a centralised P2P/B2P intermediary with strong interests in mediating the local sphere, Airbnb does not determine where their listings are ultimately located, but they can choose to focus their marketing on certain neighbourhoods and attractions and decide what to emphasise in reinforcing their 'localist' neighbourhood lifestyle tourism narrative. This underlines both the considerable power and responsibility accruing to STR platform businesses. More accountability and responsibility is called for on the part of these platforms, so as to address the inherent sustainability challenges and "the unresolved moral and ethical questions emerging therefrom" (Etter et al., 2019). This accountability should be accompanied by a focus on more context-specific and hybrid governance approaches, including self-regulatory, collaborative and inclusive mechanisms (Gurumurthy, 2018; Vith et al., 2019). Such approaches, surely more capable of capturing and building on narratives within formal deliberative channels, would improve the possibility of developing the right regulatory approach to dealing with the socio-spatial and economic unpredictability of STRs, while underpinning more sustainable accommodation platform strategies for the long term.

Acknowledgement

The authors are particularly grateful to Salvador Anton Clavé, Hug March and the anonymous reviewers for their insightful comments.

Disclosure statement

No potential conflict of interest was reported by the authors.

Funding

This research was funded by the Ministerio de Ciencia, Innovación y Universidades (reference: G60667813, programme: Retos de la Sociedad) and the Universitat Oberta de Catalunya (UOC interdisciplinary research projects).

ORCID

Julie Wilson (iD) http://orcid.org/0000-0003-2802-7275
Lluís Garay-Tamajon (iD) http://orcid.org/0000-0002-4209-3319
Soledad Morales-Perez (iD) http://orcid.org/0000-0002-8170-9286

References

Adamiak, C. (2018). Mapping Airbnb supply in European cities. *Annals of Tourism Research*, *71*, 67–71. https://doi.org/10.1016/j.annals.2018.02.008

Aguilera, T., Artioli, F., & Colomb, C. (2019). Explaining the diversity of policy responses to platform- mediated short-term rentals in European cities: A comparison of Barcelona, Paris and Milan. *Environment and Planning A: Economy and Space*, 0308518X1986228. https://doi.org/10.1177/0308518X19862286

Amore, A., de Bernardi, C., & Arvanitis, P. (2020). The impacts of Airbnb in Athens, Lisbon and Milan: a rent gap theory perspective. *Current Issues in Tourism*. https://doi.org/10.1080/13683500.2020.1742674

Ardura Urquiaga, A., Lorente Riverola, I., Mohino Sanz, I., & Ruiz Sanchez, J. (2019). "No estamos tan mal como Barcelona" análisis de la proliferación y regulación de las viviendas de uso turístico en Madrid y Barcelona. *Boletín de la Asociación de Geógrafos Españoles*, *83*(2828), 1–47. DOI: doi.org/https://doi.org/ https://doi.org/10.21138/bage.2828

Arias, A., & Quaglieri-Domínguez, A. (2016). Unravelling Airbnb: urban perspectives from Barcelona. In A. A. Russo and G. Richards (Eds.), *Reinventing the local in tourism* (p. 209). Channel View.

Artioli, F. (2018). *Digital platforms and cities: A literature review for urban research* [Cities are Back in Town Working Paper 01/2018]. Sciences-Po Urban School.

Ayuntamiento de Madrid. (2016). *La Oferta de Alojamiento Turístico en Madrid Características y Distribución Territorial*. Ayuntamiento de Madrid.

Barns, S. (2018). Smart cities and urban data platforms: Designing interfaces for smart governance. *City, Culture and Society*, *12*, 5–12. https://doi.org/10.1016/j.ccs.2017.09.006

Barns, S. (2020). *Platform urbanism: Negotiating platform ecosystems in connected cities*. Springer.

Bakardjieva, M. (2015). Do clouds have politics? Collective actors in social media land. *Information, Communication and Society*, *18*(8), 983–990. https://doi.org/10.1080/1369118X.2015.1043320

Bamberg, M., & Andrews, M. (2004). *Considering counter-narratives: Narrating, resisting, making sense*. John Benjamins Publishing.

Barrado-Timón, D., & Hidalgo-Giralt, C. (2019). Golden hordes or mere barbarians? Discourses on tourism, touristification, and tourismophobia in Madrid's Lavapiés neighbourhood. *Boletín de la Asociación de Geógrafos Españoles*, *83* (2824), 1–36. https://doi.org/10.21138/bage.2824

Barron, K., Kung, E., & Proserpio, D. (2020). The effect of home-sharing on house prices and rents: Evidence from Airbnb. *Marketing Science*. 10.1287/mksc.2020.1227.

Belk, R. (2014). Sharing Versus Pseudo-Sharing in Web 2.0. *The Anthropologist*, *18*(1), 7–23. https://doi.org/10.1080/09720073.2014.11891518

Bergen, S. (2017). *Barcelona cracks down on Airbnb rentals with illegal apartment squads*. Retrieved June 29, 2020, from https://www.theguardian.com/technology/2017/jun/02/airbnb-faces-crackdown-on-illegal-apartment-rentals-in-barcelona

Berkowitz, H., & Souchaud, A. (2019). (Self-)regulation of sharing economy platforms through partial meta-organizing. *Journal of Business Ethics*, *159*(4), 961–976. https://doi.org/10.1007/s10551-019-04206-8,

Blanco-Romero, A., Blázquez-Salom, M., & Canoves, G. (2018). Barcelona, housing rent bubble in a tourist city. Social responses and local policies. *Sustainability*, *10*(6), 2043. https://doi.org/10.3390/su10062043

Bravo, P. (2017). *El turismo puede acabar con tu ciudad … y Madrid ya se va enterando*. https://www.eldiario.es/desde-mi-bici/turismo-acabar-ciudad-Madrid-enterando_6_603049708.html

Cabrerizo, C. (2016). *La ciudad negocio: Turismo y movilización social en pugna*. Cisma Editorial.

Cabrerizo, C., Sequera, J., & Bachiller, P. G. (2017). Entre la turistificación y los espacios de resistencia en el centro de Madrid. Algunas claves para (re)pensar la ciudad turística. *Ecología Política*, *52*, 78–82.

Calzada, I. (2018). Algorithmic nations': Seeing like a city-regional and techno-political conceptual assemblage. *Regional Studies, Regional Science*, *5*(1), 267–289. https://doi.org/10.1080/21681376.2018.1507754

Cañada, E. (2019). *Trabajo turístico digno y derecho a la ciudad,* Blog de Ernest Cañada/ALBASUD. Retrieved June 08, 2020, from http://www.albasud.org/blog/es/1083/trabajo-tur-stico-digno-y-derecho-a-la-ciudad

Castells, M. (2015). *Networks of outrage and hope: Social movements in the Internet age.* Polity Press.

CNMC. (2018). *La CNMC recurre la normativa urbanística municipal de viviendas turísticas de Madrid, Bilbao y San Sebastián.* https://www.cnmc.es/2018-08-07-la-cnmc-recurre-la-normativa-urbanistica-municipal-de-viviendas-turisticas-de-madrid

Cockayne, D. G. (2016). Sharing and neoliberal discourse: The economic function of sharing in the digital on-demand economy. *Geoforum, 77,* 73–82. https://doi.org/10.1016/j.geoforum.2016.10.005

Cócola-Gant, A. (2016). Holiday rentals: The new gentrification battlefront. *Sociological Research Online, 21*(3), 1–9. https://doi.org/10.5153/sro.4071

Cócola-Gant, A., & Gago, A. (2019). Airbnb, buy-to-let investment and tourism-driven displacement: A case study in Lisbon. *Environment and Planning A: Economy and Space,* 0308518X1986901. https://doi.org/10.1177/0308518X19869012

Cócola-Gant, A., & Pardo, D. (2017). Resisting tourism gentrification: the experience of grassroots movements in Barcelona. *In: Urbanistica Tre, Giornale Online di Urbanistica, 5*(13), 39–47.

Colau, A. (2015). Mass tourism can kill a city – just ask Barcelona's residents. *The Guardian.* 2nd September.

Colliers International. (2018). *Airbnb in Europe.* Colliers International y La Haya Hotel School.

Colomb, C., & Novy, J. (2016). *Protest and resistance in the tourist city.* Routledge.

de Landa, M. (2006). *A new philosophy of society: Assemblage theory and social complexity.* Continuum.

Demailly, D., & Novel, A. S. (2014). *The sharing economy: Make it sustainable, studies 03/14.* Paris: IDDRI. https://www.iddri.org/sites/default/files/import/publications/st0314_dd-asn_sharing-economy.pdf

del Romero Renau, L. (2018). Touristification, sharing economies and the new geography of urban conflicts. *Urban Science, 2*(4), 104. https://doi.org/10.3390/urbansci2040104

Della Porta, D., & Diani, M. (1999). *Social movements: An introduction.* Blackwell.

Etter, M., Fieseler, C., & Whelan, G. (2019). Sharing economy, sharing responsibility? Corporate social responsibility in the digital age. *Journal of Business Ethics, 159*(4), 935–942. https://doi.org/10.1007/s10551-019-04212-w

Furukawa, N., & Onuki, M. (2019). The design and effects of short-term rental regulation. *Current Issues in Tourism,* 1–16. https://doi.org/10.1080/13683500.2019.1638892

Fuster-Morell, M., Espelt, R., & Renau, M. (2020). Sustainable platform economy: Connections with the sustainable development goals. *Sustainability, 12*(18), 7640. https://doi.org/10.3390/su12187640

Garay, L., & Morales, S. (2020). Decomposing and relating user engagement in festivals' virtual brand communities: An analysis of Sónar's Twitter and Facebook. *Tourist Studies, 20*(1), 96–119. https://doi.org/10.1177/1468797619873109

Garay, L., Morales, S., & Wilson, J. (2020) Tweeting the right to the city: Digital protest and resistance surrounding the Airbnb effect. *Scandinavian Journal of Hospitality and Tourism, 20* (3), 246–267. https://doi.org/10.1080/15022250.2020.1772867

García-Olivares, A. (2019), Ensamblajes Socio-técnicos y complejodad social. *Intersticios: Revista Sociológica de Pensamiento Crítico, 13*(2), 93–118.

Gerbaudo, P. (2012). *Tweets and the streets.* Pluto Press.

Gerbaudo, P., & Treré, E. (2015). In search of the 'we' of social media activism. *Information, Communication and Society, 18*(8), 865–871. https://doi.org/10.1080/1369118X.2015.1043319

George, J. J., & Leidner, D. (2019). From clicktivism to hacktivism: Understanding digital activism. *Information and Organization, 29*(3), 100249. https://doi.org/10.1016/j.infoandorg.2019.04.001

Gil, J., & Sequera, J. (2018). Expansión de la ciudad turística y nuevas resistencias. *El Caso de Airbnb en Madrid. Empiria. Revista de Metodología de Ciencias Sociales, 41,* 15–32. https://doi.org/10.5944/Empiria.41.2018.22602

Gil, J., & Sequera, J. (2018). Expansión de la ciudad turística y nuevas resistencias. El caso de Airbnb en Madrid. *Empiria. Revista de metodología de ciencias sociales, 4*(1), 15–32.

Gil, J., & Sequera, J. (2020). The professionalization of Airbnb in Madrid: Far from a collaborative economy. *Current Issues in Tourism.* https://doi.org/10.1080/13683500.2020.1757628

Gillespie, T. (2010). The politics of 'platforms'. *New Media & Society, 12*(3), 347–364. https://doi.org/10.1177/1461444809342738

Gössling, S., & Hall, C. M. (2019). Sharing versus collaborative economy: How to align ICT developments and the SDGs in tourism? *Journal of Sustainable Tourism, 27*(1), 74–96. https://doi.org/10.1080/09669582.2018.1560455

Gurumurthy, A. (2018). Policies for the platform economy: Current trends and future directions. Report by IT for Change India/International Development Research Centre (IDRC), Canada.

Gutiérrez, J., García-Palomares, J. C., Romanillos, G., & Salas-Olmedo, M. H. (2017). The eruption of Airbnb in tourist cities: Comparing spatial patterns of hotels and peer-to-peer accommodation in Barcelona. *Tourism Management, 62,* 278–291. https://doi.org/10.1016/j.tourman.2017.05.003

Hassanli, N., Small, J., & Darcy, S. (2019). The representation of Airbnb in newspapers: A critical discourse analysis. *Current Issues in Tourism,* 1–13. https://doi.org/10.1080/13683500.2019.1669540

Ioannides, D., Röslmaier, M., & van der Zee, E. (2018). Airbnb as an instigator of 'tourism bubble' expansion in Utrecht's Lombok neighbourhood. *Tourism Geographies*, *21*(1), 822–840.

Keith, M., & Pile, S. (2013). *Geographies of resistance*. Routledge.

Kitchin, R. (2017). Thinking critically about and researching algorithms. *Information, Communication and Society*, *20*(1), 14–29. https://doi.org/10.1080/1369118X.2016.11540

Lagonigro, R., Martori, J. C., & Apparicio, P. (2020). Understanding Airbnb spatial distribution in a southern European city: The case of Barcelona. *Applied Geography*, *115*, 102136–102136. https://doi.org/10.1080/1369118X.2016.11540

Latour, B. (2005). *Reassembling the social: An introduction to actor-network*. Clarendon.

Lee, D. (2016). How Airbnb short-term rentals exacerbate Los Angeles's affordable housing crisis: Analysis and policy recommendations. *Harvard Policy Review*, *10*, 229.

Leszczynski, A. (2020). Glitchy vignettes of platform urbanism. *Environment and Planning D: Society and Space*, *38*(2), 189–208. https://doi.org/10.1177/0263775819878721

Martínez-Caldentey, A., Murray, I., & Blázquez-Salom, M. (2019). En la ciudad de Madrid todos los caminos conducen a Airbnb. *Investigaciones Turísticas*, *19*, 1–27. https://doi.org/10.14198/INTURI2020.19.01

McFarlane, C. (2009). Translocal assemblages: Space, power and social movements. *Geoforum*, *40*(4), 561–567. https://doi.org/10.1016/j.geoforum.2009.05.003

Milan, S. (2015). From social movements to cloud protesting: the evolution of collective identity. *Information, Communication and Society*, *18*(8), 887–900. https://doi.org/10.1080/1369118X.2015.1043135,

Milano, C., & Mansilla, J. A. (2018). *Ciudad de vacaciones; Conflictos urbanos en espacios turísticos*. Pol·len Edicions.

Minca, C., & Roelofsen, M. (2019). Becoming Airbnbeings: On datafication and the quantified Self in tourism. *Tourism Geographies*. https://doi.org/10.1080/14616688.2019.1686767

Molas, M. (2017). Barcelona lidera el NO a l'economia col·laborativa capitalista. *Recerca. Revista de Pensament i Anàlisi.*, *21*(21), 159–164. https://doi.org/10.6035/Recerca.2017.21.10

Morales, S., Garay, L., & Wilson, J. (2020). Airbnb-mediated short term rentals, socio-spatial inequalities and geographies of resistance. *Tourism Geographies*. https://doi.org/10.1080/14616688.2020.1795712

Morales-Pérez, S., Garay-Tamajón, L., & Troyano-Gontá, X. (2020). Beyond the big touristic city: Nature and distribution of Airbnb in regional destinations in Catalonia (Spain). *Current Issues in Tourism*. https://doi.org/10.1080/13683500.2020.1780201

Mumbrú, J. (2020). Barcelona regularà el lloguer d'habitacions d'ús turístic i avisa que serà 'molt restrictiva'. *Ara.cat Societat* (02/03/2020). https://www.ara.cat/societat/Barcelona-regulara-lloguer-habitacions-turistic_0_2409359140.html

Nel·lo, O. (2019). *Els ajuntaments del canvi*. Retrieved June 12, 2020. https://www.politicaprosa.com/els-ajuntaments-del-canvi/

Paredes-Rodriguez, A. A., & Spierings, B. (2020). Dynamics of protest and participation in the governance of tourism in Barcelona: A strategic action field perspective. *Journal of Sustainable Tourism*, *28*(12), 2118–2135. https://doi.org/10.1080/09669582.2020.1791891

Pirillo Ramos, S., & Mundet, L. (2020). Tourism-phobia in Barcelona: Dismantling discursive strategies and power games in the construction of a sustainable tourist city. *Journal of Tourism and Cultural Change*. 1–19. https://doi.org/10.1080/14766825.2020.1752224

Pirone, M., Frapporti, M., Chicchi, F., & Marrone, M. (2020). *Covid-19 impact on platform economy. A preliminary outlook*. Unibo. https://doi.org/10.6092/unibo/amsacta/6471

Postill, J. (2018). Populism and social media: A global perspective. *Media, Culture and Society*, *40*(5), 754–765. https://doi.org/10.1177/0163443718772186

Puente, S. N., Maceiras, S. D. A., & Romero, D. F. (2019). Twitter activism and ethical witnessing: Possibilities and challenges of feminist politics against gender-based violence. *Social Science Computer Review*, 089443931986489. https://doi.org/10.1177/0894439319864898

Quattrone, G., Proserpio, D., Quercia, D., Capra, L., Musolesi, M. (2016). Who benefits from the sharing economy of Airbnb? *Proceedings of the 25th International Conference on World Wide Web* (pp. 1385––1394).

Ricart, E., Snihur, S., Carrasco-Farré, C., & Berrone, P. (2020). Grassroots resistance to digital platforms and relational business model design to overcome it: A conceptual framework. *Strategy Science*, *5*(3), 271–291. https://doi.org/10.1287/stsc.2020.0104

Riessman, C. K. (2008). *Narrative methods for the human sciences*. Sage.

Roman, A. (2018). Planificación urbanística del turismo: La regulación de las viviendas de uso turístico en Madrid y Barcelona. *Revista de Estudios de la Administración Local y Autonómica*, *10*, 22–39. https://doi.org/10.24965/reala.v0i10.10566

Ruano de la Fuente, J. M., Iglesias Jiménez, E., & Polo Villar, C. (2019). El Madrid vivido: los problemas urbanos desde la perspectiva de la ciudadanía en el contexto del turismo de masas. *Boletín de la Asociación de Geógrafos*, 83. https://doi.org/10.21138/bage.2826

Russo, P., & Scarnato, A. (2018). Barcelona in common: A new urban regime for the 21ts century tourist city? *Journal of Urban Affairs*, *40*(4), 455–474. https://doi.org/10.1080/07352166.2017.1373023

Sequera, J., & Nofre, J. (2018a). Shaken, not stirred: New debates on touristification and the limits of gentrification. *City*, *22* (5-6), 843–855. https://doi.org/10.1080/13604813.2018.1548819

Sequera, J., & Nofre, J. (2018b). Urban activism and touristification in Southern Europe: Barcelona, Madrid and Lisbon. In J. Ibrahim & J. M. Roberts (eds) *Contemporary left-wing activism Vol 2, Democracy, participation and dissent in a global context* (chapter 6). Taylor and Francis.

Scholz, T., & Schneider, N. (2017). *Ours to hack and to own: The rise of platform cooperativism, a new vision for the future of work and a fairer internet*. OR Books.

Slee, T. (2017). *What's yours is mine: Against the sharing economy*. OR Books.

Söderström, O., & Mermet, A. C. (2020). When Airbnb sits in the control room: Platform urbanism as actually existing smart urbanism in Reykjavík. *Frontiers in Sustainable Cities*, 15*(2),* 1–7. https://doi.org/10.3389/frsc.2020.00015,

Srnicek, N. (2017). *Platform capitalism*. John Wiley and Sons.

Theocharis, Y., Lowe, W., Van Deth, J. W., & García-Albacete, G. (2015). Using Twitter to mobilize protest action: Online mobilization patterns and action repertoires in the Occupy Wall Street, Indignados, and Aganaktismenoi movements. *Information, Communication & Society*, *18*(2), 202–220. https://doi.org/10.1080/1369118X.2014.948035.

Tong, B., & Gunter, U. (2020). Hedonic pricing and the sharing economy: How profile characteristics affect Airbnb accommodation prices in Barcelona, Madrid, and Seville. *Current Issues in Tourism*, *22*(10), 1808–1826. https://doi.org/10.1080/13683500.2020.1718619

Treré, E. (2015). Reclaiming, proclaiming, and maintaining collective identity in the# YoSoy132 movement in Mexico: An examination of digital frontstage and backstage activism through social media and instant messaging platforms. *Information, Communication & Society*, *18*(8), 901–915. https://doi.org/10.1080/1369118X.2015.1043744.

Uzunca, B., & Borlenghi, A. (2019). Regulation strictness and supply in the platform economy: The case of Airbnb and Couchsurfing. *Industry and Innovation*, *26*(8), 920–942. https://doi.org/10.1080/13662716.2019.1633278

Uzunca, B., Coen Rigtering, J. P., & Ozcan, P. (2018). Sharing and shaping: A cross-country comparison of how sharing economy firms shape their institutional environment to gain legitimacy. *Academy of Management Discoveries*, *4*(3), 248–272. https://doi.org/10.5465/amd.2016.0153

van der Zee, R. (2016). The 'Airbnb effect': Is it real, and what is it doing to a city like Amsterdam? *The Guardian*, 6 October. http://www.theguardian.com/cities/2016/oct/06/the-Airbnb-effect-amsterdam-fAirbnb-property-prices-communities

van Doorn, N. (2019). A new institution on the block: On platform urbanism and Airbnb citizenship. *New Media and Society*. https://doi.org/10.1177/1461444819884377

van Harperen, S., Nicholls, W., & Uitermark, J. (2018). Building protest online: Engagement with the digitally networked #not1more protest campaign on Twitter. *Social Movement Studies*, *17*(4), 408–423. https://doi.org/10.1080/14742837.2018.1434499

Vargas, A. (2019). *Madrid esperará el fallo del TSJM para modificar la normativa de viviendas*. Hosteltur. https://www.hosteltur.com/130959_madrid-esperara-el-fallo-del-tsjm-para-modificar-la-normativa-de-viviendas.html

Vith, S., Oberg, A., Höllerer, M. A., & Meyer, R. E. (2019). Envisioning the 'Sharing City': Governance strategies for the sharing economy. *Journal of Business Ethics*, *159*(4), 1023–1046. https://doi.org/10.1007/s10551-019-04242-4

Wachsmuth, D., & Weisler, A. (2018). Airbnb and the rent gap: Gentrification through the sharing economy. *Environment and Planning A: Economy and Space*, *50*(6), 1147–1170. https://doi.org/10.1177/0308518X18778038

Yrigoy, I. (2019). Rent gap reloaded: Airbnb and the shift from residential to touristic rental housing in the Palma Old Quarter in Mallorca, Spain. *Urban Studies*, *56*(13), 2709–2726. https://doi.org/10.1177/0042098018803261

Zeller, F., & Hermida, A. (2015). When tradition meets immediacy and interaction: The integration of Social Media in journalists' everyday practices. *About Journalism*, *4*(1), 106–119.

Third-party impacts of short-term rental accommodation: a community survey to inform government responses

Sabine Muschter (iD), Rodney W. Caldicott (iD), Tania von der Heidt (iD) and Deborah Che (iD)

ABSTRACT

Short-term rental accommodation (STRA) sharing economy platforms, such as Airbnb, give rise to externalities or negative third-party impacts in neighbourhoods. Governments worldwide continue to grapple with how to best regulate STRA platforms given such externalities, especially in the wake of COVID-19. When STRA is perceived as poorly controlled, anecdotal reports indicate that community resentment around perceived inequities and negative economic, social, and environmental impacts rise. However, little research has systematically investigated community perceptions of STRA, notably Airbnb effects at a local, non-metropolitan level, as well as preferred regulatory responses. This paper examines such community perceptions in one of Australia's top tourism destinations, the Byron Shire. An online survey of 819 residents, identified four positive, eight negative and seven mixed impacts of Airbnb on community. To redress the adverse effects and enhance the sustainable performance of STRA (including Airbnb), a majority of residents favoured several regulatory strategies such as mandatory on-site management of STRA properties and better avenues to report complaints of misconduct. However, with notable reported differences between host and non-host residents. The study thus offers possible regulatory options to support regionally-based local councils as they seek to address opposing community concerns.

Introduction

Under a broad umbrella, multiple concepts describe the sharing economy (SE), which provides opportunities to participants in terms of generating flexibility, match-making, extending reach, managing transactions, trust-building and facilitating collectivity (Sutherland & Jarrahi, 2018). The rapid digitising of global economies through mobile technology, the internet, and the cloud has given rise to a for-profit, data-centric platform - a business model bringing different groups together (Srnicek, 2017). Gössling and Hall (2019) make a point of distinguishing between the sharing and collaborative economy: "Sharing refers to predominately private, and often non-commercial transactions, while the collaborative economy focuses on mediating commercial business-to-peer exchanges, virtually always involving platforms owned by global corporations" (p. 76). Sometimes both traditional and for-profit SE models are considered jointly, or the distinction between them is becoming increasingly blurred, and the term 'hybrid' is applied (Dolnicar, 2019; Sundararajan, 2016). As a result, the joint framing of the 'real' sharing economy and the 'commercial' collaborative economy may distort perceptions of the actual contributions of each to sustainable tourism, and thus feed the political debate on how best to regulate the SE.

Some of the best-known forms of the collaborative economy are home-sharing platforms, actively promoting narratives relating to the traditional notion of sharing, human connection, non-profit or profit-sharing, and the smarter use of underutilised houses/assets. Notably, Airbnb's role in unlocking latent rental value in private homes (Sundararajan, 2016) has assisted in it becoming the world's most successful and popular home-sharing platform. Yet some hosts pursue high profit through a transformation of housing into tourist accommodation (Oskam, 2019). Thus, most accommodation platforms no longer align with the original notion of the sharing economy (Gössling & Hall, 2019). According to Kenney and Zysman (2018), Airbnb's home-sharing model of brokering the renting of rooms does not comport with the ordinary meaning of sharing. Srnicek (2017) attributes the expansionary nature of platforms such as Airbnb to their growing appetite for data and the ultimate goal of "gaining absolute dominance over its core business area" (p. 256). Airbnb involves a variety of housing micro-practices including drawing upon small individual housing assets to generate wealth for the company, and the micro-entrepreneurial Airbnb hosts through outsourcing to hosts the property cleaning and insurance costs and paying employees minimum wage (Sundararajan, 2016). However, this promotes an entirely new set of housing-related applications (Stabrowski, 2017). Oskam (2019) calls out Airbnb's lack of transparency. He states their disguise of sharing rather than renting is an intentional strategy of entering in "conflict with local attempts to establish housing policies and to regulate commercial activities" (p. 19).

In acknowledgement to the vexed issues, this paper places an individual 'local community' within a non-metropolitan context at the forefront of a two-pronged investigation to determine Airbnb's externalities. The case community is the Byron Shire, a regional tourism hotspot in Australia. Following Alyakoob and Rahman (2019), the study adopts a sustainability lens capturing economic, social and environmental aspects to help paint a fuller picture. Given the disruptive, dynamic and fast-evolving nature of the sharing/collaborative economy and their supporting platforms, a more robust evidence base with cross-sectional snapshots of specific contexts is needed (Gurran & Phibbs, 2017). The *first aim* of this paper, therefore, is to examine the positive and negative spillover impacts of Airbnb felt by members of a non-metropolitan community. The *second aim* is to investigate community members' perceptions of appropriate government regulation of STRA in their region to address the negative spillover impacts.

Participation in the SE "has real effects in multiple places on users, workers, competing producers, the communities within which sharing occurs, and the range of resources that must be consumed in order to enable such services" (Gössling & Hall, 2019, p. 82). Economists refer to these unaccounted consequences for others as a result of SE participants' as externalities or spillovers (Sundararajan, 2016). Externalities, often manifesting as negative impacts, typically trigger some form of regulation. In the case of sharing platform firms, Srnicek (2017) attributes their success to them having leapt ahead of rules. Similarly, after studying the evolving regulation of Airbnb in New York, Sundararajan (2016) concludes that most micro-entrepreneurial Airbnb hosts would not pursue their small business ideas in the presence of a stricter code. He subsequently raises the tricky question of how to create a robust regulatory infrastructure for diverse sharing economy models in a way that preserves individual freedom, provides consumer safety, prevents the minority spoiling it for the majority and avoids an unnecessary bureaucratic burden. In this light, contemporary research primarily focuses on major cities. Within the metropolis, there is growing concern over externalities - 'touristification' or the transformation of residential neighbourhoods to tourism precincts (Sequera & Nofre, 2018). Such developments drive 'gentrification' as housing markets pressurise when permanent homes convert for tourism use (Wachsmuth & Weisler, 2018) further highlighting the socio-economic issue of reduced availability of affordable housing (Crommelin et al., 2018; Lee, 2016).

However, in non-metropolitan tourism destinations, the dearth of research into community-perceived impacts of the SE is especially acute. Noted exceptions in the Australian context are Gurran et al. (2020) and Grimmer and Vorobjovas-Pinta (2020). The former highlights Airbnb's profile across 12 coastal case-study communities in four Australian states. It finds that Airbnb style platforms intersect with, and impact, local governance, neighbourhoods and housing markets in different ways, a position they conceptualise as ranging from 'pop-up' to 'invasive' tourism. The latter, considering Airbnb from a single but whole of State level, recognises its polarising effect on the Tasmanian community. Some champion the home-sharing behemoth and commend its positive impact in promoting tourism in regional areas. Others criticise Airbnb for driving up house prices, reducing available housing stock for rent, and contributing to the displacement of long-term tenants from rental properties. In the European context, Domènech and Zoğal (2020) report on the spatial distribution of Airbnb supply and its potential effects on mountainous destinations. Each study concludes that universal approaches to regulation are not appropriate. Legislators must reflect upon the differences between towns, cities and regions, and take into consideration individual socio-economic status indicators when assessing the sustainability of tourism development, and subsequent policy-making.

First, we recap the literature on Airbnb's economic, social and environmental impacts on the community. As Airbnb's negative impacts may be regarded as market failure, economic theory around addressing them through regulation are discussed. The Byron Shire context is introduced, the study's methodology outlined, with findings presented and discussed. Finally, conclusions are drawn.

Economic, social and environmental impacts of sharing economy

The United Nations' (2018) sustainable development goal (SDG) 11, advocates for cities and human settlements to be inclusive, safe, resilient and sustainable. The SDGs focus on the triple bottom line framework of sustainability with its three equally important pillars of sustainability – economic viability, ecological preservation and societal wellbeing (Mawhinney, 2002). They also align with Krippendorf's (1987) vision for a new form of tourism that "will bring the greatest possible benefit to all the participants – travellers, the host population and the tourist business, without causing intolerable ecological and social damage" (p. 106).

While the SE posits to contribute to sustainable tourism and the achievement of SDGs, a range of impacts or unintended consequences have arisen from the evolution in P2P sharing, particularly the exponential growth in the STRA sector (Cheng et al., 2020). Such effects make the SE less sustainable and often generate a 'tourismphobia' (Milano et al., 2019), spawning anti-tourism movements a growing phenomenon worldwide (United Nations, 2018). Through the web-facilitated STRA sector, often called short-term holiday letting (STHL) platforms, tourism has encroached on residential areas. Such intrusion is perceived to bring along with it, increased noise levels and at times anti-social behaviour, both generic traits associated with overtourism. This term describes destinations where hosts or guests, locals or visitors, feel that there are too many visitors and that the quality of life in the area or the quality of the experience has deteriorated unacceptably (Capocchi et al., 2019).

The literature (summarised in Table 1) identifies a range of positive and negative effects across the three pillars of sustainability (economic, social and environmental) for five key stakeholder groupings: Airbnb host residents (AHR), Airbnb visitors (AV), non-Airbnb host residents (NAHR), Approved accommodation providers (AAP), and Local government (LG) (Caldicott et al., 2020). While many of the positive and negative indicators impact all five stakeholder groups, the negative economic, social and environmental impacts may be more severe and felt more acutely by NAHRs, AAPs and LGs. Bivens (2019) arrives at a similar conclusion in his assessment of the economic costs and benefits of Airbnb expansion.

Table 1. A sustainability perspective of Airbnb's impacts (based on the literature).

Economic viability		Social wellbeing		Ecological preservation	
Positive	Negative	Positive	Negative	Positive	Negative
• AHR: Homeowners earn extra income	• AHR: Struggle to optimise pricing	• AHR, NAHR, AV: Facilitates more authentic host-guest interactions	• AHR, NAHR, LG: Non-civic behaviour, (noise, vandalism, safety)	• None reported	• AHR, NAHR, AAP, LG: Waste management issues, security, and fire and safety protocols ignored by visitors
• AHR, AV, LG: Expands accommodation offerings and promotes value competition	• AAP: Decreased demand (and prices) for low-end hotels & forces hotel price restraint	• AHR, AAP, LG: Tourists display greater destination loyalty	• AHR, NAHR, LG: Discord between resident owners & non-resident owners		
• AV: Lowers tourists' accommodation costs	• AHR, NAHR, LG: Uncertainty about Airbnb regulation & declining role of government in SE	• AV: Richer experiences than hotels across eight dimensions, though the same rate of translation into behavioural intentions	• NAHR: Converts long-term rentals causing housing shortages.		
• AHR, LG: Increases trip length of stay	• NAHR, AAP, LG: Lack of compliance with tourist regulations				
• AHR, NAHR, LG: Generates new markets and jobs & increases spending on food	• NAHR: Increased rental prices for locals				
• LG: Grows municipal revenues					
• AHR, AV, AAP, LG: Design accommodation as a platform to explore the broader destination experience					

AHR (Airbnb host resident); AV (Airbnb visitor); NAHR (non-Airbnb host resident); AAP (traditional accommodation provider); Local government (LG); SE (Sharing Economy).
Source: (Caldicott et al., 2020).

Table 2. Classification of regulation type for Airbnb.

Self-regulation (Laissez-faire)	Semi-interventionist or co-regulation	Government regulation (including prohibition)
Raising awareness via communication campaigns	Incentives for improved performance	Defining & enforcing property rights (e.g. parking, registration of activity)
Airbnb guest reviews	Subsidies and taxes (e.g. bed tax)	Enforcing regulatory constraint with penalties for non-compliance (e.g. noise)
Owners corporations	Price & quantity controls (e.g. day caps)	
	Creating institutions that reduce transaction costs involved in parties negotiating solutions to externality problems (e.g. Airbnb collecting taxes)	

Source: Nieuwland & van Melik, 2020.

Despite the spate of recent investigation, empirical research into the community context of Airbnb remains sparse, especially in the specific context of impacts to regional destinations. Discussion of sustainable tourism often ignore communities' perceptions of the effects, and it may be a challenge to find common ground amongst different community stakeholders (Hardy & Pearson, 2016).

Regulation to address negative impacts (externalities) of sharing economy

Jurisdictions require an understanding of regulatory models to address when commercial practice outpaces government policy/intervention. While informal regulation and self-regulation offer the most autonomy to industry, highly prescriptive standards to which the regulated party must comply, curtail independence. Variation from the latter command approach may cause the regulated party to suffer penalties (the control). Semi-interventionist, in-between forms involve flexible regulatory incentives for improved performance or economic regulation in the form of incentive-based instruments (e.g. taxes and subsidies) and market-based instruments (i.e. price and quantity controls) (Hemphill, 2003). The middle ground represents a co-regulatory space, where the regulator and the regulated parties collaborate in determining and achieving regulatory goals (Haines, 2006). Aside from government regulation, Sundararajan (2016) predicts an increase of regulation across three new models - peer regulation (e.g. Airbnb guest reviews), self-regulatory organisation (e.g. by owners' corporations) and delegated regulation through data (e.g. Airbnb collecting tax data).

These three basic positions align roughly with the three main options to regulate Airbnb discussed by (Nieuwland & van Melik, 2020), namely laissez-faire, semi-interventionist or co-regulation, and prohibition (the most extreme form of regulation) – see Table 2.

Regulating STRA is a challenge, and no single regulatory approach can remove the gap between regulatory expectation and the behaviour of the regulated organisation (Nieuwland & van Melik, 2020). Therefore, an appropriate mix of government regulation, co-regulation and self-regulation is required for the given set of circumstances (Gunningham, 2004).

There is no federal regulation of STRA in Australia. Instead, each of the six states has the freedom to develop their regulatory approach. Only Tasmania has enacted a state-wide statute for STRA through its Short Stay Accommodation Act 2019, which mandates registration of all STRAs. In New South Wales (NSW), Strata and tenancy laws changed in April 2020 concerning STRA. Changes to the Strata Schemes Management Act allow owners cooperation to adopt by-laws that limit STRA in their strata scheme. STRA laws, including a mandatory Code of Conduct, will apply from 18 December 2020 to impose new obligations on booking platforms, hosts, letting agents and guests. Changes to planning laws are due by mid-2021, including a new planning

Table 3. Snapshot of Byron Shire population, Visitor numbers and Accommodation listings.

	2008	2013	2016	2019
Population Byron Shire	30,347	31,609	33,400	34,574
Byron Bay	n/a	8,790	9,246	9,608
Total Visitors Numbers (in mil)[a]	1.29	1.26	1.88	2.21
Day visitors	0.6	0.6	0.91	0.99
Overnight Visitors	n/a	0.62	0.97	1.22
Visitor nights	n/a	2.94	4.04	5.50
Airbnb listings[b]				
Airbnb	n/a	n/a	1,172	3,513
Accommodation Audit listings[c]				
AAP[d]	106	n/a	n/a	81
Holiday Apartments[e]	615	n/a	n/a	671
Other[f]	400	n/a	n/a	2,573

[a]Visitor Data from November each year, provided by Destination Byron (2019) and ASB 2020.
[b]Source: Inside Airbnb November 2019. Inside Airbnb provides data solely on Airbnb property listings with those for the Northern Rivers region available at http://insideairbnb.com/northern-rivers/. The disclaimers offer more information on the methodology.
[c]Byron Shire Council Accommodation Audit (Note - Data collected in 2008 and January 2019 only).
[d]Approved accommodation providers - Hostels, Caravan Camping, Guest Houses, Hotels/Motels, & Resorts.
[e]Holiday apartments, unknown if operated by an AAP or as STRA.
[f]Including Holiday Houses, Private/Home Stays (the majority of 2019 listing registered on the Airbnb platform).

policy that applies consistent regulation of the use of premises for STRA across the whole state. A mandatory STRA premises online register is currently under development for commencement in mid-2021. Western Australia has drafted a state-wide approach to STRA regulation, and changes to the STRA laws are due to be implemented in 2021. Queensland and Victoria devolve the management of STRA to local councils. The sixth State, South Australia, is the most relaxed jurisdiction for share accommodation premised on STRA not constituting a material change in use, thereby negating the requirement for planning approval.

The Byron Shire, located in the Northern Rivers region on the far north coast of NSW, is the focal context of the study reported in this paper and described next.

The case study – Byron Shire

About the Byron Shire

The Shire which had a population of around 34,500 in 2019, with 9,600 residents in Byron Bay, is famous as a coastal tourist destination. Tourism is the leading industry contributing A$883M to the local economy in 2019 (Byron Shire Council, 2020b) with visitor numbers steadily increasing over the last eleven years (2008 to 2019) - see Table 3. Visitor arrivals of over 2.2 million from July 2018 to June 2019 total 4.73 million nights with the majority of these visitors staying overnight in Byron Bay (Destination Byron 2019) outnumbering residents by a ratio of around 220 to 1. Table 3 also captures the significant increase in STRA numbers in the Shire over the last decade, as well as the decline in the number of approved accommodation providers from 2008 to 2019 (Byron Shire Council 2020a).

Today, the township Byron Bay is one of the most expensive real estate markets in Australia. The median house price in August 2020 was $1,450,000 (compared to $550,000 in 2012), and the median rent was $770 per week. Both prices more than doubled over the last ten years (realestate.com 2020). The growth is problematic, given Byron's specific demographic. Byron suffers from higher rates of underemployment, a higher proportion of single-parent families, lower-income levels, and higher housing stress compared to other areas in NSW (Gurran et al., 2020). Of particular note is the conversion of long-term rental properties, namely apartments and houses, to STRA, listed on multiple booking platforms.

Consequently, Byron Shire is also one of Australia's least affordable regional rental-housing markets (allhomes.com.au 2020). In 2019, approximately 25 per cent of properties in the Shire were listed as STRA, predominantly on the online rental platform, Airbnb followed by Homeaway (former Stayz). Byron Bay township hosts over half of the Shire's STRA properties, comprising up to 62% of the total dwelling supply (Byron Shire Council 2020b).

STRA regulations in Byron Shire

When Airbnb commenced operation in the Shire around 2011, the Council had already introduced specific regulation for STRA, such as an urban holiday letting precinct model in 2008 to prohibit STRA in some residential areas of Byron Bay. As listings started to grow, the Council drafted an STRA Action Plan in 2014, in alignment with their Local Environment Plan 2014, prohibiting tourist and visitor accommodations in residential zones. The use of a dwelling for STRA for tourist and visitor accommodation raises legal issues for many residences knowingly used as STRA (Byron Shire Council 2020b). A local organisation representing AAPs has lobbied the NSW Government to allow regional councils to enforce stricter rules around STRAs. They suggest a limit of 30-60 nights of the year for people renting out houses or rooms, instead of the government proposed 180-365 nights (Morrow, 2018).

The present NSW government proposed day cap for hosted and non-hosted properties (NSW Government, 2019), is much higher than most Shire residents can tolerate – a position that the Council has repeatedly put the government. However, the NSW government has rejected the Council's initiatives in the past, leaving it in a 'wait-and-see' space in anticipation of a yet unscheduled, State proposal for STRA regulation. In a turn-around, in March 2019, the Council received an invitation to prepare and submit a planning proposal to the NSW government that could introduce a 90-day threshold in the most impacted towns of the Byron Shire. This document went to the State government in March 2020 (Byron Shire Council 2020a) eliciting a Departmental response for Council to provide further economic analyses, though with insufficient details to the scope.

Subsequently, in the absence of coherent STRA regulation, there are palpable tensions between different stakeholder groups. First, most Shire residents do not share the NSW government's goal of almost doubling overnight visitor expenditure in the state by 2030 (Byron Shire Council 2020a). Second, because the State government considers local infrastructure and amenity issues relating to the tourism impacts to be chiefly the responsibility of local government (ABC North Coast 2017), many residents feel unjustly burdened by tourism externalities. They pay higher water and sewerage rates to help finance the infrastructure costs associated with high visitor numbers. The Shire Mayor publicly expressed his concerns: "The proliferation of unauthorised short-term holiday accommodation is threatening the fabric of our community. In some areas, it is getting to the point where long-term residents do not know anyone in their street anymore" (Poate, 2018, p. 1). Mindful of community feeling over STRA impacts, not just in Byron Shire but across many council areas of Australia, and indeed globally, this research systematically captures residents' views. First, regarding the positive and negative spillover impacts of Airbnb specifically; and secondly, regarding appropriate government regulation of STRA for their region, more generally.

Policymakers must have current, comprehensive, valid, reliable, and evidence-based information to inform sustainable tourism practices. Given the proliferation of Airbnb within Byron Shire, this research focus aligns to that platform.

Methodology

Guided by the literature (see Caldicott et al., 2020) and in-depth key informant interviews, an informed survey instrument was developed, which contained questions relating to the following:

- Respondent status - Airbnb host and Other residents. ('Other residents', for this paper, is a label given to respondents, who are not Airbnb hosts)

- Perceived positive and negative social, economic and ecological impacts of Airbnb lettings, i.e. on housing and accommodation, local businesses, tax revenues, visitor numbers, infrastructure and neighbourhoods across the Shire
- Perceived importance of information needs about various aspects related to Airbnb
- Preferences for measures to improve regulation of the STRA sector (including Airbnb)
- Preferences for rental caps (day limits) on STRA.

All perceptions and preferences were measured using a five-point Likert scale (1 = strongly disagree to 5 = strongly agree). The survey instrument underwent pre-testing within the research team, selected academic staff, and relevant staff within the Byron Shire Council.

The research team reached out to the entire adult Byron Shire population to participate in the survey, which was openly accessible for two months. The survey link was publicised in several ways to reach across all community stakeholders: through a team member giving interviews on four radio stations; articles published in four local newspapers; a media release through the University media office; repeated survey invitations through posts on the Facebook pages of twelve community groups; the Byron Shire Council Facebook page; invitation through newsletters to members of the Chamber of Commerce, two other business networks, and, one political party. Furthermore, flyers were displayed on notice boards and at weekly markets around the Shire. Given the positive response rate (n = 819) and the broad cross-section of stakeholder engagement, the sampling method proved useful in capturing adequate distribution. English literacy and web access, as well as Airbnb lobbying, were recognised as potential bias enablers (Andringa & Godfroid, 2020). However, the team did not observe any direct mobilisation of Airbnb hosts (Hibbing et al., 2014) during this study, as when Airbnb emailed hosts across NSW in December 2018, explicitly attacking, among others, Labor Party's planned holiday-lets controls (Lovejoy, 2018). Thus, the respondent mix suggests sufficiently distribution, notwithstanding the expected slight over-representation of Airbnb hosts as 1) they are 'direct-interest' parties; and 2) the high proportion of Airbnb properties within the Shire (approximately 62% of total properties).

The 1,017 survey responses resulted in a valid data sample of 819[1] after screening for incomplete submissions. Thus, the survey captured around 2.5 per cent of the Shire's population, including views of both Airbnb hosts and non-hosts. Most questions had relevance to all respondents though matters directly relating to the Airbnb' host-experience' were limited to the self-identified hosts towards the end of the survey. Reporting of the host-perceptions are beyond the scope of this paper.

The data was then subject to the following analyses: Descriptive analysis of residents' postcodes and length of living in the Shire; principal component analysis to explore the dimensionality of perceived impacts of Airbnb; and differential analyses, such as ANOVA; and cross-tabulations. The latter sought to explore how 1) respondents' postcodes and host status associate with perceived impacts of Airbnb, and 2) Airbnb host/non-host status was associated with preferred maximum short-term rental cap and preferences to regulate STRA.

The majority of survey respondents (55%) lived within the immediate surroundings of Byron Bay, which is the central tourist hub in the Shire, followed by 18% in Ocean Shores, 13% in Mullumbimby, and 8% in Bangalow and surroundings. The average length of respondent residency within the Shire was 19 years. Out of the 819 respondents, 67% (552) were owner-occupiers of properties, while 26% (215) rented their place of residence. Furthermore, 85% of all respondents said that they were aware of STRAs within 200 m of their home, with 75% saying that these STRAs were Airbnb listings. Of the 215 respondents (26%) in rented accommodation, almost half (90, 42%) had experienced requests to leave a previous rental. Fifty-eight, or 64% of those asked to leave, reported that they knew their rental property was about to be listed on Airbnb. Although the survey did not elicit for a 'how they knew' response, permanent residents replaced by the very temporary tourist dollar has long been a common dilemma for Byron Shire renters, even preceding Airbnb and especially leading up to holiday periods. Anglicare Australia is concerned that holiday letting is creating proxy resort towns in regional Australia and adding further stress to the housing crisis (Maunder et al., 2018; White, 2020).

Table 4. Positive impacts for the community.

Airbnb leads to ...	Mean				Overall agreement (%)	
	Overall (n = 766)	Airbnb host (n = 151)	Non-host (n = 615)	Disagree*	Neither	Agree
1. Increases revenues for local businesses	3.71	4.24	3.57	11	25	64
2. Increased employment opportunities for locals	3.10	4.01	2.86	34	26	40
3. Greater variety of retail & leisure services	3.09	3.78	2.91	30	35	35
4. Increased local tax revenue	2.66	2.98	2.59	48	27	25

*Disagree = includes groups Strongly disagree and Disagree; Neither = Neither Agree nor Disagree; Agree = includes groups Agree and Strongly Agree.

Findings

Perceived impacts of Airbnb

The seeming effects of Airbnb identified by the survey respondents fell into three categories: (1) impacts that are positive for the respondents' community; (2) those that are negative for the community; and (3) those that have mixed relations across the neighbourhood. The latter, and fresh addition to the impact literature, maybe favourable for *specific* community stakeholders, having no/negligible effect or perhaps a negative impact on *other* community members. For example, Airbnb leading to more visitors in a council area is generally beneficial for STRA hosts and business/tourism operators. It most likely has little impact on those people living away from the tourist hotspot. Notwithstanding, it may be unfavourable for some adjacent locals concerned about the loss of amenity or change in the culture of their neighbourhood.

Overall, the survey results report four significant positive impacts on the Byron Shire community and eight main adverse effects. Recognisably, Airbnb has a range of implications, which may be perceived similarly or differently by Airbnb hosts and Non-hosts (Other residents). When reviewing specific stakeholder responses (hosts vs non-hosts), the mixed impacts fall under seven indicators. The following discussion expands each category with the level of respondent agreement to various statements clustered as follows: Disagree = includes groups Strongly disagree and Disagree; Neither = Neither Agree nor Disagree; Agree = includes groups Agree and Strongly Agree.

Positive impacts of Airbnb

Table 4 presents four positive impacts of Airbnb on the community as perceived by Airbnb hosts and non-hosts alike. Ranked by mean in order of 'overall agreement' they are: increases revenues for business; increases employment; promote a greater variety of retail; and, increases local tax revenues. Airbnb hosts tend to see positive impacts more favourably than non-hosts. The views diverged most intensely for the impact 'leads to increased employment opportunities for locals'. Airbnb hosts tended to agree (mean 4.01), while non-Airbnb hosts tended to be neutral (neither agree nor disagree) (mean 2.86).

Negative impacts of Airbnb

Table 5 presents eight negative impacts of Airbnb on the community as perceived by Airbnb hosts and non-hosts alike. More than three-quarters of respondents agreed on the top two negative impacts of Airbnb – the reduction of affordable housing for residents and increased traffic and parking congestion. More than two-thirds of respondents agreed on the next three main negative impacts of Airbnb on the community. Airbnb leads to 1) increased waste management problems,

Table 5. Negative impacts for the community.

Airbnb ...	Mean			Overall agreement (%)		
	Overall (n = 766)	Airbnb host (n = 151)	Non-host (=615)	Disagree	Neither	Agree
1. Reduces the availability of affordable housing for residents	4.17	3.37	4.40	15	8	77
2. Increases traffic and parking congestion	4.07	3.13	4.33	16	9	75
3. Leads to increased waste management problems	3.97	3.15	4.20	14	14	72
4. Leads to extra costs to ratepayers to provide infrastructure	3.99	3.20	4.22	15	14	71
5. Leads to increased noise levels	3.98	3.03	4.24	15	15	70
6. Adversely affects the lifestyle of neighbourhood residents	3.97	2.89	4.27	19	12	69
7. Leads to the overuse of public facilities (e.g. toilets)	3.74	2.91	3.98	21	19	60
8. Leads to increased anti-social behaviour	3.55	2.56	3.82	24	22	54

Table 6. Mixed impacts of Airbnb.

Airbnb ...	Mean			Overall agreement (%)		
	Overall (n = 766)	Airbnb Host (n = 151)	Non-host (n = 615)	Disagree	Neither	Agree
1. Provides income for Airbnb hosts	4.30	4.50	4.26	1	5	94
2. Leads to an increased number of visitors into the Byron Shire	4.21	3.99	4.28	6	10	84
3. Leads to an increased number of property investors	4.18	3.62	4.33	8	13	79
4. Offers more variety in accommodation for tourists	3.94	4.49	3.80	8	11	81
5. Increases the property prices	3.72	3.28	3.87	20	19	61
6. Enables Airbnb hosts to stay in their homes	3.38	4.17	3.18	21	32	47
7. Makes Byron Shire a more affordable tourist destination	2.81	3.61	2.61	45	20	35

2) extra costs to ratepayers to provide infrastructure, and 3) increased noise levels. Airbnb hosts tended to perceive all negative impacts less negatively than non-Airbnb hosts. The views diverged most intensely for the impact 'leads to anti-social behaviour'. Airbnb hosts tended to disagree (mean 2.56) with this statement, while non-Airbnb hosts tended to agree (mean 3.82) with it.

Mixed impacts (or broad consequences) of Airbnb

Airbnb has positive impacts on *specific* stakeholders but may have no/negligible or even a negative impact on *other* community members. Respondent perceptions of seven mixed impacts of Airbnb (ranked by mean) present within Table 6. The majority of respondents agreed that Airbnb has positive associations for the following specific stakeholders:

- For *Airbnb hosts (AHs)* in terms of income generation (94% agreed), and allowing AHs to stay in their home (47% agreed).
- For *AHs, AAPs and other business operators* in terms of bringing more visitors to the area (84% agreed).
- For *tourists* in terms of providing more variety of accommodation (81% agreed), and making the tourist destination more affordable (35% agreed).
- For *property investors* in terms of increasing the number of investable properties, thus property investors (79% agreed).
- For *general property owners* in terms of the increased property price (61%).

Notwithstanding these positive broad-stakeholder impacts, respondent expression of neutrality, or disadvantage to the same indicators for a minority of stakeholders (e.g. non-host residents), is acknowledged as important, though not widely reported. Subsequently, policy-making should consider all views.

Perceptions of a daily rental cap

Table 7 presents summaries of the duration for their preferred rental cap (day-limits) across two types of STRA property: (a) primary residence *with on-site management*; and (b) permanently non-hosted investment properties without on-site management.

Properties with on-site management

Among all five Byron Shire postcode groups, 37% of respondents felt that there should be no restrictions at all for properties *with on-site* management, meaning that these properties are available for let 365-days per year. Notably, 72% of all Airbnb hosts wanted no restrictions on such properties, compared to only 29% of non-Airbnb hosts. The majority of non-Airbnb hosts favoured a cap for *on-site* managed properties, with 31% favoured a maximum cap of 180-days on such STRA rentals, while 32% preferred a cap of less than 90-days.

Properties without on-site management

Among the five Byron Shire postcode groups, 39% of all respondents wanted 0-days rental (*full restrictions = no STRA rentals*) for properties *without on-site management*. Even 15% of Airbnb hosts wanted complete restrictions (0-days) for such properties although this was far less than the 45% of non-Airbnb hosts.

Perceptions on regulations of STRA in the Byron Shire

In recognition that Airbnb is not the only accommodation platform within the Byron Shire SE space, the survey presented nine options for regulating STRA (including Airbnb). A majority of respondents supported all nine ways of controlling STRA (see Table 8). Overwhelmingly, respondents asked for more robust avenues to report complaints of misconduct, while 84% requested appropriate enforcement of non-compliance. Overall, the Airbnb hosts appeared to demand less regulation of STRA.

Table 7. Differences regarding rental caps on STRA.

	365 days per year (No restriction)	Max. 180 days per year*	Less than 90 days per year	0 days (Not allowed at all)
A. With on-site management				
Airbnb hosts (n = 151)	72	17	11	1
% of Airbnb hosts				
Non- Airbnb hosts (n = 615)	29	31	32	8
% of Non-hosts				
Total (n = 766)	37	28	28	7
% of all respondents				
B. Without on-site management				
Airbnb hosts (n = 151)	38	26	21	15
% of Airbnb hosts				
Non- Airbnb hosts (n = 615)	11	15	29	45
% of Non-hosts				
Total (n = 766)	16	18	27	39
% of all respondents:				

*Includes two groups: Max. 180 days per year and 90 < 179 days per year.

Table 8. Ways to regulate STRA in the Byron Shire.

STRA needs regulating in the following ways …	Mean			Overall agreement (%)		
	Overall (n = 766)	Airbnb host (n = 151)	Non-host (n = 615)	Disagree	Neither	Agree
1. Adequate reporting avenues to lodge complaints of misconduct	4.51	4.02	4.63	3	7	91
2. Adequate enforcement of non-compliance	4.37	3.70	4.54	4	12	84
3. Compulsory public liability insurance to cover STRA guests and third parties for injury or damage	4.15	3.44	4.32	12	11	77
4. A bed-tax or levy for any tourist accommodation (irrespective of the accommodation type)	4.10	3.49	4.25	15	10	75
5. Restrictions on Airbnb properties without on-site management	4.06	3.08	4.30	17	8	75
6. Adequate provision of fair trade within the accommodation-provider sector	4.01	3.35	4.17	9	20	70
7. Implementation of a registration & permit system for STRA	3.99	3.01	4.24	17	8	74
8. Council-supported community advisory panel regarding STRA	3.94	3.10	4.15	13	16	71
9. Zoning restrictions for STRA in residential areas	3.86	2.73	4.14	22	10	68

Preferences for further information needs on Airbnb

As presented in Table 9, the majority of respondents within the Byron Shire agreed with the need for better public information on Airbnb-related issues, particularly impacts of Airbnb on the community's residential-rental accommodation and infrastructure.

Altogether, the differential analyses, such as ANOVA and cross-tabulations, found no difference across postcodes in perceived impacts of Airbnb and STRA regulation. However, respondents from one of the five-postcode areas (Clunes/Federal) registered a stronger desire for the implementation of a registration/permit system for STRA than residents in the other postcode areas. Regarding host status (Airbnb host and non-Airbnb host) significant differences are apparent between hosts and non-hosts were found on all items on perceived impacts of Airbnb and STRA regulation options. Airbnb-hosts tended to perceive all negative impacts less negatively and all positive impacts of Airbnb more positively than non-Airbnb hosts - a phenomenon common among stakeholders with differing financial interests (Sroypetch & Caldicott, 2018). Furthermore, Airbnb hosts tended to perceive the need for STRA regulation and information of Airbnb much less than the non-Airbnb host respondents.

Discussion

This paper purposely places the Byron Shire community residents at the forefront of an investigation of positive, negative, and mixed, triple bottom line impacts of Airbnb within the broader context of short-term rental accommodation.

The research highlights that the significant positive effects of Airbnb on the Byron Shire community perceived by most respondents were primarily economic. Firstly, there is broad agreement that Airbnb boosts revenues for local businesses and that it provides an income for Airbnb hosts. These findings align with those of others (Bivens, 2019; Siglar & Panczak, 2020). However, opinions differ somewhat regarding the role of Airbnb in providing increased employment opportunities for locals. Airbnb hosts view Airbnb's role much more favourably than other residents. Scepticism about the role played by Airbnb in local employment is also evident in the literature. Dolnicar (2019, p. 257) observes that "there is no immediate evidence of dramatic impacts on the labour market as a consequence of the rise of platform businesses". However, Sundararajan (2016) argues that the rise of crowd-based capitalism will be the demise of labour-based employment with big money going to the platforms and the labour – Uber drivers and Airbnb hosts - working for very little or nothing. On the contrary, in the case of the present study, Airbnb hosts were upbeat about their income-earning capacity.

Most respondents were, though, concerned about a range of negative impacts of Airbnb across the triple bottom line dimensions. Notably, other residents (non-Airbnb host) were more concerned about each issue than were the Airbnb hosts. In the Byron Shire, the most severely perceived negative impact identified is the socio-economic issue of reduced availability of affordable housing reflecting findings in several studies (Crommelin et al., 2018; Eccleston et al., 2019). Each of these studies reported that a high proportion of tourists led to a shortage of affordable longer-term rental properties. As Oskam (2019, p. 92) summarises, the "displacement of residents and services has started a vicious cycle which transforms neighbourhood from living environments into a commercial offer of accommodation and leisure facilities for tourist consumption". However, on the contrary Stors (2020) advocates for the social construction of new tourist sites with Airbnb hosts, and their place framings, playing a significant role in 'new' urban placemaking.

Three further perceived negative impacts relate to neighbourhood amenity. Non-Airbnb hosts, in particular, are concerned about rising short-term rental properties leading to increased traffic, congestion, and increased noise levels that adversely affect their neighbourhood lifestyles. As some of these impacts have existed for nearly 20 years (Buultjens et al., 2012; Eccleston et al.,

Table 9. Importance of information about Airbnb-related aspects.

Important to have information about …	Mean			Of importance (%)		
	Overall (n = 766)	Airbnb host (n = 151)	Non-host (n = 615)	Not important	Average important	Very important
1. Long-term impacts on residential-rental accommodation	4.20	3.46	4.40	10	12	78
2. Long-term impacts on infrastructure (e.g. roads, waste management facilities)	4.19	3.55	4.37	8	14	78
3. Long-term impacts of Airbnb on the community	4.14	3.39	4.35	9	15	76
4. The extent of compliance with existing STRA regulations	4.03	3.27	4.24	10	18	72
5. Regulations regarding Airbnb rentals (host responsibilities, guest rights)	3.94	3.33	4.10	12	19	69
6. Long-term impacts on businesses in town	3.77	3.58	3.83	8	30	62
7. Long-term impacts on approved accommodation providers	3.70	2.97	3.90	17	26	57
8. The location and type of Airbnb properties	3.40	2.49	3.65	26	21	53

Not important = includes groups Not important at all, and Of little importance; Of average importance; Very important = includes groups Very important and Absolutely essential.

2019) evidently, Airbnb is not the sole cause. However, with the shift to internet booking of STRAs, the impacts now appear exacerbated. The perception of declining liveability with the Byron Shire due to the high concentration of Airbnb in residential areas makes the platform a target reflecting broader concerns of tourism impact on residents worldwide. The character and quality of specific neighbourhoods may be changing (Petruzzi et al., 2020; Richards et al., 2019). However, the empirical evidence from this study does not support the wholesale notion of Airbnb bedevilling local neighbourhoods (A Phenomenology Collective, 2019; Zervas et al., 2017). Instead, following other commentators (Frisch et al., 2019; Grimmer et al., 2018) the reported 'mixed-impact' indicators go part-way in supporting integrated precincts that service residency, alongside leisure and work.

In terms of preferred interventions to regulate STRA, the finding of this study regarding respondents preferred rental caps on STRA is split. While the majority of respondents preferred a business/regulatory model which involves mandatory on-site management of STRA properties, the reported distinction between Airbnb hosts and other residents is new and requires further consideration. The former favour the status quo, i.e. unrestricted STRA letting; the latter favour restrictions in terms of a 180 day or 90-day limit. Nearly 50 percent of other residents (non-hosts) prefer a situation where STRA without a host present is not allowed at all! The approaches as taken in Australia, mainly *(de)regulatory* in Tasmania and *laissez-faire* in South Australia, and that of other cities around the world, particularly in the USA (*permits*) and Europe (*zone restrictions and taxes*), offer useful scenarios for further learning regarding regulatory facilitation of STRA. Albeit, each presents fresh ways to engage the community. While Airbnb is legal in such international cases, care is required to protect immediate non-host neighbours and neighbourhoods overall (Domènech & Zoğal, 2020; Grimmer & Vorobjovas-Pinta, 2020; Park, 2019).

The findings of this study suggest that locally specific regulation of the STRA sector across all three types of code (see Table 2) may alleviate several areas of stated participant concern. First, in terms of self-regulation, the results show that Byron's Airbnb hosts are less demanding for information about Airbnb-related aspects while other residents highly value such information. They are especially keen to know about the long-term impacts of Airbnb on residential-rental accommodation, on local infrastructure and the community, as well as how Airbnb hosts are complying with existing regulations.

Second, in terms of semi-interventionist or co-regulation, the majority of survey respondents reacted positively. Such an approach sanctions an activity though with certain restrictions: providing incentives for improved performance; introducing subsidies or taxes (e.g. bed-tax); promoting price & quantity controls (e.g. day caps); or creating institutions that reduce transaction costs involved in parties negotiating solutions to externality problems (e.g. Airbnb collecting taxes). In particular, the non-Airbnb hosts supported the implementation of day-caps for STRA without on-site management. The majority of respondents also support the introduction of a bed tax as one way of regulation to raise taxes from Airbnb properties.

Third, perceived as a necessity by the majority of respondents, the government should introduce regulation for the implementation of registration and permit systems for all STRA along with adequate reporting avenues to lodge complaints of misconduct, and enforcement of non-compliance of STRA.

Regulation of STRAs, and the enabling booking platforms, cannot be universal as each destination's needs and goals are quite different – as highlighted through the various State-based regulatory approaches in Australia. This study recommends that councils which experience intensifying STRAs, threatening to compromise the life-quality of residents, should be permitted to impose stricter rules and regulation to address the situation - the most extreme form of regulation (see Table 2). Local councils ought to have the autonomy to protect their community – a position currently not available to independent councils across all states in Australia. Ideally, municipal governments worldwide need to be given some opportunity by state or national governments to shape the regulation of STRA within the local area. Local governments best understand their various community stakeholder groups and can best assess the trade-off between positive, negative, and mixed impacts for the local economy, society and ecology. They can consider the concerns of the whole community - including residents, Airbnb hosts, and renters, but also property investors, AAPs, and visitors. Empowerment of local councils to promote dialogue between the broad-ranging stakeholders is preferable to a 'one size fits all', State-wide regulatory approach. It remains essential to find locally appropriate solutions; addressing community concerns, tourism demands, and housing issues, all pertinent to that local government area.

Concerning residents' information needs about Airbnb in the community, it is again thought-provoking to note the gap between Airbnb hosts and non-hosts. Airbnb hosts tended to have lower information needs than non-Airbnb hosts. Therefore, STRA regulators and administrators need to consult with both stakeholder types. Addressing the impacts of over-tourism, including Airbnb, as well as accounting for residents' preferences, is vital for destination managers. Buultjens et al. (2012) argue that to ensure a thriving destination, the entire community must accept tourism and tourists. Community approval of tourism, or social sustainability, along with economic and ecological sustainability, underpins the UN's 2018 sustainable development goals. Thus, accounting for the mediating role of residents' perceptions of tourism development can significantly improve management strategies (Gannon et al., 2020). Similarly, mitigating unjustified fears and a potential moral panic over new developments can promote innovative opportunities for stakeholders. Despite open consultation and public participation processes, not all stakeholders' concerns will be identified or subsequently addressed to the likes of those stakeholders (Caldicott et al., 2014; Ravenscroft, 2020).

Conclusion

The sharing economy started idealistically, intending to connect people with other people's underused assets, which could benefit the environment and society more widely. However, more recently, the sharing economy has come under criticism as being more selfish than sharing. In the case of Airbnb, many of its listings are not actually by homeowners letting out spare bedrooms but are by professional landlords using the platform to get around existing regulations and get higher rents from daily, rather than long-term, rentals. According to real estate attorney Phyllis Weisberg, chair of the Cooperative & Condominium Law Committee of the New York City Bar, "There is something fundamentally wrong with a business model that encourages people to breach their obligations and responsibilities. This is a selfish kind of economy where people will just do this to make as much money as they can until they get caught" (Goodale, 2015, p. 1). The backlash against the sharing/selfish economy has spurred a more in-depth look at the priorities and moral underpinnings of the sharing economy. It also raises the need to investigate its externalities. Through this paper, we explore ways to mitigate the negative and promote the positive impacts within the Byron Shire.

The paper principally explores STRA (including Airbnb) as providing both opportunities and challenges for a non-metropolitan community. It notes the influence of lobbyists and advocates on both sides, which feed the evolving debate over the regulation of STRA. In such regard, this study also provides evidence around residents' preferred ways to regulate STRA and the relative importance to the community of STRA-related information. Common in some metropolitan holiday hotspots, the likes of Amsterdam, Barcelona and Venice, the shortage of available housing for purchase or rental combined with the increase in property prices and rents have disrupted the social fabric of the community. Subsequently, this study reinforces the notion that STRA platforms, notably Airbnb, have highly emotional impacts upon host communities in both metropolitan and non-metropolitan tourist hotspots.

Shifting local to national strategic thinking, *beyond economic imperatives*, is crucial for core community, cultural, and environmental values to survive and receive consideration as equals necessary in a balanced social-ecological system (Milano et al., 2019; Ravenscroft, 2020; Sroypetch & Caldicott, 2018). Dynamic change and action going forward must be the primary focus towards fulfilling the requirements of local stakeholders involved in tourism operations while contemplating how best to manage for sustainable development goals within business and community - inspiring, new management practices within and beyond the tourism industry. Some distressed communities may seem completely lost to non-sustainable tourism development, primarily brought on through unintended consequences of a market disruptor. However, addressing the critical equilibrium between ecology, societal wellbeing and economics can bring back and strengthen community; promoting resilience against further internal and external shocks.

Limitations and further research

Although the research team made every effort to encourage survey participation by all adult Byron Shire residents, the proportion of Airbnb hosts in the sample (20%) is higher than that of the wider Byron Shire population (estimated at around 6%[2]). Respondents who are Airbnb hosts or benefit economically from Airbnb, or those who are actively opposed to Airbnb (i.e. in neighbourhood groups or personally impacted by nearby Airbnb rentals) maybe slightly over-represented. Additionally, the study focused on only one local government area out of 129 in NSW and 547 across Australia. While the area studied is a renowned tourism hotspot, the findings cannot be generalised. The research thus calls for a widened scope, through a larger-scale study, to confirm data broadly applicable to more local government areas and beyond Australia. Replicating the research methodology across other towns in NSW/Australia will assist in building a comparable data snapshot(s) and develop a more comprehensive understanding of why different regions might need various STRA regulations.

Further follow-up research is needed to understand how the COVID-19 pandemic moderates the impact of STRAs on a local community. During the Australian six-week lockdown from 23 March to 15 May, nearly all of Byron's economy links to tourism and hospitality, ninety per cent of shops, hotels and restaurants in Byron Bay were closed. However, in April 2020, even with the COVID-19 restrictions, the pre-COVID-19 stock of 3,500 or so Airbnb listings for the Byron Shire continued. This was despite the significant loss of international visitors. The anomaly may be due to Byron Bay becoming the 'go-to domestic destination' for many domestic travellers after easing of NSW intra-state lockdown-regulations and the tightening of interstate-border restrictions (Kirpatrick, 2020). Thus, the impacts of Airbnb on Byron – positive, negative, and mixed - appear to be ongoing and inviting further research. Such studies might assess the differential impact now that the influx of tourists is mainly domestic.

Future research is also warranted to explore the emotional impacts of Airbnb on host communities, which is another form of unintended, third party effect STRA has on community residents. The high number of Airbnb rentals tends to displace long-term rentals, continuously and economically challenging renters' sense of wellbeing. White (2020) suggests, although a common phenomenon, it is exacerbated by the COVID-19 impacted economy and decreased job market insecurities.

Disclosure statement

No potential conflict of interest was reported by the author(s).

Notes

1. The sample size relating to each key finding reported in the above sections varies as not all 819 participants answered all pertinent questions.

2. Around 1600 Airbnb hosts account for around 3,500 Airbnb listings in the Shire. The population of adults (>18 years of age) in Byron is approximately 28,000.

Funding

This article was supported by Southern Cross University, School of Business & Tourism Cluster Grant.

ORCID

Sabine Muschter (iD) http://orcid.org/0000-0002-3852-8842
Rodney W. Caldicott (iD) http://orcid.org/0000-0002-0560-9515
Tania von der Heidt (iD) http://orcid.org/0000-0002-9852-8764
Deborah Che (iD) http://orcid.org/0000-0002-5274-9502

References

A Phenomenology Collective (2019). Cultivating activism in the academy: a Deleuzoguattarian exploration of phenomenological projects. *Qualitative Inquiry*. https://doi.org/10.1177/1077800419836692.
ABC North Coast (2017). *Byron Bay tourism crunch: Mayor warns of a backlash if growth isn't curbed*, Australian Broadcasting Commission, viewed 2 February, http://www.abc.net.au/news/2017-08-18/byron-wants-brakes-on-tourism/8820984.
allhomes.com.au (2020). *Byron Bay (NSW 2481) suburb infomation*, viewed 9 August, https://www.allhomes.com.au/ah/research/byron-bay/12715210.
Alyakoob, M., & Rahman, M. S. (2019). Shared prosperity (or lack thereof) in the sharing economy. (17 May) Available at, https://doi.org/http://dx.doi.org/10.2139/ssrn.3180278.
Andringa, S., & Godfroid, A. (2020). Sampling bias and the problem of generalizability in applied linguistics. *Annual Review of Applied Linguistics*, 40, 134–142. https://doi.org/10.1017/S0267190520000033

Bivens, J. (2019). The economic costs and benefits of Airbnb: no reason for local policymakers to let Airbnb bypass tax or regulatory obligations. View this report at epi.org/157766, Economic Policy Institute., https://www.epi.org/files/pdf/157766.pdf.

Buultjens, J., White, N., & Neale, K. (2012). Collaborative destination management planning: a case study of Byron Bay, Australia. *Journal of Travel and Tourism Research (Online)*, *12*(1), 18–33. http://ezproxy.scu.edu.au/login?url=https://search-proquest-com.ezproxy.scu.edu.au/docview/1439928137?.

Byron Shire Council. (2020a). *Draft Byron Shire Sustainable Visitation Strategy 2020 - 2030*, Byron Shire Council, viewed 26 August, https://www.byron.nsw.gov.au/files/assets/public/hptrim/economic-development-industries-development-tourist-strategies-sustainable-visitation-strategy-2019-2029/byron-shire-draft-sustainable-visitation-strategy-2020-2030-public-exhibition-version.pdf.

Byron Shire Council. (2020a). *Planning proposal for short term rental accommodation in Byron Shire*, Byron Shire Council, viewed 10 February, https://byron.infocouncil.biz/Open/2020/02/PLAN_20022020_AGN_1151_WEB.htm.

Caldicott, R. W., Scherrer, P., & Jenkins, J. (2014). Freedom camping in Australia: current status, key stakeholders and political debate. *Annals of Leisure Research*, *17*(4), 417–442. viewed 2014/11/27, https://doi.org/http://dx.doi.org/10.1080/11745398.2014.969751>.

Caldicott, R. W., von der Heidt, T., Scherrer, P., Muschter, S., & Canosa, A. (2020). Airbnb – exploring its triple bottom line impacts. *International Journal of Culture, Tourism and Hospitality Research*, *14*(2), 205–223. https://doi.org/10.1108/IJCTHR-07-2019-0134

Capocchi, A., Vallone, C., Pierotti, M., & Amaduzzi, A. (2019). Overtourism: a literature review to assess implications and future perspectives. *Sustainability*, *11*(12), 3303. https://www.mdpi.com/2071-1050/11/12/3303. https://doi.org/10.3390/su11123303

Cheng, M., Houge Mackenzie, S., & Degarege, G. A. (2020). Airbnb impacts on host communities in a tourism destination: an exploratory study of stakeholder perspectives in Queenstown, New Zealand. *Journal of Sustainable Tourism*, Published online 25 August, 1–19. https://doi.org/10.1080/09669582.2020.1802469.

Crommelin, L., Troy, L., Martin, C., & Parkinson, S. (2018). *Technological disruption in private housing markets: the case of Airbnb. Australian Housing and Urban Research Institute Limited Melbourne*. http://www.ahuri.edu.au/research/final-reports/305.

Destination Byron (2019). *Byron visitor economy snapshot June 2019*, Destination Byron, viewed 25 January. http://www.destinationbyron.com.au/research/.

Dolnicar, S. (2019). A review of research into paid online peer-to-peer accommodation: launching the Annals of Tourism Research Curated Collection on peer-to-peer accommodation. *Annals of Tourism Research*, *75*, 248–264. https://doi.org/10.1016/j.annals.2019.02.003

Domènech, A., & Zoğal, V. (2020). Geographical dimensions of airbnb in mountain areas: the case of Andorra. *Journal of Rural Studies*, *79*, 361–372. https://doi.org/10.1016/j.jrurstud.2020.08.051

Eccleston, R., Warren, N., Verdouw, J., Flanagan, K., Eslake, S. (2019). *A blueprint for improving housing outcomes in Tasmania*, Institute for the Study of Social Change, University of Tasmania, viewed 16 June. https://www.utas.edu.au/__data/assets/pdf_file/0009/1074609/Insight-Three-Housing-Web-Version.pdf.

Frisch, T., Sommer, C., Stoltenberg, L., & Stors, N. (2019). *Tourism and everyday life in the contemporary city.*, Taylor & Francis. https://books.google.co.th/books?id=88uGDwAAQBAJ.

Gannon, M., Rasoolimanesh, S. M., & Taheri, B. (2020). Assessing the mediating role of residents' perceptions toward tourism development. *Journal of Travel Research*, *In Press*, https://doi.org/10.1177/0047287519890926

Goodale, G. (2015). *With big growth for the sharing economy, has it become selfish?*, The Christian Science Monitor, viewed 26 August. https://www.csmonitor.com/USA/Society/2015/0321/With-big-growth-for-the-sharing-economy-has-it-become-selfish.

Gössling, S., & Hall, M. (2019). Sharing versus collaborative economy: how to align ICT developments and the SDGs in tourism? *Journal of Sustainable Tourism*, *27*(1), 74–96. https://doi.org/10.1080/09669582.2018.1560455

Grimmer, L., & Vorobjovas-Pinta, O. (2020). Maintaining the status quo: regulating Airbnb in Tasmania. in C-S Ooi & A Hardy (eds), *Tourism in Tasmania.*, Forty South Publishing. pp. 195–208, https://www.utas.edu.au/__data/assets/pdf_file/0011/1283366/book-tourism-in-tasmania.pdf.

Grimmer, L., Massey, M., Vorobjovas-Pinta, O. (2018). *Airbnb is blamed for Tasmania's housing affordability problems, but it's actually helping small businesses*, The Conversation Media Group, viewed 20 March. https://theconversation.com/airbnb-is-blamed-for-tasmanias-housing-affordability-problems-but-its-actually-helping-small-businesses-91566.

Gunningham, N. (2004). *Best practice rail safety regulation*, National Centre for OHS Regulation, viewed 17 November. https://openresearch-repository.anu.edu.au/bitstream/1885/43219/2/RailSafetyFinalVersion.pdf.

Gurran, N., & Phibbs, P. (2017). When tourists move in: how should urban planners respond to airbnb? *Journal of the American Planning Association*, *83*(1), 80–92. https://doi.org/10.1080/01944363.2016.1249011

Gurran, N., Zhang, Y., & Shrestha, P. (2020). Pop-up' tourism or 'invasion'? Airbnb in coastal Australia. *Annals of Tourism Research*, *81*, 102845. https://doi.org/10.1016/j.annals.2019.102845

Haines, F. (2006). *Regulatory failures and solutions: a characteristic analsyis of meta-regulation. paper presented to the Annual Meeting, Law and Society Association, Baltimore, MD, USA*, July 6-9, viewed 17 November, https://minerva-access.unimelb.edu.au/bitstream/handle/11343/34947/67730_00004200_01_Meta-regulation_paper.pdf?.

Hardy, A., & Pearson, L. (2016). Determining sustainable tourism in regions. *Sustainability*, 8(7), 660–678. https://doi.org/10.3390/su8070660

Hemphill, T. A. (2003). Self-regulation, public issue management and marketing practices in the US entertainment industry. *Journal of Public Affairs*, 3(4), 338–357. https://doi.org/10.1002/pa.162

Hibbing, J. R., Smith, K. B., & Alford, J. R. (2014). Differences in negativity bias underlie variations in political ideology. *The Behavioral and Brain Sciences*, 37(3), 297–307. nohttps://doi.org/10.1017/S0140525X13001192

Kenney, M., & Zysman, J. (2018). *Work and value creation in the platform economy.*, Berkeley University of California. viewed 10 June, https://brie.berkeley.edu/sites/default/files/brie_wp_20184.pdf.

Kirpatrick, D. (2020). *Gridlock holiday: which town is NSW's most wanted?*, News Corp, Australia, viewed 19 November, https://www.northernstar.com.au/news/gridlock-holiday-which-town-is-nsws-most-wanted/4142232/?.

Krippendorf, K. (1987). *The holiday makers - understanding the impact of leisure and travel.*, Butterworth Heinemann.

Lee, D. (2016). How Airbnb short-term rentals exacerbate Los Angeles's affordable housing crisis: analysis and policy recommendations. *Harvard Law & Policy Review*, 10, 229. http://heinonline.org/HOL/Page?handle=hein.journals/harlpolrv10&div=13&g_sent=1&collection=journals.

Lovejoy, H. (2018). 'Airbnb mute on its political campaign', *The Byron Echo*, 27 December, viewed 16 November, 2020. https://www.echo.net.au/2018/12/airbnb-mute-political-campaign/.

Maunder, S., Thomas, K., Merkell, H., & Drewitt-Smith, A. (2018). *Holiday letting forcing people out of regional long-term rentals, says charity.*, Australian Broadcasting Commission. viewed 16 November. https://www.abc.net.au/news/2018-05-01/holiday-letting-forcing-out-tenants-says-anglicare/9710336.

Mawhinney, M. (2002). *Sustainable development: understanding the green debates*. Blackwell Science.

Milano, C., Novelli, M., & Cheer, J. M. (2019). Overtourism and tourismphobia: a journey through four decades of tourism development, planning and local concerns. *Tourism Planning & Development*, 16(4), 353–357. https://doi.org/10.1080/21568316.2019.1599604

Morrow, C. (2018). *Rental plan frustration*, Byron Shire News, News Corp, Australia, viewed 31 December, <<https://www.byronnews.com.au/news/rental-plan-frustration/3446990/>.

Nieuwland, S., & van Melik, R. (2020). Regulating Airbnb: how cities deal with perceived negative externalities of short-term rentals. *Current Issues in Tourism*, 37(7), 811-25. https://doi.org/10.1080/13683500.2018.1504899

NSW Government. (2019). *Short-term rental accommodation - a new regulatory framework*, NSW Department of Planning, Industry and Environment and Department of Customer Service, viewed 26 August. https://www.planningportal.nsw.gov.au/exhibition/proposed-short-term-rental-accommodation-reforms.

Oskam, J. A. (2019). *The future of Airbnb and the "sharing economy": the collaborative consumption of our cities.*, Channel View Publications, Bristol, UK. https://doi.org/10.21832/9781845416744.

Park, M. (2019). The sharing economy, regulations, and the role of local government. *International Journal of Tourism Cities*, 6(1), 158–174. https://doi.org/10.1108/IJTC-08-2019-0122

Petruzzi, M., Marques, G., Carmo, M., & Correia, A. (2020). Airbnb and neighbourhoods: an exploratory study. *International Journal of Tourism Cities*, 6(1), 72–89. vol. ahead-of-print, https://doi.org/10.1108/IJTC-08-2019-0119

Poate, S. (2018). *Airbnb fires on mayor over fresh holiday lets comments*, News Corp, viewed 14 February. https://www.northernstar.com.au/news/airbnb-fires-on-mayor-over-fresh-holiday-lets-comm/3389383/.

Ravenscroft, T. (2020). *Travel as we knew it is over" says Airbnb co-founder*, Dezeen.co, viewed 25 June. https://www.dezeen.com/2020/06/23/travel-coronavirus-airbnb-co-founder-brian-chesky/?.

realestate.com (2020). *Byron Bay 2481*, www.realestate.com.au. https://www.realestate.com.au/neighbourhoods/byron-bay-2481-nsw.

Richards, S., Brown, L., & Dilettuso, A. (2019). The Airbnb phenomenon: the resident's perspective. *International Journal of Tourism Cities*, 6(1), 8–26. https://doi.org/10.1108/IJTC-06-2019-0084

Sequera, J., & Nofre, J. (2018). Shaken, not stirred: new debates on touristification and the limits of gentrification. *City*, 22(5-6), 843–855. https://doi.org/10.1080/13604813.2018.1548819.

Siglar, T., Panczak, R. (2020). *Ever wondered how many Airbnbs Australia has and where they all are? We have the answers*, The Conversation Media Group, viewed 20 February, https://theconversation.com/ever-wondered-how-many-airbnbs-australia-has-and-where-they-all-are-we-have-the-answers-129003.

Srnicek, N. (2017). *Platform capitalism.*, John Wiley & Sons.

Sroypetch, S., & Caldicott, R. W. (2018). Backpacker tourism in Fiji as a sustainability intervention; will they sink or swim?. In J Cheer & AA Lew (Eds.), *Tourism, Resilience and Sustainability: Adapting to Social, Political and Economic Change* (pp. 260–279). Routledge.

Stabrowski, F. (2017). People as businesses': Airbnb and urban micro-entrepreneurialism in New York City. *Cambridge Journal of Regions, Economy and Society*, 10(2), 327–347. https://doi.org/10.1093/cjres/rsx004

Stors, N. (2020). Constructing new urban tourism space through Airbnb. *Tourism Geographies*, arXiv.org, 2(CSCW), 1–29, https://doi.org/10.1080/14616688.2020.1750683

Sundararajan, A. (2016). *The sharing economy: the end of employment and the rise of crowd-based capitalism.*, The MIT Press. https://mitpress.mit.edu/books/sharing-economy.

Sutherland, W., & Jarrahi, M. H. (2018). The sharing economy and digital platforms: a review and research agenda. *International Journal of Information Management, 43*, 328–341. https://doi.org/10.1016/j.ijinfomgt.2018.07.004

United Nations (2018) *The sustainable development agenda*, The United Nations, viewed 27 September, https://www.un.org/sustainabledevelopment/development-agenda/.

Wachsmuth, D., & Weisler, A. (2018). Airbnb and the rent gap: gentrification through the sharing economy. *Environment and Planning A: Economy and Space, 50*(6), 1147–1170. https://doi.org/10.1177/0308518X18778038

White, L. (2020). *Byron Bay region's 'hidden' homelessness issues made worse by Airbnb and holiday-letting*, Australian Broadcasting Commission, viewed 30 August, https://www.abc.net.au/news/2020-08-04/byron-bay-hidden-home-less-worsened-by-airnbnb-holiday-letting/11485572.

Zervas, G., Proserpio, D., & Byers, J. W. (2017). The rise of the sharing economy: estimating the impact of Airbnb on the hotel industry. *Journal of Marketing Research (Research), 54*(5), 687–705. http://ezproxy.scu.edu.au/login?url=http://search.ebscohost.com/login.aspx?direct=true&db=buh&AN=125577949&site=ehost-live. https://doi.org/10.1509/jmr.15.0204

Social consequences of Airbnb: a New Zealand case study of cause and effect

Chris Ryan and Linglong Ma

ABSTRACT

This study of impacts of Airbnb in a small coastal town in New Zealand was initiated by a need to create housing for those displaced during the summer. The research involved a survey of approximately one-quarter of the households and detailed interviews with 25 local respondents. It was found that approximately 17% of households experienced household stress due to housing costs. However, it was concluded that the impact of Airbnb, while highly visible, is a symptom of wider social factors than simply being a cause of immediate in housing usage and impacting hotel occupancy rates. Context is important in terms of communal ties and residents' senses of place as short-term occupancy of property becomes a norm. The wider housing market is a determinant of rents and differences between seasonal daily rents derived from tourists and those paid by more stable renters. The de-industrialisation of cities for gentrification has become the de-urbanisation of leisure and a desire for landscape rich destinations, made easier by physical accessibility by transport and informational accessibility through the internet. It is also the outcome of political processes.

Introduction

The history of Airbnb is easily accessible through internet browsers. It is also a history that clearly demonstrates the potential of the internet as, within a decade from 2008/9 to 2019, the company grew from renting air mattresses to its initial 3 clients to be a business with a valuation of over US$38 billion (Schleifer, 2019). The core of this paper lies in research that sought to measure the impact of Airbnb on the housing rental market of the New Zealand coastal resort town of Raglan. In the summer of 2016/17 anecdotal evidence emerged that customary long-term rental agreements were being reduced in numbers and duration as property owners sought to earn rental income from summer visitors prepared to pay higher nightly fees for short duration stays. Among other signs, long-term residents of Raglan were found to be hiring space at the Raglan camp site during the summer, and tourism operators were finding difficulties in recruiting seasonal employees because of a shortage of affordable accommodation.

This paper is also embedded in the hierarchical analytical system of the micro, meso and macro (Dopfer & Potts, 2004), whereby the micro here is represented by the individual stories of informants describing their concerns as they sought rental accommodation. The macro is represented by the aggregated impact at a community level while the generalisation of the principles found in the study contribute toward a wider understanding of the impacts peer-to-peer housing rental schemes have had on holiday destinations represents the meso.

This paper comprises sections that initially draw on a wider literature that examines the impact of Airbnb and peer-to-peer accommodation services. It is found that the experience of Raglan is not unique, but equally Raglan has some specific features that make for an interesting case study. One specific feature is that the town has retained a strong sense of community represented by *Raglan Naturally* documentation briefly discussed below. Indeed the project was initiated by the Raglan Community Board's sub-committee – the Whaingaroa Raglan Accommodation Project (WRAP) as it sought to find solutions consistent with community objectives. (Whaingaroa is the original Maori name for the settlement – and means the "long pursuit" to note the landing of the Tanui waka or canoes when reaching New Zealand). However, as the research dug deeper into the issues, the more complex they appeared, and as described below the use of Airbnb was part of a wider social process connected to issues of housing demand and supply in addition to the influence of internet growth.

The research revealed a process of greater commercialisation as the internet expands the market place. A demanding market able to comment directly on the professionalism of accommodation providers drives standards up, and prices. The letting of holiday accommodation attracts investors attracted by returns on property, land and property is sold, and units are upgraded. The ambience of place begins to change, impacting on the lives of local residents as gentrification occurs. Senses of community may be under threat as the places from which residents derive meaning change. Changes in land use and property prices are subject to political and economic factors, and points of disruption may emerge that change the nature of places and population. Hence, while this research was commenced by an attribution of impacts to Airbnb, such a view is now thought to be mistaken.

Much of the existing research into the impacts of Airbnb is arguably constrained. Most studies relate to spatial changes within a city, of how property values change, and populations move. It is not, however, simply a problem of land use. As the physical assets of community change so too do the interactions between people. Cultural and social change also occurs. Most studies described in the literature review relate to zones within cities, and little has seemingly been written on the impact on smaller communities, especially those that have sought over two decades to develop communal values on ideas of what is the nature of their community and what it is they wish to protect. In that sense, Raglan in New Zealand, serves as an interesting case of a community grappling with potentially disruptive change.

Literature review

On entering the search term "Airbnb" into Google Scholar, over 49,000 academic papers are quickly identified, of which half have been published from 2015 to 2019. One reason has been the growing interest of researchers in the gentrification effects of the holiday property market, its impacts on land use patterns and on the patterns of longer-term rentals (Gant, 2016; Wachsmuth & Weisler, 2018). The process of gentrification has attracted significant attention and can be divided into phases of abandonment of properties, regeneration, displacement, revitalisation and renaissance, and the outcome has come to be associated with regraded areas of trendy cafes, bars and the sipping of lattés (Slater, 2006). Past studies have associated this process with the arrival of Airbnb and equivalent peer-to-peer (P2P) social media. Various factors account for this. As noted above, a greater commercialisation of the holiday rental market has eventuated as professional investors specifically purchase apartments and other accommodation to obtain higher rates of return on property made possible by short duration rental practices, and this, in turn, attracts more inbound investment. A symbiotic relationship exists where retail, café and restaurant development occurs to take advantage of the presence of higher income consumers, thereby making yet more attractive the zones of overnight rental accommodation to holidaymakers.

The initial vision of people making a marginal increment to their income by renting rooms has thus morphed into a significant business venture as landlords chase higher returns from temporary holidays lets of complete homes or apartments. This has created what Wachsmuth and Weisler (2018) termed a "rent gap" between gentrified and other properties in the same zone, but impacts extend beyond this. Evidence suggests that rents in general increase across the locale because of Airbnb. Wachsmuth and Weisler (2018) present data from New York to support the contention, while Cócola-Gant (2016) provided evidence of local property ownership and rental usage being dissipated through the process he terms "collective displacement". Analysing Airbnb data sets for Barcelona, he indicates that properties taken out of the housing stock form only 2.2% of the total housing in that city, but there are spatial inequalities, and clusters of Airbnb properties exist in areas attractive to tourists such as in the historic part of the city. These form a spatial cluster where 16.8% of the housing stock was used for vacation lets.

González-Pérez (2020) identifies similar processes occurring in Palma, Majorca, but additionally suggests that the gentrification of Palma's historic centre predated the arrival of Airbnb with properties being converted into hotels while cheaper property prices attracted young professionals seeking accommodation relatively close to places of work. Gu and Ryan (2008) comment on the same process taking place in Beijing's hutong prior to the 2008 Beijing Olympics. In one sense, the arrival of Airbnb represents a continuation of past processes, but further intensifies the process by involving more people. Herein lies the issue of property prices.

Cócola-Gant and Gago (2019) examined the housing and property market in Alfama, the historic area of Lisbon. They found two main impacts followed Airbnb. First, properties were purchased by professional investors and short-term rentals (STRs) accounted for a quarter of all housing by 2016. The second implication was a significant increase in feeling of insecurity and displacement concerns among long-term renters. In this sense the findings of Celata and Romana (2020) are of significance because they make a distinction between the more gentle process of gentrification and the more drastic residential depopulation of historic centres due to P2P services in Italian cities. It is notable that in these case studies of Rome, Florence, Venice, Palma, Lisbon and Barcelona the context is one of the gentrification of old historic centres, but the processes are not confined to the Mediterranean. Gurran et al. (2020) find not too dissimilar processes along Australia's coastline in their examination of 16 resort areas. They apply the nomenclature of "pop-up" to "invasion" in their description of holiday property development.

Guttentag (2015) points to one reason as why this has occurred. Defining Airbnb as a "disruptive innovation" he notes that disruptive innovations often outpace legal frameworks. From this perspective, he notes that often Airbnb accommodation is illegal in not meeting various regulations, and indeed may not be visible to the authorities. Such illegalities include noncompliance with regulations imposed on motels and hotels with reference to fire prevention and safety, and more commonly the avoidance of paying taxation on the income earned. Some apartments located in primarily residential areas may, by the very act of carrying out a commercial activity, be flouting zoning regulations and ignoring regulations requiring businesses to be licensed. Guttentag (2015) notes the reaction of subsequent prohibition of rental properties that rent accommodation for periods of less than 30 days in cities such as San Francisco and Paris. Other commentators have found some evidence of residents' complaints about the noise created by occupants of Airbnb apartments and houses (e.g. Leland, 2012, Said, 2012).

Much of the global debate over Airbnb has been paralleled in New Zealand. In the report *Economic Effects of Airbnb in New Zealand* (Deloitte Access Economics, 2018), it is noted that in 2017 there were 578,000 stays booked in Airbnb properties in New Zealand with hosts accommodating 1.5 million guest nights in 225 different locations. Airbnb guests, it was estimated, spent NZ$781.4 million, accounting for approximately 2.8% of all tourist expenditure. However, the growth of Airbnb was welcomed in New Zealand for a number of reasons. By 2016, continuous growth in New Zealand's inbound tourism had outpaced the provision of summer accommodation in key locations. This was particularly noticeable in the late February period of Chinese New Year when New Zealand experienced peak visitation inflows from China. The then Prime Minister, John Key, also held the tourism portfolio, and publicly argued that Airbnb properties would be able to meet the accommodation shortfall.

Nonetheless, New Zealand commentators were raising many of the same concerns found globally, albeit within a context that differed in some ways. In the case of New Zealand there were precursors to Airbnb due to the tradition of what New Zealanders call a "bach" or "crib". Initially the New Zealand "bach" was a beach side accommodation of little sophistication offering cheap seaside holidays for their owners and friends (McCarthy, 1998; Page, 2008). Over time properties were improved by their owners and with the advent of national media and especially in the 1990s with the advent of the internet, services such as bookabach.com emerged whereby owners rented them to acquaintances and others. Initially the primary purpose was the building of family memories during the long summer holiday period that commenced before Christmas and continued for almost two months: a process commenced in the 1930s with the introduction of paid holiday leave, better public transport and private car ownership (Atkinson, 2012; Schänzel et al., 2005). But as property prices increased and holiday patterns changed, the nature of holidaying also began to change (Schänzel et al., 2005), and properties were upgraded and commercialised. National guidelines of quality were subsequently generated by national bed and breakfast associations and these systems were well established by the time Airbnb was introduced in the country.

A second feature that meant New Zealand (and Australia) differed from other countries was that both economies depended on immigration. Immigration, especially in Auckland, was perceived to be pushing up house prices and the costs of renting, albeit not to the extent popularly believed (Hyslop et al., 2019). At the lower end of the market, there was, however, evidence of people being priced out of the market and a growing level of homelessness was increasingly apparent as those sleeping rough on many streets became more evident. Income inequality was also becoming far more evident as New Zealand had generally followed neo-liberal economic policies, one feature of which was no capital gain taxation on profits made from the sales of houses if a purchase and subsequent sale was completed – a policy only lightly changed in 2015 under the "bright-line" rules which effectively means capital gains taxation is only paid if the house is "flipped" within five years of the initial purchase. However, for most parts the purchase of additional homes by those who could afford such activity was a tax sponsored activity.

A third factor was that by 2017 the commercial accommodation sector in some locations such as Auckland and Queenstown faced the imposition of tourist bed taxes. The sector thus felt it was being disadvantaged compared to the peer-to-peer services that were not originally subject to the same taxation. Fourth, stories of property investment for Airbnb renting fed perceptions of additional inequalities in the housing market by creating potential business property tax avoidance. For their part Campbell et al. (2019) identified clusters of Airbnb densities and suggested that such spatial clustering represented a challenge to local authorities in terms of identifying properties that should be incurring business rather than residential rates. The wealth gap was growing prior to 2019, as evidenced by Scott (2019, cited by Radio NZ) linking the growing use of properties for Airbnb with a doubling in the numbers of families on the Queenstown waiting list for a house in the period 2015 to 2019, while Cheng et al. (2020) reiterated the concerns of tourism employers within the city not being able to find accommodation for seasonal employees.

Certainly, the launch of Airbnb in New Zealand in 2015 was associated with existing changes in the holiday accommodation marketplace. As Table 1 indicates, from approximately 1990 to 2020 three periods of change can be identified, and in each period significant changes occurred that led to a much more professional holiday rental market that reinforced property development and the emergence of property being seen as an asset on which rates of return were

Table 1. Micro- meso- and macro- dimensions in Airbnb expansion.

Perspective	Characteristics	Change Agents	Features
Micro Perspectives 1990c-2010c	Local Regional	Egalitarism morphs to inequality under impact of neo-liberal economics Technical innovation Impact on housing	Based on bach and campgrounds Emergence of internet based systems Limited impact on local housing market – either on renting or purchasing properties
Meso Perspectives 2010c-2020c	Regional National	Neo-liberal policies create income hierarchical systems Right of centre policies encourage immigration to generate growth Technical innovation accelerates Impact on housing	Greater inequalities in income and wealth distribution Increased immigration, emergence of land banking and ghost housing Faster internet connection (3 G & 4 G) Growth in international and domestic tourism Housing boom and property development Significant impacts on local rental markets
Macro Perspectives 2015c-2020c	Regional National International	Economic growth generates tourism growth Commercialisation Technological innovation Impacts on housing Government policy of intervention begins to emerge	Tourism booms and bottle-necks in accommodation emerge Property investment is professionalised and rental upgrades occur Repetition of patterns emerge nationally in tourist hot spots Increases in value of desirable holiday accommodation Introduction of fast band internet on a national scale – 5 G starts Significant impact on local rental markets is found nation wide Taxation regimes are increasingly examined at governmental levels

being sought. Hence periods of micro, meso and macro change occurred. These changes include increases in property prices, especially in the north part of New Zealand, due to continued immigration and possibly outflows of money from China (Chancellor et al., 2016; Hyslop et al., 2019). In 2019, the government also reinforced the professionalism of renting properties through legislation aimed at improving insulation and other improvements – which also again led to people requiring rates of return on investment (Bierre & Howden-Chapman, 2020; Telfar-Barnard et al., 2017). At the same time there were incidences of land-banking and "ghost housing" being reported (ghost houses are those purchased simply to obtain capital gain but which are left empty, and in China these are termed "nail houses"). Slowly, the conversations about services such as Airbnb became a national debate and tourism was being identified as a source of increasing property prices (Tsui et al., 2019).

On the other hand, local authorities were welcoming the economic impacts associated with the additional numbers of visitors that Airbnb was reputed to generate. Hunter (2019a, b), drawing on AirDNA data, reported that in Rotorua home-owners had an income of NZ$32.8 million in

2018/19 with similar income being generated for Tauranga. While it can be suggested that the data may be over-estimations because they fail to take into account expenditure switching behaviours in that visitors may have used alternative accommodation, and that not all Airbnb entries are of private households, what is of importance is that local authorities perceive Airbnb was generating positive economic impacts for their regions. Whether these monetary flows are sufficient to induce them to impose bed taxes and business rates is a more problematical issue. In January, 2019, it was estimated that of the 8300 Airbnb properties being listed in Auckland, some 3800 were liable for the bed tax that was being levied, but of this latter figure only 1285 had been identified by Council staff. However, Airbnb's own data indicated there were 11,300 active listings in the City and over half were being rented for more than 33 nights a year (Keall, 2019). However, if the rental relates to a room in a house occupied by the home-owner, the owner does not become liable for the bed-tax. In short, keeping track of businesses is difficult, especially as rentals can appear and disappear relatively rapidly as many renters are not involved on a full-time basis.

Within the theoretical framework of frames of analysis, a distinct sequencing of events can be seen to emerge that in ways that indicate temporal systems in the aggregation effects of peer-to-peer (P2P) services as evidenced in Table 1.

Table 1 comprises three primary rows, labelled micro, meso and macro perspectives within indicative periods, each with four columns. The three terms are derived from systems theory and the work of Dopfer et al. (2004) in evolutionary economics. The concept has a temporal, evolutionary perspective, and regards economic system as sets of complex rules and retaining capabilities of innovative change. The terminology has been interpreted as the levels of the individual, the macro is the aggregate of the micro, and the meso the origin and propagation of new rules (Dopfer et al., 2004, p.268). Dopfer and Potts (2004) extend the model by seeking to carefully define the ontology of evolutionary economics, and by drawing attention to the notion that processes are rule driven.

Mody et al. (2019) similarly identify the stages with reference to Airbnb. For them the micro represents the individual units, the meso being Airbnb as a distribution system, and the macro being the competition between Airbnb as a brand and other accommodation providers and brands. For their part Prayag et al. (2020) apply the terminology as the micro being the individual actors in Airbnb transactions and the nature of the innovative practice, the meso represents a series of socio-technical regimes (Prayag et al., 2020, p. 2), and the macro the "landscape developments" associated with the "technological transformations are embedded within wider social and economic systems" (Prayag et al., 2020, p. 2).

For the purposes of this paper and following Ryan's (2020) concepts of determination of destination management, the core processes lie in political decision taking and New Zealand's swing to the neo-liberal concepts of Roger Douglas, the country's Finance Minister from 1984 to 1988, and the architect of "Rogernomics" (Keizer & Muysken, 1997, Brownlow & Batstone, 2007). It was these neo-liberal policies that effectively reinforced wealth inequalities and the role of property ownership in wealth creation in New Zealand. Property prices also arguably rose due to the open immigration policies that followed, particularly under the Key government. Additionally, the development of the internet made overseas ownership property ownership easier, and also made more accessible immigration into New Zealand through on-line services. The "meso" therefore took the form of the forces of neo-liberalism, property pricing, immigration and internet development to radically change the "micro" orientation prior to about 2010 to disrupt the process (of which Airbnb was a beneficiary) to create a totally different "macro" by 2020.

The process has led to what are in effect self-reinforcing mechanisms whereby outcomes become drivers in cyclical reiterations. The tax regimes relating to housing has given rise to what Broome terms "Residential Capitalism", which he describes as "the foundation of low and lower middle income household wealth in New Zealand" (Broome, 2008, pp. 346). Those regimes included offsetting mortgage interest against tax, and additionally freedom from paying capital gains taxation as previously noted. In addition those renting property could claim expenses against taxable income – and thus the situation described by Broome intensified in the following decade until finally, in 2015, tax reforms imposed taxation on sales of property where ownership had not previously endured for five years. However, in the absence of a capital gains tax, property purchase for the purposes of creating Airbnb assets continues in New Zealand as a speculative activity (Prayag et al., 2020; Rehm & Yang, 2020).

Much of the above analysis of possible impacts of disruptions such as Airbnb follows a relatively conventional pattern of tourism and social media induced change in the housing market being determined by broad economic-political forces, but the evidence of gentrification points to yet an even wider context – that of the sense of community. As described in the next section, Raglan is a small, and until now a relatively cohesive community based on its vibrant summer environment as a surfing and adventurous location appealing to those loving the outdoors. One can observe that the literature of place attachment and community has much in common. Mannarini and Fedi (2009) proposed five dimensions of place attachment – namely: (a) a shared place of interaction premised on mutual respect and shared values, (b) an affective community, that is a place of emotional bonds to people and place, (c) the ordinary community, that is the usage of facilities that are familiar to the people, (d) the place of participation, of politics and culture that creates a sense of solidarity and finally an organised community – a place of neighbourhoods, centres and areas such as the cluster of shops. In short, as theories of place attachment denote, the community is a physical place imbued with memories, family histories and associations that have symbolic importance for residents and provide sense of identity and meaning (Ramos-Tumanan, 2019, Ryan, 2020).

The development of gentrification – the upgrading of buildings and spaces, and with property development comes the disestablishment of old patterns of life thus represents a disruption in the previous sense of place. Butler (2007, p. 162) regards gentrification functioning "as an important way of understanding the mediations between global processes and flows, on the one hand, and the construction of identities in particular localities, on the other." Gentrification can be interpreted as a slow process of change whereby historically private sector investment is ploughed into the restoration and conversion of older buildings into residences desired by an upwardly mobile professional class that in the process displaces the prior lower income groups found resident in such locales (Brown-Saracino, 2013). In her original work on London, Glass (1964) suggests that while gentrification is easily identified by its outcomes, it is not so easily defined by its causes. She attributes the cause to the de-industrialisation of the city, and argues it is an evolving ideological shift from suburbs to inner city areas made possible by changing patterns of work. In the case of Raglan it is suggested that it is the result of a growing affluent class able to shift from the city to previously marginal coastal areas not for work, but leisure patterns. The cause lies in increases in middle- and upper class incomes, improvements in accessibility, and the realisation that leisure assets can also be monetary assets. Given this, the gentrification process intrudes on and commences a displacement process that impinges on residents' senses of place attachment and community.

For his part, Theodori (2005) using interactional perspectives, offers a bridge between the two concepts of place attachment (much used in tourism) with that of community (also common in the tourism literature following Murphy's (1985) seminal work) by observing understandings of community as being territory-free (an association of individuals across boundaries) and territory-based (associations formed by common spatial use). He defines community "as a place-oriented process of interrelated actions through which members of a local population express a shared sense of identity while engaging in the common concerns of life" (Theodori, 2005, p.662-663). Such definitions are applicable to Raglan as described below.

The context of the study

The seaside town of Raglan on the west coast of the Waikato in New Zealand's north island is well known to surfers because it possesses the longest left hand break in the southern hemisphere. The town has a population of approximately 3,300, and has enjoyed a reputation for being "laid back", a place to relax: an image reinforced by the community and being featured in classic surfing films such *The Endless Summer* (1966) and the more recent Indie award winning adventure sports film, *Last Paradise* (2011) Its ambience is further reinforced by a local population of artists, potters and photographers who take inspiration from its landscape and natural harbour, within which orca and other sea mammals can be spotted. Historically agriculture was a primary industry, but tourism has become increasingly important to the town since the beginning of the second millennium (Ryan, 2019).

As noted, the town is known for its strong sense of community, perhaps strengthened for being at the end of state highway 25 that links it to Hamilton, the major city in the Waikato, some 45 minutes' drive to the east. As the Waikato economy has thrived, so the professional classes of Hamilton have "discovered" Raglan, which now also serves as a commuter provider for Hamilton. The town's sense of identity has been public since about 1999 when the township, led by its Community Board, undertook a number of public meetings to establish a vision for the community as tourism began to make its presence felt (Ryan & Cooper, 2004). Those meetings led to the first statement of its *Raglan Naturally* documentation in which the community drafted its vision of what it wanted for the residents, and equally important, what it did not want. That document has been revisited at least four times, and the most recent version was published in 2019 and is available as a public document on http://www.raglannaturally.co.nz/raglan-naturally-draft-plan/. The documentation and associated discussions are easily accessible to Raglan's population with the township having its own social media pages and the local newspaper, the *Raglan Chronicle* being an important internet based medium that reports views and stances to create an informed local population.

These public processes and the emergence of a strong consensus on the need to create a sustainable natural environment, and to create policy based on research inclusive of local interests has created a strong impact on the polices of the Waikato District Council, which has effectively incorporated several aspects of the *Raglan Naturally* documentation into its District Plan. As evidence of the community's sustainability credentials one can look at the expertise of Xtreme Zero Waste – a community led recycling programme recognised nationally as a leader in sustainable waste management, and which successfully recycles at least 75% of all waste generated in the community. Other distinguishing features of the town include its policies of adhering to local ownership of retail outlets where possible, and its resistance to having the presence of large national chains of retailers including large supermarkets.

The Raglan housing and rental market

With increasing incomes in the Waikato, wider car ownership and improvements in the state highway system, Raglan grew as a commuter town, and as a seaside recreational asset for the Waikato. Day-trip activity from Hamilton had long been established by the late 1990s, but as the motorway system improved and house prices climbed in the major conurbations of Auckland and Hamilton, Raglan began to attract the purchasers of holiday homes. According to the rates data held by the Waikato District Council, of the 1800 households in the Raglan area, 715 houses have owners not normally resident in Raglan.

As noted in Table 1, a growing inequality of income and wealth ownership has emerged since 2000 in New Zealand. In 2018, the top 10% of wealth owners owned 53% of all wealth, whereas the lowest 50% of the population owned but 4% of the total wealth (Stats NZ, 2019). A key determinant of this trend toward higher Gini coefficients in New Zealand has been the significant increase in house values, and one aspect of this has been the buying of property not as homes, but as investments on which the owners wish to make a rate of return in a period when capital gain on housing has tended to outstrip interest rates on bank deposit accounts.

This has been very evident in Raglan, where, in the period from 2007 to 2017, it has been estimated that Raglan's population increased from 2,670 to 3,240. Corelogic (2018) data indicates that the number of residential properties available in 2018 numbered 1,834 with an additional 201 being vacant. One immediate cause of the increase in house prices and rentals is the fact that in the period 2007 to 2017 the population increased by 21%, but the numbers of available houses increased by only 5% (Strateg.ease, 2018). Assessments of rents can be found by assessing rentals on sites such as trademe.co.nz. Strategease (2018, p. 5) note "The number of rental properties listed on "Trade Me" has declined markedly in recent years and the median rent has risen by 30% (from NZ$340 to NZ$440 per week) since 2016" thereby exceeding the average rent of NZ$354 per week for the whole of the Waikato District Council region. To add to the problem, projections for "population growth to 2046 would seem to imply a need for a further 1,284 dwellings, representing an increase of 63% over the current numbers of homes" (Strateg.ease, 2018, p. 5).

The importance of tourism to Raglan

Tourism has undoubtedly grown in Raglan, and while actual visitation numbers are lacking on a regular basis, nonetheless ample evidence for such numbers exist. It is known that during summer the amount of waste collected can peak during the summer months (Xtreme Zero Waste, 2017, 2018). Another statistic is derived from smartphone records collected for a report commissioned by the Waikato District Council in 2018 from Qrious, the then data analytics subsidiary of Spark, one of New Zealand's leading telco companies. Using these data Morgan (2018) cites visitor numbers of 145,000 during the period November 2016 to March 2017. Another statistic is the number of Airbnb listings that appear in the Raglan region. In 2018/19 these were 167% higher than during the comparable summer months of 2016/17. Campbell et al. (2019) interactive map of Airbnb offerings per head of resident population shows that the area around Raglan has one of the highest such densities in New Zealand. (https://malcolmhcampbell.shinyapps.io/AirbnbCensusNZ/)

Airbnb and the Raglan rental market – the emergence of housing stress

In Raglan, bed and breakfast accommodation was a long established form of holiday provision, and many providers were already using internet based services such as Bookabach, bachcare, and nzstays. These services had, in many cases, also established principles of best practice and property owners registered akin to New Zealand's official Qualmark accreditation scheme, and multiple registrations were common. Nonetheless, the emergence of the international peer-to-peer provider, Airbnb, initiated a change in the Raglan market place for rented accommodation, and according to local estate agents the provision of longer-term rented accommodation effectively dried up as owners took to the internet for summer lets.

Research method

A sequential mixed methods approach was adopted of the form QUANT QUAL for pragmatic and research objective reasons. The sequencing and initial research timetable was determined by the need of WRAP's committee to collect data to make application for project funds relating to social housing. For that, the funding agency required statistical data on the level of displacement of renters, the housing stress being experienced, and the causes of that stress.

Consequently a questionnaire was developed based on concepts of housing stress as discussed below. The second qualitative stage was generated by the research team to provide qualitative data that examined the reasons for answers provided in the first quantitative stage. By its nature, social stress represents psychological perceptions of the effects of induced change as much as the specific search for alternative accommodation. Thus the research was oriented toward trying to assess to what extent commonalities existed in processes of adaptation to change and what was considered as "serious degrees of stress". These procedures are consistent with the principles of mixed methods research proposed by John Cresswell in his various works on mixed methods research (Clark & Creswell, 2008; Creswell, 2011).

"Household stress" is a recognised term that relates to (a) whether the cost of housing is high relative to household income and/or (b) the degree of crowding that exists in a household. The Australian Housing and Urban Research Institute also refers to the 30:40 ratio, that is when a household is in the bottom 40% of income earners and is paying more than 30% of its income on housing costs. For those above the 40% criterion and who pay more than 30% of their income on housing, it is assumed that this is a matter of choice and hence they are not defined as suffering "housing stress". While for the most part studies have considered levels of indebtedness (e.g. Hlaváč et al., 2012; Nepal et al., 2010), others have added psychological considerations that include depression or the impacts of children's behaviour due to household deficiencies (e.g. Fuller et al., 1993; O'Connor et al., 2015).

The questions used for the survey were determined after four meetings and various revisions by the WRAP Committee. The first section of the questionnaire sought information on the nature of the respondent's current accommodation, and whether they were renting, owned outright, or still had a mortgage. They were asked about the rent or mortgage being paid. The section therefore included questions such as "how much rent are you paying?", "What proportion of after tax income does that represent?" Equivalent questions related to mortgages. Additionally, respondents were asked about the nature of their accommodation. As indicated below, some were found residing in garages, cars and barns. Questions were tied to the number sharing the accommodation, and the numbers of rooms, bathrooms and toilets. These questions permitted an assessment of overcrowding in terms of bedroom usage and sleeping arrangements. In short – the questions drew on past research pertaining to measures that act as proxies for potential stress, and additionally measures of displacement by asking about duration of property accommodation and type of accommodation being used.

The second section posed a series of questions about concerns and indices of possible "housing stress". Recognising that stress is an emotional response to financial pressures of meeting rents or mortgage payments, and (as found in the evidence) concerns about increasing rates (property taxes) of mortgage free pensioners wholly dependent on state pensions, questions were generalised about how much stress respondents felt about renting, owning or potentially hoping to buy properties in Raglan. Because generational issues exist about the concerns of whether younger people have the capability of buying properties due to the very high property price/income ratios found in New Zealand (Opit et al., 2020), the final section asked for basic socio-demographic data including ethnicity, income as well as age and gender. In addition the final part of the questionnaire was left blank but with an invitation to write any additional comments respondents might wish to make. The questionnaire was then delivered to a sample of randomly selected households in Raglan based on streets and areas, and subsequently collected by calling on those households.

The second part of the study used qualitative analysis based on data derived from 25 respondents who replied to advertisements placed in Community House in Raglan and in the *Raglan Chronicle*. The advertisement stated the purpose of the research, but generally the Raglan community was already aware of the research because the WRAP committee had provided a series of articles in the local newspaper (*Raglan Chronicle*) and indeed the paper had printed the questionnaire. One of the authors then spent several days at Community House and at the local library to "button-hole" potential respondents and questioning was completed after 25 respondents had been interviewed based on the concept of saturation, wherein it was felt insufficient new data was being gained (Braun & Clarke, 2019; Weller et al., 2018). This last exercise was also supplemented by interviewing estate agents in the town to obtain their views on trends in housing, and attempts were also made to contact property developers associated with a new housing development at the Rangitahi Peninsula. Information was also provided by the economic development officers of the Waikato District Council.

Given that the literature draws attention to determinants of housing stress that include occupation, family structure, income, type and size of accommodation, levels of income and housing costs, and other demands on income and emotional reactions, questioning began by asking how long people had lived in Raglan. It effectively asked for an informant's history of living in Raglan and their connection with the community before specifically asking them their thoughts about tourism, the pressure it imposed on housing and to what extent and how they were affected by Raglan's housing situation. Given the local publicity about the WRAP project respondent were usually more than willing to talk about these issues if they had the time. Some permitted follow up phone calls.

The sample

A total of 395 completed questionnaires were received. This number represented 21.5% of the total households. However, of the total households, 201 are generally unoccupied. Hence of the regularly occupied properties, the response rate was approximately 24%. The total number of people covered by the survey was estimated as being 979. There were 752 adults involved in households that ranged from 105 households with one occupant to one home with ten people. The numbers of children between the ages of 12 to 18 years totaled 66, and additionally, there were 161 children under the age of 12 years. Based on an estimated population size of about 3,240 (the 2018 census data were not then currently available) this means the survey covered approximately 30% of the population. For simple statistical tests assuming the probability level of significance of 0.05 at the desired power level of 0.8, this sample size is sufficiently rigorous (Ellis, 2010) for analysis at a general level.

Findings

The quantitative study

As indicated the quantitative survey covered a series of issues, and the findings are therefore reported in the sequence of examining housing costs, the consequence of those costs, housing stress being experienced, and the factors thought to account for that stress? This more holistic approach was adopted to assess just how readily were Airbnb and P2P services being identified as a source of problems being experienced as against other potential determinants of stress.

Specific questions pertaining to "housing stress" were asked using a five point scale labelled from "not stressed at all to "being very stressed". The mean scores on these types of items and the frequency counts on some of these scores are shown in Table 2

It can be seen that about 16.5% stated they were "anxious" or "very anxious" about finding somewhere to live (of the 327 who answered the question), and about 15% (of 329 respondents) expressed similar levels of concern about meeting either rent or mortgage payments. Almost a quarter of respondents noted significant levels of concern about actually being able to own a house in Raglan in the next five years. Of those who were renting a house and who answered the question (n = 136), 62% (n = 84) indicated that they did not feel secure about their rental arrangements.

Table 2. Descriptive statistics on housing stress.

	No	Mean	Std. Dev	No Stress	Little Stress	Mild Stress	Anxious	Very Anxious
Are you stressed by being unable to find a place to live?	327	1.81	1.34	222 (67%)	20 (6%)	30 (9%)	29 (9%)	25 (8%)
Are you stressed by the cost of your rent or mortgage?	329	1.95	1.25	179 (54%)	53 (16%)	49 (15%)	29 (8%)	19 (6%)
Are you stressed by your view of your future opportunity to buy or build a house?	306	2.28	1.45	133 (43%)	59 (19%)	34 (12%)	41 (13%)	36 (12%)
How likely are you to be able to buy or build a home in Raglan in the next 5 years?	272	2.02	0.98	Never 92 (34%)	Unlikely 99 (36%)	Hope to 51 (19%)	Will Definitely 27 (9%)	
If you are renting, do you feel secure in your current housing situation?	136			Yes 52 (38%)		No 84 (62%)		
If you own your home, or you are paying a mortgage, do you feel secure in your current housing situation?	252			197 (78%)		52 (22%)		

Table 3. Index of crowding.

	Frequency	Percent	Valid Percent	Cumulative Percent
Very low (<0.5 person per room)	31	8.0	21.4	21.4
Low (1 person per room)	85	21.9	58.6	80.0
Moderate (<2 people per room)	13	3.3	9.0	89.0
High (2-3 people per room)	12	3.1	8.3	97.2
Crowded (3+ people per room)	4	1.0	2.8	100.0
Total	145	36.7	100.0	
Missing	250	63.3		
Total	395	100.0		

When these data are cross-tabulated with socio-demographic data some basic life-stage variables are indicated, albeit it not always at statistical significant levels and the sub-samples are relatively small. For example, from anecdotal evidence it seems that those in their late 20 s are potentially vulnerable to higher levels of concern if they have young children at school. They have no wish to move away from Raglan because of concerns over their children's education and friendship patterns and are particularly vulnerable if one of the adult members is no longer fully employed and they have recently had a child. A combination of lower income and extra expenses would seem to be at play here. For example respondent 101 noted "We do not want to leave. The kids are settled in Raglan so we live in whatever is available!"

Another potentially vulnerable group would seem to be those about the age of 70 years old who have retired. There is slight evidence to suggest a cycle whereby the newly retired at 65 years feel relatively comfortable in the initial period of their retirement, but about five or so years into their retirement they are finding that there are increasingly dipping into past savings to meet costs. However, after an age of about 80 or 85 years they appear to have adapted to the situation, or are now accessing additional benefits available to them. Comments that highlighted these issues included respondent 29 who commented that they "we're going backwards in retirement funds", and respondent 34 who noted "We are thinking of leaving Raglan due to retirement and downsizing."

Another measure of housing problems is also the nature of accommodation and levels of over-crowding in a home. The first measure is relatively objective in that there are other issues if people are living in tents, garages or barns, while the second measure might be said to be more subjective. However, the first measure is also problematic in that such people on the verge of degrees of homelessness may not be easy to reach and indeed might be unwilling to answer questionnaires. In this instance it was found that of the 395 respondents, nine failed to describe where they were living and 39 indicated other than a conventional house. Thus three were sleeping in a shed, three in a car, three in a garage, and 11 in a "tiny house", eight in an out-house or cabin – and various other forms of non-standard accommodation including a barn to form a total of 39 (about 10%) being in other than a conventional house.

With reference to the type of house being occupied, the questionnaire included questions about numbers of occupants, rooms, bedrooms, toilets and washing facilities. As noted in the definitions of "housing stress", one potential source of stress may be due to a feeling that the current property being occupied is simply not large enough in terms of providing facilities for those occupying it. The sample showed that 14% of the sample were living in households that contained more than 4 people. Hence one method of assessing potential inadequacy of housing conditions is to divide the number of bedrooms by the number of occupants to assess to what degree three or more people need to share a bedroom. Consequently a five-fold classification was created as shown in Table 3. This shows that 11.1% of the homes contain more than 2 people sleeping in the same bedroom.

However, the tests of statistical significance revealed little pattern of stress between this measure of over-crowding and feelings of stress. Further, the sub-samples are not sufficiently large enough to permit conclusions with any degree of certainty.

One factor that can induce stress is the actual level of rent or mortgage being paid as a proportion of income. Of those paying rent, 127 respondents provided some data about the rents that they were paying. The rents ranged from one person paying NZ$1 per week to one other paying NZ$590 per week. The lowest levels were found to be associated with those living in buses or garages and the payments seemed to be linked to having access to washroom and similar facilities. Using the SPSS feature of "trimmed means" when the top and bottom 2.5% of the sample are excluded to calculate a mean score, the mean rent being paid by respondents was NZ$267 per week. The median rent was NZ$300. Given the mean Airbnb rent of NZ$134 per night the financial inducement for property owners to rent a property during the summer period can be observed, but arguably it is not wholly conclusive when one considers the need for high occupancy rates and the costs associated with those occupancy levels. However, for Bookabach.com at NZ$243 per night, even if using a property management group such as Bachcare.com the temptation to rent a property over the summer period may be greater, especially if week long rentals are being achieved. One caveat for comments relating to Airbnb is, however, that fact that they are more oriented toward the renting of a single bedroom within a house occupied by the owner than is Bookabach.com.

For those paying rents, it was estimated that the rents were accounting for about 44 to 47% of household weekly income before savings and leisure spending but after other general weekly costs of utilities, food, and transport costs were accounted for. Mean weekly 'discretionary' household income for those renting property was estimated as being about NZ$300 in monetary terms, and it was found that savings tended to be low. Those paying mortgages were earning considerably more with an income of about NZ$1000 weekly household disposable income after core costs were accounted for and mortgage payments were accounting for approximately one-third of such income. However, it must be noted that there does appear to be a skew toward the older members of the population in the sample. Two-thirds of the sample were over the age of 45 years, and this age group included many who had either paid off a mortgage, or had relatively low mortgage payments, and hence had higher discretionary income.

Such calculations carry several caveats. To simply ask for the level of personal income in New Zealand is to invite high levels of non-response, and also to obtain a figure that is potentially misleading. Personal incomes are also arguably insufficient when seeking to analyse at a household level. Again, it may not be assumed that occupants of a household would necessarily be aware of the incomes of others within the household. Of those providing information, 233 responded to the question by providing details of household 'discretionary income', of whom 109 were paying rent. A proxy for total household income was calculated by adding rents or mortgages to the discretionary income. It must be noted that this is little more than a proxy and by definition excluded those who own houses and have no mortgages. Excluding monies paid on rent the mean weekly discretionary household income was NZ$383 (the median was NZ$300) and rents as a percentage of mean income was 47% and of median income 44%. This highlights that many households are not in a position to save significant sums in order to pay the required deposits on homes. Consequently it was found that the aspiration to buy a home in Raglan is uncommon among those renting properties.

The questionnaire permitted other reasons to be assessed, and among those who are renting, specific impacts potentially attributable to Airbnb include those who already know that they have to leave their rented accommodation prior to the Christmas/New Year/Summer holiday period, and also those who have what were termed as "short-term rental contracts" in that they are less than 12 months in duration. The other reasons are more general in nature, but do reflect the conditions of a local housing market and its increasing costs that are partly due to the added demand for accommodation being caused by tourism (see Figure 1).

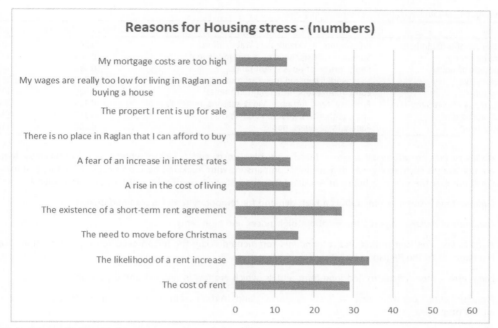

Figure 1. Reasons for Housing Stress.

Qualitative data

The interview data were analysed by first reading and re-reading the text, thereby creating a consensual thematic analysis of the text. Second, use was made of textual analysis software, namely QDA Miner and WordStat 8.0.

Among those interviewed was a female over the age of 65 years, who had lived in Raglan for more than 20 years, but who had worked as a carer. Having been on low wages for most of her life at the time of the interviews she was living in a van because despite promises, long-term rentals had not materialised and equally other promised rentals had been converted to Airbnb lettings. Even those who had properties out for letting on P2P media recognised the problems this was causing. As one property owner put it " ... for the people who were renting in Raglan, it's unfortunate that people who have properties will turn those people out of their homes just so they can make extra money over the holiday period. I think it's very unfortunate and say that that happens because in the winter months, they are quite happy to let those people back in the homes ... I don't really like that, but that's just my opinion." However, the speaker went on to state that she would not rent out a room on Airbnb, but yet again she suggested that faced with increasing rates and trying to live on a pension she understood why people would rent rooms on Airbnb. Similarly another property owner stated he rented out on Airbnb to help pay mortgage fees, and others facing housing stress also voiced recognition of why some people used Airbnb to supplement incomes to meet mortgage and rates costs. The one group who did incur criticism to some degree were those who retained empty homes for much of the year.

While such comments are generally congruent with the quantitative findings and are valid in that respect, textual analysis software was used to see if some degree of generalisation might be possible. Using coherence measures QDA Miner identified the themes shown in Table 4.

The coherence measure is described by Weidemann (2015, p.92). Essentially the process creates comparisons of semantic content between adjoining segments of text, and in this instance 500 passes was undertaken (Reider et al, 1999). The table can be re-interpreted as representing eight inter-connecting themes: *viz*:

Table 4. Themes within the text (coherence measures).

Theme	Key words	Coherence Measure	Frequency
To buy an affordable house	Costs, rents, Auckland, Pay, Wage, afford	0.345	181
Summer time	Summer, tourists, holiday, accommodation	0.344	171
Hundreds of dollars	Rents, prices of house, thousands	0.335	140
Place to live	Live, work, Hamilton, need to move, hard (to find)	0.328	231
Long-term	Long, hard, properties, long-term rental	0.326	138
Property price, property rent	Property, rent, Airbnb, holiday seasons, prefer to rent	0.323	206
Local authorities	Local authorities, government, kind	0.313	144
Family lived	Family lived, years, home	0.306	130

Ability to buy an affordable house – faced with high costs and a lack of choice, and insufficiently high enough wages such ability was diminishing. Comparisons with Auckland housing prices are made, and for a small number the sale of a house in Auckland was the only way to afford a smaller house in Raglan.A

Summer-time – summer time brings a high demand for temporary rental accommodation.

Hundreds of dollars – again a theme about high prices and high rents.

Place to live – difficult to find and respondents commented about the forced need to move to locations like Hamilton, or to the Raglan camp site.

Long-term – very difficult to find long-term rentals, which are few in number and expensive.

Property price, property rent – just expensive and Airbnb rentals are often preferred by those letting properties.

Local authorities – some asked if there was a need for local authorities or government to supply social housing, or provide additional benefits to permit people to but properties or stay in rented accommodation.

Family lived – references being made to the duration of time that respondents had lived in Raglan.

Given the logical "tightness" of these themes, the tables of similarity indices showed high levels of connectedness (maximum similarity = 1.0) and 3 D similarity mapping simply produced "blobs" of overlapping text. Alternative measures simply showed the dominance of three phrases – namely "Accommodation", "Airbnb" and "Property Prices." A conventional manner of identifying themes is to create a word map or word cloud, and after some cleaning of the text including the deletion of confirmatory phrases such as "yeah" and "uh" (which were frequent in the text), Figure 2 resulted. The software package, WordStat 8.0, permits the researcher to revise text to clarify synonyms, and then the size of words indicates importance (here judged by frequency), centrality (by spatial positioning) and clustering (by colour).

The domination of the words "People" and "Raglan" in the resultant word points to a key factor confirmed by earlier research – namely Raglan is a desirable place in which to live. It has "friendly people", a strong sense of community, a desirable "laid-back" life style, a relaxed ambience, local ownership of shops, and is set in a beautiful landscape of beach and harbour. It is also slightly isolated.

The role of Airbnb was mentioned several times. Many participants held to the view that listing properties on social platforms and online accommodation services like Airbnb and Bookabach.com could bring more revenue than renting solely to long-term tenants. The general view was this was an easy way for property owners to obtain extra revenue to pay for the mortgage, cover their own vacation costs, or to cope with increasing bills.

"… the idea landlords take a look at the 42 days of the summer when you're renting your property out for a night more than you rent out a week. You make your entire mortgage for the year in 42 days and you've got credit card details if they make any damages, Airbnb or Bookabach will get you back (costs incurred through damage)."

"Because most people that buy property are putting them on Airbnb or holiday rentals. So they can have much more money that way. It's all started to happen once people realize that they can make more money on Airbnb or holiday home. So, which means there are fewer properties for the locals who rent."

Figure 2. Word Cloud from transcripts.

Some home owners showed the extent to which some would go to list on Airbnb or Bookabach in the interviews. For example, one home owner was converting their garage for renting out on Airbnb. The participant considered it to be "a great way" to gain revenue.

Discussion

Past literature relating to the impact of Airbnb on destinations has tended to concentrate on issues including the percentage of households being used for rental properties, the changing usage of housing, the impact on hotel occupancy rates, the impact on prices being charged for accommodation, and the impact on the numbers of tourists being attracted to an area. Relatively little research has been undertaken of how residents have been impacted by such changes. In studying this topic, a number of factors emerge. First, it is suggested that context is important. There are significant differences between a large urban area such as Boston or London, and a small community of some 3,300 people such as Raglan. Secondly, size of population and area does impact on senses of community and hence place attachment (Mannarini & Fedi, 2009). Among those impacts are the formal and informal patterns of leadership and degrees of homogeneity existing within the Community. In Raglan, there is the formality of a Community Board that has legal recognition and the leadership of that community has continuity through commitment to the principles ensconced in the documentation, *Raglan Naturally*, that informs Local Authority Planning procedures. That documentation has consistently sought to retain Raglan's ambience, low rise buildings and local ownership of retail units and environmental schemes. It is also evident that the residents recognise the problems created by success in tourism and a growing desire by others to visit and live in the town.

Third, in terms of the impacts that Airbnb and similar schemes might have on property rents and house prices – they are factors that affect the demand side of the equation. In Raglan, the tourist demand for summer accommodation exacerbates a situation where the demand for housing from the local population had already outstripped the building of new housing. Thus, while tourism is highly visible in its impacts, it is, in this case, a secondary factor in the local property market as is the case of Queenstown. Thus another variable when seeking to consider the impacts of Airbnb is that of housing demand independent of tourism.

One obvious solution to relieve the pressure on house prices is to build more housing, and in 2016 a new development was approved for the Rangitahi Peninsula across the habour. The target is to build 500 homes over time. Stages one and two indicate well over 200 homes on the plans (www.rangitahi.conz, 2019) were quickly sold. However, anecdotal evidence suggests that about 50% of purchasers were from out of Raglan. The prices of these houses far outstrip the ability of local residents to buy these properties, thereby attracting more affluent purchasers who wish to reside in the popular seaside town. It is likely that many out of town purchasers will, in fact, rent the properties to tourists when not in occupancy as one means of paying mortgages. Hence the attractiveness of the town, when combined with tourism, is helping to generate a process of gentrification, which is fourth variable that must be considered.

The findings suggest that gentrification and the association with Airbnb is part of the process of place and place attachment change. Originally gentrification was perceived as part of the de-industrialisation of the city (Glass, 1964), but arguably in the post-industrial society of the 21st century it has become a revitalisation of the marginal places of landscape beauty for the purposes of recreation. To recreation can also be added the monetary elements of capital gain and income supplementation by summer lets. From this perspective social media entities such as Airbnb increasingly are seen not as an initiator of change, but as a supplement and reinforcement of more significant economic and social change. The observable results are an upgrading of properties and additions to holiday accommodation.

In turn, this identifies a fifth factor involved in the study. That is the role of political ideologies and frameworks established by political processes. The initial study was prompted by a community's response to observable housing stress and a need to establish a business case for social housing schemes to cope with that stress. Various proposals emerged including a need for residential homes for older residents and modes of payment whereby a form of reverse mortgage permitted the elderly to use their existing property to pay for care while releasing a home for rental. Alternative suggestions would include "rent to buy" proposals and the involvement of charitable groups such a Habitat for Humanity and the religious based foundations. Further, some respondents indicated a willingness to forgo Airbnb revenues in order to be good neighbour. Neo-liberal governmental policies, nonetheless, had led to a growth of immigration as an easy means generating economic growth, and balancing budgets had meant reductions in welfare services and additionally, a reluctance to impose what were regarded as too high a level of minimal wages. This has led to wealth inequities noted above, and the arguably over-active housing market.

It is concluded that Airbnb and its impacts are as much a symptom of wider issues as a cause of problems the community faces. First, the basic issue is that population growth has exceeded the increase in the numbers of units of accommodation being built. Second, improvements in infrastructure and ease of obtaining data via the internet has improved the physical and knowledge accessibility relating to the acquisition of purchasing property in Raglan. Third, economic growth in New Zealand combined with the inequalities in the wealth that growth has created a situation where out of town ownership has significantly increased to a point where approximately one-third of homes are owned by non-residents. Tax regimes have in some instances been a motive for adopting this form of wealth enhancement as against other forms of investment or business start-up (Rehm & Yang, 2020). A fourth factor has been the attractiveness of Raglan for inbound migrants seeking what they regard as a quintessential New Zealand combination of relaxing life-style and beautiful landscapes.

Taken together these issues represent a micro, meso and macro change identified by Dopfer and Potts (2004), and hence Raglan's growth arises because it was ideally placed to take advantage of the radical changes that were occurring in the wider economy. The micro changes existed on both the demand and supply side. Using Slater's (2006) terminology, displacement of long-term renters occurred, replaced by holiday lets, while evidence existed of purchases of property by individuals from out of town to take advantage of the opportunities provided by Airbnb. By the same token Airbnb was also able to take advantage of the same changes, and this congruence of mutual advantage enabled many property owners to gain financially. However, such gains are associated with costs. The proponents of Airbnb will point to research that indicates that the service has little negative impact on hotel rack rates (Zervas et al., 2017) and that it does attract additional tourism thereby generating new expenditure flows in a community (Sperling, 2014). Much therefore depends on the pattern of leakages, but if, as in Raglan, a third of homes are owned by non-residents, then leakages will tend to be high.

Hence the importance of strong ties within the local community. The study shows that many residents are aware of the problems holiday rentals pose for the less affluent members of the community. The very WRAP initiative is indicative of this awareness. In a post Covid-19 era of low interest rates and, in the light of tourism data in 2020, few constraints on New Zealand domestic tourism demand, more might be tempted to pursue such a path. The initiative by the community in establishing the WRAP programme is indicative of a meso change, as also is the permitting of the Rangitahi housing construction. These represent operational and organisation changes in the "socio-technical" environment as described by Prayag et al. (2020).

If, therefore, Airbnb and its impacts are symptoms of wider social and technological change, then possible responses may well require social intervention from governments. Other studies propose restrictions on the number of days a property may be rented for short-term stays, and differential property taxes that distinguish between rentals for long-term stays and those for short-term stays. In essence, such policies exist where a property short-term let attracts a business property tax, where a long-term rental attracts a non-business lower property tax. Finally, it is concluded that any analysis of the impact of Airbnb needs a wider lens than simply regarding it as purely a feature of the tourism demand for accommodation.

Acknowledgements

The research was undertaken within the United Nations World Tourism Organization's programme of the International Network of Sustainable Tourism Observatories. The research was funded by funds from the Waingaroa Raglan Accommodation Project, The WEL Energy Trust and the University of Waikato Summer Research Programme for students.

Disclosure statement

No potential conflict of interest was reported by the authors.

Funding

This work was supported by WRAP Project (Raglan);University of Waikato Summer Scholarship.

References

Atkinson, N. (2012). Call of the beaches' rail travel and the democratisation of holidays in interwar New Zealand. *The Journal of Transport History*, 33(1), 1–20. https://doi.org/10.7227/TJTH.33.1.2

Bierre, S., & Howden-Chapman, P. (2020). Telling stories: The role of narratives in rental housing policy change in New Zealand. *Housing Studies*, 35(1), 29–49. https://doi.org/10.1080/02673037.2017.1363379

Braun, V., & Clarke, V. (2019). To saturate or not to saturate? Questioning data saturation as a useful concept for thematic analysis and sample-size rationales. *Qualitative Research in Sport, Exercise and Health*, 18(1-2), 1–16.

Broome, A. (2008). Neoliberalism and financial change: The evolution of residential capitalism in New Zealand. *Comparative European Politics*, 6(3), 346–364. https://doi.org/10.1057/cep.2008.15

Brownlow, G., & Batstone, C. (2007). Institutions, entrepreneurship and economic performance: Reinterpreting rogernomics. *Journal of Interdisciplinary Economics*, 18(2–3), 149–176. https://doi.org/10.1177/02601079X07001800203

Brown-Saracino, J. (2013). *The gentrification debates: A reader*. Routledge.

Butler, T. (2007). For gentrification? *Environment and Planning A: Economy and Space*, 39(1), 162–181. https://doi.org/10.1068/a38472

Campbell, M., McNair, H., Mackay, M., & Perkins, H. C. (2019). Disrupting the regional housing market: Airbnb in New Zealand. *Regional Studies, Regional Science*, 6(1), 139–142. https://doi.org/10.1080/21681376.2019.1588156

Celata, F., & Romana, A. (2020). Overtourism and online short-term rental platforms in Italian cities. *Journal of Sustainable Tourism*, Pre-print. https://doi-org.ezproxy.waikato.ac.nz/10.1080/09669582.2020.1788568

Chancellor, W., Abbott, M., & Carson, C. (2016). A study of the factors influencing residential house prices in Auckland and New Zealand. *New Zealand Journal of Applied Business Research, 14*(1), 55.

Cheng, M., Mackenzie, S. H., & Degarege, G. A. (2020). Airbnb impacts on host communities in a tourism destination: An exploratory study of stakeholder perspectives in Queenstown, New Zealand. *Journal of Sustainable Tourism, 21*(3), 1–9. https://doi-org.ezproxy.waikato.ac.nz/10.1080/09669582.2020.1802469

Clark, V. L. P., & Creswell, J. W. (2008). *The mixed methods reader.* Sage.

Cócola-Gant, A., & Gago, A. (2019). Airbnb, buy-to-let investment and tourism-driven displacement: A case study in Lisbon. *Environment and Planning A: Economy and Space,* 0308518X19869012.

Cócola-Gant, A. (2016). Holiday rentals: The new gentrification battlefront. *Sociological Research Online, 21*(3), 1–9. http://search.proquest.com/docview/19266793

Corelogic. (2018). *Property data and analytics.* Report on the Raglan Housing Market prepared for Strateg.ease and Waikato District Council.

Creswell, J. W. (2011). Controversies in mixed methods research. *The Sage Handbook of Qualitative Research, 4,* 269–284.

Deloitte Access Economics. (2018). *Economic effects of Airbnb in New Zealand Analysing consumer benefits and economic contribution.* Deloitte.

Dopfer, K., Foster, J., & Potts, J. (2004). Micro-meso-macro. *Journal of Evolutionary Economics, 14*(3), 263–279. https://doi.org/10.1007/s00191-004-0193-0

Dopfer, K., & Potts, J. (2004). Evolutionary realism: A new ontology for economics. *Journal of Economic Methodology, 11*(2), 195–212. https://doi.org/10.1080/13501780410001694127

Ellis, P. D. (2010). *The essential guide to effect sizes: Statistical power, meta-analysis, and the interpretation of research results.* Cambridge University Press.

Fuller, T. D., Edwards, J. N., Sermsri, S., & Vorakitphokatorn, S. (1993). Housing, stress, and physical well-being: Evidence from Thailand. *Social Science & Medicine (1982)), 36*(11), 1417–1428. https://doi.org/10.1016/0277-9536(93)90384-g

Glass, R. (1964). Aspects of change. In J. Brown-Saracino (Ed.), *The gentrification debates: A reader* (pp. 19–30). Routledge.

González-Pérez, J. M. (2020). The dispute over tourist cities. Tourism gentrification in the historic Centre of Palma (Majorca, Spain). *Tourism Geographies, 22*(1), 171–191. https://doi.org/10.1080/14616688.2019.1586986

Gu, H., & Ryan, C. (2008). Place attachment, identity and community impacts of tourism—the case of a Beijing hutong. *Tourism Management, 29*(4), 637–664. https://doi.org/10.1016/j.tourman.2007.06.006

Gurran, N., Zhang, Y., & Shrestha, P. (2020). Pop-up 'tourism or 'invasion'? *Annals* of Tourism Research, *81,* 102845. https://doi.org/10.1016/j.annals.2019.102845

Guttentag, D. (2015). Airbnb: Disruptive innovation and the rise of an informal tourism accommodation sector. *Current Issues in Tourism, 18*(12), 1192–1217. https://doi.org/10.1080/13683500.2013.827159

Hlaváč, P., Jakubík, P., & Galuščák, K. (2012). *Household stress tests using microdata.* CNB Financial Stability Report, 2013.

Hunter, Z. (2019a, June 23). Airbnb hosts make $32.8m but rental market takes hit. *The Daily Post.* The Knowledge Basket. https://www-knowledge-basket-co-nz.ezproxy.waikato.ac.nz/databases/newztext-newspapers/search-newztext-newspapers/view/?sid=2002559&d12=nzh02%2Ftext%2F2019%2F06%2F24%2FROT-DBp-n-zh-airbnbrotorua-18.html

Hunter, Z. (2019b, July 6). Tauranga Airbnb hosts pocket $33.5 million in 11 months. *New Zealand Herald.* https://www.nzherald.co.nz/property/news/article.cfm?c_id=8&objectid=12241396

Hyslop, D., Le, T., Maré, D. C., & Stillman, S. (2019). *Housing markets and migration–Evidence from New Zealand.* MOTU Report No. 19/14. MOTU Economic and Public Policy Research.

Keall, C. (2019, January 23). Council's secret weapon in war on Airbnb cheats. *New Zealand Herald.* https://www.nzherald.co.nz/business/news/article.cfm?c_id=3&objectid=12194725

Keizer, P. K., & Muysken, J. (1997). *The future of the welfare state: Reflections on Rogernomics.* METEOR, Maastricht research school of Economics of TEchnology and ORganizations.

Leland, J. (2012, July 21). They can list, but they can't hide. *The New York Times.* http://www.nytimes.com/2012/07/22/nyregion/stuyvesant-town-sleuths-keep-vigil-against-illegal-hoteliers-in-their-midst.html

Mannarini, T., & Fedi, A. (2009). Multiple senses of community: The experience and meaning of community. *Journal of Community Psychology, 37*(2), 211–227. https://doi.org/10.1002/jcop.20289

McCarthy, C. (1998). A summer place: Postcolonial retellings of the New Zealand Bach. *Jouvert: A Journal of Postcolonial Studies, 2,* 1–19.

Mody, M., Hanks, L., & Dogru, T. (2019). Parallel pathways to brand loyalty: Mapping the consequences of authentic consumption experiences for hotels and Airbnb. *Tourism Management, 74,* 65–80. https://doi.org/10.1016/j.tourman.2019.02.013

Morgan, C. (2018). *Whaingaro a Raglan: Planning for tourism.* Presentation/Economic Development Waikato District Council. University of Waikato Management School.

Murphy, P. E. (1985). Tourism: A Community Approach, New York: Methuen.

Nepal, B., Tanton, R., & Harding, A. (2010). Measuring housing stress: How much do definitions matter? *Urban Policy and Research, 28*(2), 211–224. https://doi.org/10.1080/08111141003797454

O'Connor, K., Stoecklin-Marois, M., & Schenker, M. B. (2015). Examining *Nervios* among immigrant male farmworkers in the MICASA study: Sociodemographics, housing conditions and psychosocial factors. *Journal of Immigrant and Minority Health, 17*(1), 198–207.

Opit, S., Witten, K., & Kearns, R. (2020). Housing pathways, aspirations and preferences of young adults within increasing urban density. *Housing Studies, 35*(1), 123–142. https://doi.org/10.1080/02673037.2019.1584662

Page, J. (2008). A history of bach tenure in New Zealand. *Legal History, 12*, 177.

Prayag, G., Ozanne, L. K., Martin-Neuninger, R., & Fieger, P. (2020). Integrating MLP and 'after ANT'to understand perceptions and responses of regime actors to Airbnb. *Current Issues in Tourism*, 1–18.

Radio NZ. (2019). *Airbnb likely cause of high rents in Queenstown – researcher.* https://www.rnz.co.nz/news/business/387548/airbnb-likely-cause-of-high-rents-in-queenstown-researcher

Ramos-Tumanan, M.-A. (2019). *Place attachment of tourists and place meaning by residents: Cases from Anhui China* [Ph.D. thesis]. University of Waikato Management School.

Rehm, M., & Yang, Y. (2020). Betting on capital gains: Housing speculation in Auckland, New Zealand. *International Journal of Housing Markets and Analysis.* https://doi.org/10.1108/IJHMA-02-2020-0010

Reider, G. A., Cernusca, M., & Hofer, M. (1999). Coherence artifacts in second harmonic microscopy. Applied Physics B: Lasers & Optics, 68(3).

Ryan, C. (2019). *Housing Stress: To what extent does tourism exacerbate the issues relating to property prices and rentals in Raglan? A report for the WRAP initiative.* Unpublished Report: Waikato INSTO Research Project, The University of Waikato Management School.

Ryan, C. (2020). *Advanced tourism destination management.* Cheltenham: Edward Elgar Publishing.

Ryan, C., & Cooper, C. (2004). Residents' perceptions of tourism development: The case of Raglan, New Zealand. *Tourism Review International, 8*(1), 1–17. https://doi.org/10.3727/154427204774809529

Said, C. (2012, June 10). Short-term rentals disrupting SF housing market. *San Francisco Chronicle.* http://www.sfgate.com/realestate/article/Short-term-rentals-disrupting-SFhousing-market-3622832.php

Schänzel, H. A., Smith, K. A., & Weaver, A. (2005). Family holidays: A research review and application to New Zealand. *Annals of Leisure Research, 8*(2–3), 105–123. https://doi.org/10.1080/11745398.2005.10600965

Schleifer, T. (2019, March 19). Airbnb sold some common stock at a $35 billion valuation, but what is the company really worth? *Vox Recode.* https://www.vox.com/2019/3/19/18272274/airbnb-valuation-common-stock-hoteltonight

Slater, T. (2006). The eviction of critical perspectives from gentrification research. *International Journal of Urban and Regional Research, 30*(4), 737–757. https://doi.org/10.1111/j.1468-2427.2006.00689.x

Sperling, G. (2014). How Airbnb combats Middle Class Income Stagnation. https://www.stgeorgeutah.com/wp-content/uploads/2015/07/MiddleClassReport-MT-061915_r1.pdf

Strateg.ease. (2018, August). *Housing study: Report for Whaingaroa-Raglan housing affordability project.* Strateg.ease/EnFocus Resource Management and Public Policy.

Telfar-Barnard, L., Bennett, J., Howden-Chapman, P., Jacobs, D. E., Ormandy, D., Cutler-Welsh, M., Preval, N., Baker, M. G., & Keall, M. (2017). Measuring the effect of housing quality interventions: The case of the New Zealand "rental warrant of fitness. *International Journal of Environmental Research and Public Health, 14*(11), 1352. https://doi.org/10.3390/ijerph14111352

Theodori, G. L. (2005). Community and community development in resource-based areas: Operational definitions rooted in an interactional perspective. *Society & Natural Resources, 18*(7), 661–669. https://doi.org/10.1080/08941920590959640

Tsui, K. W. H., Tan, D., Chow, C. K. W., & Shi, S. (2019). Regional airline capacity, tourism demand and housing prices: A case study of New Zealand. *Transport Policy, 77*, 8–22. https://doi.org/10.1016/j.tranpol.2019.02.007

Wachsmuth, D., & Weisler, A. (2018). Airbnb and the rent gap: Gentrification through the sharing economy. *Environment and Planning A: Economy and Space, 50*(6), 1147–1170. https://doi.org/10.1177/0308518X18778038

Weidemann, G. (2015). *Text mining for qualitative research in the social sciences: A study on democratic discourse in Germany.* Springer VS.

Weller, S. C., Vickers, B., Bernard, H. R., Blackburn, A. M., Borgatti, S., Gravlee, C. C., & Johnson, J. C. (2018). Open-ended interview questions and saturation. *PloS One, 13*(6), e0198606. https://doi.org/10.1371/journal.pone.0198606

Xtreme Zero Waste. (2017). *Waste collection statistics, 2016 to 2017.* Xtreme Zero Waste.

Xtreme Zero Waste. (2018). *Waste collection statistics, 2018 to 2019.* Xtreme Zero Waste.

Zervas, G., Proserpio, D., & Byers, J. W. (2017). The rise of the sharing economy: Estimating the impact of Airbnb on the hotel industry. *Journal of Marketing Research, 54*(5), 687–705. https://doi.org/10.1509/jmr.15.0204

Airbnb impacts on host communities in a tourism destination: an exploratory study of stakeholder perspectives in Queenstown, New Zealand

Mingming Cheng, Susan Houge Mackenzie and Gebeyaw Ambelu Degarege

ABSTRACT

Airbnb's disruptive impacts on tourism destinations have been well acknowledged but systematic examination is still lacking. This study investigates these impacts on host communities from the perspectives of tourism destination stakeholders including Airbnb hosts, traditional accommodation providers, local residents and policy makers in Queenstown, New Zealand. Underpinned by social representation theory, the results of fourteen semi-structured interviews confirm the complexity of Airbnb growth, which is characterised by multiple and conflicting interests, and potential paradoxes in destination management policies. This research highlights the advantage of using multiple stakeholder perspectives by providing a more holistic and critical understanding of Airbnb's impacts. It offers a starting point to inform the ongoing debate regarding sustainable tourism development in destinations with globally disruptive entities.

Introduction

The rapid growth of Airbnb worldwide has created unprecedented challenges for the tourism and hospitailty sector (Cheng, 2016; Dolnicar, 2019). Airbnb is a peer-to-peer (P2P) internet platform that, for a fee, connects travellers with local hosts offering short-term accommodation. Local hosts can share their home or entire residence with guests. The rapid growth of Airbnb, and similar short-term accommodation providers, has disrupted tourism destinations and established new ways of doing business (Guttentag, 2015). On one hand, there is growing evidence that Airbnb can provide a range of benefits, such as creating meaningful local-guest encounters, broadening the supply of accommodation options, and generating additional incomes for locals in destinations with a relatively high cost of living (Guttentag & Smith, 2017; Pforr et al., 2017). On the other hand, local communities, hotel owners and policymakers have voiced concerns over the dramatic growth of Airbnb (Nieuwland & Van Melik, 2020; Richards et al., 2019; Stuart, 2017). Airbnb has been accused of threatening the safety and affordability of host communities, violating government safety procedures and creating housing shortages (Fang et al., 2016; Koh & King, 2017; Nieuwland & Van Melik, 2020).

Empirical evidence has begun to emerge examining the various impacts of Airbnb. These include its economic (e.g. Dogru et al. (2017)), socio-cultural (e.g. Richards et al. (2019)) and environmental impacts (e.g Cheng et al. (2020)). While these studies provide a foundation for understanding the complex set of impacts associated with Airbnb, these tend to be analysed in isolation rather than holistically across stakeholders within a destination. The fragmented nature of this knowledge may lead to an unblanaced view or misunderstanding of the Airbnb phenomenon and as such, prevent local boidies (e.g. councils, taxation offices) from identifying the various concerns across multiple stakeholders so as to inform the development of evidence-based policies (Cheng & Edwards, 2019). As such, research on the impacts of short-term accommodation providers across multiple stakeholders is urgently needed to systematically examine the wider range of stakeholder perspectives on this emerging issue (Jordan & Moore, 2018). As such, this study directly responds to calls by Cheng (2016) and Prayag and Ozanne (2018) to broaden the knowledge of Airbnb's impacts by incorporating a holistic approach to investigate the perspectives of multiple stakeholders. It seeks to illustrate how these multiple perspectives provide greater options in terms of response strategies.

Therefore, this study employs social representation theory with the aim of: (1) identifying the perspectives of multiple stakeholders on the impacts of Airbnb on hosting communities in a rapidly-developing tourism destination (Queenstown, New Zealand), and (2) identifying stakeholders' response strategies in relation to these impacts. Social representation theory was chosen because it facilates a deeper understanding of how multiple social actors (e.g. diverse stakeholders) perceive social and cultural phenomena (e.g. Airbnb) from "an emic, contextual and process-oriented perspective" (Monterrubio & Andriotis, 2014, p. 290). More importantly, it helps to identify how these perceptions drive stakeholder attitudes and behaviours (Potter & Litton, 1985).

Literature review

Social representation theory

Social representation theory (SR) has been frequently used to interpret the impacts of tourism on destinations. SR attempts "to elucidate the social process involved in the everyday, active construction of the world by participants, and to show how attitudes, beliefs and attributions are formed in terms of these socially derived frameworks" (Potter & Litton, 1985, p. 81). The theory is concerned with collective representations of a community and how social constructions of phenomena are created, and recreated, in everyday interactions (Moscovici, 2001). Social representations reflect a community's social structures, local meanings, popular narratives, and cultural traditions (e.g. Murray, 2002). In the context of tourism, SR suggests that resident perceptions of tourism impacts are "informed by direct experiences, social interaction and other information sources such as the media" (Fredline, 2006, p. 139). Thus, SR can provide an understanding of how community stakeholders perceive and react in a collective manner to various tourism phenomena. It differs from *social exchange theory* in that it recognises people's perceptions and behaviours cannot always be attributed to logical or rational thought processes based on simple cost-benefit analyses. Rather, SR posits that perceptions are often dictated by instinct and practical consciousness (Sharpley, 2014; Suess & Mody, 2016).

The use of SR in tourism has largely focused on segmenting local community members based on their support for the industry. For example, Andriotis and Vaughan (2003) identified three groups of local community members including (1) advocates, (2) the socially and environmentally concerned and (3) economic sceptics. The authors suggest that segmentation is a good starting point for tourism planners when engaging with local communities. However, such application is increasingly being contested due to its limited ability to capture how locals develop their understanding of social realities (Suess & Mody, 2016; Weaver & Lawton, 2013). Suess and Mody (2016) argue that SR in tourism should be applied by recognising the social and cultural contexts underlying locals' perceptions, attitudes and behaviours towards tourism impacts. At its most fundamental SR helps tourism scholars to explore "multiple stakeholder realities and key aspects

Table 1. Summary of representative research on peer-to-peer accommodation impacts.

Level	Theme	Example	References
Macro	Socio-political	Regulatory or Legal	Ferreri and Sanyal (2018); Uzunca and Borlenghi (2019)
		Housing Supply and Affordability	Lee (2016) Schäfer and Braun (2016) Gurran and Phibbs (2017)
	Socio-economic	The Local Economy	Dogru et al (2020); Fang et al. (2016)
	Socio-technical	New Technologies of Hospitality	Zach et al (2020)
	Socio-ecological	Sustainability	Cheng et al (2020)
Meso	Hospitality/tourism industry	Hotel Occupancy and Revenues	Oskam and Boswijk (2016) Zervas et al. (2017)
	Destination	The Overall Supply of Accommodation Options	Nadler (2014)
		Respond to Peak Demand/crisis	Hajibaba et al (2017); Farronato and Fradkin (2018)
		Local Housing Impacts	Wachsmuth and Weisler (2018)
		Local Residents' Quality of Life and Public Safety Concerns	Gurran and Phibbs (2017) Nieuwland and van Melik (2020)
Micro	Host/Guest	Employment Opportunities and Income For Local Hosts	Ikkala & Lampinen (2015)
		Host-Guest Encounters	Tussyadiah and Pesonen (2016); Cheng and Zhang (2020)
		Alternative Experiences for Visitors	Shaheen et al. (2012)
		Temporary Employment Lacking Social Safeguards	Schor and Fitzmaurice (2015)
		New Travel Pattern	Tussyadiah and Pesonen (2016)
		Discrimination	Cheng and Foley (2018) Kakar et al. (2017)

Notes: Themes are adapted from Prayag and Ozanne (2018).

of group and individual identity that dictate tourism-related behaviours and perceptions" (Monterrubio & Andriotis, 2014, p. 290). The current study was contextualised in this emic, process-oriented perspective of SR in order to develop new knowledge regarding multiple stakeholders' perspectives on Airbnb impacts. This approach enhanced the understanding of how these perceptions lead to diverse attitudes, outcomes, and response strategies across multiple community stakeholders.

Peer-to-peer accommodation impacts and responses

Due to the enormous growth of short-term peer-to-peer (P2P) accommodation in the last decade, the impact of these has received increasing attention from researchers and practitioners. This growth has created distinct challenges and impacts for different stakeholders. Table 1-summarises the various impacts of P2P accommodation in the extant literature from a micro-meso-macro level framework. These impacts span economic, sociocultural, environmental and political domains.

At the micro level, P2P research has mainly focused on host-guest relationships. Since its inception, Airbnb has been portrayed as generating additional employment opportunities and income for local hosts (Fang et al., 2016) and facilitating positive host-guest encounters (Tussyadiah & Pesonen, 2016). In particular, Airbnb has been recognised for providing alternative experiences for visitors in a convenient, economically-competitive manner (Shaheen et al., 2012). Mody et al. (2019) also found that, on balance, local residents perceived Airbnb as having more positive than negative impacts. Notwithstanding these findings, scholars are increasingly concerned with questions surrounding Airbnb's negative impacts. Using social exchange theory, Stergiou and Farmaki (2019) showed that local residents' negative perceptions of Airbnb were largely related to socio-economic and environmental impacts. Researchers have also speculated about whether P2P accomodation will increase temporary employment that may lack important social safeguards (e.g. social security coverage) (Schor & Fitzmaurice, 2015), and highlighted potential discrimination and community well-being issues (Cheng & Foley, 2018; Kakar et al., 2017). Studies on Airbnb hosts have also increased by examining the role of hosts in guest-host encounters (Cheng & Zhang, 2019) such as their morality and responsibility (Farmaki et al., 2019). Cheng and Foley (2019) identified how Airbnb's algorithmic management practices may dimish Airbnb hosts' sense of control.

At the meso level, research has largely focused on how P2P accommodation impacts traditional accommodation providers. In general, literature consistently supports the notion that Airbnb threatens conventional accommodation providers (Choi et al., 2015), particularly lower-priced providers (Oskam & Boswijk, 2016). Zervas et al. (2017) found that, for example, in Texas, USA, Airbnb negatively impacted hotels' annual revenues by 8–10%. Dogru et al. (2020) revealed that, while Airbnb listings adversely impacted key hotel metrics (e.g. RevPAR, ADR), they did not negatively impact occupancy rates. Although not all destinations have experienced P2P accommodations as a direct competitor to traditional accommodation providers, research indicates that Airbnb-style accommodations are likely to threaten budget hotels in the short to medium-term future (Koh & King, 2017). Applying transaction cost theory, Akbar and Tracogna (2018) argue that hotels can buffer these impacts by revising business models to leverage their superior capacity via integrated platforms that account for frequency and uncertainty.

Research also suggests that Airbnb may broaden accommodation options and enable tourism destinations to respond more effectively to peak demand (Juul; Nadler, 2014) or crisis (Hajibaba et al., 2017) by providing alternative accommodations. In some cases, Airbnb has been perceived as supporting the 'green economy' by tapping into under-used resources (e.g. spare rooms) to combat excess consumption (Airbnb, 2017). However, these claims are challenged by scholars who argue that, rather than utilising underused resources, Airbnb encourages conversion of longer-term rental stock to short-term accommodation, thereby reducing affordable local housing options (Kakar et al., 2017). From a community perspective, Airbnb has also been found to increase tourist traffic in residential areas, which can impact residents' quality of life and raise public safety concerns (Gurran & Phibbs, 2017; Nieuwland & van Melik, 2020).

At the macro level, research has primarily focused on legal and regulatory interventions associated with P2P accommodations and more recently, sustainability (Cheng et al, 2020). These studies have reported how Airbnb providers may reap unfair benefits by manipulating existing regulatory frameworks to avoid government regulations and associated fees and taxes (Guttentag, 2015). This emerging economy may also challenge the integrity of social governance and consumer safety (e.g. via lower accommodation safety standards) (Juul; Rauch & Schleicher, 2015). These issues have created a range of regulatory responses to Airbnb globally. While some cities have completely banned Airbnb, other regulatory authorities are struggling to balance corporate interests with public good (Ferreri & Sanyal, 2018). As an intermediary with significant global economic influence, Airbnb has the ability to define rules and assign risks (Dredge & Gyimóthy, 2015; Ferreri & Sanyal, 2018). Recent research indicates that under the neoliberal discourse of entrepreneurship, Airbnb and their local hosts are actively lobbying governments to deregulate P2P accommodation providers (Ferreri & Sanyal, 2018).

In response to the adverse impacts of Airbnb, a range of measures have been proposed in the literature, ranging from conservative to more proactive approaches (Gurran & Phibbs, 2017; Nieuwland & Van Melik, 2020). Thus far, policy approaches have largely focused on seeking to better differentiate between residential and commercial properties in order to assess whether Airbnb requires new legislation, or if it falls under current legal frameworks. Responses have included zoning revisions, residential development controls, establishing clear Airbnb operating conditions, assessing taxes and fees, and assessments of neighbourhood safety, liability and insurance terms (Lee, 2016; Pforr et al., 2017). Hotelier responses have focused primarily on competing with P2P providers by adapting their business models, developing more authentic,

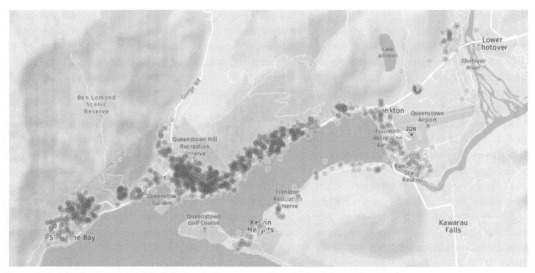

Figure 1. Spatial distribution of Airbnb listings in Queenstown, New Zealand (December 2017).

localised experiences, and exploiting Airbnb's shortcomings (e.g. variable safety standards) rather than competing on price (Alrawadieh et al., 2020; Richard & Cleveland, 2016).

The current literature on P2P accommodation has thus far provided a number of valuable insights into select areas of impacts and the responses to these. Notwithstanding, this literature has largely focused on issues associated with P2P providers in isolation, rather than holistically across stakeholders in a particular destination. Literature in this area can be enhanced by exploring the complex and nuanced sociocultural and economic perceptions of Airbnb impacts across multiple stakeholders within the same destination. Thus, the current study aimed to contribute to this growing area of literature by examining these diverse perspectives through in-depth interviews with a range of stakeholders in a rapidly-growing tourism destination: Queenstown, New Zealand.

The research context: Queenstown, New Zealand

Queenstown is a mountainous four-season tourism destination in the South Island of New Zealand that has experienced a rapid increase in visitors over the past 10 years. It has grown from 20,548,732 guest nights in 2010 to 29,731,631 in 2017 (Statistics New Zealand, 2019). Although Queenstown hosts over 2.6 million international guest nights per year (Jenkins, 2018), it has less than 40,000 permanent residents (Statistics New Zealand, 2018). The rapid growth in tourists has not only stimulated an increase of traditional accommodation providers in Queenstown but also, more recently, a rapid growth in Airbnb listings. In 2017, Queenstown had over 4,226 Airbnb listings (see Figure 1 for a spatial overview of Queenstown Airbnb listings). Concurrent with this increase in Airbnb listings, local and national media in New Zealand have charged Airbnb with inflating prices in the local rental market, inconveniencing local residents and creating difficulties for local workers seeking longer term accommodation (Brown, 2017; Kuprienko, 2018; Williams, 2017). Between 2015 and 2017, these issues drew considerable media attention, with the tensions between Airbnb and other stakeholders being characterised as a 'battle' (Brown, 2017).

Diverse stakeholder responses to the issues identified herein complicate our understanding of Airbnb's impacts on a given tourism destination. As such, Queenstown provided a valuable case study context in which to investigate diverse stakeholders' perspectives of Airbnb's impacts on

Table 2. Research participant profiles.

Pseudonym	Stakeholder type	Role/position
Host1	Airbnb Host	Host
Host2	Airbnb Host	Host
Host3	Airbnb Host	Host
Host4	Airbnb	Host
Community5	Community	Long term renter
Community6	Community	Home owner
Hotel7	Hotel	General Manager
Community8	Community	Long term renter
Community9	Community	Home owner
Hotel10	Hotel	General Manager
Hotel11	Hotel	General Manager
Hotel12	Hotel	General Manager
Council13	Policy maker	Council member
Council14	Policy maker	Council member

host communities. At the time of writing, two New Zealand councils (Auckland and Queenstown Lakes District) had proposed or introduced new legislation for regulating short-term P2P accommodation, including higher tax rates and tighter operating regulations. In Auckland, hosts who rented properties more than 28 days of the year were required to pay a portion of the Accommodation Provider Targeted Rates. These were previously only charged to commercial accommodation providers, on top of residential rates (Auckland Council, 2020).

Method

As personal experiences were central to the aims of this study, a qualitative constructivist approach was selected (Charmaz, 2005). This approach is not designed "to build universal laws but to develop fresh insights about a phenomenon and to offer theoretical propositions where little is known" (Matteucci & Gnoth, 2017, p. 50). Based on the existing literature, we identified four main categories of stakeholders including (1) Airbnb hosts, (2) traditional accommodation providers, (3) community members and (4) policy makers (e.g. Jordan & Moore, 2018). Individuals with "substantial experience" or "considerable insight" (Charmaz, 2001, p. 676) into these four categories were recruited. They included: (i) an Airbnb host in Queenstown for at least two years, (ii) an accommodation provider in Queenstown for at least two years, (iii) a Queenstown community member for at least five years who was unaffiliated with Airbnb and (iv) a Queenstown policy maker (i.e. council member) who was unaffiliated with Airbnb. A snowballing method (Bryman, 2012) was employed in the recruitment process which began via the Chamber of Commerce. A total of 14 semi-structured interviews with these various stakeholders was conducted including four Airbnb hosts ($n = 4$); four hotel operators ($n = 4$); four local community members that were unaffiliated with Airbnb ($n = 4$); and two policy makers from local council that were unaffiliated with Airbnb ($n = 2$). All hotel-based participants were general managers from lower/mid-range to high-end hotels. Table 2 outlines the profiles of the research participants.

Individual semi-structured interviews lasting between 25 and 45 minutes were conducted face-to-face and audio recorded. The interviews focused on two main topics. First, participants were asked to discuss their perspectives on Airbnb's impacts in Queenstown. Second, participants were asked what they thought were the best response strategies for supporting and/or mitigating these impacts. In line with social representation theory, these two overarching questions sought to understand the perceived impacts across diverse stakeholders, but also how these perceptions were linked to various response strategies and outcomes. Interviewing continued until theoretical saturation was reached (Bryman, 2012). The study adopted Legard et al.'s

Table 3. Example of thematic analysis process.

Open Codes	Sub-theme	Theme
The concerns around Airbnb are more about the impacts it is having on housing of the staff and the staff migration from hotels to Airbnb. ...people are finding that it is more profitable for them to use their places for Airbnb	• Staff recruitment and retention issues • Housing shortage	• Negative economic impacts

(2003) approach to saturation, whereby it is achieved when the researchers had gained "a compelling understanding of the participants' perspectives" (p. 152).

All interviews were audio-recorded, transcribed, coded and analysed using *thematic analysis* (Braun & Clarke, 2006). Thematic analysis involves a number of analytic steps starting with the researchers immersing themselves in the data, in this case by reading and listening to the transcripts numerous times. After this initial immersion process, the researchers generated initial codes, and then expanded these into themes ((Creswell, 2007) see Table 3). The themes were then reviewed in relation to codes and raw data, and finally defined and formally labelled (Braun & Clarke, 2006)). Braun and Clarke (2006) write that the thematic analysis process is cyclical or iterative, rather than linear. That is it involves constant comparison and analysis of the data throughout research process (e.g. statements and incidents were compared with other statements and incidents).

Results

Data analysis revealed that stakeholders' perspectives of Airbnb's impacts are characterised by the following themes: economic impacts (positive and negative), socio-cultural impacts (positive and negative), political impacts, and environmental impacts (see Figure 2). Each of these themes will be discussed in more detail complimented with a set of representative quotes.

Positive economic impacts

Stakeholders perceived a range of positive economic impacts resulting from Airbnb, such as extra income, family-friendly employment opportunities, reduction of costs associated with house maintenance and repairs as well as complementary responses to current tourist growth. Hosts consistently focused on the extra income and family-friendly employment opportunities generated by Airbnb. Hosts portrayed Queenstown as a very expensive place to live and so relied upon supplemental income from Airbnb to pay for essential items such as mortgages and children's education, as well as enabling them to save for the future. Hosts also saw Airbnb as providing local residents with opportunities to experience their own family holidays by gaining rental incomes from their homes while away. Hosts viewed Airbnb as offering more flexible, family-friendly employment than other alternatives in the destination. As Host 2 explained: [Hosting works better than] *a different employment situation or a different situation with your family style or anything... I guess if we didn't have Airbnb, I might have to work full time, so it does take that pressure off.*

Hosts also felt that Airbnb helped to reduce house maintenance and repair costs, which meant they could keep their property in a better condition than long-term renting options. Hosts reported that opportunities to inspect and clean their home on a regular basis prevented damage they felt would be caused by seasonal or long-term tenants. Despite the uncertain nature of Airbnb bookings, hosts perceived Airbnb to be a better option than a more stable, longer-term rental income. Host 1 explained, *"I think for the property, personally, I think it's looked after better when it's* [rented via] *Airbnb and not long-term because you're in there every week or*

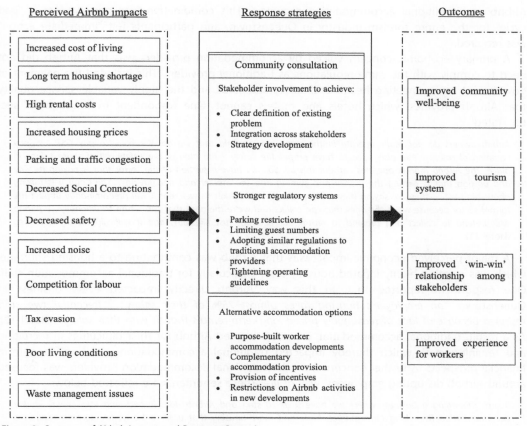

Figure 2. Summary of Airbnb Impacts and Response Strategies.

few days; it's been fully cleaned and maintained; whereas log-term rentals, you don't; it's not maintained as well." Policy makers also perceived that Airbnb was a potentially complementary response to current tourist growth and an important element within the local tourism system. They felt that Queenstown's existing infrastructure was under significant pressure to cope with the rapid growth of tourism. One respondent explained, *"the economic effects of Airbnb are more favourable as it maintains the whole income locally"* (Council 14).

Nevertheless, traditional accommodation providers did not preceive Airbnb as a unique economic threat to their business. Rather, they viewed it as simply another accommodation option that catered to a specific market segment, which could impact them to varying degrees based on their own target market. However, they were united in their belief that Airbnb is not adequantely regulated and that Airbnb creates an *unfair playing field* for commercial providers. Traditional accommodation providers felt that Airbnb hosts should be required to operate under the same existing legal frameworks as hotels and motels. While they reported that Airbnb's presence was disrupting the traditional accommodation sector as well as existing business systems, providers also noted that this was not an immediate economic concern for them because accommodation suppliers in Queenstown currently could not meet tourist demand.

Negative economic impacts

Stakeholders believed that Airbnb is linked to a range of negative economic impacts. This is primarily due to the intertwining impacts of housing and labour, which creates a conflict between

Airbnb and traditional accommodation providers. This combination was portrayed as a "bad cycle" for the entire tourism industry in Queenstown, and participants felt "immediate action" was required.

A primary economic concern voiced by accommodation providers was that Airbnb did not need to comply with the same regulations as traditional providers. This included the payment of government taxes, meeting health and safety standards and the highly variable service quality that Airbnb provides, which hotels and motels cannot. One respondent from the hotel sector stated:

> Airbnb owners do not really operate in the same playing field that we do. We have to pay GST, ... pay commercial rates... We also have to have proper fire safety - fire alarms, fire safety, all of those things in place. The Airbnb market operates without this all. So, you have a portion of the sector that is paying its way and portion that is getting the money and coming into the market and not paying... The Council is talking about big tax ... they are saying they will levy the Airbnb market as well, but it will predominantly impact the formal sector because we're the ones that can collect and we're the ones that can return traditionally... Airbnb will pretend to collect and pretend to return but actually, just like GST, and it will slip through the net. (Hotel 11)

A major perceived economic impact was that Airbnb was contributing to a housing shortage, which was creating highly inflated housing costs particularly for traditional accommodation staff. One respondent reported that, in this way, Airbnb directly impacted every business in Queenstown: "an employee's housing takes almost 75% of their salary... [recently] two staff resigned because of lack of reasonably priced long-term rentals that fit with their salary" (Hotel 12). As a result, traditional accommodation providers blamed Airbnb for their difficulties in recruiting and retaining staff, which thereby impacted traditional accommodation providers' long term financial prospects. A further concern from the traditional accommodation providers was focused around Airbnb disrupting employees' way of life. These sentiments are reflected below:

> [I am] managing a business where we have 9 to 10 staff and Airbnb does impact and takes away worker accommodation from long term market. More and more housing that used to be worker accommodation is now being taken by Airbnb; so long-term rents are up and availability of long-term accommodation for workers is down. Therefore, our staff find it really hard to find an affordable place to stay. So, you have got, [hotel] prices are down, and profit is down, and we have to pay staff more because their prices have gone up. They cannot afford to live here. (Hotel 11)

> I did not move to Queenstown to live in a place where people who are working with me are ... living with six in a bedroom, and one of the major reasons that they are doing that is 10% of the stock is Airbnb... it all comes to where the staff live, how long they stay for, what sort of environment they live in, so for [staff] health and welfare, those things to do [impact me] but, no, Airbnb does not affect me from a business perspective at all. (Hotel10)

> The concerns around Airbnb are more about the impacts it is having on housing of the staff and the staff migration from hotels to Airbnbs. Queenstown is suffering from a shortage of rental housing; it is a big issue because the city has very low density of housing and people are finding that it is more profitable for them to use their places for Airbnb versus [long-term] rent. (Hotel 12)

Some accommodation providers had a further concern that, in addition to losing staff due to accommodation shortages, some staff would move from employment with traditional accommodations into Airbnb supported employment (e.g. cleaners). This was another unanticipated area of perceived conflict reported between traditional accommodation and Airbnb: competition for labour. From one hotelier's point of view, Airbnb created opportunities for people to move away from hotels and motels and work for Airbnb hosts instead. Such labour shifts may be the result of the prevailing loss taxing system in relation to Airbnb services that has resulted in payments of 'untaxed cash' for existing services catering to traditional accommodation providers, such as cleaning services. In this way, Airbnb was perceived to have disrupted an existing supply chain for traditional accommodation providers, rather than creating new or innovative opportunities.

Airbnb is just an income stream and it is an easy income stream. Why they would want to self-regulate? They do not live in the world of regulation that I do in a hotel. They take cash, stick it in their pocket, don't declare, don't pay tax on it, don't pay rent ... up until of late when things are getting a bit tougher - why would they self-regulate? (Hotel 10)

Despite wider assumptions that Airbnb negatively impacted the hotel market in terms of rates and revenues, traditional accommodation providers in the current study did not uniformly report this perception. With the continuous growth in visitors to Queenstown, respondents from high-end hotels did not report experiencing threats from Airbnb as they had maintained high occupancy rates. However, less expensive accommodation providers, such as motels and serviced apartments which cater to relatively similar market segments as Airbnb, reported negative impacts. As one community member who worked in the tourism industry observed:

Hotels and motels are quite negative about Airbnb. I think there is at least noise [i.e. complaints] coming out from them ... but I think their occupancy rate is pretty high at the moment so they're probably not so worried because they're not affecting their bottom line as much. (Community 6)

One provider took a broader historical perspective on Airbnb, as he reflected on possible futures for Queenstown. He believed that oversupply would happen at some point in the future, but would then correct itself. He commented that *"each destination has a cycle ... with new investment in Queenstown on hotels, what will happen if tourist numbers drop?"*

Queenstown always has a downside and a lot of people don't understand it because they've only seen this current side. There is another side. If we then have another two or three hotels built ... and the circle [visitor numbers] goes down, and we've got Airbnb and the numbers we have, it would be difficult [for hotels], but then some of the Airbnb's may not be Airbnb's [if that happens] and [home owners] go back to long term renting or whatever. (Hotel 7)

Positive socio-cultural impacts

The positive sociocultural impacts reported by stakeholders signified perceptions of social change, including creating a range of accommodation options and cultural exchange platforms, and providing unique, enriching visitor experiences. Perhaps unsurprisingly, all of the Airbnb hosts believed that Airbnb had significant positive personal and community impacts in Queenstown. From a socio-cultural perspective, hosts felt that Airbnb created more authentic experiences than staying in a hotel. This was reflected in their observations of both being a host and then using Airbnb during their own holidays. As one host reported:

We travel a lot as a family I would always choose Airbnb over a hotel personally because you get time to hang out with family and it is just such a richer experience, you know, than staying in a hotel. (Host 2)

In particular, hosts thought that Airbnb provided novel opportunities to show visitors the 'Kiwi [New Zealand] family experience', which they felt seldom happened in other traditional accommodations. In this sense, hosts perceived that Airbnb served as a cultural exchange platform for both hosts and guests, which gave reciprocal opportunities to understand other cultures and ways of living. As one host explained:

It is really lovely to meet people from different cultures and they express a real appreciation about being hosted by a family and they love the space, they love privacy, they love not being in a hotel and that is rewarding for us ... So it does mean you have good relationship with different cultures and it is rewarding to offer [visitors] something other than a hotel - they get a glimpse of what life is like for a Kiwi family. (Host 1)

Interestingly, traditional accommodation providers also believed that there were positive socio-cultural impacts for both Airbnb hosts and guests.

There is probably some fantastic cultural exchange and some sharing of culture that is really positive and lovely for people to experience more, and more the 'Kiwi way', and for New Zealanders to experience other cultures, and I think that's extremely healthy - I don't think there is any issue with that. (Hotel 11)

Negative socio-cultural impacts

Despite these positive impacts, hosts felt that some aspects of Airbnb could disrupt normal daily life and social routines. They attributed these potential disruptions to cultural differences between hosts and guests (Host4). Hosts also reported an awareness of negative community perceptions that Airbnb may contribute to housing shortage and increased rental costs, parking, traffic congestion, and waste management in Queenstown. However, hosts questioned whether Airbnb, and similar providers, were the root or sole cause of such problems, as one host noted:

> ... families are leaving [Queenstown] because they can't find rentals or afford a house, and the parking issue and traffic issue is definitely big, but I'm not sure that [Airbnb] is ... a basic cause of these increases. I am not sure how much the increase in houses prices has to do with Airbnb. There are a lot of foreign investors buying houses in Queenstown and they are not available for local families to use them. People are just come using homes that are not even rented in between ... a lot of foreign investors are doing that [and legislation] should be tightened up. (Host1)

Hosts emphasised the need to look at the 'bigger picture' in terms of key overarching destination issues (e.g. low salaries, high rents, a growing population) beyond just Airbnb providers, as discussed here:

> Airbnb is not purely to blame for the shortage of accommodation. Queenstown has always been known for high rent, greedy property owners, even ... in commercial buildings, because you are always going to get someone [renting]. Unfortunately, some people have to charge a high amount because 'I have to cover my mortgage.' In Queenstown, you're not paid as much [and], if you want to be here, people are working at $17 per hour and of course, it's hard to pay rent of what, like, $200-250 a week [for one room]? (Host 3)

Local community members expressed divergent views on Airbnb's impacts. Negative impacts attributed to Airbnb included housing and parking shortages; congestion and over-crowding; increases in waste, disruptive noise, competition for residential and commercial spaces; or feeling disconnected from one's own neighbourhood. For example, some community members felt strongly that the growth of Airbnb in Queenstown had negatively influenced the lives of residents and potentially contributed to a loss of "Kiwi culture" in Queenstown, as reflected below:

> ... noise, traffic, parking, kids not feeling safe, cars driving around so you cannot [walk around], kids cannot bike around easily. Neighbours, you know, if your neighbours are changing every night, when you've got these people partying next door ... one of the complaints [against Airbnb] was noise and it's always hard to get noise control out, so that's every night. (Community6)

Conversely, some community members had neutral or positive impressions of Airbnb impacts in their neighbourhood. These community members appreciated the economic and cultural gains brought by Airbnb at both personal and community levels. One of the local respondents stated:

> Personally, I don't think there are any negative impacts associated with Airbnb specifically. We have neighbours who Airbnb their home and that has not impacted on us. They do their spare room; they do not do the whole house. Once or twice, we hosted for them on weekends that they needed to go away and did not want to cancel and that was lovely really, two lovely couples, who did have lovely enjoyable weekends and we sat down with these people three hours each, enjoyable visits. We have thought about renting our house out [on Airbnb]. (Community 9)

Overall, local community perceptions of Airbnb appeared to be heterogeneous and largely dependent on personal experiences in highly localised areas.

Political impacts

Stakeholders did not portray political impacts of Airbnb as definitively negative or positive. Rather, data clearly highlighted both the challenges and opportunities for local policy makers and regulatory authorities. As Queenstown had only recently proposed, but not enacted, regulations to govern Airbnb rentals at the time of the study, policy makers were focusing on self-regulation due to a lack of tax enforcement policies. One barrier to change was that any change would be unlikely to impact those already in the 'system' (i.e. who had already obtained resource consent). One respondent noted that it was difficult to identify "hard legal ground" (Council13) with regard to Airbnb, while others cited a lack of successful models upon which to operate. According to one policy maker, "in the changing world, it is difficult to define the model [that Queenstown needs]" (Council14). Before revising regulations, policy makers felt they needed a much clearer vision of both the existing problem and Queenstown's ideal future.

Notwithstanding, local policy makers believed that, rather than being the cause of all problems, Airbnb was part of larger, more complex growth issues. Respondents suggested that it was important to look at the Airbnb phenomena more broadly within the larger tourism system, and to view it as a potential symptom of Queenstown's larger growth issues.

> If the housing crisis is what we want to solve, then let's look at the housing crisis. Let's not look at little symptoms around it, like Airbnb, which is something we're doing. (Council13)

As such, policy makers wanted to involve more stakeholders and gather more data before forming final opinions or changing policies in relation to Airbnb, as one respondent explained:

> I do not think Airbnb is close to the priority. I think we are just reacting in the best way we can, but it is not proactive. I feel that public discussion involving all stakeholders about the existing context is essential before things become more complicated. One of the major drawbacks in relation to Airbnb is lack of data on 'what' and 'how many'. (Council 14)

This statement reflected a key reason why respondents felt it was so difficult to reach consensus on Airbnb impacts and response strategies: Airbnb did not disclose key data, such as visitor nights. The lack of data from Airbnb also made it harder for policy makers to monitor whether the hosts were following or breaching regulations, and to assess the full extent of Airbnb rental activity. Even in instances when hosts clearly breached regulations, policy makers often lacked sufficient information to take evidence-based enforcement action.

> There is lack of transparency and lack of information whether the host is hosting from a commercial gain perspective, or allowing friends and families to stay in the properties that they are not gaining financially from, or blocking out [calendar nights] for themselves to use their own property for Christmas and New Year type of thing. (Council 13)

From policy makers' perspectives, Airbnb was generally perceived as an accommodation provider that, like other tourism services, could have both positive and negative impacts on the local community and other tourism services. As such, Airbnb was portrayed as an integrated part of the tourism services that catered to visitor needs.

Environmental impacts

The environmental impacts was less discussed by the respondents. The environmental impacts mainly focus on additional waste generated for residential and commercial spaces, creating increasing pressures for waste management.

> We've got some Airbnb where we are, [we live on site], and their rubbish fills up, they've got somebody who's been given property manager role to come around and clear the bin, but they only do it once in two, three weeks, it's pretty unsightly (Hotel 1).

Stakeholder responses and strategies

Based on stakeholder's perspectives of Airbnb's impacts, each participant was further asked to reflect on what they thought the best responses and strategies were to either support or mitigate Airbnb impacts. A variety of responses and strategies were proposed by respondents to address the perceived impacts of Airbnb, ranging from relatively 'soft' regulatory approaches to 'strict' law enforcement.

Overall, the importance of developing appropriate and timely strategies that adequately addressed Airbnb issues and balanced tourism sector interests with hosts and the larger community was emphasised. The fundamental strategies for addressing impacts of Airbnb revolved around management functions including community consultation and informed stakeholder involvement, increased regulation, providing incentives for hotels to develop purpose-built worker accommodation, and provision of purpose-built worker accommodations by the government.

Community consultation

The most frequently proposed reponse was providing regular and meaningful community consultation opportunities, as reflected below:

> I think some community consultation led by the council would be really good. We have a tendency to adopt strategies before we consult our community; if we do consult our community it is normally through a kind of quick survey. I think actually having some kind of forum where people can talk about issues and share their experience would make it valuable. (Host 2)

The other suggestion is to engage all stakeholders in a more integrated manner. One host explained the perceived benefits of this approach across stakeholders:

> ... get the stakeholders involved, get hoteliers involved, get the Airbnb hosts involved, get the council involved and ... say what are the issues that we are currently facing because I am sure all of us have a different experience so [the] neighbour of an Airbnb host may have a different experience to the host. (Host 2)

Local policy makers also believed there was a need to clearly define the 'problem' and overall community vision through stakeholder involvement.

> [We] should try getting all stakeholders in the room and [have] one 'proper' facilitated session about what we want to see as a community. (Council 14)

Regulation

Strengthening regulatory systems was another strategy recommended by a range of stakeholders to address perceived Airbnb impacts. Community members were in favour of "regulating actions instead of restricting" (Community6). This approach involved enacting tighter regulations on how Airbnb hosts can operate, rather than blanket bans on Airbnb hosting. A host also underlined "the need to have better governance over who is doing it [hosting Airbnb] and how they are doing it; I think regulation needs to be in place" (Host2). Traditional accommodation providers asserted that assuming Airbnb would self-regulate was misguided and not viable:

> The customer wants Airbnb, and Airbnb want to stick their money in their pocket, and I cannot see ... who else is in the position to regulate that, apart from the government or the council. (Hotel 10)

Hence, council-driven enforcement that tightened regulations across a number of areas, such as parking or guest numbers, was suggested. Community and policy makers also reinforced that safety concerns, for hosts and guests, and resident quality of life underpinned their desire to see increased Airbnb regulations. For example,

> I think homestay[s] should be regulated to the extent that it is safe; just basic things, like making sure you have fire escapes ... fire alarm that kind of thing, and something like parking [that] does not start to impinge on the street ... so just kind of basic amenity ... Parking, home safety ... If people are using Airbnb for a large part of the year, they should probably think about providing parking. (Community 6)

> There needs to be control in place for both sides to ensure that community is operating in a way that we want to operate. (Council 13)

Some participants went further to suggest that Airbnb hosts should be subject to the same regulations as traditional accommodation providers to ensure economic equity.

> Capture formally those that are wishing to put their property in Airbnb and put them through the same controls regulations as everybody else; play like formal sector and pay the same rates; pay commercial rates and do it properly. (Hotel 11)

To illustrate this perspective, the hotel manager equated the current uncontrolled Airbnb system to unfair working conditions: *"It is like saying, do you treat a part-time employee differently from a full-time employee?"* (Hotel 11). Interestingly, some hosts shared the perspective that they should operate more like a traditional accommodation provider.

> The first thing we have to do is to pay additional rates - which, absolutely, why we would not? - but certainly, we have to. We are certainly becoming a commercial entity. I think that is absolutely valid and then [requiring you to] get a resource consent. (Host 2)

Alternative options

Many participants identified that, while Airbnb was perceived to contribute to housing shortages, it was unclear to what degree these shortages were casued by Airbnb activity versus rapid population growth in the Queenstown region. As this issue appeared to be multifaceted, various stakeholders identified a need for alternative longer-term accommodation provisions by both policy makers and traditional accommodation providers. Participants suggested both public and incentivised private worker accommodation developments.

> I am a little over people who always blame governments or councils. If I had enough money, I would build workers accommodation... The council should be building more purpose-built accommodation for workers. (Host 3)

> If you could reduce the cost to build somehow, then people will be prepared to build worker accommodation ... or incentivise and facilitate accommodation for people working in town. (Hotel 7)

Some 'increased supply' and 'mixed use' responses were already in progress, and included specific exclusions on Airbnb activities as a result of perceived issues associated with housing shortages.

> We got special housing areas throughout our district... which will include affordable housing inside of that, so Queenstown has got its own growth when we compare it nationally... It is a new sub-division within that sub-division. You will not be allowed to run Airbnb. (Council 13)

Overall, in terms of accountability for addressing perceived Airbnb impacts, the local council was identified as the major actor responsible for policy making and solutions, as reflected by one host: *Personally, I think that is not my responsibility to solve that [housing shortage] problem, that is the council's responsibility* (Host4). Accommodation providers affirmed the view that changes needed to start at the level of public government stating, *"Action would have to start from the government. The government has to regulate and penalise"* (Hotel 12). Hotel managers also suggested that the hotel industry could play a role in these solutions. *"The hotel/motel industry association needs to understand how they can look to provide the required alternatives or solutions"* (Hotel 8).

Discussion and conclusion

Guided by social representation theory, this research identified diverse stakeholder perspectives on Airbnb impacts and illustrated how these perspectives led to different response strategies and anticipated outcomes. This research suggests that the impacts of Airbnb are complex, reflect diverse stakeholder interests and experiences, and encompass a range of economic, sociocultural, and political dimensions.

Theoretical implications

Previous tourism research employing social representation theory has largely relied on quantitative measures of impacts and focused on consequences, such as support for tourism, rather than processes (e.g. Suess and Mody (2016)). This is problematic as it treats community stakeholders as a single entity with homogenous attitudes (Moyle et al., 2010) and thereby overlooks the potenital for heterogenous perspectives on tourism across stakeholders. This study extends applications of social representation theory to the P2P accommodation context by focusing how disruptive accommodation processes are being contested, interpreted, and integrated into the traditional tourism eco-system. Understanding how various stakeholders interpret and form perspectives on Airbnb facilitates a more nuanced amd critical understanding of this phenomenon.

This study also extends sustainable tourism and P2P accommodation literature in relation to the on-going debate regarding how tourism can develop sustainably in destinations with a global disruptive player, such as Airbnb (Dolnicar, 2019). Current research on P2P accommodation generally examines Airbnb impacts in isolation by focusing on one aspect of impacts, such as hotel pricing strategies (e.g. Zervas et al. (2017)). This approach results in fragmented knowledge that lacks a holistic perspective on sustainable tourism destinations. The current study highlights the need for fuller pictures of P2P accommodation impacts across diverse stakeholders in various localities to inform longer-term destination visions and policy(von Briel & Dolnicar, 2020). In the absence of a holistic perspective, policy makers may struggle to envision effective strategies for dealing with issues arising from P2P accommodations. This is particularily important given the lack of data sharing and transparency reported in the current study, and research suggesting that Airbnb may be actively engaging 'Airbnb advocates' to lobby governments under its entrepreneur umbrella (Ferreri & Sanyal, 2018). These issues add further complexity and challenges to understand stakeholder perspectives and reinforce the need for reliable, transparent information regarding Airbnb's supply and demand in Queenstown and other global destinations.

The research also identifies new perspectives on existing dialogues related to organisational aspects of the sharing economy. The current literature largely focuses on how Airbnb's organisation processes impact hosts as an informal employee (Cheng & Foley, 2019; Sundararajan, 2014). This literature does not recognise how the sharing economy can restructure the current workforce for both traditional and sharing economy providers by shifting workers from the formal labour force (e.g. hotel workers) into a more informal labour force (e.g. P2P accommodation support services, such as cleaners). The current study highlighted how this shift, and associated issues of worker welfare and employment stability, may create less visible, but significant impacts on tourism and hospitality workers. These findings underscore the importance of future research examining the broader labour impacts of Airbnb across stakeholders.

Practical implications

Contextually, this study contributes further empirical evidence to inform global debates regarding Airbnb's impacts and potential management approaches from non-European and non-American perspectives (Nieuwland & Melik, 2020). In a fast-growing tourism destination, an increasing number of Airbnb listings might not necessarily result in decreases for traditional accommodation providers (Cheng et al., 2020). With increasing accommodation demand in Queenstown, the direct impacts of Airbnb on traditional accommodation providers were not perceived to create immediate negative economic impacts. However, more indirect impacts were identified in Queenstown, in terms of altering labour force structures. For instance, Airbnb made employee recruitment and retention more difficult in Queenstown due to both alternative work-force opportunities (e.g. P2P accommodation support services) and housing shortages, which made longer-term accomodation unaffordable. These findings highlight the importance of examining broad geographical perspectives to fully capture the dynamics of Airbnb (Grimmer et al., 2019; Guttentag, 2019)

Practically, our findings suggest that the commonly promoted "top-down strategies transferable from one city to another" (Ferreri & Sanyal, 2018) may be of questionable value given the complex impacts Airbnb has on a destination and contextual factors unique to that destination. In this study context, Queenstown is a rapidly growing mountainous tourism resort with significant accommodation constraints. Thus, at least in a short-term, Airbnb is filling gaps in the accommodation market and functions in relative harmony with the hotel sector. However, this study also highlights a range of potentially negative community impacts, such as disputing ways of life, increasing rental costs, and inadequate regulatory frameworks. These social, economic and regulatory issues are compounded by a lack of clear data upon which to evaluate the size and scope of Airbnb in a destination, and thereby establish impact metrics and appropriate policy changes. This is important because, as stated above, some perceived impacts of Airbnb are often embedded with existing destination issues. For instance, while many Queenstown stakeholders perceived various impacts as a direct consequence of Airbnb, policy makers did not view Airbnb as the root of all problems, but rather part of larger growth issues. Thus, one of the most complex issues reported in this study was the need for regulators to identify ways to disentangle perceptions of Airbnb's impacts from other issues affecting rapidly growing tourism destinations.

While unique theoretical and practical insights were gained, our study is not without limitations. The findings from various stakeholder groups may not apply to other stakeholders in different destinations. Research with a wider range of participants in a range of tourism destinations may refine and/or challenge these findings. In addition, future approach to quantify the impacts identified herein provide a helpful baseline for policy development and monitoring, particularly for scenario planning. Finally, collecting data with a more diverse range of stakeholders and using a longitudinal research design can provide more in-depth, potentially distinct, stakeholder perspectives.

Disclosure statement

No potential conflict of interest was reported by the authors.

References

Airbnb. (2017). Airbnb: Helping travel grow greener. https://press.atairbnb.com/app/uploads/2017/03/Airbnbandsustainabletravel2017.pdf

Akbar, Y. H., & Tracogna, A. (2018). The sharing economy and the future of the hotel industry: Transaction cost theory and platform economics. *International Journal of Hospitality Management*, *71*, 91–101. https://doi.org/10.1016/j.ijhm.2017.12.004

Alrawadieh, Z., Guttentag, D., Cifci, M. A., & Cetin, G. (2020). Budget and midrange hotel managers' perceptions of and responses to Airbnb. *International Journal of Contemporary Hospitality Management*, *32*(2), 588–604. https://doi.org/10.1108/IJCHM-01-2019-0015

Andriotis, K., & Vaughan, R. D. (2003). Urban residents' attitudes toward tourism development: The case of Crete. *Journal of Travel Research*, *42*(2), 172–185. https://doi.org/10.1177/0047287503257488

Auckland Council. (2020). Rating of providers of online accommodation properties. https://www.aucklandcouncil.govt.nz/property-rates-valuations/your-rates-bill/Pages/accommodation-provider-targeted-rate.aspx

Braun, V., & Clarke, V. (2006). Using thematic analysis in psychology. *Qualitative Research in Psychology*, *3*(2), 77–101. https://doi.org/10.1191/1478088706qp063oa

Brown, T. (2017). Queenstown council to vote on Airbnb cuts. https://www.radionz.co.nz/news/national/343295/queenstown-council-to-vote-on-airbnb-cuts

Bryman, A. (2012). *Social Science Research Methods*. (4th ed.). Oxford University Press.

Charmaz, K. (2005). Grounded theory in the 21st Century. Applications for advancing social justice studies. In N. Denzin & Y. Lincoln (Eds.), *The Sage handbook of qualitative research* (pp. 507–535). Sage.

Cheng, M. (2016). Sharing economy: A review and agenda for future research. *International Journal of Hospitality Management*, *57*, 60–70. https://doi.org/10.1016/j.ijhm.2016.06.003

Cheng, M., Chen, G., Wiedmann, T., Hadjikakou, M., Xu, L., & Wang, Y. (2020). The sharing economy and sustainability–assessing Airbnb's direct, indirect and induced carbon footprint in Sydney. *Journal of Sustainable Tourism*, *28*(8), 1083–1017. https://doi.org/10.1080/09669582.2020.1720698

Cheng, M., & Edwards, D. (2019). A comparative automated content analysis approach on the review of the sharing economy discourse in tourism and hospitality. *Current Issues in Tourism*, *22*(1), 35–15. https://doi.org/10.1080/13683500.2017.1361908

Cheng, M., & Foley, C. (2018). The sharing economy and digital discrimination: The case of Airbnb. *International Journal of Hospitality Management*, *70*, 95–98. https://doi.org/10.1016/j.ijhm.2017.11.002

Cheng, M., & Foley, C. (2019). Algorithmic management: The case of Airbnb. *International Journal of Hospitality Management*, *83*, 33–36. https://doi.org/10.1016/j.ijhm.2019.04.009

Cheng, M., & Zhang, G. (2019). When Western hosts meet Eastern guests: Airbnb hosts' experience with Chinese outbound tourists. *Annals of Tourism Research*, *75*, 288–303. https://doi.org/10.1016/j.annals.2019.02.006

Dogru, T., Mody, M., Suess, C., Mcginley, S., & Line, N. D. (2020). The Airbnb paradox: Positive employment effects in the hospitality industry. *Tourism Management*, *77*, 104001 https://doi.org/10.1016/j.tourman.2019.104001

Creswell, J. W. (2007). Qualitative inquiry and research design: Choosing among five approaches. Thousand Oaks: Sage

Dogru, T., Hanks, L., Ozdemir, O., Kizildag, M., Ampountolas, A., & Demirer, I. (2020). Does Airbnb have a homogenous impact? Examining Airbnb's effect on hotels with different organizational structures. *International Journal of Hospitality Management*, *86*, 102451. https://doi.org/10.1016/j.ijhm.2020.102451

Dogru, T., Mody, M., & Suess, C. (2017). The hotel industry's Achilles Heel? Quantifying the negative impacts of Airbnb on Boston's hotel performance. *Boston Hospitality Review*, *5*(3), 1–11.

Dolnicar, S. (2019). A review of research into paid online peer-to-peer accommodation: Launching the Annals of Tourism Research curated collection on peer-to-peer accommodation. *Annals of Tourism Research*, *75*, 248–264. https://doi.org/10.1016/j.annals.2019.02.003

Dredge, D., & Gyimóthy, S. (2015). The collaborative economy and tourism: Critical perspectives, questionable claims and silenced voices. *Tourism Recreation Research*, *40*(3), 286–302. https://doi.org/10.1080/02508281.2015.1086076

Fang, B., Ye, Q., & Law, R. (2016). Effect of sharing economy on tourism industry employment. *Annals of Tourism Research*, *57*, 264–267. https://doi.org/10.1016/j.annals.2015.11.018

Farmaki, A., Stergiou, D., & Kaniadakis, A. (2019). Self-perceptions of Airbnb hosts' responsibility: a moral identity perspective. *Journal of Sustainable Tourism*, 1–21. Online First

Farronato, C., & Fradkin, A. (2018). The welfare effects of peer entry in the accommodation market: The case of airbnb (No. w24361). National Bureau of Economic Research.

Ferreri, M., & Sanyal, R. (2018). Platform economies and urban planning: Airbnb and regulated deregulation in London. *Urban Studies*, *55*(15), 3353–3368. 0042098017751982. https://doi.org/10.1177/0042098017751982

Fredline, E. (2006). Host and guest relations and sport tourism. In H. Gibson (Ed.), *Sport tourism: Concepts and theories*. Routledge.

Grimmer, L., Vorobjovas-Pinta, O., & Massey, M. (2019). Regulating, then deregulating Airbnb-The unique case of Tasmania (Australia). *Annals of Tourism Research*, *75*, 304–307. https://doi.org/10.1016/j.annals.2019.01.012

Gurran, N., & Phibbs, P. (2017). When tourists move in: how should urban planners respond to Airbnb?. *Journal of the American Planning Association*, *83*(1), 80–92. https://doi.org/10.1080/01944363.2016.1249011

Guttentag, D. (2015). Airbnb: disruptive innovation and the rise of an informal tourism accommodation sector. *Current Issues in Tourism*, *18*(12), 1192–1217. https://doi.org/10.1080/13683500.2013.827159

Guttentag, D. (2019). Progress on Airbnb: A literature review. *Journal of Hospitality and Tourism Technology*, *10*(4), 814–844. https://doi.org/10.1108/JHTT-08-2018-0075

Guttentag, D., & Smith, S. (2017). Assessing Airbnb as a disruptive innovation relative to hotels: Substitution and comparative performance expectations. *International Journal of Hospitality Management*, *64*, 1–10. https://doi.org/10.1016/j.ijhm.2017.02.003

Hajibaba, H., Karlsson, L., & Dolnicar, S. (2017). Residents open their homes to tourists when disaster strikes. *Journal of Travel Research*, *56*(8), 1065–1078. https://doi.org/10.1177/0047287516677167

Ikkala, T., & Lampinen, A. (2015). Monetizing network hospitality: Hospitality and sociability in the context of Airbnb. In Proceedings of the 18th ACM conference on computer supported cooperative work & social computing (pp. 1033-1044).

Jenkins, M. (2018). *Sustaining tourism growth in Queenstown*. Auckland.

Jordan, E., & Moore, J. (2018). An in-depth exploration of residents' perceived impacts of transient vacation rentals. *Journal of Travel & Tourism Marketing*, *35*(1), 90–101. https://doi.org/10.1080/10548408.2017.1315844

Kakar, V., Voelz, J., Wu, J., & Franco, J. (2018). The visible host: Does race guide Airbnb rental rates in San Francisco? *Journal of Housing Economics*, *40*, 25-40.

Koh, E., & King, B. (2017). Accommodating the sharing revolution: a qualitative evaluation of the impact of Airbnb on Singapore's budget hotels. *Tourism Recreation Research*, *42*(4), 409–421. https://doi.org/10.1080/02508281.2017.1314413

Kuprienko, D. (2018). Queenstown housing crisis bites, tourism giants buy staff accommodation. https://www.stuff.co.nz/business/103017338/queenstown-businesses-plan-more-staff-accommodation-as-housing-crisis-bites

Lee, D. (2016). How Airbnb short-term rentals exacerbate Los Angeles's affordable housing crisis: Analysis and policy recommendations. *Harv. L. & Pol'y Rev*, *10*, 229.

Matteucci, X., & Gnoth, J. (2017). Elaborating on grounded theory in tourism research. *Annals of Tourism Research*, *65*, 49–59. https://doi.org/10.1016/j.annals.2017.05.003

Mody, M., Suess, C., & Dogru, T. (2019). Not in my backyard? Is the anti-Airbnb discourse truly warranted?. *Annals of Tourism Research*, *74*(C), 198–203. https://doi.org/10.1016/j.annals.2018.05.004

Monterrubio, J. C., & Andriotis, K. (2014). Social representations and community attitudes towards spring breakers. *Tourism Geographies*, *16*(2), 288–302. https://doi.org/10.1080/14616688.2014.889208

Moscovici, S. (2001). Why a theory of social representation?. In K. Deaux & G. Philogène (Eds.), *Representations of the social: Bridging theoretical traditions* (pp. 8–35). Blackwell Publishing.

Moyle, B., Glen Croy, W., & Weiler, B. (2010). Community perceptions of tourism: Bruny and Magnetic islands. *Asia Pacific Journal of Tourism Research*, *15*(3), 353–366. https://doi.org/10.1080/10941665.2010.503625

Murray, M. (2002). Connecting narrative and social representation theory in health research. *Social Science Information*, *41*(4), 653–673. https://doi.org/10.1177/0539018402041004008

Nadler, S. S. N. (2014). *The sharing economy: what is it and where is it going?* Massachusetts Institute of Technology.

Nieuwland, S., & Melik, R. v. (2020). Regulating Airbnb: How cities deal with perceived negative externalities of short-term rentals. *Current Issues in Tourism*, *23*(7), 811–825. https://doi.org/10.1080/13683500.2018.1504899

Oskam, J., & Boswijk, A. (2016). Airbnb: the future of networked hospitality businesses. *Journal of Tourism Futures*, *2*(1), 22–42. https://doi.org/10.1108/JTF-11-2015-0048

Pforr, C., Volgger, M., & Coulson, K. (2017). *The Impact of Airbnb on WA's Tourism Industry*. Retrieved from

Potter, J., & Litton, I. (1985). Some problems underlying the theory of social representations. *British Journal of Social Psychology*, *24*(2), 81–90. https://doi.org/10.1111/j.2044-8309.1985.tb00664.x

Prayag, G., & Ozanne, L. (2018). A systematic review of peer-to-peer (P2P) accommodation sharing research from 2010 to 2016: progress and prospects from the multi-level perspective. *Journal of Hospitality Marketing & Management*, *27*(6), 649–678. https://doi.org/10.1080/19368623.2018.1429977

Rauch, D. E., & Schleicher, D. (2015). Like Uber, but for local governmental policy: The Future of local regulation of the "sharing economy." *George Mason Law & Economics Research Paper*. 1-61

Richard, B., & Cleveland, S. (2016). The future of hotel chains: Branded marketplaces driven by the sharing economy. *Journal of Vacation Marketing*, *22*(3), 239–248. https://doi.org/10.1177/1356766715623827

Richards, S., Brown, L., & Dilettuso, A. (2019). The Airbnb phenomenon: the resident's perspective. *International Journal of Tourism Cities*, *6*(1), 8–26. https://doi.org/10.1108/IJTC-06-2019-0084

Schor, J. B., & Fitzmaurice, C. J. (2015). 26. Collaborating and connecting: The emergence of the sharing economy. In L. Reisch & J. Thogersen (Eds.), *Handbook of research on sustainable consumption* (pp. 410). Edward Elgar.

Shaheen, S. A., Mallery, M. A., & Kingsley, K. J. (2012). Personal vehicle sharing services in North America. *Research in Transportation Business & Management*, *3*, 71–81. https://doi.org/10.1016/j.rtbm.2012.04.005

Sharpley, R. (2014). Host perceptions of tourism: A review of the research. *Tourism Management*, *42*, 37–49. https://doi.org/10.1016/j.tourman.2013.10.007

Statistics New Zealand. (2018). Queenstown-Lakes District Census Data Summaries

Statistics New Zealand. (2019). Overseas guests boost South Island accommodation. https://www.stats.govt.nz/news/overseas-guests-boost-south-island-accommodation

Stergiou, D. P., & Farmaki, A. (2019). Resident perceptions of the impacts of P2P accommodation: Implications for neighbourhoods. *International Journal of Hospitality Management*, 102411. https://doi.org/10.1016/j.ijhm.2019.102411

Stuart, R. (2017). Sydney is Airbnb's Australian boomtown, but not everyone is celebrating the website's success. http://www.abc.net.au/news/2017-01-31/airbnb-booming-in-sydney-but-it-could-be-pushing-up-rents/8223900

Suess, C., & Mody, M. (2016). Gaming can be sustainable too! Using Social Representation Theory to examine the moderating effects of tourism diversification on residents' tax paying behavior. *Tourism Management*, *56*, 20–39. https://doi.org/10.1016/j.tourman.2016.03.022

Sundararajan, A. (2014). What Airbnb gets about culture that Uber doesn't. *Harvard Business Review, 11*.

Tussyadiah, L., & Pesonen, J. (2016). Impacts of peer-to-peer accommodation use on travel patterns. *Journal of Travel Research*, *55*(8), 1022–1040. https://doi.org/10.1177/0047287515608505

Uzunca, B., & Borlenghi, A. (2019). Regulation strictness and supply in the platform economy: the case of Airbnb and Couchsurfing. *Industry and Innovation*, *26*(8), 920–942. https://doi.org/10.1080/13662716.2019.1633278

von Briel, D., Dolnicar, S. (2020). The evolution of airbnb regulation-An international longitudinal investigation 2008–2020.

Wachsmuth, D., & Weisler, A. (2018). Airbnb and the rent gap: Gentrification through the sharing economy. *Environment and Planning A: Economy and Space*, *50*(6), 1147–1170. https://doi.org/10.1177/0308518X18778038

Weaver, D. B., & Lawton, L. J. (2013). Resident perceptions of a contentious tourism event. *Tourism Management*, *37*, 165–175. https://doi.org/10.1016/j.tourman.2013.01.017

Williams, D. (2017). Queenstown's Airbnb crackdown explained. https://www.newsroom.co.nz/2017/11/12/59807/queenstowns-airbnb-crackdown-explained

Zach, F. J., Nicolau, J. L., & Sharma, A. (2020). Disruptive innovation, innovation adoption and incumbent market value: The case of Airbnb. *Annals of Tourism Research*, *80*, 102818 https://doi.org/10.1016/j.annals.2019.102818

Zervas, G., Proserpio, D., & Byers, J. W. (2017). The rise of the sharing economy: Estimating the impact of Airbnb on the hotel industry. *Journal of Marketing Research*, *54*(5), 687–705. https://doi.org/10.1509/jmr.15.0204

COVID-19 pandemic exposes the vulnerability of the sharing economy: a novel accounting framework

Guangwu Chen, Mingming Cheng, Deborah Edwards and Lixiao Xu

ABSTRACT

The outbreak of the COVID-19 pandemic has resulted in a global economic recession, but little is known about the impact it has had on the informal economy, including the peer-to-peer rental market. This study assessed the financial loss of Airbnb listings for its hosts in Greater Sydney, Australia. Findings show that comparing August 2020 to January 2020, the pandemic resulted in 89.5 per cent income loss for Airbnb hosts (about 14 million) with hosts suffering about 6.5 times more than the Airbnb platform itself. However, many Airbnb hosts are not eligible for the financial aid being offered by the NSW State Government or the Australian Federal Government. The study further demonstrates the vulnerability of the sharing economy during a time of crisis. It contributes empirical evidence to the widening public debate on the sharing economy's contribution to sustainable tourism and decent work (SDG 8), and reduced inequalities (SDG 10), and, most importantly, it raises concerns over taxation and social protections for informal employees. Methodologically, this study contributes to the literature by presenting a comprehensive income accounting framework to analyse this segment of the workforce's financial performance, which can serve as benchmark for tax estimation and financial aids.

Introduction

The outbreak of the COVID-19 pandemic has resulted in a significant number of related infections and deaths across the globe. It has also impacted global economies and resulted in widespread job losses. While evidence has started to emerge, which quantifies the broader economic impacts of COVID-19, less is known about its impacts on things such as the sharing economy, including the peer-to-peer (P2P) rental market. The "sharing economy implicitly refers to the sharing of capacity-constrained physical assets (e.g. cars, rooms, and bicycles)" (Wirtz et al., 2019, p. 455). P2P rental, as part of the sharing economy, has enjoyed dramatic growth in the last decade, creating a new era of disruptive and alternative economic growth where underutilised resources can be used (for a fee) without the need to own them. As a strong contributor to the diversification of tourism's accommodation value chain, Airbnb demonstrates its capacity for reducing inequalities as it engages local residents by providing them with opportunities for new and additional sources of income. By increasing access to such underutilised resources, Airbnb contributes to Sustainable Development Goal 8 (decent work and economic growth) and Sustainable Development Goal 10 (reduced inequalities) (UNWTO, 2020). However media coverage has shown that the travel bans associated with COVID-19 across the globe have had significant negative impacts on P2P rental, particularly the income loss experienced by hosts (ABC News, 2020a). This is an issue, which is likely to widen inequalities.

The impacts of COVID-19 on Airbnb hosts are particularly staggering, not only because of the nature of Airbnb work (work on demand) but also due to their limited entitlement to various forms of government support (ATO, 2020a). Concerns about this sharing economy workforce were highlighted even before the pandemic began; particularly in relation to issues such as safety, income stability and employment protection (Sundararajan, 2017). These concerns have only been heightened as a result of the impacts of COVID-19. While various media outlets have reported the detrimental impacts of the pandemic on the sharing economy, there has been little data presented to support such claims. Without a rigorous evaluation of the impacts on the sharing economy workforce (including Airbnb hosts) it is difficult for stakeholders (including government) to establish baseline data from which to respond to these types of negative impacts, including the issue of provision of government subsidies or support.

Against this backdrop, using a novel income accounting framework, this study systematically assesses the income loss of Airbnb hosts at both spatial and temporal scales in Sydney under two waves of the pandemic. Sydney is one of the largest metropolitan cities in Australia and Airbnb has become an increasingly attractive income source for many local residents with 41,338 Airbnb listings in January 2020. This research contributes to the sharing economy and tourism literature in times of crisis by providing empirical evidence in relation to the economical sustainability of the sharing economy. Methodologically, it contributes by proposing a novel accounting framework to assess Airbnb listing income, which opens avenues for future research to examine the financial impacts of similar digital, peer-to-peer platforms on its workforce.

This article starts with a review of existing literature on the relationship between the sharing economy and sustainable development goals (SDGs) and employment issues associated with the sharing economy, followed by the impact of COVID-19 on Airbnb hosts and the accounting framework. The research design sections then detail the accounting framework used in this study based on the data of Airbnb listings in Sydney, followed by the result and discussion sections on the vulnerability of the sharing economy. This article concludes with the implications for the wider sharing economy beyond this study.

Literature review

The sharing economy and sustainable development goals (SDGs)

The wide implications rising from the rapid growth of the sharing economy businesses have been linked to various sustainable development goals (SDGs). While the sharing economy businesses including Airbnb at the beginning have been framed as an alternative pathway to sustainable future, multiple concerns have already been identified during their course of development. Indeed, the relationship between Airbnb and SDGs, more broadly the sharing economy, is far from being straightforward.

Early studies have suggested that the sharing economy businesses can provide flexible work arrangement and employment opportunities as well as reduce the impacts of production and consumption, offering an alternative to existing consumption practices. These can contribute to decent work and economic growth (SDG8), responsible production and consumption (SDG12) and Climate action (SDG13) (Andreoni, 2019). However, while acknowledging the positive impacts brought by the sharing economy on SDGs, research has identified the potential negative impacts, such as job insecurity, and platform capitalism (Table 1). For example, Cheng et al.

Table 1. Positive and negative impacts of the sharing economy in relation to Sustainable Development Goals.

Sustainable Development Goals	Positive Impacts	Negative Impacts
Goal 8: Decent Work and Economic Growth	Opportunities for new and additional sources of income, and flexible work arrangement (Mas and Pallais, 2017).	Lack of social protection and job security (Malos et al., 2018).
Goal 10: Reduced Inequalities	Addressing the injustice and inequalities of market economies (Cohen and Kietzmann, 2014).	Corporate co-option that emphases a neoliberal paradigm (Marqusee, 2015). Benefiting mainly the middle- or upper-income levels (Andreoni, 2019).
Goal 11: Sustainable Cities and Communities	Less resource-intensive by re-circulating under-utilised space (Cheng, 2016). Increase personal relationship, trust and community bonds that enhances the social sustainability (Richardson, 2015).	"Omen companies may use the 'sharing economy' as a marketing gimmick to disguise profit-motivation and exploitation under the pretence of making the society a better place" (Mi and Coffman, 2019, p1)(These include gentrification, speculation in the housing market and disruption of the social fabric of neighbourhoods (see e.g. Wachsmuth and Weisler(2018)).
Goal 12: Responsible Consumption and Production	New lifestyle to engage in alternative consumption and sustainable lifestyle Raise awareness about sustainability and over-consumption so that more collaborative and community-based approaches can be adopted (Möhlmann, 2015).	Rebound effect: the money saved could be re-spent thus driving extra consumption and production (Frenken and Schor, 2017). The increased affordability can induce consumption that have impacts on hyper-consumption, water generation and population (Andreoni, 2019).
Goal 13: Climate Action	Through a reduction in the total resources required and it helps reduce pollutants, emissions and carbon footprints (Cheng et al., 2020a).	Carbon footprint associated with induced consumption (Cheng et al., 2020a).
Goal 17: Revitalize the global partnership for sustainable development	Airbnb has created the facility/platform to build business partnerships (e.g. Airbnb and the International Olympic Committee (IOC) partnership).	Platform capitalism: platforms such as Uber and Airbnb, take advantage of data collection, aiming to become monopoly-like platforms (Srnicek, 2017).

(2020) highlight that while Airbnb can provide opportunities for extra income and flexible work arrangement (SDG 8), it has the potential to reduce community bonds and collaborations (SDG 11). More importantly, recent years have witnessed discrepancies that exist between the expected benefits of Airbnb and the application of Airbnb's business model. Cui et al.(2020) highlight that while Airbnb seems to reduce gender equity, its personal information-based business model (e.g. profile picture) can potentially create racial disparities. Martin (2016) also suggests that due to wide affordability of the products in the sharing economy, there is increasing expansion of consumption resulting in increasing pressure on environment. Indeed, as Andreoni (2019) suggests, "the present structure of the sharing economy has the risk to generate effects going in a direction that is opposite to that established in the Sustainable Developments Goals." (P.576). Table 1 presents various positive and negatives impacts of the sharing economy in relation to SDGs.

Employment in the sharing economy

Employment issues in the sharing economy have received increasing attention in the last few years. This attention has included government inquiries due to the wider public concerns on wages and employment conditions of their workforce (Ravenelle, 2017). This type of employment is associated with digital, service-based, and on-demand platforms (Haripershad and Johnston, 2017; Palos-Sanchez and Correia, 2018), often labelled as on-demand workforce for "a just-for-now remedy" (Peticca-Harris et al., 2020).

The academic literature has long debated the benefits and shortcomings for the current workforce of the sharing economy, particularly related to P2P accommodation markets (Dogru et al., 2020). On one hand, the sharing economy accords its workforce more flexibilities (Mas and Pallais, 2017) to have control over the financial and personal aspects of work (Ravenelle, 2017). For example, Airbnb hosts are free to decide the availability of their listings as they choose, whereas employees from the hotel industry would not be able to do so. In addition, compared to traditional employment, the sharing economy workforce do not need to sign long-term contracts so they can take advantage of flexible work conditions (Berg, 2015; Friedman, 2014).

While these benefits have been recognised, researchers are also concerned with the income security associated with this on-demand employment, where social insurance is largely absent (Malos et al., 2018). Srnicek (2017) suggested that Airbnb and many other platforms operate by outsourcing as much of their costs as possible, aiming to turn into a monopoly-like platform, with employees hyper-exploited. Indeed, many workers are not entitled to unemployment insurance, workers compensation and disability insurance, work-related health insurance, and retirement pensions, which are part of traditional employment (Corujo, 2017). This is largely due to the fact that the platforms associated with the sharing economy have passed the financial and social risks on to the workers (Friedman, 2014), and these workers are not the formal employees of these platforms (Tran and Sokas, 2017). Indeed, by lowering entry barriers without considering a worker's previous experience, P2P sharing platforms can attract the maximum number of potential independent contractors and pass the whole responsibility on to them as individual business owners (Malos et al., 2018). This work nature consequently minimises the external regulation over the relationship between employer and employees - but more seriously, because these transactions happen across borders, "it becomes unclear which jurisdictions' regulations apply to the work being transacted" (Graham et al., 2017) (p.140).

When the COVID-19 pandemic kicked in, these workers were widely reported to be hit the hardest. According to a survey of AppJobs - a digital platform that compares App-based jobs - over half of these workers lost their jobs. What made this situation worse was that many of these workers were not eligible for government support.

COVID-19 and Airbnb hosts

Airbnb's workforce (Airbnb hosts) is not immune to the pandemic. With pandemic-related travel restrictions around the world, there has been a collapse in Airbnb bookings. While the Airbnb announced they would contribute $250 million (US) to support Airbnb hosts around the world who had experienced COVID-19-related cancellations, the policy only covers nights booked on or before March 14 with a check-in between March 14 and May 31, 2020. It is also limited to cover only 25 per cent of the total rental income loss (Airbnb, 2020a). Airbnb has also provided a $17 million (US) "Superhost Relief Fund" for hosts who show strong reliance on Airbnb as a vital source of income; however, only some veteran 'Superhosts' can access this benefit (Airbnb, 2020b). What is even more worrying is that many Airbnb hosts are not entitled to the financial support initiatives being provided by many governments the world. Despite an extensive search, the authors of this paper could find no data indicating what percentage of Airbnb hosts rely on the platform as their main source of income. However, there is evidence that most Sydney-based hosts are ordinary residents at the early stage of Airbnb's growth (Airbnb, 2013), who rely on the extra income from

Airbnb to make ends meet including mortgage payments and renting and staying in their home (Airbnb, 2020b). However, at the time of this study, our research estimates that there are 6,452 (53.5%) hosts with multiple listings which are likely to be professional hosts (Dolnicar and Zare, 2020). These professional hosts use Airbnb for commercial profits, who typically have a mortgage with their space (Dolnicar and Zare, 2020). Dolnicar and Zare (2020) predict that these professional hosts will be likely to decline and turn to long-term rental market as a result of the pandemic.

In Australia, the federal government announced a $130 billion JobKeeper payment to help retain jobs and support businesses affected by the significant economic impact caused by the Coronavirus. Around six million workers received a fortnightly payment of $1,500 (before tax) through their employer (AustralianGovernment, 2020c). Unfortunately, many gig economy workers or freelancers, including Airbnb hosts, did not qualify to claim this financial aid. Research shows that the sharing economy, including P2P rental, can help ease unemployment by providing extra income (Fang et al., 2016). However, with the ongoing pandemic, many Airbnb hosts who heavily rely on Airbnb as a vital source of income can be placed in a difficult situation. Against this backdrop, this research quantifies the financial impacts of COVID-19 on Airbnb hosts in Sydney, Australia. It further discusses implications for government and suggests directions for future research.

Accounting frameworks for Airbnb hosts' income

Ways to assess the income of Airbnb listings have received increasing attention from both industry practitioners and academics, as the accurate assessment of Airbnb listings' income can provide various stakeholders with important evidence to formulate strategies including price strategies (Kwok and Xie, 2019) and taxation (Dalir et al., 2020). By accounting for the income of Airbnb listings and then comparing the results with the long-term rental market in Sydney, Gurran and Phibbs (2017) concluded that "Airbnb listings may fall outside of existing land use regulations or evade detection until neighbours complain" (p.80). A similar approach has also been adopted by Yrigoy (2019) to estimate the impacts of Airbnb listings on residential rentals to calculate the revenue of Airbnb listings in Palma, Spain.

However, the accounting framework of Airbnb listings' income is not straight forward as Airbnb does not share its transaction data with the public. Previous studies have failed to take the booking service fee charged by the Airbnb platform into consideration by simply using the price as the proxy, thereby overestimating a host's rental income (e.g. Yrigoy (2019) and Gurran and Phibbs (2017)). As such, to build a comprehensive accounting framework for Airbnb listings' income, at least three critical pieces of information need to be taken into consideration. They are:

1. Spatial and temporal income distribution
2. The number of cancellations. This is particularly important during the pandemic period when cancellations happen more frequently (Hu and Lee, 2020)
3. The income distribution between hosts and the Airbnb platform.

By taking these three critical pieces of information into consideration, this study has clearly outlined each element of the accounting framework in the research design so that future researchers can replicate this accounting framework to examine the financial impacts of similar online peer-to-peer platforms.

Research design

Data

Eight months' worth of information on Airbnb listings in Sydney (January to August 2020) was obtained from Inside Airbnb (http://insideairbnb.com/). The initial number of Airbnb listings was

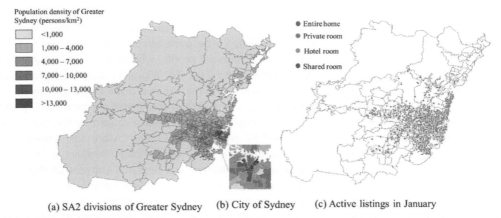

(a) SA2 divisions of Greater Sydney   (b) City of Sydney   (c) Active listings in January

Figure 1. Geographical boundary of Greater Sydney (including SA2 (a) and City of Sydney (b)), and active listings in January 2020(c).

41,338 (Jan.), 40,434 (Feb.), 39,670 (Mar.), 37,845 (April), 37,562 (May), 36,901 (June), 36,057 (July) and 31,391 (Aug.). After data cleaning, we excluded the listings without comments in the corresponding month, and only kept the listing with active comments, which are termed as active listings hereafter. As the number of review comments were used as a proxy for the estimation, they include the cancelled booking with the key phrases "automatically cancelled" in review comments. In order to avoid over-estimation, we have also deleted the cancellation numbers from active listings which are 115 (Jan.), 96 (Feb.), 89 (Mar.), 85 (April) and 83 (May) based on the comment with the key phrase "automatically cancelled"; however, under the Australian travel ban, there were no cancellations recorded during June to August. The data of listings contains a variety of information of Airbnb listings including the listing's ID, location, room type, price per night, minimum number of nights, reviews per month, detailed review comments, listings per host, and availability. Price of the listings per night, reviews, and minimum nights required to stay are used as the proxy to estimate the income of Airbnb hosts, although it can only be estimated as the lower limit of the income, as Airbnb guests can stay more nights than the minimum nights required (Cheng et al., 2020a).

Geographical boundary

The Greater Sydney area is adopted as the geographical boundary (Figure 1), and the census tract Statistical Area Level 2 (SA2) subdivisions of the Australian continent are taken from the Australian Statistical Geography Standard (ASGS) published by the Australian Bureau of Statistics (ABS) (ABS, 2011). We aggregate Airbnb listings into a SA2 level based on their location (latitude and longitude coordinate). The Greater Sydney area is comprised of 312 SA2 regions but the active listings are concentrated at 247 SA2 regions. The city area (Figure 1b) has the highest density with a population of more than 211,000 people (ABS 2020). The active listings are mostly located at the densely populated regions (Figure 1c), and the two dominant room types of Airbnb listings are for the entire home and private rooms. Listings offering a shared room or a hotel room are rare in Sydney.

Method

The calculation of income includes two parts: 1) the booking service charge imposed by the Airbnb platform, and 2) the room service charge payable to the Airbnb host. Four key types of information are utilised in this study to assess the financial loss of Airbnb listings, including net

Table 2. Explanation of each data type of Airbnb listings.

Type	Explanations
Net number of review comments per month $(r_{i,j})$	All the Airbnb guests left a review or automatic review after they stayed. The number of reviews can be an indicator of the minimum number of Airbnb guests staying at a property. This number deducts the number of cancellations.
Price of Airbnb listing $(p_{i,j})$	The price of individual Airbnb listings per night.
Minimum nights required $(n_{i,j})$	The minimum nights required by Airbnb hosts when making a booking.
Last active comments	An indicator of whether the Airbnb listings are still active

number of review comments per month, price of Airbnb listings, minimum nights required, and last active comments (Table 2).

The first step taken to assess the income of the Airbnb platform and its hosts is to calculate the booking total price per month for a listing, which is consistent with Cheng et al.(2020a)'s algorithm:

$$b_{i,j} = (p_{i,j} \cdot n_{i,j} + s_{i,j} + c_{i,j} + t_{i,j}) \cdot r_{i,j}$$ Eq.1

Where $b_{i,j}$ is the booking total price per month (AUD\$) of listing i for the month j; $p_{i,j}$ represents the average price per night of listing i for the month j; $r_{i,j}$ is the net monthly number of reviews, and it already deletes the cancellation records. The cancellation is captured based on the comment with the key word "automatically cancelled"; $n_{i,j}$ is the minimum nights required. The service fee $s_{i,j}$ is usually charged along with the booking total price $(b_{i,j})$. The cleaning fee $c_{i,j}$ only applies once even though the guest may stay more than one night, which should be differentiated from hotels. The occupancy tax $(t_{i,j})$ collection and remittance should also be taken into account, and it varies across different cities depending on local policies.

Two tax schemes typically apply to Airbnb hosts depending on the regulations in different cities. One is occupancy tax. "In areas that Airbnb has made agreements with governments to collect and remit local taxes on behalf of hosts, Airbnb calculates these taxes and collects them from guests at the time of booking" (Airbnb, 2020c). The other one is subject to income taxes (Dalir et al., 2020), which are not collected from a booking. Airbnb hosts are required to declare their income as part of their annual income tax assessment, and if "the host is carrying on an enterprise renting out commercial residential premises, such as a commercial boarding house, a different income tax obligation applies" (ATO, 2020b).

The booking total only represents the lower limit of the total booking income for Airbnb hosts as Airbnb guests can stay longer than the minimum nights required. The income of Airbnb hosts needs to be shared between the Airbnb platform and its hosts. The host's revenue does not share part of the service fee and tax; thus the host's income is:

$$h_{i,j} = (p_{i,j} \cdot n_{i,j} + c_{i,j}) \cdot r_{i,j}$$ Eq.2

The Airbnb platform's income is the booking service fee $s_{i,j}$. This part contains the guest service fee (up to 14.2 per cent) and the host service fee (3 per cent for the host) which together represents up to 17.2 per cent of the booking subtotal (the nightly rate plus the cleaning fee and additional guest fee [if applicable] but excluding Airbnb fees and taxes). Here we adopt the assumption that 13 per cent (average 10 per cent for the guest service fee and 3 per cent for the host service fee) of the booking subtotal from Cheng et al.(2020a)'s calculation. More relevant details are available on Airbnb's website: (https://www.airbnb.com.au/help/article/1857/what-is-the-airbnb-service-fee).

In order to demonstrate the calculation and reproductivity of the income accounting framework, a demonstration case study is provided in Appendix 1 (Supplementary Material) based on an anonymous Airbnb listing in Sydney, along with uncertainty analysis.

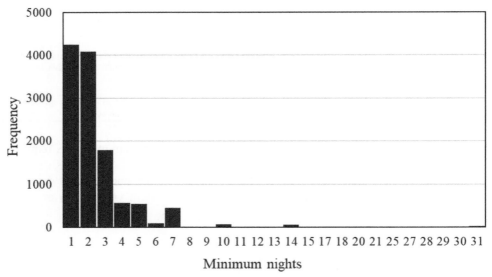

Figure 2. Histogram of minimum nights required in January.

Uncertainty in the income accounting framework

Length of stay

We adopt the "minimum nights" for the length of stay. InsideAirbnb applies a value of 3 nights per booking where no public statements are made about length of stay,[1] when estimating occupancy rates. However, we cannot obtain detailed information on length of stay and thus "minimum nights" offers a reference that represents a lower limit value of the estimation. Figure 2 provides a histogram of minimum nights in January as a reference.

Review rate

Users are not required to leave reviews. Thus, review numbers extracted based on comments may underestimate numbers of actual bookings. However, there is no perfect solution for this issue even though assumptions could be introduced. For example, InsideAirbnb's "San Francisco Model" chose a review rate of 50 per cent;[2] Marqusee(2015) used the rate of 72 per cent; Budget and Legislative Analyst's Office used a value of 72 per cent in San Francisco for a low impact scenario and a medium impact scenario, and introduced a review rate of 30.5 per cent for a high impact scenario (BLAO, 2015). However, to the best of our knowledge, there is no available data that could be used to convert reviews to numbers of bookings; thus we do not modify our model by introducing a review rate. We define active listings as those that received at least one review, which represents the lower limit of the estimation.

We have also compared our estimation with three real-world cases. The error of booking total between our estimation and the three listings is 3.5 to 3.7 per cent (see details in Appendix 1, Supplementary Material).

First and second wave of COVID-19 in Greater Sydney

In order to identify the periodical impacts of the pandemic on Airbnb hosts, we further break the period into the first and second wave of COVID-19 in Greater Sydney. To identify the first and second waves, we break down the confirmed cases on a daily basis and consider government responses (Figure 3). When the first case of COVID-19 was confirmed in late January, the Australian government decided to issue a travel ban to mainland Chinese visitors, to commence

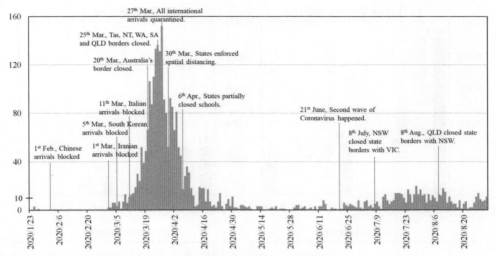

Figure 3. Australian Government responses and confirmed cases in Greater Sydney.
Source: The Department of Health, New South Wales (NSW) government (NSWGovernment, 2020a)

on February 1 2020 (AustralianGovernment, 2020b). In February, there were no new confirmed cases in Australia. However, confirmed new cases began significantly increasing in March. The Australian government then issued a series of travel bans to Australia for international visitors from places such as Iran, South Korea, and Italy (ABC News, 2020b). Finally, the Australian border was closed to all international travellers on March 20 (AustralianGovernment, 2020a). Various Australian states also followed by introducing strict border closures on March 25 (ABC News, 2020c). Australia reached 158 cases on March 27 when the federal government announced they would thereafter place all international returned residents into mandatory quarantine. The new daily confirmed cases began decreasing following this initiative and by the end of May, no new cases of confirmed local transmission were recorded. This is the point at which the first wave was considered by most people to have ended in Greater Sydney.

The second wave began in June with the number of confirmed cases of locally acquired transmission still below 10 per day. These numbers soon began rising more rapidly with 20 confirmed cases per day being recorded by the end of July. This was of great concern, particularly because another Australian city, Melbourne, was experiencing a surge in the number of confirmed cases. As a result, on July 8, 2020, the New South Wales State Government issued a state border closure with Victoria for first time in 100 years (NSWGovernment, 2020b). Queensland also initiated border closures to travellers from COVID-19 hotspots (including NSW) on August 8, 2020 (ABC News, 2020d). This point in time is generally considered the start of the second wave of COVID-19 for Greater Sydney.

Results

Number of active listings

Findings in Figure 4 show that Airbnb hosts have suffered significant reductions in listings since the outbreak of the COVID-19 pandemic but the degree of these losses have varied across different room types. Overall, active Airbnb listings in Sydney dropped to 7,540 in February compared to 12,067 in January. In March, there were 4,715 active listings, a reduction of 60.9 per cent compared to January, and this number decreased to 2,575 in June, a 78.7 per cent drop from January. In the second wave of COVID-19 from June to August, there was an increase from 2,575

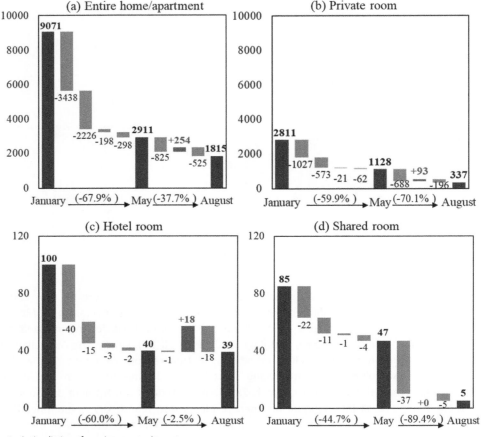

Figure 4. Active listings from January to August.
*Detailed data from January to August is available in Appendix 2 (Supplementary Material, the Excel file, Dataset S1-1).

to 2,940 and then a drop to 2,196. The overall number has a 46.8 per cent decrease in August compared to May, representing a further loss of active listings in the second wave.

As shown in Figure 4, the rapid decline of "entire home/apartment" and "private room" bookings from January to March are largely a result of the Australian government's border closure to Chinese tourists and the subsequent restrictions on all travellers, regardless of nationality. From March to May, the decline curve tends to flatten and then bounce back slightly. This is because at that stage, most of the Airbnb guests were domestic and COVID-19 was largely perceived to be under control in Australia. However, due to the outbreak of the second wave in June and the state border closures between Victoria, NSW and Queensland in July and August, the number decreased again.

Hosts with single and multiple listings both suffer significantly from COVID-19, particularly those offering an entire home/apartment or a private room (Figure 5) in the first wave. For the entire home/apartment, the active hosts with single listings decreased by 58.6 per cent while hosts with multiple listings decreased by 76.3 per cent from January to May.

However, in June, with the start of the second wave, multiple listings bounced back by 5.9 per cent compared to May, but the hosts with a single listing still kept decreasing by 50.3 per cent. They both witnessed an increase of 11.9 per cent and 12.4 per cent respectively from June to July, and then a drop by 17.4 per cent and 26.1 per cent from July to August respectively. This is because the ease of restrictions and the reopening of economy with a better understanding of COVID-19 in the second wave.

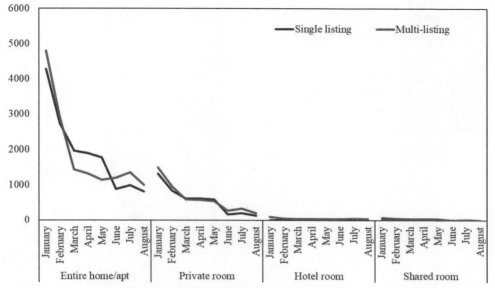

Figure 5. Active hosts with single or multiple listings from January to May 2020.

The private room listings also display a similar trend like the entire home/apartment. These results echo the hypothesis suggested by Dolnicar and Zare(2020) that some hosts with multiple listings, are likely to be professional hosts. These professional hosts tend to maximise their profits and as a result, these hosts might have turned their Airbnb listings into long-term rentals to avoid the risks associated with COVID-19. In contrast, hosts with a single listing are more resilient to the crisis as these hosts are more likely to have other incomes because the earning from a single listing is not likely to be enough to cover daily expenditure, thus having to expose themselves to potential safety risks by living with guests. Most importantly, the Australian border closures have resulted in a sharp decrease in tourism during this period.

Income loss of Airbnb hosts

In January, the Sydney Airbnb market was prosperous with a total revenue of 17.8 million dollars including 15.7 million dollars for hosts. Eight suburbs have an income more than $500,000 per month on average in January. Hosts from the suburbs of Pyrmont-Ultimo and Haymarket-The Rocks in the inner city as well as Bondi Beach, Manly, Fairlight, Avalon and Palm Beach have a total income of more than $700,000 each (Figure 6). Bondi, Tamarama, Bronte, Surry Hills, Potts Point and Woolloomooloo are popular tourist areas and/or shopping centres with a total income of more than $500,000.

However, during the first wave, with the increasing number of positive cases in Sydney and Australia's travel bans, Airbnb hosts' income loss was about 10 million AUD less and 63.8 per cent lower in May than that in January (Figure 7). The inner city of the Greater Sydney has 80.8 per cent decrease of hosts' income compared with May to January. This area used to have the most concentrated active Airbnb listings as it not only has the bustling shopping centres but also many popular tourist attractions including the Sydney Opera House, Sydney Harbor Bridge and China Town. The other tourist attractions and shopping centres such as Bondi Junction and the Sydney beach suburbs also had a 43.5 per cent decrease of income from January to May 2020.

The findings of this research also show that suburbs with a high concentration of Chinese ethnic groups have been hit hard. Hurstville, which is known as a Chinese concentrated suburb,

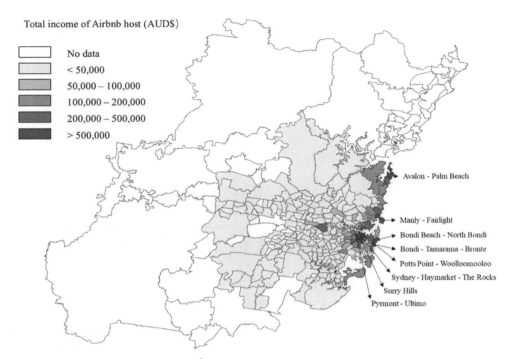

Figure 6. Income of Airbnb hosts by census tract[3] in January 2020.
*Detailed data from January to August is available in Appendix 2 (Supplementary Material, the Excel file, Dataset S2) and figures for hosts' income are compiled in multiple media GIFs file.

has witnessed a 68.2 per cent decrease in May compared to January. That could be as a result of a decline in demand by international students with associated reduced demand from those students' friends and family (visiting) as a result of the incoming traveller restrictions.

In the second wave of COVID-19 in Australia, Airbnb hosts' income loss was about $4 million and was 71.1 per cent lower in August than in May (Figure 8). The inner city of Greater Sydney has a further 67.6 per cent decrease of hosts' income compared with May to January. Popular beachside suburbs and Bondi Junction also experienced an 85.6 per cent decrease.

By contrast, 50 SA2 areas in outer suburbs have seen a reverse growth in income during the second wave. There are three reasons that can explain this: 1. some areas have increasing active listings such as "Cherrybrook" where active listings increase from 1 to 5 listings (Table A5, Appendix 1, Supplementary Material); 2. Some areas have maintained the same active listings but an increase in price such as "Ashcroft – Busby – Miller" (Table A6, Appendix 1, Supplementary Material); and 3. the lost listings in some suburbs are replaced by more expensive listings such as "Belmore – Belfield" (Table A7, Appendix 1, Supplementary Material).

Discussion and implications

The financial losses experienced by Airbnb hosts are estimated to be approximately 6.5 times greater than the losses incurred by the Airbnb platform itself. This echoes the wide concern that the flexibility of gig employment also comes with the risk of economic fluctuations for workers; particularly during time of economic crisis (Friedman, 2014). As Airbnb hosts are informal employees of Airbnb (Sundararajan, 2014), the Airbnb platform transfers their risks through outsourcing room services to Airbnb hosts. When there is an economic boom, there seems to be a win-win situation, where both Airbnb platforms and Airbnb hosts are able to generate income;

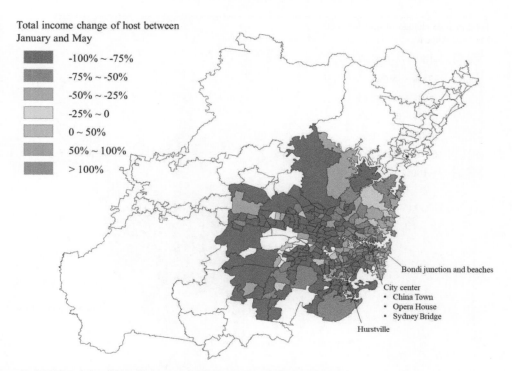

Figure 7. Spatial statistics of Airbnb's income change in the first wave of COVID-19.
*Interactive maps: (1) Income of Airbnb's host from January to August (AUD$1000)://www.datawrapper.de/_/Yh74G/; (2) The change of hosts' income between May to January (%)://www.datawrapper.de/_/gC6Wm/; (3) The change of hosts' income between August to May (%)://www.datawrapper.de/_/aP4A5/

however, as this study shows, during the COVID-19 crisis Airbnb hosts can be burdened by a loss of income that will have implications for ongoing mortgage repayments and other debts.

In addition, compared to an employee's average salary, the daily income of Airbnb hosts can range from 17 to 146 per cent of the wage of a full-time employee depending on room types (Australian adult's income averages $221 per day) (ABS, 2020). A significant proportion of the income derived by Airbnb hosts is usually re-spent on satisfying the needs of guests, and contributing to the economy and employment in many other sectors as well as contributing to government revenue in the form of goods and services taxes (Cheng et al., 2020b).

Indeed, the fast-developing sharing economy was initially introduced as an alternative business model to the traditional economy, which is able to create employment as well as supplement residents' income, aligning with SDG 8. Subsequently, with the rapid development of Airbnb, many hosts became professional hosts, relying on their rental revenue as their main source of income. There is no evidence to suggest that the Australian government has established effective means by which to estimate the amount of tax that Airbnb hosts should pay. In the current tax system at the time of writing, the Australia Taxation Office relies on Airbnb hosts to self-declare their income for the sharing economy activities in their tax return. This self-declaration system encourages Airbnb hosts to avoid self-reporting as a small business, thus resulting in many of the Airbnb hosts not being able to claim financial aid. At the same time, this self-declaration system can also lead to possible action of Airbnb hosts choosing not to register an ABN to avoid paying tax. Therefore, despite Airbnb hosts experiencing a 100 per cent loss in income, their JobKeeper applications were declined by the Australian Taxation Office (e.g., https://community.ato.gov.au/t5/COVID-19-response/Cash-Flow-Boost-for-Airbnb-Hosts/td-p/76460).

Against this loophole, this study provides a comprehensive income accounting framework for P2P accommodation business at both spatial and temporal scale. The framework enhances the

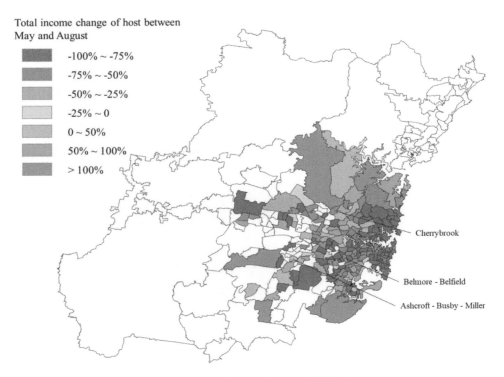

Figure 8. Spatial statistics of Airbnb's income change in the second wave of COVID-19.
*50 SA2 areas in outer suburbs that have a reverse growth in income from May to August are listed in Appendix 2 (Supplementary Material, the Excel file, Dataset S3).

income transparency of Airbnb hosts, which may serve as a baseline for future tax accounting and reforms. It also informs policymakers about the underestimation of income losses of free-lancers and gig economy workers in the tourism industry, adding empirical evidence in relation to possible adjustment of new JobKeeper unemployment subsidies. As such, this study highlights the need for the Australian government to reform the current system to integrate gig economy work-ers into the social welfare system as the sharing economy is going to stay and potentially quickly bounce back. Whilst it seems a good idea to pay as little tax as possible by avoiding such statuses it has implications in situations such as this. It is also something the government should work to reform in order to protect such businesses in the future, as P2P economy is here to stay.

In addition, the financial impacts of the COVID-19 outbreak on local communities raises signifi-cant concerns as to how the sharing economy can contribute to sustainable tourism. Consistent with Gössling and Michael Hall(2019)'s study, this research highlights that while the sharing econ-omy can generate employment this can also have significant implications for social trade-offs and rebound effects. The financial impacts can further jeopardise the informal employment opportuni-ties in the sharing economy leading to an erosion of the traditional social contract in employment, thereby reducing the sharing economy's ability to contribute to Sustainable Development Goals (8 and 10) for decent work and reduced inequalities as well as sustainable cities and communities.

As described by the International Labour Organization (ILO), decent work should cover four pillars: employment creation, social protection, rights at work, and social dialogue (Winchenbach et al., 2019). However, in the current climate, the P2P economy faces a significant barrier to pro-viding social protections and stable income for those working in the gig economy. Our study provides timely empirical evidence to support the critical engagement with the role of tourism in relation to decent work as Baum et al.(2016) highlighted that employees should be at the centre of the sustainable tourism debate, particularly concerning the informal sector, where limited social protection usually occurs. Our study aligns with previous research which finds that contributing to SDG 8 in tourism is not simply about the creation of jobs, but also about the quality of that employment (Winchenbach et al., 2019). It calls for a re-evaluation of the existing framework of broad decent work standards by integrating the informal economy into the formal economy and paying special attention to the distinctive nature of the sharing economy (Heeks, 2017).

With COVID-19 showing signs of being under control in Australia, our study shows that the outer suburbs of Greater Sydney have begun to bounce back, albeit slower than those that are located closer to the centre of Sydney. With international travel restrictions and residents being encouraged to holiday domestically, it is reasonable to hypothesise that Airbnb in regional areas will demonstrate more resilience and recover more quickly than in the cities.

Conclusions

This study provides a timely assessment of income losses of Airbnb hosts under the ongoing COVID-19 pandemic up to the end of August 2020. It offers empirical evidence demonstrating how economic risks are transferred from the sharing economy platforms onto their informal employees (such as Airbnb hosts) while these informal employees are not eligible for many employment-based social insurance or justice programs. This study raises concerns regarding the vulnerability of workers in the sharing economy and the industry sector's contribution to sustainable tourism and decent work goals.

Indeed, this comprehensive income accounting framework offers a starting point to further engage in the sustainability discourse of the rapidly evolving tourism industry during the pandemic. This requires an accurate assessment of income to address issues in relation to employment and decent work (SGDs 8) (Winchenbach et al., 2019). In particular, the demonstration case study based on an anonymous Airbnb listing provides future researchers with a guide for how to perform the income framework, and enhances the reproducibility of this research. As such, this framework can have wider applications beyond tourism to advance interdisciplinary research.

Despite this research's important contribution to the extant literature, this study is not without limitations. First, the study only assesses the income loss of Airbnb hosts in Sydney. Further studies that can assess Airbnb loss on a global scale will be able to provide a more accurate picture of the global impact of COVID-19 on the sharing economy workforce. Secondly, at the time of writing this article, Sydney continues to experience a second wave of COVID-19 and there is potential for further waves. A longitudinal study would therefore be promising to provide further empirical evidence to assess the resilience of the sharing economy. This study has not considered the effect of gentrification (see e.g. Wachsmuth and Weisler(2018)). While Airbnb may provide some residents with opportunities for new and additional sources of income, it may be detrimental to others, such as long-term tenants, who are pushed out of their neighbourhood. It is important to note that while Airbnb hosts are the most important part of Airbnb business models, there are other stakeholders in its business models such as the cleaner hired by hosts. Further research taking a holistic view of the supply chain of Airbnb will enable a better understanding of the full impact of COVID-19 on Airbnb. Lastly, further research that can combine various data, such as Airbnb's tax returns to the Australian Tax Office could provide a more accurate framework for stakeholders to formulate a variety of strategies. Further research into the complexity issue of the sustainability of the sharing economy is encouraged.

Notes

1. Source: http://insideairbnb.com/sydney/#
2. Source: http://insideairbnb.com/about.html#disclaimers

3. "Census tract" is an area roughly equivalent to a neighborhood established by the Bureau of Census for analyzing populations.

Disclosure statement

No potential conflict of interest was reported by the authors.

Funding

This project is funded by the China Postdoctoral Science Foundation (Grant 2020M680440) and Curtin Faculty of Business and Law Support for Revise and Resubmit Journal Papers.

References

ABC News. (2020a). Coronavirus cancellations, toilet paper shortages leave Airbnb hosts nervous. https://www.abc.net.au/news/2020-03-18/coronavirus-cancellations-leave-airbnb-hosts-nervous/12063266

ABC News. (2020b). Coronavirus travel ban for Italy, Iran, China and South Korea extended amid global pandemic. https://www.abc.net.au/news/2020-03-12/coronavirus-travel-ban-extended-global-pandemic/12049448.

ABC News. (2020c). Coronavirus border closures see thousands of grey nomads, travellers stuck in caravan parks. https://www.abc.net.au/news/2020-03-25/coronavirus-sees-travellers-stuck-in-caravan-parks/12088742.

ABC News. (2020d). Queensland borders close to COVID-19 hotspots Victoria, NSW and ACT. Here's what it means for you. https://www.abc.net.au/news/2020-08-07/queensland-closes-borders-covid-19-hotspots/12534156.

ABS. (2011). Australian Statistical Geography Standard (ASGS): Volume 1 - Main Structure and Greater Capital City Statistical Areas, ABS Catalogue Number 1270.0.55.001, (July 2011). ed. Australian Bureau of Statistics, Canberra, ACT, Australia.

ABS. (2020). 6302.0 - Average Weekly Earnings, Australia. Australian Bureau of Statistics. https://www.abs.gov.au/ausstats/abs@.nsf/mf/6302.0

Airbnb. (2013). New Study: Airbnb Community Contributes AUD $214 Million to Sydney and its Suburbs, Brings Tourists to New Neighbourhoods. https://www.airbnb.com.au/press/news/new-study-airbnb-community-contributes-aud-214-million-to-sydney-and-its-suburbs-brings-tourists-to-new-neighbourhoods#:~:text=The%20study%20indicates%20that%20the,to%20help%20make%20ends%20meet.

Airbnb. (2020a)., $250M to support hosts impacted by cancellations. https://www.airbnb.com.au/resources/hosting-homes/a/250m-to-support-hosts-impacted-by-cancellations-165.

Airbnb. (2020b). Answers to your questions about the Superhost Relief Fund.

Airbnb. (2020c). In what areas is occupancy tax collection and remittance by Airbnb available? https://www.airbnb.com.au/help/article/2509/in-what-areas-is-occupancy-tax-collection-and-remittance-by-airbnb-available.

Andreoni, V. (2019). Sharing economy: Risks and opportunities in a framework of SDGs. In: Filho, W., Azuk, A. (Eds.), Sustainable cities and communities. Encyclopedia of the UN Sustainable Development Goals. Springer.

ATO. (2020a). Cash flow boost for Airbnb hosts. ATO: Australian Taxation Offiece. https://community.ato.gov.au/t5/COVID-19-response/Cash-Flow-Boost-for-Airbnb-Hosts/td-p/76460.

ATO. (2020b). Renting out all or part of your home. ATO:Australian Taxation Office. https://www.ato.gov.au/general/the-sharing-economy-and-tax/renting-out-all-or-part-of-your-home/.

AustralianGovernment. (2020a). Border restrictions. https://www.pm.gov.au/media/border-restrictions.

AustralianGovernment. (2020b). Continuing travel ban to protect Australians from the coronavirus. https://www.pm.gov.au/media/continuing-travel-ban-protect-australians-coronavirus.

AustralianGovernment. (2020c). JobKeeper payment. https://treasury.gov.au/coronavirus/jobkeeper.

Baum, T., Cheung, C., Kong, H., Kralj, A., Mooney, S., Nguyễn Thị Thanh, H., Ramachandran, S., Dropulić Ružić, M., & Siow, M. L. (2016). Sustainability and the tourism and hospitality workforce: A thematic analysis. *Sustainability*, 8(8), 809. https://doi.org/10.3390/su8080809

Berg, J. (2015). Income security in the on-demand economy: Findings and policy lessons from a survey of crowdworkers. *Comparative Labor Law & Policy Journal*, 37, 543.

BLAO. (2015). *Analysis of the impact of short-term rentals on housing. Policy Analysis Report of City and County of San Francisco*. Budget and Legislative Analyst's Office. https://sfbos.org/sites/default/files/FileCenter/Documents/52601-BLA.ShortTermRentals.051315.pdf.

Cheng, M. (2016). Sharing economy: A review and agenda for future research. *International Journal of Hospitality Management*, 57, 60–70. https://doi.org/10.1016/j.ijhm.2016.06.003

Cheng, M., Chen, G., Wiedmann, T., Hadjikakou, M., Xu, L., & Wang, Y. (2020a). The sharing economy and sustainability – Assessing Airbnb's direct, indirect and induced carbon footprint in Sydney. *Journal of Sustainable Tourism*, 28(8), 1083–1099. https://doi.org/10.1080/09669582.2020.1720698

Cheng, M., Houge Mackenzie, S., & Degarege, G. A. (2020b). Airbnb impacts on host communities in a tourism destination: An exploratory study of stakeholder perspectives in Queenstown, New Zealand. *Journal of Sustainable Tourism*, Ahead-of-print, 1–19. https://doi.org/10.1080/09669582.2020.1802469.

Cohen, B., & Kietzmann, J. (2014). Ride On! Mobility business models for the sharing economy. *Organization & Environment*, 27(3), 279–296. https://doi.org/10.1177/1086026614546199

Corujo, B. S. (2017). The 'Gig'economy and its impact on social security: The Spanish Example. *European Journal of Social Security*, 19(4), 293–312. https://doi.org/10.1177/1388262717745751

Cui, R., Li, J., & Zhang, D. (2020). Reducing discrimination with reviews in the sharing economy: Evidence from field experiments on Airbnb. *Management Science*, 66(3), 1071–1094. https://doi.org/10.1287/mnsc.2018.3273

Dalir, S., Mahamadaminov, A., & Olya, H. G. T. (2020). Airbnb and taxation: Developing a seasonal tax system. *Tourism Economics*, Online first. https://doi.org/10.1177/1354816620904894.

Dogru, T., Mody, M., Suess, C., McGinley, S., & Line, N. D. (2020). The Airbnb paradox: Positive employment effects in the hospitality industry. *Tourism Management*, 77, 104001. https://doi.org/10.1016/j.tourman.2019.104001

Dolnicar, S., & Zare, S. (2020). COVID19 and Airbnb – Disrupting the disruptor. *Annals of Tourism Research*, 83, 102961. https://doi.org/10.1016/j.annals.2020.102961

Fang, B., Ye, Q., & Law, R. (2016). Effect of sharing economy on tourism industry employment. *Annals of Tourism Research*, 57, 264–267. https://doi.org/10.1016/j.annals.2015.11.018

Frenken, K., & Schor, J. (2017). Putting the sharing economy into perspective. *Environmental Innovation and Societal Transitions*, 23, 3–10. https://doi.org/10.1016/j.eist.2017.01.003

Friedman, G. (2014). Workers without employers: shadow corporations and the rise of the gig economy. *Review of Keynesian Economics*, 2(2), 171–188. https://doi.org/10.4337/roke.2014.02.03

Gössling, S., & Michael Hall, C. (2019). Sharing versus collaborative economy: How to align ICT developments and the SDGs in tourism? *Journal of Sustainable Tourism*, 27(1), 74–96. https://doi.org/10.1080/09669582.2018.1560455

Graham, M., Hjorth, I., & Lehdonvirta, V. (2017). Digital labour and development: Impacts of global digital labour platforms and the gig economy on worker livelihoods. *Transfer (Brussels, Belgium)*, 23(2), 135–162. https://doi.org/10.1177/1024258916687250

Gurran, N., & Phibbs, P. (2017). When tourists move in: How should urban planners respond to Airbnb? *Journal of the American Planning Association*, 83(1), 80–92. https://doi.org/10.1080/01944363.2016.1249011

Haripershad, S., & Johnston, K. (2017). *Impact of the gig economy (Uber and AirBnB) in South Africa, ECSM 2017 4th European Conference on Social Media* (p. 146). Academic Conferences and Publishing Limited.

Heeks, R. (2017). Decent Work and the Digital Gig Economy: A Developing Country Perspective on Employment Impacts and Standards in Online Outsourcing. Crowdwork, Etc. Development Informatics Working Paper, 71.

Hu, M. R., & Lee, A. (2020). Airbnb, COVID-19 Risk and Lockdowns: Global Evidence.

Kwok, L., & Xie, K. L. (2019). Pricing strategies on Airbnb: Are multi-unit hosts revenue pros? *International Journal of Hospitality Management*, 82, 252–259. https://doi.org/10.1016/j.ijhm.2018.09.013

Malos, S., Lester, G. V., & Virick, M. (2018). Uber drivers and employment status in the gig economy: Should corporate social responsibility tip the scales? *Employee Responsibilities and Rights Journal*, 30(4), 239–251. https://doi.org/10.1007/s10672-018-9325-9

Marqusee, A. (2015). Airbnb and San Francisco: Descriptive Statistics and Academic Research. Project: Amendments Relating to Short-Term Rentals. https://commissions.sfplanning.org/cpcpackets/2014-001033PCA.

Martin, C. J. (2016). The sharing economy: A pathway to sustainability or a nightmarish form of neoliberal capitalism? *Ecological Economics, 121*, 149–159. https://doi.org/10.1016/j.ecolecon.2015.11.027

Mas, A., & Pallais, A. (2017). Valuing alternative work arrangements. *American Economic Review, 107*(12), 3722–3759. https://doi.org/10.1257/aer.20161500

Mi, Z., & Coffman, D. (2019). The sharing economy promotes sustainable societies. *Nature Communications, 10*(1), 1214. https://doi.org/10.1038/s41467-019-09260-4

Möhlmann, MJJoCB. (2015). Collaborative consumption: determinants of satisfaction and the likelihood of using a sharing economy option again. *Journal of Consumer Behaviour, 14*(3), 193–207. https://doi.org/10.1002/cb.1512

NSWGovernment. (2020a). COVID-19 in NSW - up to 8pm 19 October 2020. https://www.health.nsw.gov.au/Infectious/covid-19/Pages/recent-case-updates.aspx.

NSWGovernment. (2020b). NSW and Victorian border closures. https://www.nsw.gov.au/news/nsw-and-victorian-border-closures.

Palos-Sanchez, P. R., & Correia, M. B. (2018). The collaborative economy based analysis of demand: Study of Airbnb case in Spain and Portugal. *Journal of Theoretical and Applied Electronic Commerce Research, 13*(3), 85–98. https://doi.org/10.4067/S0718-18762018000300105

Peticca-Harris, A., deGama, N., & Ravishankar, M. (2020). Postcapitalist precarious work and those in the 'drivers' seat: Exploring the motivations and lived experiences of Uber drivers in Canada. *Organization, 27*(1), 36–59. https://doi.org/10.1177/1350508418757332

Ravenelle, A. J. (2017). Sharing economy workers: Selling, not sharing. *Cambridge Journal of Regions, Economy and Society, 10*(2), 281–295. https://doi.org/10.1093/cjres/rsw043

Richardson, L. (2015). Performing the sharing economy. *Geoforum, 67*, 121–129. https://doi.org/10.1016/j.geoforum.2015.11.004

Sundararajan, A. (2014). What Airbnb gets about culture that Uber doesn't. *Harvard Business Review*, 2014–11-27. https://hbr.org/2014/11/what-airbnb-gets-about-culture-that-uber-doesnt

Sundararajan, A. (2017). *The sharing economy: The end of employment and the rise of crowd-based capitalism.* MIT Press.

Tran, M., & Sokas, R. K. (2017). The gig economy and contingent work: An Occupational health assessment. *Journal of Occupational and Environmental Medicine, 59*(4), e63–e66. https://doi.org/10.1097/JOM.0000000000000977

UNWTO. (2020). Tourism for SDGs. UNWTO: United Nation World Tourism Organisation, http://tourism4sdgs.org/.

Wachsmuth, D., & Weisler, A. (2018). Airbnb and the rent gap: Gentrification through the sharing economy. *Environment and Planning A: Economy and Space, 50*(6), 1147–1170. https://doi.org/10.1177/0308518X18778038

Winchenbach, A., Hanna, P., & Miller, G. (2019). Rethinking decent work: The value of dignity in tourism employment. *Journal of Sustainable Tourism, 27*(7), 1026–1043. https://doi.org/10.1080/09669582.2019.1566346

Wirtz, J., So Kevin Kam, F., Mody Makarand, A., Liu Stephanie, Q., & Chun HaeEun, H. (2019). Platforms in the peer-to-peer sharing economy. *Journal of Service Management, 30*(4), 452–483. https://doi.org/10.1108/JOSM-11-2018-0369

Yrigoy, I. (2019). Rent gap reloaded: Airbnb and the shift from residential to touristic rental housing in the Palma Old Quarter in Mallorca, Spain. *Urban Studies, 56*(13), 2709–2726. https://doi.org/10.1177/0042098018803261

Index

Note: Figures are indicated by *italics*. Tables are indicated by **bold**. Endnotes are indicated by the page number followed by 'n' and the endnote number e.g., 20n1 refers to endnote 1 on page 20.

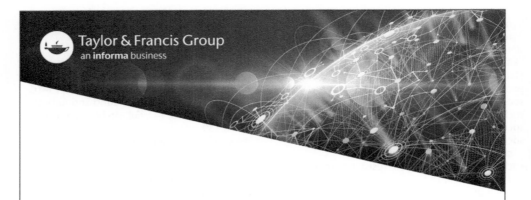

Taylor & Francis eBooks

www.taylorfrancis.com

A single destination for eBooks from Taylor & Francis with increased functionality and an improved user experience to meet the needs of our customers.

90,000+ eBooks of award-winning academic content in Humanities, Social Science, Science, Technology, Engineering, and Medical written by a global network of editors and authors.

TAYLOR & FRANCIS EBOOKS OFFERS:

A streamlined experience for our library customers

A single point of discovery for all of our eBook content

Improved search and discovery of content at both book and chapter level

REQUEST A FREE TRIAL
support@taylorfrancis.com

Routledge   CRC Press